# Multidimensional Mind:
## Remote Viewing in Hyperspace

# Multidimensional Mind:
## Remote Viewing in Hyperspace

Jean Millay, Ph.D.

*Foreword by*
Stanley Krippner, Ph.D.

North Atlantic Books
Berkeley, Califonia
A Universal Dialogues Book

To
Darrell Lemaire

# Multidimensional Mind: Remote Viewing in Hyperspace

Published by
North Atlantic Books
P.O. Box 12327
Berkeley, California 94712

*Multidimensional Mind: Remote Viewing in Hyperspace* is sponsored by the Society for the Study of Native Arts and Sciences, a non-profit educational corporation whose goals are to develop an educational and cross-cultural perspective linking various scientific, social and artistic fields; to nurture a holistic view of the arts, sciences, humanities and healing; and to publish and distribute literature on the relationship of mind, body and nature.

1-55643-306-9
Printed in H.K

Library of Congress Cataloguing-in-Publication Data

```
Millay, Jean
      Multidimensional   Mind : Remote Viewing in Hyperspace
/ by Jean Millay
         p. cm.
      ISBN 1-55643-306-9  (pbk. : alk. paper)
      1. Parapsychology.   I. Title
   BF 1031.M547   1999                          98-35635
   133. 8--dc21                                     CIP
```

## Permission has been granted for the use of the following materials in *Multidimensional Mind:*

Some of the illustrations resulting from our many telepathy trials and remote viewing experiments appeared in Kane,B., Millay,J. & Brown,D., "Silver Threads: 25 Years of Parapsychology Research" (Praeger, an imprint of Greenwood Publishing Group, Westport, CT,1993). These images are reprinted with permission. (In that book, the photos are numbered 6.1-6.12.) Results of some of these same telepathy trials were published earlier in this author's dissertation (1978); in The Humanistic Psychology Review [1981]; and in the conference proceedings of the First, Second, and Eleventh International Conference on the Study of Shamanism and Alternate Modes of Healing. These conference proceedings were published by Independent Scholars of Asia, Inc., Berkeley, CA. (Heinze, R-I., Ed.) (1983-1994).

## The cartoons that enliven these pages are reprinted with permission, including:

* "Home" by James Thurber; copyright ©1943 James Thurber. Copyright ©1971 Rosemary A. Thurber. From "Men, Women and Dogs", published by Harcourt Brace.
* "Siva, Lord of Destruction" The New Yorker Collection, Copyright ©1982 Lee Lorenz from cartoonbank.com. All Rights Reserved.
* "Relax Completely" by Gahan Wilson, reprinted by permission. Copyright ©1978 Gahan Wilson.
* "Miracle" and "Dolphins" reprinted by permission. Copyright ©1998 Sidney Harris.
* "Peanuts" permission granted by Charles Schultz, reprinted by permission of United Feature Syndicate, Inc., Copyright ©1960.
* "Alley Oop" by V. T. Hamlin, reprinted by permission. Copyright ©1963 NEA Service, Inc. T.M.

* Russell Targ granted permission to reprint the drawings made by Uri Geller and this author during the experiments conducted at SRI in 1973. (Originally published by Targ, R. & Puthoff, H., "Information Transmission Under Conditions of Sensory Shielding", in Nature 252 [1974]: 602-607.)

* Artists involved in the remote viewing experiments have provided permission to print their work, including James Dowlen, Tom Byrne, Gregory Schelkun, Sola Patricia Smith.
* Permission granted from Luis Gasparetto to print paintings he channeled from artists while in trance, October: 4,1980.
* Photo of Amelia Garcia taken in 1928, courtesy of her daughter, Amelia Rose Garcia (1998).
* Photo of Jean Millay on back cover, courtesy of PCA International, Inc. (1999).
* Permission granted from Marge King to print a photo of the Light Sculpture in use by students in her science class (1972).
* Permission granted to quote a verse from "Tao Te Ching by Lao Tzu, A New English Version," with Foreword and Notes by Stephen Mitchell. Translation Copyright ©1988 by Stephen Mitchell. New York: HarperCollins Publishers,1999.
* Permission granted to quote verses from "Rhymes for Rap" (Nostradamus and Fat Cat Rule) Copyright ©1989 Donald R. Douglas.
* Permission granted to reprint "Birds in a Brewing Storm" Copyright © Jesse Allen by courtesy of Vorpal Gallery, San Francisco and New York.
* Other contributions for which permission was kindly given include the photographs of Dean Brown, Ph.D., by Don Parker, Ph.D.; the high-voltage photography of Uri Geller by Henry Dakin (previously published in Dakin, H.S. "High-Voltage Photography," San Francisco: H.S. Dakin Co.,1974); and diagrams by Saul-Paul Sirag and Ruth-Inge Heinze, Ph.D..

# ACKNOWLEDGMENTS vii

My appreciation and gratitude extend to five generations. My grandparents, Will and Alpha Penrose, introduced me to the love of the wide-open spaces in nature and to their spirit world after death. My parents, George and Grace Beers, supported me emotionally and economically through many unemployed years while I studied art and practiced remote viewing. My sister, Marge King, challenged me to write as intelligibly as possible about these issues that defy logical explanations. My children, Mara and Mitchell Mayo, increased my information and direct experiences in mind-to-mind communication; and my grandchildren, Serena Mayo, Tylea Decker, and Kahili Hahn, demonstrated that communication before birth was also possible. To them and to the generations to follow, I dedicate this work.

My intense appreciation and gratitude extend also to several mentors, without whom this work would not have been completed. First, the world famous Indian classical musician Alla Rakha introduced me to the deeper realms of mind-to-mind communication, long before this formal research began. Later, there were many days of philosophical discussions that physicist and Sanskrit scholar Dean Brown, PhD, was willing to spend with me. He understood that my thinking processes were dominated by images, so he thoughtfully designed his explanations to create pictures in my mind. In that way I could begin to comprehend at least some of the vast information he holds about the nature of the universe. The premier humanistic psychologist and great teacher Stanley Krippner, PhD, guided me through my PhD program and beyond. Through the many years of our friendship, I have seen how his spiritual integrity has been a beacon of light for all of his students. Anthropologist and noted world explorer Charles Brush, PhD, offered help and encouragement that was fundamentally important to me at those times when the scope of the project seemed beyond me. My dear friend and mentor, the late Shelby Parker, was always emotionally supportive. Through her generosity she provided the means for the new computer and printer to begin this manuscript.

The encouragement, deep friendship, and spiritual and intellectual support from the noted anthropologist Ruth-Inge Heinze, PhD, kept me writing when I was discouraged. Her organization of the *Annual International Conferences on the Study of Shamanism and Alternate Modes of Healing* has kept the field alive. When there did not seem to be enough outside interest in the subject to continue to report research, she published all the proceedings of the conferences herself, and these books have become a major source of reference for scholars today. Her decision to join Richard Grossinger, PhD, of North Atlantic Books as co-publisher has literally made this final work possible. I am intensely grateful to them both. No book can be completed without the help of editors, and several people helped with this at different times, including Marge King, Don Douglas, Kathy Glass and Ruth-Inge Heinze, PhD. The cover was designed by Joanne Kamiya, and I especially appreciate the much needed advice and emotional support she has given me over the many years of our friendship.

Two different organizations generously provided grants that kept the computer and the printer going with their expensive supplies and made it possible to photocopy the four hundred original telepathy trials to save them from the ravages of time. A grant from The Thanks Be To Grandmother Winnifred Foundation kept the project alive at an early age, and provided a much-needed scanner. A grant from the Institute of Noetic Sciences provided necessary expense money to continue the project.

More than one hundred and forty people participated in the various telepathic, remote viewing, and precognition experiments that we conducted over a period of many years. No research can be done alone, and for their interest and help, I am most grateful. They are listed alphabetically in Appendix B. The best research comes from the need to know, rather than the need to prove. All our participants volunteered because they, too, wanted to gain a better understanding of mind-to-mind communication. For them and for all the others who explore the multidimensional realms of human consciousness and share their findings, much thanks and appreciation.

In order to write about these realms beyond spacetime, I have needed space and an extended period of uncluttered time. These are invaluable for the extension of focus. The spiritual environment, the encouragement to continue in the creative process, the loving space we share and enjoy, have all been provided by my loving companion, Darrell Lemaire. Our own profound experiences of spiritual mind-to-mind communication have easily spanned distances of three hundred miles and more. His deep love and acceptance of "what is," his teaching of "there are no limits," are greatly cherished.

—Jean Beers Millay
Doyle, California, 1998

# TABLE OF CONTENTS

# FOREWORD

## by Stanley Krippner, PhD

Modern science, by and large, has been extremely antagonistic regarding parapsychology since its establishment in the 1880s, and this "gap of hostility" probably has widened rather than narrowed (Keen, 1997, p. 290). The Society for Psychical Research, founded in England in 1882, was the first major organization to attempt the scientific assessment of what are now called "psi phenomena," usually defined as organism-environment and organism-organism interactions in which it appears that information or influence has occurred that cannot be explained by means of mainstream science's understanding of sensory-motor channels (Radin, 1997). Hence, these reports are *anomalous* because they appear to stand outside the modern scientific concepts of time, space, and force.

Psychology is the scientific study of behavior and experience; parapsychology (or "psi research") studies apparent anomalies of behavior and experience—those existing apart from currently accepted explanatory mechanisms that account for organism-environment information and influence flow. Psi phenomena are usually grouped under the headings of "extra-sensory perception" (ESP), "psi gamma," or "receptive psi," in which anomalous information flow is reported, and "psychokinesis" (PK), "psi kappa," or "expressive psi," in which anomalous influence flow is reported. A dream about an unusual event that is actually occurring at the same time as the dream would be a possible example of receptive psi, while a possible example of expressive psi would be the reported movement of a physical object at the same time that someone claims to be "willing" that object to move.

The Parapsychological Association, founded in 1957 and an affiliate of the American Association for the Advancement of Science since 1969, consists of about three hundred members in some thirty different countries. This group tends to exclude from its membership people who make dogmatic statements about anomalies; indeed, it has gone on record as stating that labelling an event as a psi phenomenon does not constitute an explanation for that event, but only indicates an event for which a scientific explanation needs to be sought (Parapsychological Association, 1989).

The Parapsychological Association also has emphasized that "a commitment to the study of psi phenomena does not require assuming the reality of 'non-ordinary' factors or processes" (Ibid, p. 2). Despite these disclaimers and cautionary statements, parapsychology has been referred to by scholarly critics as a "pseudoscience" (Stanovich, 1985, pp. 159-162), a "deviant science" (Ben-Yehuda, 1985), and a "spiritual science" (Alcock, 1986, pp. 537-565) that is incompatible with the modern scientific worldview. Indeed, parapsychologists have been accused of harboring a hidden agenda in their work:

> The anomalies are for most parapsychologists only the means to an end; ultimately, they hope, these specimens will demonstrate once and for all that science as we know it is badly mistaken in its materialistic orientation and that human existence involves an ineffable, nonmaterial aspect that may very well survive the death and decay of the physical body. As long as the need exists to find meaning in life beyond that which is forthcoming from a materialistic philosophy, the search for the paranormal will go on. (Alcock, p. 563)

It is against this background that Jean Millay's *Multidimensional Mind* assumes importance in the ongoing discourse. Dr. Millay places her perspective on psi phenomena directly within the context of what is already part of mainstream science—perception, communication, memory, intelligence, and the natural environment. Mining her own massive research project for examples, she uses these gems to illustrate her position regarding such hypothetical constructs as remote viewing, resonance, and non-local spacetime.

For Dr. Millay, the multidimensional nature of mind requires a multidisciplinary approach for its description and perhaps, eventually, its understanding. Drawing from such diverse sources as humanistic and transpersonal psychology, quantum physics, dream research, Eastern texts, and shamanism (e.g., Bohm, 1980; Braud, 1984; Child, 1985; Griffin, 1997; Harman, 1988; LeShan, 1984; Tart, 1975; Taussig, 1987), Dr. Millay sees psi as a complex system, a mosaic in which many variables are constantly interacting. These variables range from one's state of consciousness during a psi phenomenon, to the state of consciousness of others involved in the psi interaction, to the status of solar and terrestrial fields at the time of the psi occurrence.

Toulmin (1982) writes that "postmodern science puts us in a position to reverse the cosmological destruction wrought by modern science, from AD 1600 on. The world view of contemporary, postmodern science is one in which practical and theoretical issues, contemplation and action, can no longer be separated; and it is one that gives us back the very unity, order, and sense of proportion...that the philosophers of antiquity insisted on" (p. 264). This reunification of the worlds of humanity and nature is not a task for psi research alone, but the "new parapsychology" has a unique opportunity to play a vital role in this historic mission. In the meantime, *Multidimensional Mind* falls within the parameters of Toulmin's description, as does Dr. Millay's imaginative vision of humankind and its possibilities.

# References

Alcock, J. (1986). Parapsychology as a "Spiritual Science." In P. Kurtz (Ed.), *A Skeptic's Handbook of Parapsychology* (pp. 537-565). Buffalo, NY: Prometheus.

Ben-Yehuda, N. (1985). *Deviance and Moral Boundaries: Witchcraft, the Occult, Science Fiction, Deviant Sciences and Scientists*. Chicago: University of Chicago Press.

Bohm, D. (1980). *Wholeness and the Implicate Order*. London: Routledge and Kegan Paul.

Braud, W. G. (1994). Reaching for Consciousness: Expansions and Complements. *Journal of the American Society for Psychical Research, 88*, 185-206.

Child, I. L. (1985). Psychology and Anomalous Observations: The Question of ESP in Dreams. *American Psychologist, 40*, 1219-1230.

Griffin, D. R. (1997). *Parapsychology, Philosophy, and Spirituality: A Postmodern Exploration*. Albany: State University of New York Press.

Harman, W. W. (1988). The Postmodern Heresy: Consciousness as Causal. In D. R. Griffin (Ed.), *The Reenchantment of Science: Postmodern Proposals* (pp. 115-128). Albany: State University of New York Press.

Keen, M. (1997). A Skeptical View of Parapsychology. *Journal of the Society for Psychical Research, 61*, 289-303.

LeShan, L. L. (1984). *From Newton to ESP: Parapsychology and the Challenge of Modern Science*. Wellingborough, Northamphire, England: Turnstone Press.

Parapsychological Association. (1989). Terms and Methods in Parapsychological Research. *Journal of Humanistic Psychology, 29*, 394-399.

Radin, D. I. (1997). *The Conscious Universe: The Scientific Truth of Psychic Phenomena*. San Francisco: HarperSanFrancisco.

Stanovich, K. (1985). *How to Think Straight about Psychology*. Glenview, IL: Scott, Foresman.

Tart, C. T. (1975). *States of Consciousness*. New York: E.P. Dutton.

Taussig, M. (1987). *Shamanism, Colonialism, and the Wild Man: A Study in Terror and Healing*. Chicago: University of Chicago Press.

Toulmin, S. (1982). The Emergence of Post-modern Science. In M. J. Adler (Ed.), *The Great Ideas Today, 1981* (pp. 68-114). Chicago: Encyclopedia Brittanica.

# INTRODUCTION

Each of us has experienced some event during this lifetime that revealed the existence of dimensions of reality beyond our usual assumptions about space and time. For some of us it may have been triggered by a traumatic event or a near-death experience. For some it may have been stimulated by a dream; or it may have come as a psychic communication from a loved one. For others, it was the result of meditation, of learning to discipline the naturally noisy mind into a profound silence.

The reason I can say with assurance that it will happen to all of us at some time is not because I claim this to be a mysterious "psychic" prediction on my part, but because many respected scientists have reported solid research about psi phenomena. There is a large literature available for study. (1) Scientific research from many disciplines can show clearly that the true nature of our consciousness is multidimensional and a fundamental part of our multidimensional universe. We can no longer conform to the limitations of 19th and 20th century materialistic ideas about what it means to be human. Our current manifestation in a three-dimensional body is a *projection* of this multidimensional consciousness. While our brain/mind contains a vast collection of DNA memories, healthy cell memories, mythological memories, and experiential memories, it also keeps track of its own space and time. Our multidimensional consciousness, however, is much more than the body/brain/mind it sets in motion. It is beyond the conventional three-dimensional measurements. Multidimensional consciousness is not even limited by the four dimensions of spacetime. It can provide the mind (with its sensory systems and their memories) with information beyond the reach of the physical body, beyond the knowledge of the mind. Researchers of psi phenomena from all over the world have shown this to be true, while many of us continue to study why and how it is possible. It is time to pay attention to the results of this research, and to contemplate what it means for all of us.

You may have been taught that it is not possible for one person to receive an image from another telepathically. The leaders of academic circles during the 19th and 20th centuries assumed that only the measurable was "real," and mind-to-mind communication was considered to be beyond the measurable. We now know that this idea is wrong. The 21st century will be dominated by increased understanding of the capacities of human consciousness, and the potentials of this knowledge for dynamic evolution.

Illustrated below are images that have been successfully transmitted directly from mind to mind by lovers who were totally isolated from each other. Each target, used for testing telepathy, was randomly chosen from a pool of one hundred possible targets. The sender was required to redraw the target and to write about what she was thinking during the eight minutes of testing time. The receiver was asked to draw and to write about whatever came to his mind during that same time. These people were not professional psychics. They participated in our experiments because they hoped to improve their communication with each other. This is the only example in four hundred telepathy trials in which red zig-zag lines were drawn, and both the sender and receiver drew them at the top. The concept of a person in pain and a red "O" are also matched.

All fields of human study and endeavor—education, medicine, biology, botany, physics and technology—will be changing as this vast potential of multidimensional consciousness becomes realized within each of us. We are co-creators in the ongoing game of evolution. There is no need to be limited by the old mythologies of history. We are free to explore the multidimensional realms available to our awareness.

### TARGET

"—And number FOUR is the King! WOK!"

*(cut from Marvel Comics)*

**Box Score:**

**Blind Match = 4**
**Similarities = 6**

### SENDER

"Action, violence, comedy, dumb."

"Focused at first on WOK."

*(The sender wrote these words on the back of the drawing.)*

### RECEIVER

"Man yelling, seems to be in pain...."

"Pain is main impression."

*(The receiver wrote these words on the back of the drawing.)*

**Team #8 - TARGET - Trial #3**
**February 28, 1975**

*(Photo from a magazine listed in Appendix A.)*

**Box Score:**
**Blind Match = 0  —  Similarities = 0**

**Team #8 - SENDER - Trial #3**

"Serene,
calm,
watery.
Peaceful,
moody."

**Team #8 - RECEIVER - Trial #3**

"Bold number
on some sort of oval plate.
Resembles motocross
number on a bike."

Illustrated above is an example of an unsuccessful telepathy attempt by the same team. Naturally, not all of the team's thirty trials were as remarkable as the one on the first page, though their scores ranged from 40% to 12%. In these experiments, we certainly expected some to be missed completely, and about 25% of our four hundred telepathy trials fell into this category of unsuccessful attempts. However, when you consider that most skeptics assume that telepathy never happens, the actual rate of total failure is quite low. In addition, the five outside independent judges (using forced-choice blind matching techniques) matched 25% of the telepathy trials correctly. The other 50% of the trials were only partially correct, and so some judges were able to match them and some were not. (Under each target is a box score for the number of correct matches for the two types of judging—blind matching and similarities matching.) However, the statistics are based only on the hits vs. the misses of the blind matching, and these are shown on a graph in Chapter Four.

We studied every response in detail and found the most information about the processes of mind-to-mind communication among the 50% of the trials that were only partially correct. This led to a careful analysis of the types of responses, as well. The four hundred telepathy responses and thirty-five remote viewing (RV) responses did provide us with in-depth information, not only about the mental processes involved, but also about our projections, our memories, and our multiple personalities. In Chapter Two we have tried to present all this in as simple a format as the complexities of the information allow

We have no need to prove to anyone that something happens when we close our eyes to ask for a vision. Those of us who have practiced drawing, painting, sculpture, or film making over the years have an intimate relationship with visions. We have learned how to quiet the verbal mind, how to focus total intention on the intelligence of the visual system, and how to wait for a vision to reveal itself. Since we all can explore our own potentials to expand our telepathic ability, perhaps the examples shown in the next few chapters will encourage you in your own personal explorations. We also wish to show where you can go wrong in such experiments, so you are not led astray by your own mental projections. Perhaps we can help you sort out what your mind projects from what you actually perceive.

There is an old saying that "seeing is believing," but it is also true that "if you really don't believe it, you won't see it." And we could add another saying to that: "If you do believe it, you might see it, even if it is not there to be seen." Hard-line skeptics, unwilling to believe what is demonstrated in the research, have called successful RV and telepathy "just good guessing." They have closed their eyes to the richness of their own multidimensional minds.

Since different people might use the same words with different meanings, we have attempted to clarify the way we use certain terms. The concepts defined in the next few pages include: 1) mind-to-mind communication and other psi phenomena; 2) the electromagnetic properties of our bodies and brains, and learning voluntary control of them through biofeedback; 3) various states of consciousness, such as meditation, trance, out-of-the-body; and 4) the multiple dimensions of the hyperspace and its relationship to non-local mind. For those who are not familiar with these terms, we recommend that you at least scan the next few pages, and perhaps refer back to them when you encounter a process that is unfamiliar to you. Those people who are familiar with these concepts jump to Chapter One.

## TECHNICAL AND THEORETICAL CONCEPTS ABOUT OUR MULTIDIMENSIONAL MINDS

**1. Mind-to-Mind Communication** — This phenomenon has been given various terms over the centuries. In 1886, Frederic W. H. Myers coined the term *"telepathy"* (feeling at a distance) to include all the processes of communication of emotions, ideas, mental images, sensations, or words from one individual to another that were beyond the reach of the normal senses. (2) In 1930, Upton Sinclair used the term *"mental radio"* to describe the work he did with his wife, Mary Craig Sinclair. (3) By 1947, J. B. Rhine, PhD, was using the term *"ESP,"* which stands for *"extra-sensory perception."* (4) In 1973, at Stanford Research Institute (SRI), Russell Targ and Hal Puthoff, PhD, developed the term *"remote viewing."* (5) They wanted to create some cognitive distance between their scientific experiments and other terms associated historically with the occult. Elizabeth Rauscher, PhD, used the term *"remote perception,"* because all the senses can receive information, not just vision. (6) The Parapsychology Association continues to use the term *"psi phenomena"* to cover all psychic activity, including telepathy, clairvoyance, channeling, precognition, psychokinesis (PK), remote viewing (RV), etc. Some researchers are now using the term *"anomalous cognition."*

**2. Telepathy** — I prefer to use the word *"telepathy"* for our experiments in which we used target pictures pasted on 3" x 5" cards. (The illustrations on pages 1 and 2 are examples of this type.) One hundred picture cards were always in the target pool from which the *sender* chose one randomly after the *receiver* was settled in a different room. The sender was asked to draw and to write what s/he was thinking about during the sending period. The isolated receiver was asked to draw and to write about whatever came to mind during this same period. Both of them had a set of ten differently colored marking pens. Eighteen different pairs of people *(teams)* completed four hundred free-response telepathy trials between 1974 and 1980. The conditions varied when the teams wanted to reverse their roles

of sender/receiver, but only the 355 trials consistent with the original protocol were used for the statistics.

**3. Remote Viewing** — We used the term *"remote viewing"* (RV) when a whole environment was the official target (indoor or outdoor). These experiments were done according to the SRI terminology, though our methodology differed from theirs somewhat. We conducted thirty-five RV trials over a period of fifteen years, with each series of trials slightly different in its protocol. It is important to realize that the targets for both types of studies (telepathy and RV) are vastly different, even though the mental processes are basically the same. For remote viewing the teams are separated not by rooms, but by many miles. Except on two occasions, the outbound team and the remote viewer were never closer than ten miles. Several sessions were done from a distance of nearly three thousand miles, and the greatest separation was eight thousand miles.

The illustration below is an example of this type of mind-to-mind communication. We expected to send and receive images of scenic places where tourists usually go. The cat is not an expected RV target site. The dog is not an expected RV response. The photo of the hungry cat was taken during the last five minutes of an RV experiment between Maui, Hawaii and Santa Rosa, California. James Dowlen was nearly three thousand miles away when he did this drawing of the hungry dog in his studio. The cat was a stray with a litter of nursing kittens. She had camped out on the porch of the rented cabin where I stayed during my visit to Maui. After our outbound team had left the "official" target site for that day, we arrived at the cabin to find this cat. My partner had brought cat food for her (not french fries as Dowlen's drawing suggests), but I was annoyed because of the timing of the distraction. The sending period was not quite over. However, because I was keeping track of all events as they happened during that hour, I photographed the cat as well.

When I returned to San Francisco, I was amazed to see Dowlen's very specific drawing (below). My RV partner

***TARGET***
***March 23, 1984***

Photo by Millay in Maui, Hawaii.

*(This hungry cat rushed into the room and sat by the refrigerator.)*

A DOG IS BEGGING FOR FOOD
ANNOYANCES FROM the PLATE OF FOOD...

***REMOTE VIEWER***
***James Dowlen***
in California, 3,000 miles away

"A dog is begging for food. Annoyances from a plate of food..."

in Maui is a cat lover. He would have taken the stray cats home with him, except for the ninety-day quarantine requirement for moving animals to the mainland. Dowlen is a dog lover. He does not have a cat. The transfer of animal type in the drawing is understood because memory is often projected onto the brief vision from the hyperspace. (See definition #21 page 12.) This was only one of several remarkable RV responses Dowlen had done for this series. The others are shown in Chapter Three.

**4. Sensory Perception vs. Extra-Sensory Perception—**
In this study we can show that *sensory perception* is at the heart of telepathy and that it is incorrect to continue to use the term *"extra-sensory"* to refer to one special extra sense that is dedicated to psychic perception. The concept implied by the term actually blocks the understanding of how the process works. Besides using the five generally acknowledged senses separately, we also use them in various combinations to arrive at additional information. Dean Brown, PhD, has listed more than fifty senses in his book, *Cosmic Law.* (7) Many of the senses on his list are related to the idea of *resonance.* It is far too simplistic to continue to refer to psi phenomena as though it were ESP, or a sixth sense. After all, each of the five senses has several subsystems. For example, the sense of touch can detect temperature, texture, pressure, etc., and uses different nerve endings for each of these sub-systems. Rods and cones provide information to the sense of sight differently. Visualization and visual memory, which can take place with eyes open or closed, are included in the sense of sight even though they involve projections from within, rather than resulting from light coming into the eye from the outside. In Chapter One we illustrate ten combinations of sensory perceptions because they are revealed in the results of our research. Each sense has its own perceptual ability, probably related to the individual's dominant cognitive style.

I believe that the term *"anomalous cognition"* is also inaccurate because psi is not abnormal, or improper, as the dictionary defines the meaning of *anomalous.* I believe that mind-to-mind communication is a natural activity of consciousness, and in subsequent chapters we attempt to illustrate this from the examples of our research. The term *"parapsychology"* is also an inappropriate name. Jeffrey Mishlove, PhD, agrees. In his book *Roots of Consciousness* he writes, "I am refraining from using that term in this book, along with the related term *paranormal.* Such terms may have caused damage to a field whose subject matter is, in my view, properly conceived of as *normal* and *psychological."* (8) Indeed the study of the human mind must now include its natural multidimensional characteristics.

**5. Teams** — A telepathic team is composed of a *sender* and a *receiver.* All teams in our studies volunteered and chose their own partners. The only requirements for acceptance into the study were that subjects had already established some rapport with each other, and that they were willing to commit themselves to the time necessary to complete all of the sessions (the telepathy and brainwave biofeedback training). Eight of the first eleven teams in the 1974 study were students at California State University at Sonoma (CSUS) in Cotati. Two teams included one student with a partner who was not a student. The average age of the students was mid-twenties. Another team had friends who were involved in the project. They asked to be included, though they were not students and were older, about mid-thirties. One team was a married couple with two children. The rest of the teams were composed of roommates, buddies, or lovers. By the following summer, two of the couples were married, but the others had separated. In the later 1980 study, the five teams, #12 to #16, were all male/female couples. Their ages ranged between thirty and fifty. One team from that group was married. The others were lovers, co-workers, or good friends. One additional team, at the TV recording studio, consisted of one sender and two receivers. Their results were not included with these statistics. For remote viewing experiments, there was more than one *sender* and/or more than one *receiver.* The make-up of the different RV teams is described in more detail in Chapter Three.

**6. Targets** — A target is whatever is chosen to be *sent* telepathically to the viewer. For remote viewing, the entire environment became the target site. For our telepathy, we used as targets pictures cut from all types of magazines. They were pasted on 3" x 5" cards so the picture on the back would not create confusion about the actual target intended, and placed in envelopes. The *monitor* would shuffle the target envelopes and spread them out in front of the sender, ask the sender to choose one randomly from the target pool, and announce the beginning of each trial. The receiver would draw whatever came to mind. This is called *"free-response telepathy,"* as opposed to "card guessing." One hundred targets were in the target pool at the beginning of each session. When attempting telepathy, it is best to have no idea whatsoever about the target, because it is the strange, unexpected, image that may be accurate.

We discovered the major difficulties of using cards for targets when my son Mitchell Mayo was recovering from an illness at age ten. Since he took an interest in telepathy, we practiced with the five black symbols on the Zener cards to pass the time (used extensively by J. B. Rhine). At first we had little success. Finally, we assigned an emotion (i.e., mad, sad, or glad) to each symbol. After that our transmission rate improved. The exercise had an unexpected benefit. It allowed both of us to express emotion without the other one taking it personally, since the emotions were relegated to the symbolic images as abstractions. Even with that benefit, we soon tired of the same old cards. Simple targets repeated over and over again are boring. You can remember them all, so you can imagine them all. Memory and imagination create a noisy interference in the clarity of mind, and clarity is necessary for telepathy. Card targets create static in the signal to noise ratio.

Free-response telepathy is a better approach. However, a major problem of free-response telepathy was revealed in a study by Hardy, Harvie, and Koestler. (9) In 1975, they conducted a number of experiments to test telepathy using simple line drawings. For controls, they did a "mock" experiment by asking two separate groups of people to make simple line drawings from memory, with no attempt to send or receive them telepathically. When they compared the two sets of drawings from the control groups, they found almost as many similarities as were found in their telepathic attempts.

Here is the problem with this type of experiment. If we ask thirty people to draw twelve pictures of whatever came to mind and then compare all 360 pictures together, we might very well find about as many matching ideas and images among them as one might find among line drawings used during telepathic attempts. This does not prove that their telepathy set was matched only by chance. It does illustrate that many of us derive our pictures from a similar memory base. When we learned to read, the pictures with the words became *word-picture-symbols.* These early symbols are still in our memories. When we are asked to draw something, the earliest learned memories are often the images that rise to the surface first. The list of common pictures might read as follows: house, tree, flower, stick figure or face, animal, mountain, sun, bird, boat, fish, car. No matter how many line drawings might be made from memory by people from the same culture, many images would naturally match, because of our shared memories from school textbooks, colorbooks, or other common sources. Early and shared memories are discussed in Chapter Six.

In our study we hoped to avoid the confusion between actual telepathy and the synchronicity of shared memory. That is why we created such a large target pool with so many very different images. Pictures were collected from any source available, such as postcards, hand-made drawings, and comic books. Most of them were cut from a variety of magazines with photographs of people, nature, things, paintings, drawings, or decorative words. Since the couples in our study were expected to respond differently to the same images, we asked the sender to redraw the randomly chosen target in its colors, rather than with only black outlines (a few black and white targets were included in the pool for contrast). Since we were exploring ways that communication between couples might be improved, we needed a record of what the sender might actually be thinking during the sending period. Sometimes the sender was *not* thinking about the target, and occasionally the receiver's response would follow that variance from the target in a similar way.

If you want to begin this practice at home, before going to the trouble of cutting a lot of pictures out of magazines, I recommend that you buy a deck of children's flash cards with one colored picture on one side and the word that goes with it on the other. Have someone else put them in security envelopes, so you don't know what is there. Remove the ones you have already used from the deck, and shuffle the rest of them each time you use them.

**7. Sending Period** — In our telepathy trials, the sending period was eight minutes long, divided into three sections. We found that if the sending period was too long, the thoughts of the participants would wander. If it was too short, the receiver might not feel tuned in sufficiently to receive an image.

As soon as the team arrived for the session, they would spend a few minutes meditating or just relaxing together. Often they had just come from school or another busy activity and needed to slow down or to eat something. After that they each would be given ten blank 3" x 5" cards and ten colored marking pens. In the presence of the monitor, they wrote their names and the date on all the cards and numbered them from one to ten. The monitor examined them and directed the participants into different rooms. Two minutes were spent in quiet contemplation before the monitor asked the sender to select a target randomly from the pool. Then during the first timed period (two minutes) the sender would contemplate the target before beginning to redraw it. During this time, the isolated receiver could draw or write whatever came to mind. Four minutes were timed for the drawing. The monitor would then announce there were two more minutes to write on the card whatever they were thinking about. At that point they were to sit quietly to clear their minds before the next target card was chosen. The only words spoken would be by the monitor.

Those instructions, such as, *"Begin drawing," or, "You have two minutes to write about your thoughts,"* etc., were predetermined and did not change during any of the sending periods. After five trials were completed, the monitor would ask the receiver to return so they all could compare responses and targets and discuss their feelings about the session. During that time, the monitor recorded each numbered trial with each response made during that sending period. The next set of five trials began as soon as both team members felt they were ready.

**8.  Set and Setting** — The *set* refers to the state of mind of the participants and to the strength of their intentions to communicate. The *setting* refers to the environment used in the study. Therefore the setting was designed to encourage a relaxed state of mind of the participants. Neither the early study nor the later one was done in a formal laboratory, with monitors in white lab coats. The setting was always friendly and casual.

The 1974-75 study was conducted in an apartment near the college that was chosen for the convenience of the students who had volunteered to spend the many hours it took to complete the study. The apartment had cushions, a foam mattress, and bag chairs on the floor, all nicely covered in soft fabrics or fake fur. A five-foot painting of a microscopic view of soft blue butterfly scales hung on the wall. There was a dining room table with chairs, and food was always available for hungry students. Each student was asked to color a mandala pattern designed to focus the visual system. This was also used to shift the focus of attention from verbal to nonverbal activity, while waiting to practice interhemispheric brainwave biofeedback *(IH synch)*. The interpersonal *(IP team synch)* sessions began right after *IH synch* sessions, when each person had relaxed as much as possible. The receiver's room also had velvet pillows on a foam mattress on the floor. There was a large tie-dyed blue velvet wall hanging, and a handmade rug in the same colors. Soft music, without dramatic changes to distract the meditation, was played continuously to mask any possible outside noises. One student, Michael Mahon, volunteered to do foot rubs before the sessions for those who needed the extra chance to relax. Relaxation was always the priority during these sessions. Noise or confusion in the subject room was eliminated since it could cause error in the results.

There was one exception to the informal setting. Each of the five teams of the 1980 study agreed to go in turn to the University of California Medical Center Langley Porter Psychophysiology Laboratory (UC Lab) in San Fran-cisco, where the EEG chart recording and computer analysis could be used. We didn't wear white lab coats there either, and we tried to make the subject room as comfortable and as casual as possible, in spite of the formality of the whole environment. The telepathy and biofeedback training sessions for the rest of that study were conducted at Henry Dakin's Washington Research Institute (WRI) in San Francisco in an apartment that had carpeting and was arranged for the comfort of the participants.

**9.  Qual** — Qual includes more than the set of the participants, and more than the idea of setting. (10) Qual includes the whole emotional environment, the passing train, and the "psychic soup" of all the people involved in the experiment. It includes what is still wandering through the thoughts of the participants before the experiment, beyond the set of their intentions (i.e., the unfinished term paper or the errands they must do when the experiment is over). The qual  includes the weather outside as well as the emotional state of the monitor, such as the attention devoted to operating the machines and his/her level of sensitivity to the needs and comfort of the participants.

For our experiments in 1974, the most important qual had been established already by Eleanor Criswell, EdD. She is a professor of Humanistic Psychology at CSUS, and was then president of the California Biofeedback Society. She had set up a program for students to work toward a special degree in parapsychology. The interest in this program was so extensive that students came from all over the country to study with her. The time, place, and environment were perfect for my study as well. Criswell had set the stage, and the students who arrived were ready to participate in any ongoing psi research. Thirty people volunteered for my study after seeing a demonstration of the *Stereo Brainwave Biofeedback Light Sculpture* (page 10).

**10.  Sensory Shielding** — It is important for those  who seriously want to know if they can transmit messages from mind to mind to be protected from distractions and any sensory clues that might confuse the experiment. We made sure our participants would not be compromised because of inadequate shielding during their telepathy attempts. In the past, the researchers were most concerned about this so they or their participants could not be accused of cheating. In our own experience we found that the best place to receive a telepathic message is in an electromagnetically shielded room that blocks out all distractions and encourages meditation. We did not have such a room, but we did block distractions and kept our teams separated and shielded, which was what they also wanted.

**11. Box Score** — The blind matching score (**BMS**) is listed under each target illustrated in subsequent chapters. It represents how many of the five independent judges were able to match that particular response with its target. The similarities matching score (**SMS**) takes into account six types of similarities matched by other independent judges (e.g., **d** = drawing, **s** = shape, **cl** = color, **w** = word, **m** = mood, **cn** = concept).

Example: When three of the five judges matched the response with the target and only shape and color were similar, the box score would read like the one below:

BMS = 3 — SMS = s, cl

Since there were three cards for each of the many trials for judging similarities (target, sender's drawing, and receiver's response), the task was very time-consuming. The only people who would volunteer for such a job were truly interested in psi phenomena. So these judges were given an additional chance to mark a set of trials as a "hit," in case none of the six similarities seemed to match. This was called the "subjective" choice. The total average of this was 35% of the 290-trial set and 57% of the 65-trial set. However, the subjective score was not included here because it was added to allow the volunteers a way to express their enthusiasm for psi without compromising their judgments about the actual similarities we wished to study.

The table below lists the results of the similarities judging for both the 1974-75 studies (290 trials) and the 1980 trials (65 trials).

| Similarities Matching Scores | 290 trials | 65 trials |
|---|---|---|
| Similar lines or drawing | = 12% | = 8% |
| Similar shape (list of 20 types) | = 32% | = 51% |
| The same color (10 colored pens) | = 23% | = 55% |
| Exact word or descriptive words | = 23% | = 41% |
| Similar mood (list of 20 moods) | = 19% | = 24% |
| Similar concept (list of 20 concepts) | = 21% | = 26% |

The people who judged the similarities for the first study were not the same people who judged the 1980 study. Judges also demonstrate some differences in they way they look at events. However, except for the lower score for drawing similarity, the 1980 teams showed substantial increases in the other similarity scores, especially shape, color, and word. The 1980 teams also had a larger BMS score. Theirs was 33.6% compared to 23% for the 1974-75 studies. Though there were fewer trials in 1980, those five teams raised the total score to 25%. Perhaps one reason the 1980 teams had higher scores was because they were older and had become more involved with their own spiritual practices. The judges who used blind matching later reported that they looked primarily for ideas or concepts that matched, rather than for shapes or colors that matched. As you can see, the similarities judges found that only 21% of the 290 trials matched in concept. Yet the similarity of shape reached 32%. Perhaps the imaging system was a stronger receptor than the conceptual one for most of our participants, because we had requested drawings first and then verbal responses. (11)

**12. Consciousness** — This word has been used to mean so many different aspects of the human psyche that now it must be defined by any author before it can be used. It can refer merely to the act of being aware, or awake, as in the question we might ask of someone who is just waking up, "Are you conscious?" Others have used the term to refer to that timeless aspect of ourselves, that part of us which is in tune with God. That has been called our "higher consciousness." The higher consciousness is said to be able to bring events and ideas into awareness from beyond space and/or time. It is also responsible for creative insight, intuition, spiritual and transcendental visions, etc. Freud used the term "unconscious" to refer to repressed memories. From hypnosis the term "pre-conscious" refers to the memories that may arise spontaneously into awareness. They have been just below the surface of awareness, and when the mind stops talking to itself and relaxes, the pre-conscious thoughts have an opportunity to rise to the surface. Ruth-Inge Heinze, PhD, reports there are also states of dissociation, in which a person is not aware of the present moment in space and time, but may be very much aware of other dimensions, as in trance states or out-of-the-body states. Shamans or mediums may attain such states while a discarnate spirit speaks through them. (12) When they return awareness to the present spacetime frame, they may be totally unaware of what happened while their attention was focused on another dimension.

With all of these possible uses for the words about consciousness, it is necessary to establish a different term for each different state. We explored many different types of psi experiences in our studies so several terms will be used. We shall refer to ordinary waking consciousness as *"awareness."* We shall refer to the material that was forgotten or just below the surface of awareness, but which arises into awareness during the relaxation period just before telepathic trials (or during hypnosis), as the *"pre-conscious."* And we shall refer to our higher consciousness that provides information to our sensory awareness from beyond space and/or time (from the hyperspace) as the *"superconscious"* or the *"psyche."* This is also our spiritual nature, our relationship to the Great Mystery of the Universe, our relationship to God. If any deep *subconscious* material surfaces at all, it might be represented only by symbols at the level of awareness, so we shall use the term *"symbolic"* when images from the subconscious are received in our telepathic responses. We shall use the term *"trance"* for a state of intense concentration, augmented by the conditional descriptions of *"light trance"* or *"deep trance."* Deep trance can be induced by drums, music, certain herbs, or by a trained hypnotist. The *light trance* is often self-induced, and is sometimes used in telepathy. Different types of trance are discussed in Chapter Five.

It is rare for the activity of the *superconscious* to reveal the unseen dimensions as light in a photograph. Illustrated below are pictures taken of Dean Brown when he was in a highly creative state. Don Parker, PhD, was using standard Polaroid 600 film in his home camera. When Parker saw the first picture, he thought there was something wrong with his camera, so he took another one. However, other pictures taken later with the same film pack were quite normal. For these pictures, there was only one overhead light on in the room and it was not moving. The chair in the background is not blurred. In the photo on the left, Brown's figure can be seen glowing; on the right, the lights seem to be moving in several directions. Ordinary logic has not explained these anomalous photographs.

There are some lights, some energies around the body that can be measured with considerable accuracy. The series of photos illustrated on the opposite page was taken from an infra-red computer monitor. Joanne Kamiya learned to focus attention on the flow of blood in her body through the use of a skin temperature biofeedback device. This series shows her raising the temperature of her hands just by directing her focus of attention on the feeling of warmth in them.

**13. Biofeedback** — Biofeedback is a system of feeding back information from the body that is ordinarily unconscious to the personality. Thirty years ago, Joe Kamiya, PhD, found that a person could identify the frequencies of brainwave signals, as measured from the scalp, and gain conscious control of them. Since that time, biofeedback has been used by therapists to help people improve their health through learning voluntary control of various electrically measurable parameters of the human nervous system (e.g., emotions with Galvanic Skin Response [GSR] machines; muscle tension with EMG machines; cold hands and feet with skin temperature machines; high blood pressure and heart rate with pulse monitors; and brainwaves with EEG machines). (13)

This medical model for the use of biofeedback has been widely accepted over the years and has been extremely useful. However, in an educational setting, biofeedback can be used in an entirely different way as a tool for self-discovery. Students can discover for themselves just how thoughts affect their bodies. Also, different modalities of biofeedback can enhance the ability of students to focus attention in different ways.

In 1982, I had an opportunity to use a variety of biofeedback equipment for several weeks with a fifth-grade class. Through learning to relax the muscles in his

On rare occasions, we have seen that a person in a high-energy state of creativity may affect the exposure of photographic film. Some types of film "see" more of the visible spectrum than most of us do. This may or may not be one example, but it does suggest a possibility. One might think that someone was swinging a lantern with multiple lights, but that did not happen.

Photographs by
Don Parker

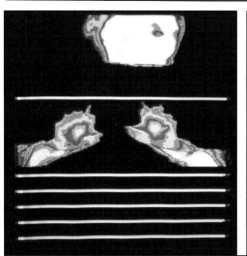 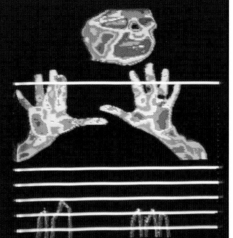 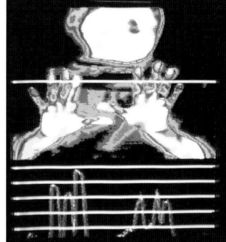

**Joanne Kamiya demonstrates her ability to raise the temperature of her hands through the force of her intention.**
She moves the infra-red light of her body around, as she wills the flow of blood to be increased to the tips of her fingers. In the first image,
her cold fingertips are black. The second image shows that as she begins to focus the feeling of heat into her hands, her face cools off somewhat.
When the temperature of her hands increased ten degrees, they began to show white and her face also warmed up again.
Photographs by Richard Lowenberg and Jean Millay

forehead through biofeedback with an EMG, a good student controlled his headaches. His grades improved even more, so he was later transferred into the gifted program. Through learning to control his emotions using the GSR, an average student was no longer afraid to speak in front of the class, and later he made the honor roll for the first time. Through learning to stabilize his faster brainwave frequencies, a hyperactive student increased his ability to focus attention and was able to improve his reading level and his self-confidence. The addition of biofeedback lessons in the classroom can allow students to learn about the electromagnetic dimensions of their thoughts and feelings and the effects their emotions have on their health. This study, and others conducted by Marge King in her high school science classroom, are detailed in Chapter Six. (14)

From ancient times, shamans have studied the interaction between thoughts and health. Rolling Thunder, a Native American, told us that he had to process the bite of a rattlesnake as part of his training to become a medicine man. Many have learned to walk on fire without getting burned. (15) Voluntary control of a variety of physical functions has been a goal of meditators for centuries. Electronic machines can assist in the learning of self-control.

**14. The Portable Brainwave Analyzer** — In the late Sixties, only large institutions could afford and house EEG machines, which filled a whole room. In 1969, R. Timothy Scully, PhD, developed the portable Aquarius Electronics Alphaphone™. In 1971 he built an advanced version which was the brainwave analyzer. The analyzer sorted brainwave frequencies into four categories and provided

sound signals to identify them. With two of these analyzers, plus the isolation switches, I was able to create the *Stereo Brainwave Biofeedback Light Sculpture* (*Light Sculpture*). It had reciprocal designs carved in eight Plexiglas panels that would light up with different colors in response to four brainwave frequency ranges for two separate sets of signals. (See pages 10 and 40.) With this, along with the warbling feedback sound that came directly from the analyzers, I found that I could synchronize the two signals from my own head (from electrodes placed at symmetrical places on both sides). The feedback tones accompanied feelings of deep meditation and sometimes resulted in profound creative insight. Because of personal psi experiences that were quite powerful, Scully and I both wondered if it would be possible for two people to learn to synchronize their brainwaves with each other to improve telepathic communication. The formal studies that provide the background for this book began in 1974.

**15. Brainwave Frequency Categories** — The standard designation for the number of cycles per second is Hertz (Hz). The frequency ranges are listed below. Frequencies above 20Hz are sometimes called Gamma.

| below 4Hz | 4Hz to 7Hz | 8Hz to 12Hz | 13Hz to 20Hz |
|-----------|------------|-------------|--------------|
| **Delta** | **Theta** | **Alpha** | **Beta** |

7Hz to 13Hz
(This was the expanded alpha range
we used for biofeedback and for
the EEG synchronization scores.)

The *Stereo Brainwave Biofeedback Light Sculpture* changes its colors and patterns with changes in thoughts. On the left is the pattern that appears when both signals are in the alpha range. On the right is the pattern that appears when the left signal is in alpha and the right one is in theta. Mandala patterns are used so the visual focus is not distracted when the lights change.

Photos by Richard Hendrickson, PhD

We used Scully's portable machines from 1972 to 1982. They were quite accurate within the range of 4Hz to 20Hz, but they were not designed to measure anything faster. We did see frequencies up to 36Hz on the chart recorders at the UC Medical Center's Langley Porter Psychophysiology Laboratory (UC Lab) in San Francisco. (Faster frequencies were reportedly measured by a Japanese laboratory from two boys who exhibited psychokinesis [PK], but we could not confirm that when these same boys visited the Washington Research Institute (WRI).

**16. Brainwave Synchronization** — Simultaneous alpha signals, as measured from symmetrical places on both sides of the head, were called relative interhemispheric synch (relative *IH synch*). When the simultaneous alpha signals were in the same frequency and also in phase, or with a slowly varying phase angle, they were called absolute *IH synch*. These words carried the concept easily to all participants, though the technical term for absolute synch was "phase coherence."

The two brainwave analyzers fed information into the phase comparator for additional analysis. The participants could see the relationship between the patterns of their right and left brainwave signals in colored light mandalas on the *Light Sculpture*. (Two of the ten possible brainwave patterns are illustrated above.) The feedback tones from all three instruments included a warbling sound from each brainwave analyzer that indicated the frequency being measured, and two mellow AUM tones from the phase comparator, one of which indicated simultaneous alpha and the other phase coherence. When the participants trained to improve their percent-time scores of alpha with their eyes closed, only the sound signals were used.

We had hoped to find a synchronization between two people who were telepathic. Simple simultaneous alpha between two people was not precise enough to show us what we were looking for. Only the tones from the phase comparator were helpful for training synchronization between two people. The interpersonal simultaneous alpha we called *"IP team* relative *synch."* When the simultaneous alpha signals were also in phase, we called it *"IP team* absolute *synch."* At the beginning, *IP team synch* of either kind seemed to occur so infrequently for some of our teams that it was not easy for the partners to identify it, but three teams seemed to join in phase coherence naturally.

However, all of the twenty-two volunteers learned to improve their individual ability to produce alpha rhythms in *IH synch*. Only a few of the teams showed improvement in *IP team synch*. Their final telepathy scores did not necessarily match that same improvement. We could not answer our original question about whether training helped or hindered their telepathic ability. The overall telepathy scores for blind matching were not statistically significant at 23%, since chance would be 20% with the method of scoring we used. Yet we found a statistically significant correlation between the average *IP team* absolute *synch* scores and the team telepathy scores ($p < .01$). Those teams which had the highest scores in *IP team synch* also had above-chance scores in their telepathy. (See Chapter Four.)

These results encouraged us to continue exploring our questions, though many were still unanswered, and more had been generated. In 1980, the Institute of Noetic Sciences (IONS) provided us with a small grant that allowed us to use the electroencephalogram (EEG) chart recorders and computer analysis at the UC Lab. Under the supervision of Joe Kamiya, PhD, and with the computing expertise of James Johnston, PhD, we recorded the brainwaves of five additional volunteer teams.

Johnston compared the blind matching scores of the entire set of telepathy trials with the *ratio* of EEG phase coherence. He found that the statistical correlation was higher than before at $p < .001$. (16) His statistics included 355 trials completed by sixteen different teams. With the additional teams and trials, the average telepathy score increased to 25%. Because of this strong statistical correlation, we decided to examine the results of our telepathy in greater detail.

As a result of an intensive examination of the telepathic responses, we can illustrate some of the problems we all have in communication with each other, and the problems we have in perception of what we think is an external reality and what we project from our internal mental activity. So much of what we perceive is just the *mind's reflections from our own projections.* One of the benefits of telepathic attempts is that the misty edge between projection and reception is stretched out much further so that we can examine it better and in more detail. That misty edge goes by so fast in ordinary perception that we often miss it, taking our projections as though they represented an external consensus "reality." Knowing this, the creative game of self-discovery can begin anew by developing a variety of ways to perceive the inner and outer worlds. Becoming flexible in different ways of focusing attention is a key to the expansion of our intelligence.

One first response to an experience of brainwave synchronization with a friend is to assume that you both think the same way. The assumption, of course, is that you both think the way that *you* do. All your own mentations might be projected onto the other until your own reality is all there is. If your projections continue without confirmation, the relationship may soon end, when you are shocked to find that your friend does *not* think the way you do. The decision to truly communicate begins as you and your partner encourage each other to share interpretations of the same experience. The next response is to compare your dominant cognitive styles and symbols. You think in pictures, he thinks in words, for example. Your symbol of love and caring is to offer a cup of tea. Since he was burned as a child by someone accidentally spilling a cup of tea on his arm, this will not be a symbol of love and caring for him. He would prefer a gentle word and a touch. It is in these details of follow-up conversation that the power of brainwave synchronization can be experienced more deeply. Additional technical details of the brainwave synchronization part of the study are included in Chapter Four.

> **From 355 telepathy trials completed by sixteen different teams, we found a statistically significant correlation (p < .001) between team average telepathy scores and their team average scores in alpha phase coherence (IP Team Synch).**

**17. Psychic Soup** — All the thoughts of all the participants of a telepathic event might be intermingled. When the sender stops sending, and tunes into the receiver, she can get a feeling of the receiver's response. The monitor's thought field is also part of the soup. When groups of people participate in remote viewing experiments, parts of the thoughts of many are woven into the responses. (See pages 96 to 100.) The active attention of many people simultaneously seems to be able to influence the outcome of some events. (See page 141.) We have observed that it is possible for the brainwaves of one person to influence those of another. A monitor, who becomes extremely analytical or anxious while studying the readout of the brainwave analyzers, might unconsciously block the *synchronization* of participants. As soon as he reestablishes his own inner calm, the synchronization of the participants might then continue. (Experimenter effect must be taken into account in the study of EEG. Any distraction can shift the frequencies of the EEG that is being observed.) (See page 142.)

Psi experiences of all kinds are natural to life and death and have always been an essential part of life before technology. A few scientists are beginning to explore psi phenomena as it might be related to many types of resonances, field-consciousness effects, quantum physics and geomagnetic fluctuations. Early results show that we do seem to be interconnected among multidimensional pathways.

**18. Local Sidereal Time (LST)** — James Spottiswoode, PhD, found a relationship between LST and success of telepathy experiments. He writes: (17)

> The Earth rotates on its axis every 24 hours exactly with respect to the sun; this is known as a solar day. But due to the fact that the Earth is also orbiting the sun once per year, 24 hours is not the period of the Earth's rotation with respect to the distant stars. That period, called a sidereal day, is slightly shorter—23 hours and 56 minutes long. It is the time required for the distant stars to return to exactly the same position when viewed by an observer at a fixed location on the Earth's surface. The time at any location with respect to the sidereal rotation period is known as Local Sidereal Time.

**19. Geomagnetic Fluctuations** — Sun spots and solar flares produce changes in the electromagnetism reaching Earth, resulting in disrupted radio signals, for example. Studies of the negative effects that solar flare activity may have on the success of telepathy have been reported. (18) These effects and those linked with Local Sidereal Time are discussed in Chapter Four.

**20. Non-Local Spacetime** — Physicist and Sanskrit scholar Dean Brown has provided this definition of non-local spacetime:

> The domain of the non-local is the realm where time and space do not operate. For instance, mathematics, great art, and psi experiences are outside of spacetime. De Chardin called it the noösphere. The quantum physicist David Bohm called it the holo-movement. In the non-local, everywhere is here; every when is now; every point is the center of the universe. Normal day-to-day perception is usually seated in spacetime. But *REAL* experiences are out of spacetime. This is the domain of the archetypes, the domain of reality that underlies true communication (resonance).

It is important to hold the idea of non-local spacetime when contemplating the results of all psi phenomena. We and others who study and conduct research in this field use the term extensively. Non-local spacetime may seem impossible in our logical material existence, but in the super-consciousness of non-duality, or oneness with the universe, non-local spacetime becomes experiential.

**21. Hyperspace** — Saul-Paul Sirag has described the multidimensionality of the hyperspace as follows: (19)

> The idea that space is more than three-dimensional is at least as old as Plato, who, in his *Parable of the Cave* suggested that we usually identify ourselves with our three-dimensional shadows rather than with the higher-dimensional beings we really are. This idea was rejected by Aristotle and subsequent generations of physicists. Recently, however, theoretical physicists working on unified field theory have found it necessary to postulate the physical reality of hyperspace, defined as a space of more than three dimensions (3-d). These proposed physical hyperspaces are 10-d or 26-d or even higher-dimensional spaces....
>
> In 1864, Maxwell unified electricity and magnetism in such a way that he produced an electromagnetic theory of light. This unification made the startling proposal that visible light is merely a tiny part of the electromagnetic spectrum. Similarly, because we today are unifying all the forces, something new, analogous to light, should come out of our endeavors. I propose that a theory of consciousness is but a small part of a spectrum of realms of consciousness....

At a 1996 conference called "Towards a Science of Consciousness: The First Tucson Discussions and Debates," Sirag expanded on his hyperspace theories. His paper is entitled "A Mathematical Strategy for a Theory of Consciousness." (20)

The idea that ordinary reality is embedded in a higher-dimensional reality is a traditional theme of fiction, philosophy, and religion. Now this idea is being seriously entertained by physicists attempting to unify the physical forces: electromagnetism, the weak and strong nuclear forces, and gravity.

The hyper-dimensional form of unified field theory views all force fields and matter fields as existing in a hyperspace of more than four dimensions. The spacetime of ordinary reality is, therefore, merely a four-dimensional projection of this hyperspace.

The physical hyperspace may, of course, be embedded in a larger space with even richer structures. If we postulate that the mental realm is a hyperspace which embeds physical hyperspace, then a unified theory of mental and physical events becomes possible. Paranormal phenomena may be defined as events which seem to disregard the limits of ordinary spacetime reality. Such events, however, may be understood as normal events in the hyperspace. These events seem unusual because the spacetime projection provides only a partial view of the hyperspace events.

Sirag's diagram below provides us with a way of visualizing the concept that the hyperspace body has a *projection* into the spacetime body, and the spacetime body has a *lifting* into the hyperspace body, which is the realm of the superconscious. All of us have a hyperspace body and a spacetime body. This diagram helps us to visualize and to understand how psi is a natural part of the cosmic order of things.

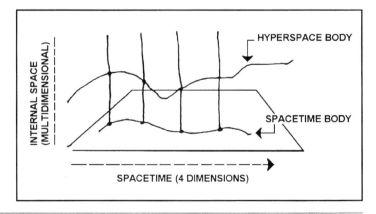

# CHAPTER ONE — SENSORY PERCEPTION

The term *"sixth sense"* has been in the language for so many years that most people think it is the vehicle of psi experiences, or that it is a special capacity only psychics have. Since there are so many more senses than the five major ones we usually think of, the term "sixth sense" is misleading. Touch, for example, is a general label for a collection of separate sensory nerve endings that discriminate temperature, texture, pressure, etc. Hearing includes not only the frequencies and amplitudes of sound waves, it also anticipates melodies and rhythms, and can discriminate the nuances necessary for the brain to interpret the meaning of language. That old concept of a "sixth sense" not only limits our understanding of all of our senses, but it also implies—as does the term *"ESP"* (extra-sensory perception)—that there is a special sense organ somewhere in the body or brain that accounts for psychic activity. None has been found. Actually, the senses we have and use all the time are the ones that have the remarkable ability to feel and to know things at a distance. Each sense transmits its individual impressions to assigned receptors in the brain. Each reception is translated through its own unique memories and associations. Sometimes sensory perceptions can conflict with each other. Sometimes they combine to form new insights, because the possible combinations of sensory perceptions are very numerous. We are able to demonstrate ten different types of sensory perceptions using as illustrations the words and pictures from the four hundred telepathy trials of our studies over the years.

The perceptions of our sensory systems can become extremely sensitive and discriminating. Think what it may be like to be a composer of music. If you are one, you know, but if you are not, just imagine for a moment that you are. You are composing a symphony for fifty musicians to play. You must be able to consider the blend of sounds among the different stringed instruments, and the timing for each of them to become part of the background or to dominate the melody in turn. There are the horns and the woodwinds which also must play their part in the exact harmony that you wish to hear. The percussions must be on the beat with the right sound at the right time. What kind of hearing is required? How much sensitivity must the ears have to be able to send sounds to the brain for discrimination and judgment? Next you choose to add a chorus of fifty people. There are altos, basses, sopranos, plus a few soloists. The notes for each group have to be written into the score in exactly the right way for the total effect. Now just imagine that the final music is the sublime *Ninth Symphony* by Beethoven. He devoted his life to the sound of music, but the triumph of this symphony is more than sounds; it touches the spirit of all who have heard it around the world. He was totally deaf at the time. The knowledge of musical sound was within him.

Consider the mother who wakes up in the middle of the night, knowing that her son has just been killed in a war on the other side of the world. For his whole life she was lovingly tuned to his needs. Her sensitivity to him was aware, even in sleep, to respond when his spirit came to tell her goodbye. She had within her the love and knowledge of his heart.

Illustrated below is the randomly chosen target picture (left), the sender's drawing (center), and James Dowlen's telepathic response (right). He has drawn a head—not quite human, not quite animal—with pointed ears. He drew the Ankh, but put it on the top of the head where the crown is in the target, and drew both hands holding a paintbrush. Four of the visual elements of the target appeared to him telepathically. From childhood on, he has filled stacks of notebooks with his drawings from life, and he can draw any fleeting image that arises in his mind. For Dowlen, the knowledge of imagery is within him.

*TV Team - TARGET*
*3/15/77*

*Egyptian wall painting*

*TV Team - SENDER*

"Ancient Egypt Ankh"

*TV Team - RECEIVER*
*James Dowlen*

## TELEPATHY RESULTS DEMONSTRATE HOW SENSORY IMPRESSIONS ARE RECEIVED

All of the senses can receive impressions telepathically from the hyperspace, translate them according to the memories associated with the current dominant level of thought, and thus make them available to conscious awareness. The senses can do this independently, or they can cooperate to build up additional information.

In this book we show that *sensory perception* is at the heart of telepathy and why the term "extra-sensory" is incorrect and blocks the understanding of the actual process of the activity. We also show that much of what we perceive, whether it is by telepathy or directly in front of us, is part of what we project onto the external world. What we think we perceive is often dominated by the way our minds reflect that projection back to us. In these telepathic attempts some of these problems of ordinary face-to-face communication can be demonstrated. We hoped to find out *what actually happens* when we try to communicate telepathically. Why is the response right when it is right? Why is it wrong when it is wrong? How can we improve the potential of such communication? Most of the people who volunteered to help with the study had experienced psi at one time or another. Some of it was very puzzling. For that reason that we subjected all the results to different types of judging. The judging for similarities **(SMS)** exposed the variety of sensory perceptions that were missed in the process of blind matching **(BMS)**. The box scores under the targets compare the two and are explained on page 7.

**1. The Senses of Smell and Taste** are sometimes reported by psychics when doing remote viewing or when looking for lost children. Since our targets were only pictures pasted on 3" x 5" cards the senses of smell and taste were not evoked, and I do not have any examples of them. We did try to conduct a group experiment once to include the sense of smell with the picture targets. Many things went wrong. After a film canister containing a smelly substance had been randomly chosen from a box of ten of them for the "official target smell," another film canister containing a few drops of nail polish remover (acetone) fell over in the box. Gradually the acetone leaked out, dominating all the other odors in the area. Joanne Kamiya gave the only response to smell we received during that session. Her drawing did not match the official target: but it did look like the object of the sender's attention; a building (with the same shape as the box containing our collection of smells). She drew windows on it, in the same arrangement as the spots of flowers on the box, and something toxic leaking out the bottom. I believe that a study using targets of smell and taste would show that sensory perception can be evoked in all the senses. For that experiment, however, we should choose receivers who have these senses highly developed, such as florists or cooks.

**2. The Sense of Touch** was often evoked for some of our receivers. When it was, the sense of feelings in the body was directly related to the images of the targets. Below, the receiver of Team #16 writes that she "...felt pressure in center forehead...." This seemed to evoke the image of the circle on the forehead of the jaguar priest in the target.

**Team #16 - TARGET Trial #4 - 8/14/80**
Ancient Mayan painting

BMS =1 - SMS = s, cl, cn

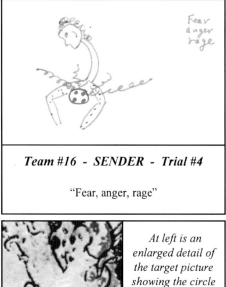

*Team #16 - SENDER - Trial #4*

"Fear, anger, rage"

*At left is an enlarged detail of the target picture showing the circle in the center of the forehead.*

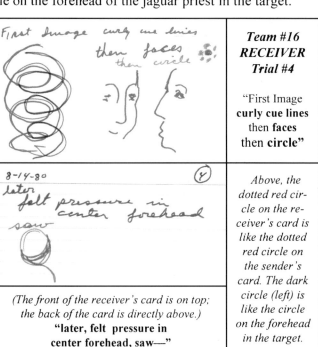

*(The front of the receiver's card is on top; the back of the card is directly above.)*
**"later, felt pressure in center forehead, saw—"**

*Team #16 RECEIVER Trial #4*

"First Image **curly cue lines** then **faces** then **circle**"

*Above, the dotted red circle on the receiver's card is like the dotted red circle on the sender's card. The dark circle (left) is like the circle on the forehead in the target.*

**Team #4 - TARGET - Trial #8**
**2/26/75**

"THE RICHARD M. NIXON
THREE-DOLLAR BILL"
*(cartoon from MAD Magazine)*

**BMS = 4 - SMS = s, cl, m**

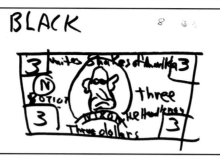

**Team #4 - SENDER - Trial #8**

"He is:

Depressed, Sad case,
Heckle! Sick,
Oh, No!"

**Team #4 - RECEIVER - Trial #8**

"Something with a **charge** on it.
Humorous—maybe **morbid humor.**
Had an impact.
Curvy lines, not angular."

**3. The Sense of Qual** is the quality of the mood induced in the viewer by the target or the sender. The similarities judges found a 19% *mood* similarity in the 290 trials completed by the students. A list of twenty different moods was used to categorize the qual, such as peaceful, violent, sexy, active, gentle, fearful, humorous, etc. In the illustration above, the humorous mood was easily matched by both types of judges (blind match and similarities). The receiver of Team #4 writes, "...Humorous—maybe morbid humor...." His drawing of three heads and three bodies expressed the target concept of three, which is repeated many times on the three-dollar bill. In a different set, when the target was an African woman sitting in the sand with hungry children near her, this same receiver writes, "Mood is somber. Picture of a woman looking... out into the distance...." He often sensed the quality of the mood of a target. Others seemed to miss or ignore the qual entirely.

**4. The Sense of Empathy** is another factor that we often overlook when we think of the five senses. Nevertheless, it is quite common for us to feel what other people feel, whether they are calm, anxious, or excited. It is now common to learn voluntary control of emotional states using biofeedback instruments. For example, a galvanic skin response (GSR) machine measures the minute amounts of sweat from the fingertips. An emotional reaction will increase the amount of sweat, which the instrument registers. We also register the emotions of others when they are close to us. While the receiver of Team #4 expressed the qual of the target without identifying with it, the receiver of Team #1 seems to have identified, or empathized, with the possible emotions of the man looking down into a cave at a monster. Below, the receiver of Team #1 writes that she felt she was "...looking down..." and that she "felt cold chill" and saw a "circular pattern...." Several receivers seemed to provide empathic responses to the targets that included emotional material in them. (See pages 27 and 34 for other examples.)

**Team #1 - TARGET - Trial #3**
**12/18/74**

"KLIK KLIK   By my troth!
a Mammoth Demon!  Colorless...Eyeless...
...A lifelong **Cave-Dweller!**"

*(Cartoon from Marvel Comics)*

**BMS = 1 - SMS = s, cl, m**

**Team #1 - SENDER - Trial #3**

"Colorless

lifeless

teeth

pinchers"

**Team #1 - RECEIVER - Trial #3**

**"One time felt like I was at the top of
spiral staircase looking down**

**felt cold chill**—then

**circular pattern** swirling across by field of
vision. Again—turning, revolving."

**Team #16
TARGET
Trial #3**

*8/14/80*

*Western
Pronghorn.
See
Appendix A.*

**BMS = 4
SMS = cl, w,
m, cn**

**Team #16 - SENDER - Trial #3**

"round
full **dog**'s head
horns"

**Team #16 - RECEIVER - Trial #3**

"First image of dark animal—
got caught up in drawing—lost image
**Heard or felt sound—as if a barking animal**"

**5.  The Sense of Hearing** was mentioned by a few receivers in relation to picture targets, though it was not common. In our remote viewing a receiver found that she would *hear* in her mind several relevant things that resulted in images or comments. In the illustrations above, the receiver writes, "...Heard or felt sound—as if a barking animal." For some unknown reason, the sender describes the animal as having a "full *dog's* head." The sender doesn't name the animal, and seems to have some confusion about what kind of animal it might be.

In one of the SRI series, remote viewer Hella Hammon reported seeing "an **'A'** frame that goes squeak, squeak." In that session, the outbound team had gone to a playground and sat on a swing with rusty hinges. (21)

The sense of hearing is one that can be tested more extensively with good results. In 1968 I was in New York City, attempting to receive an image from my daughter Mara who was staying with her aunt, Marge King, in California. Researcher Thelma Moss, PhD, had chosen as a target picture a painting by Salvador Dali. The Dali painting was full of a variety of symbolic images. The only one I

"saw" was an animal with "V" shapes, similar to flames on a burning giraffe in the background. I missed the dominant image, which was a tall woman with one leg full of bureau drawers. However, we did much better with "hearing" the music. I had sent Mara a list of the twelve records we both had. These included The Grateful Dead, The Beatles, symphonies by Beethoven and Tchaikovsky, and others. We agreed to play a specific record by Ravi Shankar at the same time before we began, so we could "tune in" to the same resonances. At the end of the visual part of the experiment (at a specific time), she was to choose a record from the list, and I would attempt to report what it was. When she did, I knew instantly that she was playing a record by The Beatles, but it was unfamiliar to me. I knew the exact song was *not* one we had in common. King had just bought the record for the many teenagers in her household, and they were all dancing and singing to "send" it to me. The song was "Your Mother Should Know" from a newly released album. This change in the pre-arranged protocol of the experiment suggests that the sense of telepathic hearing also used judgment. I expected something I knew from the list, but from three thousand miles away I could tell that the song was one I had not "heard" before.

**Team #6 - TARGET - Trial #7
11/12/74**

*The target is a cartoon from the New Yorker Magazine and is covered under a copyright © 1973 Saxon. Permission to print it is unavailable at this time. However, the sender included the important elements of the original, though her drawing is cruder, done very quickly in the short time allowed for the sending period. The response to the concept of a broken computer monitor is "no picture" and news of a broken oil pipeline.*

**BMS = 0 - SMS = cl, w, m**

**Team #6 - SENDER - Trial #7**

"Now what do I do?  Everything is **broken.**
Waiting.  Maybe he doesn't know how they
work.  Maybe he is a robot."

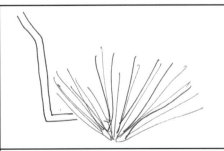

**Team #6 - RECEIVER - Trial #7**

"**No 'picture'** only impressions vague
and sinister.  Perhaps an impression
of some kind of oil pipeline spill."

**6. The Sense of Concept** is a most important part of our available senses. Before children learn language, they learn concept. For example, a sixteen-month-old child had just arrived at her grandmother's house after a very long trip with her parents in an old-fashioned automobile. Since she didn't yet know what the "arms" of grandmother's big sofa were called, she referred to them as "fenders." Another child, only a few months older, lived with her parents in a third-floor apartment. There was no elevator, so after the mother had taken the child (plus traveling toys and stroller) up to the apartment, she would go back down for the groceries. She always said, "I'll be back," before leaving the apartment, to assure the child that she would not be gone long. Once as she opened the door to go, the child asked, "Mommy, will you I'll-be-back?" It was clear that the two-year-old had learned the whole sound for the concept, but she may not yet have distinguished the meaning of individual words. This early learning of concept can be examined closely in the results of our telepathic experiments. (A discussion of early memory is in Chapter Six.)

The judge of similarities was given a list of twenty simple concepts, such as buildings, landscapes, growing things in nature, humans, animals, birds and bugs. This was to be a helpful guide when considering concept similarities. The first 290 trials had 21% concept similarities. The 65 trials had 26% concept similarities.

In the illustration above, the receiver of Team #14 responds to the target picture of a statue of a person with the concept of a "statue" of a person, but his response mentions a large

*Team #14 - TARGET*
*Trial #10*
*8/15/80*
*Guardian of a Canopic Urn from King Tut's Tomb*

BMS = 4 - SMS = s, cl, cn

*Team #14 - SENDER*
*Trial #10*

"Tut—the boy King"

*Team #14 - RECEIVER*
*Trial #10*

"**Statue** of Balzac by Rodin —cigar store Indian"

one in bronze by Rodin (which he has seen on the Stanford campus near his home) and a large wooden statue. Neither are like the target picture, which is a small statue covered in gold, and was taken from the Egyptian tomb of Tutankhamen (from 1350 BC).

The target below is a photograph of the bas-relief of Ashurbanipal killing a lion from his horse. This pose is similar to that of St. George killing a dragon, which is a common image painted many times throughout centuries of Christianity. Today, the dragon has been translated into cartoons where heroes fight them over and over again. A song describes Puff, a Magic Dragon, and the symbol is transformed into a friendly dragon that is familiar to this receiver. In these responses, conceptual transformations are made instantaneously from culture to culture. The concept of a lion is transformed into a dragon. The statue from an ancient tomb becomes a modern statue. The broken monitor on the previous page relates to something broken.

*Team #5 - TARGET - Trial #10*
*12/17/74*
*Ashurbanipal, King of Assyria, 668 - 626 BC*

BMS = 4 - SMS = d, s, w, m, cn

*Team #5 - SENDER - Trial #10*

"Warrior—Animals"

*Team #5 - RECEIVER - Trial #10*

"**Fire-breathing dragon**—Puff? book dragon, Magic—Andre Morton"

**Team #9**
**TARGET**
**Trial #4**

**12/16/74**

*Earth from*
*the moon.*
*NASA*
*photograph.*

**BMS = 2**
**SMS = w, m,**
**cn**

**Team #9**
**SENDER**
**Trial #4**

"View of the
**world**
from
the moon.

Space,
curves,
cloud
formations."

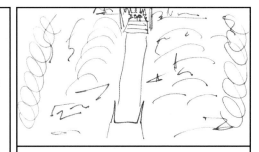

***Team #9 - RECEIVER - Trial #4***

"Going down road
on some sort of coach toward castle.
**World spinning around—rolling hills.**"

**7. Verbalization** is not considered one of the *sense* organs of the body, yet a very important part of the brain is devoted to our ability to communicate verbally. I include it here in the chapter about sensory perception because we can demonstrate that the exact words used in the target, or by the sender, arise in the mind without the receiver actually hearing them. Both the sender and the receiver were asked to write about their thoughts during the same experimental time period. The exact words or other words that described the target were matched 23% of the time in the 290 trials and 41% in the 65 trials. Even if more than one exact word was used by the receiver (see page 20), only one point was given for word similarity (just as only one point was given in cases where there was more than one matching color, shape, mood, or concept). Words that accurately described the target or the sender's drawing, but were not used by the sender, were also included in the judging of word similarities. For example, five targets with pictures of flowers were named directly by four receivers, while another drew and named a "mandala."

Above is an example in which the exact word used by the sender was also used by the receiver. The first impression of the receiver of Team #9 was of a road in the center of the page. He is "going down road..." through the center, which is often used as a symbol for allowing the mind to travel through the center of the brain into the hyperspace. He also received impressions of a "...*world* spinning around—rolling hills." Both comments add to the verbal description of the photograph of the Earth from the moon. The sender's drawing suggests the many curves in the receiver's drawing, along with the rolling movement.

In the example below, the receiver's response includes the words "reaching out...hand...," which describe the major element of the target, even though those words are not used by the sender or in the target. The receiver's drawing is more accurate than the sender's drawing. The hand is in the same position on the card, with fingers out, as in the target. The concept of opposites is also indicated. The lady fears her opposite instead of being attracted to him.

***Team #4 - TARGET - Trial #9***
**2/26/75**
"FOOLS! You dared invade
the dark domain of SKOL—"
*(Cut from Marvel Comics)*

**BMS = 5 — SMS = d, s, w, m, cn**

***Team #4 - SENDER - Trial #9***

"Colorful
Oh, My ! Nasty.
Poor lady.
Mean   Beastly
Ogrely"

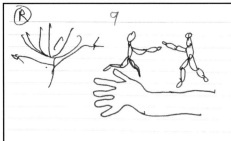

***Team #4 - RECEIVER - Trial #9***

"Branching
**Reaching out**
antlers
**hand**
Attraction between opposites"

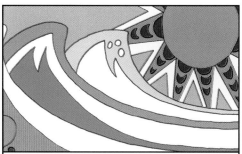

*Team #6 - TARGET - Trial #3*
*11/12/74*
*Cut from magazine listed in Appendix A.*

**BMS = 2 — SMS = d, cl, w, m, cn**

*Team #6 - SENDER - Trial #3*

"Heavenly, colorful, peaceful,
what a nice place to be."

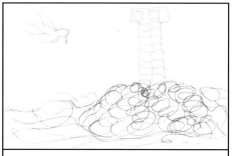

*Team #6 - RECEIVER - Trial #3*
"1st: Bird soaring.
2nd: Man in front of plane (jet).
3rd: **Lighthouse & ocean setting.**
4th: Race horse & race track.

Eventually a picture of
**a lighthouse at sea** emerged."

In the trials where the correct words were used, the image might not be accurate, as in the illustration of the world. In the trials where the drawing would be a good match, the words would often be very different from the target. These examples indicate how the various mental systems can operate independently and/or cooperatively. By providing information from different systems, they can create mental confusion. When this happens, some of us choose to depend on one reliable system and to ignore or suppress the information from the other systems. Instead, we could learn to increase the sensitivity of each of the sensory systems and to combine their different contributions to increase the intelligence available to us. Future educators might teach techniques to focus all systems.

For example, when I have trouble remembering the name of an absent person, I can usually visualize him/her in my mind very clearly. That often works to bring the name to mind. However, if the visualization is too vivid, the verbal association is less attached to it, and the memory of the name is gone. Eventually, I learned to shift my attention away from the image, and to think about something else. That allows the verbal faculty more dominance so the appropriate connection can take place. Then I can expect the right name of the person to come into my awareness.

In the illustration above, the receiver of Team #6 responds with "lighthouse & ocean setting" to the image of a stylized sun over ocean waves. The curved lines of the sun's rays in the target are repeated in the rocks and in the building blocks of the lighthouse. Even though the receiver lists a number of images, he writes, "...Eventually a picture of a lighthouse at sea emerges." This is an important clue to the way images arrive in the visual system during telepathy attempts. Often there are many as we free-associate, until one strong image dominates. Some can be described in words and others can only be drawn.

In the illustration below, the concept of a temporary structure in a prison camp is registered as a camping tent from the receiver's memory. The concept of two war prisoners talking outside the structure is translated into two cats fighting with bloody claws and fur and blood on the ground. This response was easily matched.

Hidden from guards, prisoners talk

*Team #9 - TARGET - Trial #10*
*11/26/74*
"Hidden from guards, prisoners talk"
*(War-time news photograph, see Appendix A.)*

**BMS = 5 — SMS = d, s, cl, w, m, cn**

hidden from guards prisoners talk

*Team #9 - SENDER - Trial #10*

"Hidden from guards, prisoners talk."

*Team #9 - RECEIVER - Trial #10*

"**Tents**—Cat fight"

**Team #9**
**TARGET**
**Trial #9**
**11/26/74**

"The Uncanny
Badger"
by *John
La Farge*
(1897)

**BMS = 3**
**SMS = d, cl,**
**w, m, cn**

JOHN LA FARGE'S "THE UNCANNY BADGER" (1897)

**Team #9**
**SENDER**
**Trial #9**

"**Blues &
greens -
water** fall
(animal
fuzzy,
**brown.**)"

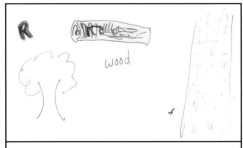

**Team #9 - RECEIVER - Trial #9**

"Wood. **Browns** Black
possibly a tree or log.
**Water—Blues**.
Sense of lost."

In the illustration above, the receiver of Team #9 wrote three of the same words that the sender had written: "...browns...water...blues." His drawing also includes a waterfall. In this case, both the words and the image relate to the same idea, a waterfall. The target has only a little bit of green in it. The sender mentions green, though she doesn't use it in her drawing, but her partner uses green in his drawing of a tree. Even though his response does not include the badger, he adds at the end, "...sense of lost." The receiver may be feeling lost by identifying with the environment, or he might assume the presence of a human or an animal in the target picture, even though he doesn't draw one.

A different example of the sense of verbalization is illustrated below. The receiver has drawn only a few lines that seem unrelated. We do not see any recognizable objects in them. However, he writes, "After looking at my drawing, I began seeing a person looking at something—possibly the sea." Now if we use our imaginations, we could visualize that a person looking out to sea might have eyes that seem to be staring, or to have a vacant look. In

that way we might be able to match what he wrote with the target showing the empty eyes of the skull. Actually, two of our judges did match this trial correctly. What is interesting to us about this response is that his report suggests he has used visualization to receive his image while his eyes were open. That means that his inner image might have been superimposed over the top of his drawing of lines—that is, it was projected from within. This receiver had a very difficult time drawing anything. Most of his attempts were very sketchy, yet he did choose at least one right color out of the ten available 50% of the time.

This receiver of Team #11 also responded with word similarities in seven of his twenty trials. The average similarity of words for the eleven teams in the first 290 trials is only 23%, his score of 35% is one of the highest of all of them. Most of his words were broadly descriptive rather than exact, because his partner wrote very little. Even when he drew and labeled a flower when the target was a flower, his partner did not use that word. Two of the teams in the 1980 study scored as high as 60% in word similarity, but most of those scores were for descriptive words also.

**Team #11**
**TARGET**
**Trial #4**
**11/11/74**

*Photo of an
ancient skull.*
Man, Myth,
and Magic
*magazine.*

**BMS = 2**
**SMS = cl,**
**w, m, cn**

**Team #11 - SENDER - Trial #4**

"sinister, death, dark, ghosts, goblins,
frightening feeling of skulls and spirits
flying from the air toward me."

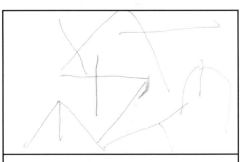

**Team #11 - RECEIVER - Trial #4**

"after looking at my drawing,
**I began seeing a person**
looking at something, possibly the sea—"

*Tom Byrne* — *REMOTE VIEWER*

"DOES THE EYE SEE?"

**8. The Sense of Sight** was represented in our study in a dominant way, because the image of the target was specifically requested. Both the senders and receivers were asked to draw pictures about the messages being sent and received. For the judging of similarities, three scores were requested for images: drawing, shape, and color. The total shape similarity score for the first eleven teams, completing 290 trials, was 32%; the same color was 23%; the same type of drawing was 12%. The total scores were differently distributed for image similarities among the five teams participating in the 1980 study. Drawing achieved only 8%, while color went as high as 55% and shape was 51%. For judging shape similarities, a chart of twenty line/shape styles was given to the judges to be used as a guide only. That chart included common shapes, such as round, square, triangular or scattered, and straight, curled, or sketchy lines. The chance of matching a shape or line from this list would be one in twenty. At the beginning of every session, each team member was given a box of marking pens with the same set of ten colors in each one. The drawings might be done with one or many colors, so the chance scores for matching color could have been very complex. Therefore, no matter how many colors were matched, the similarities judges counted only one color similarity, even when the same three colors were in the sender's drawing as were in the receiver's drawing. Also, if the target had many colors, and the receiver matched only one of them, the chance of that happening would be less remarkable, yet a score of one color similarity would be given. These prob-

**What is it that sees those images that the physical eye does not see?**

lems, inherent in the judging of color in the days before computer analysis was available, are clearly visible in the subsequent illustrations. Sometimes the participants would feel more comfortable using their own pencil or pen for drawing, rather than color, but all trials were included in the scoring.

During a remote viewing experiment, artist Tom Byrne drew the image illustrated at left. While he was drawing images being sent to him from ten miles away, he wondered how he could be seeing those images. This is a major question that we all have, and there are many unique belief systems to account for what may seem to be the unaccountable. Among South American shamans, there is a "deer spirit" who sees and brings the information back to the seer. For Christian mystics, God, a patron saint, or an angel may provide information through direct intervention in one's thoughts or prayers. Among humanistic and transpersonal psychologists, mind-to-mind communication is a natural process within natural law.

Those who study physics today agree that there are many dimensions beyond the four dimensions of spacetime, but they disagree about how many there may be. (22) Whether there are as few as seven dimensions beyond spacetime, or as many as forty-eight or more, these multiple dimensions constitute the hyperspace of our larger reality. If consciousness is made up of brain stuff (atoms, molecules, electromagnetism), then it also must have as many dimensions as any other sub-atomic particle in the universe. Spiritual people of most religions accept the idea that the soul is infinite and eternal. When we define the soul as an essential part of consciousness, and combine that with the scientific concept of the hyperspace, we find that the vast potential of the superconscious becomes available to us all. It can no longer be ignored by those who seriously study science, especially human science. Today, concepts of consciousness must be included in education, not rejected as though they belonged to a "religion." The natural evolution of mind proceeds with those who are able to expand the horizons of human thought.

The assumption among the closed-minded is that psi is impossible. For them "ESP" becomes a sarcastic abbreviation for "Error Some Place." Any positive evidence of psi

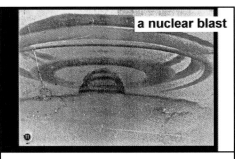

Team #10 - TARGET - Trial #3
12/2/74
*Photograph of a nuclear test.*

BMS = 5 - SMS = d, s, cl, w, cn

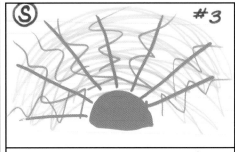

Team #10 - SENDER - Trial #3
"hot colors—blast
destruction"

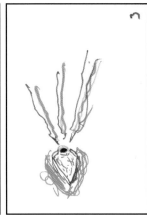

*Team #10
RECEIVER
Trial #3*

"Lots of
**sun energy**
coming from
& going into
an Eye."

reported in the literature was said to be fraud or self-delusion. No matter how carefully the scientific protocol had been followed, some skeptics would always project their own beliefs of error onto the results. Parapsychologists have struggled in vain for years to overcome this kind of thinking. But when the famous cosmologist Carl Sagan, PhD, declared that parapsychology was "pseudoscience," (23) classes in parapsychology in public schools were canceled all across the country with no public debate allowed.

However, since each of us involved in these experiments had experienced some form of telepathy at some time in our lives, we could ignore the skeptics and simply set out to explore our own potential abilities. We were motivated to find out *why* telepathy is successful some of the time and *why* our visions do not conform to the target at other times. That is why for us the errors have been equally interesting. Now, after twenty years of pondering the results of this research, we can share some ideas that have risen to the surface of our understanding. For one thing, telepathic attempts show us our pre-conscious projections. For another, we find that the intelligence of the visual system has far greater potential than most people, including

educators, have imagined. It is time to encourage students to explore their visual intelligence systems for themselves.

In the judging of similarities, the receiver's drawing was considered similar only if a number of elements matched either the target or the sender's drawing. In the illustration above, the drawing was rated as a similarity. In the target, the energy of the blast is circular; however, the sender of Team #10 draws it as though it were rays of the sun. Her receiver also draws the rays from a center image in a similar way, but he does not identify the image as the sun. Instead he writes, "lots of *sun energy* coming from and going into an eye," which could be a more accurate way to match the concept of the nuclear blast. The sender's drawing is an example of how the memory of images can be superimposed over the target picture she is looking at and can dominate the response to it. When such a shift occurs in the image we see directly, it is also natural for the same type of shift to take place when the image is received telepathically.

In the illustration below, the response to color changes to black when the target is black. Here the image and the words seem to have no relation to each other at all. Both the visual and verbal systems are working independently.

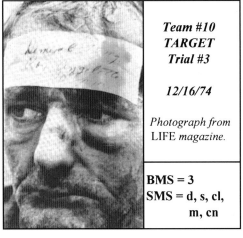

*Team #10
TARGET
Trial #3*

*12/16/74*

*Photograph from
LIFE magazine.*

BMS = 3
SMS = d, s, cl,
m, cn

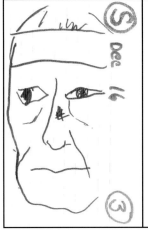

*Team #10
SENDER
Trial #3*

"Man
beaten up.
Bandage
on head.
Pain,
sorrow."

Team #10 - RECEIVER - Trial #3

"Glass of milk at 1st."

**Team #9 - TARGET - Trial #8**
**12/16/74**
*Cut from a magazine listed in Appendix A.*

BMS = 1 - SMS = d, s, cl, m

**Team #9 - SENDER - Trial #8**

"A ringed bull—
bright colors on his back—
suns and stars."

**Team #9 - RECEIVER - Trial #8**

"Norseman breathing fire."

To demonstrate that the visual system actually does see things that the eyes do not see, look closely at the visual elements in the illustration above. In the target, there are four circles in the band around the neck of the bull. The receiver of Team #9 drew four circles in the headband, though they are a different color. The receiver drew the horns, the red eyes, and yellow angular lines. There are many visual similarities in this one trial. This is definitely a non-random telepathic event. It represents direct mind-to-mind communication. These images do not occur at any other time in the entire set of four hundred trials. However, the receiver does not name the drawing as a brightly colored bull in a yellow and red background. He calls it a "Norseman breathing fire."

In spite of the many visual similarities, four of the five judges did not match it. Instead they all matched the Norseman with a different target in that same set of five trials; a picture of a magician's face painted white, blue, with red accents. The four judges later reported that they looked for evidence of concept similarity more than visual similarity when attempting to do blind matching.

In the cartoon by Charles Schultz, left, Linus describes what he imagines he "sees" in the changing shapes of clouds. Perhaps the way we interpret what we "see" in the hyperspace is a bit like the way we "see" images in the clouds. When the shape and/or color arrive in the mind from the hyperspace telepathically, our visual memory automatically freely associates with the partial images. Charlie Brown represents the viewer with very little self-confidence. The images his memory projects are not as elaborate as the ones Linus describes, and he is afraid the others will laugh at him. (24)

Above, the receiver of Team #9 is confident. He enjoys the game of telepathy and so he is able to draw what he *sees,* whether or not it seems weird. The results, though not the same subject as the target, demonstrate the extensive ability of the visual system. All of our participants were encouraged to express whatever came to mind during the experimental time period. They, as well as we, were fascinated by what the actual results might be, whether they were right or wrong. In the next few pages of illustrations, many shape similarities are shown. Keep in mind that the cloud-watching spirit is part of the responses of the receivers, senders, and judges alike. Even the reader is not immune to such imaginative projections into shape similarities.

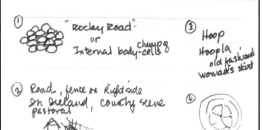

**Team #15 - RECEIVER - Trial #1**

"(1) 'Rocky Road' or Internal clumps of body cells.
(2) Road, fence on right side.
    In Ireland, country scene, pastoral.
(3) Hoop — Hoopla. old-fashioned woman's skirt."

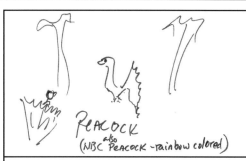

**Team #15 - SENDER - Trial #1**

"Peacock
(also NBC peacock—rainbow colored)"

**Team #15 - TARGET
Trial #1 - 8/9/80
"Birds in a Brewing Storm"**

*Copyright © Jesse Allen
Reproduced by courtesy of
The Vorpal Gallery, San Francisco
and New York City.*

**BMS = 0 — SMS = s, c, m**

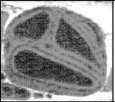

*At left is an enlarged detail of a rock at the bottom of the Jesse Allen painting. The shape is similar to the divided circle in the receiver's response #4.*

Allen's work were put into the target pool, though only three of them were randomly chosen as targets in the whole study. The intricate detail that Allen included in his paintings is difficult to reproduce here, but these large paintings are a great joy to see directly, especially for anyone who has ever seen auras, or energy patterns swirling in multidimensions in the spaces between people, animals, and plants. They are exhibited at the Vorpal Galleries in San Francisco and New York City.

The receiver of Team #15 has drawn several shapes and concepts that are similar to the target in the illustrations above. The dynamic backgrounds of Jesse Allen's marvelous paintings are often covered with circles in descending sizes swirling in elaborate patterns of energy. (25) The receiver of Team #15 has captured the idea of many circles grouped together in her first response. In her fourth response, she has drawn circles within circles, divided into sections. These elements can also be seen in the enlarged detail of the rock (above). In her third response, she writes about a hoop, while in the second one, she has included the idea of a country scene. This highly stylized painting with birds and trees could imply a country scene. Several greeting card-sized reproductions of

The illustration below is an additional example of how the verbal and visual intelligence systems can operate very differently from each other. The response is similar to the sender's pictures in drawing, color, and concept. The sender drew heads in red and brown lines, but left the eyes as open oval shapes. The receiver also left the eyes as open oval shapes in his drawing of a head. He uses red and green lines, and though there is green in the target picture, the sender did not use it. But the spray of white from the top of the head in the target picture is not totally lost on the receiver. He has drawn a spouting whale on top of the head he drew, but his other words are unrelated to his drawing.

**Team #13
TARGET
Trial #7

8/19/80**

*Reproduction of a painting of Hindu Deities.*

**BMS = 3 — SMS = d, s, cl, m, cn**

**Team #13
SENDER
Trial #7**

"Indian Gods."

**Team #13
RECEIVER
Trial #7**

"Penguin Whale Black & white. Green hills."

**Team #2 - TARGET - Trial #2**
**2/27/75**
*See Appendix A.*

BMS = 4 - SMS = d, s, cl, w

**Team #2 - SENDER - Trial #2**

"I merely tried to repeat, **'long red** hair,'
mentally & see *[partner]* looking at
**my long red** hair."

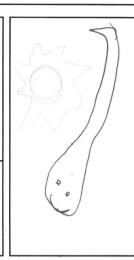

**Team #2
RECEIVER
Trial #2**

"**Red** snake.
That's all.

It was hard to
do this one.
A yellow sun
came later."

In the illustration above, the sender's response to the target indicates that she is very proud of her own long red hair, which everyone agrees is quite beautiful. Her roommate has drawn a *long red* snake in response. The snake's eyes are similar to those of the lady with red hair, but the snake is smiling and looks happier. In this example, an exact word is given along with drawing, shape, and color similarities.

In the illustration below, however, the same team provided another look at the visual system in action. The concept of a temple is not similar, but the shape and color are. The receiver writes, "...Then when she started drawing, saw a brown object—solid—so did horse." The horse seems to be tied to a hitching post, but with some imagination the post is shaped like an archway. Her visual system has received an image that was similar in shape and color, but her attention is still influenced by thoughts of horses at the mental level, and by her interest in dancing ("...tu-tu, ballet") at the pre-conscious level. Among her thirty telepathic trials she drew or mentioned horses several times in response to unrelated targets, and referred to dance ideas in four different trials (see page 65).

Experienced psychics learn to look for different aspects of the target before settling on one idea. Our teams of students were not trained psychics, though they had experienced some psi events previously. However, before the semester ended, some of them had discovered for themselves a few strategies that improved their responses.

Several parapsychologists have initiated training programs to improve psi performance. Relaxation is the first thing to learn; ways of clearing the mind of one's other activities are next; after that just allow the resonance of the other person to come into consciousness. When a monitor sits with the receiver during the experiment, s/he may ask certain questions to help the receiver look for different aspects of the target, whether that target is a picture, a slide, a movie, or an environment. In the latter type of experiment, the monitor may ask the viewer to move back thirty feet to see more of the environment, or to float over the scene to see it from above, or to move in closely so that s/he can see more details. These suggestions help relate the

**Team #2 - TARGET - Trial #4**
**2/27/75**

*Mayan Temple*

BMS = 4 - SMS = s, cl, w

**Team #2 - SENDER - Trial #4**

"Tried to envision *[partner]* walking around
the arch of old Aztec ruin,
climbing over rocks to get there,
exploring the whole ruin, feeling the rock."

**Team #2 - RECEIVER - Trial #4**

"1st saw Mary—colored zinnia—
then a tu-tu (ballet).
Then when she started drawing
**saw a brown object—solid**—so did horse."

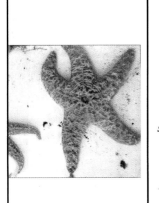

*Team #4*
*TARGET*
*Trial #4*

*2/26/75*

*Photo of starfish from unknown source. See Appendix A.*

BMS = 1 — SMS = d, s, m

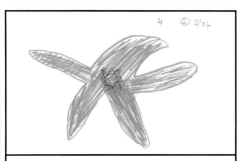

*Team #4 - SENDER - Trial #4*

"5 points—stars— sea
5-star (button peyote)—Movement
Pentagram—Shiny—beautiful—graceful
rough, tough, hard."

*Team #4 - RECEIVER - Trial #4*

"People in active concentrated activity.
Mood is kind of light—not heavy.
Not a whole lot of color. Definite
concentrated intention—work—play
—business or sports or something."

information that otherwise might seem to be fragmented to the viewer.

Often the visual association is made so quickly that it is very difficult to separate it from the simple shape that has flashed so briefly in the mind. After that the ability to reassess the identity of the image has been compromised by the prevailing memory association. In the illustration above, the receiver of Team #4 has captured the shape very well. It seems that he has "seen" the shape of the starfish and related it to a person in motion, which it does resemble in outline. However, he has shown in previous examples that he is quite capable of drawing better-shaped heads. Even though he refers to people in these drawings, their heads do not greatly differ from just a shorter starfish appendage.

We observed an unusual process of imaging with Uri Geller during the SRI experiments, and I have often wondered about it. Once he drew a bunch of circles, wondering whether the target might be drops of water or grapes (the target was a bunch of grapes, but he put the stem on the bottom, as though his images were upside down). Later, the SRI team (Russell Targ and Hal Puthoff) set up some metal-bending experiments for Geller. They decided to "warm up" with a couple of telepathy exercises first. The SRI security department wanted to test Geller's ability to "read" anything through a room with a lead shield. During the first trial, Targ and I were sending a message from within the room. Geller and Puthoff were on the outside, near the hall. At that moment, several noisy people in the hall created a distraction, and Geller passed with no images. So the director put Geller in the shielded room, where there would be no distractions, and the rest of us were outside. Targ asked the director to draw the target picture. He

chose to draw a Christmas tree with a star on the top. This drawing was put up on the south wall. Soon I could feel that Geller had part of the image but was unsure about it, so I concentrated on the star. Geller burst out of the room with some enthusiasm, knowing that he had it right. He told us that he was facing east, with one hand on the south wall. His first image was of a two-story flight of stairs. Later he "saw" the star, and put it in the sky, over the stairs. At that point, he rotated his drawing and knew that it was a tree and that the star should be at the top. This trial was not part of the regular SRI series, and I don't know whether or not the SRI team kept those drawings.

My sketches as I remember that experience are below. Is it possible that an image is received directly in the occipital visual center (upside down or sideways), depending on the direction of reception? The visual association center (or other part of the brain) interprets the image through a memory, unless the image is so abstract that it remains upside down. As exploration of psi advances, this question about the direction of perception could be tested easily with appropriate protocol using experienced subjects.

*Simulated drawing of a Christmas tree from a target used for an RV warm-up exercise with Uri Geller at SRI in December, 1973.*

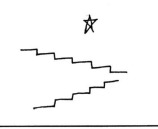

*Simulated drawing of two-story flight of stairs from one made by Geller in response to the Christmas tree "target" at SRI in December, 1973.*

In our studies, however, we did not consider exploring such subtleties of upside-down or right-angle reception. Our participants were beginners with uncertain telepathic ability, and none of our targets were that abstract. We could only hope that the environment and the qual were positive enough to encourage some evidence of actual mind-to-mind communication between friendly couples.

With that consideration, we were happy to see so many shape similarities. Illustrated above and below are further examples of the visual system

LUCAS VAN LEYDEN'S "MARY WITH CHILD"

***Team #6***
***TARGET - Trial #1***
***1/10/75***
*Mary with infant Jesus.*

**BMS = 0 - SMS = s, cl**

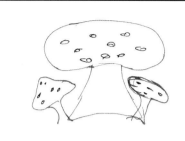

***Team #6 - SENDER***
***Trial #1***

"Serene, Pensive"

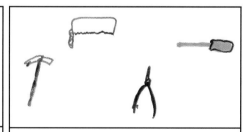

***Team #6 - RECEIVER - Trial #1***

"Singular impression of mushroom —
or maybe mushroom cloud"

*The mushrooms and the drawing of the heads have similar shapes. For many students at the time, the mushroom symbolized a powerful medicine for life; the mushroom cloud symbolized the end of life.*

seeing something not seen by the eyes. The sender of Team #6 drew the heads of the Madonna and Child very crudely. The receiver's drawings follow the shapes, but they are simply translated as mushrooms. The only other time in the four hundred trials that a mushroom was given as a response was to a target that was also the head and shoulders of a person. That target was a black and white photograph of a Native American medicine man. The mushroom drawing response to it was quite small (with no baby mushroom on its lap), though there was another drawing of a small key. The receiver of Team #1 writes, "... Main impression is something with mushroom shape." We could consider the shape to be the most important element in both responses or we could consider the conceptual importance of the mushroom in Native American spiritual medicine. (In the early 1970s, CSUS [called "Sonoma State"] was often referred to as "Altered State." Later on when activists de-

manded better food in the cafeteria, it was called "Granola State.") In any case, none of the judges matched the Mary and Jesus target with the mushroom response though the shape is similar to the sender's drawing, but three judges did match the Native American medicine man target with its mushroom response though it had less shape similarity.

The response below by the receiver of Team #10 includes a saw, a hammer, and a pair of pliers, which have color and shape similarities to the drawing by the sender. The tools might be considered an oblique conceptual relationship to Jesus, the carpenter. In addition, the receiver may have identified with the target when the only thing he writes is, "I feel drained." Three of the judges did match this one. Though the statue is ancient, the sender, receiver, and monitor thought this was a statue of Christ, even though the martyr is not on a cross. Memory is such a powerful overlay, none of them questioned that assumption.

***Team #10***
***TARGET***
***Trial #10***

***12/2/74***

*Photo of part of an ancient marble statue.*
*See Appendix A.*

**BMS = 3**
**SMS = s, cl, w, m**

***Team #10***
***SENDER***
***Trial #10***

"sadness, grief, death, grey, loss"

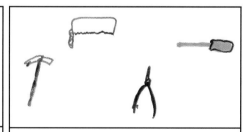

***Team #10 - RECEIVER - Trial #10***

"I feel drained"

*←— Detail of receiver's pliers enlarged to show shape & color similarity to sender's drawing.*

*This illustration is from a 1961 study by R. Pritchard called "Stabilized Images on the Retina." (27) He built a miniature slide projector to fit on a contact lens so eye movements could not track the image. Parts of the image faded into smaller, meaningful sections.*

"Paranormal phenomena...seem unusual because the spacetime projection provides only a partial view of the hyperspace events."

Saul-Paul Sirag

Partially correct images occur frequently during telepathic attempts, and they have been reported by other researchers as well. (26) It is time to take this into consideration when trying to understand the telepathic process. The eyes must track an image to see it, or to hold it all in memory. The telepathic eye cannot track the way the physical eye does. When Pritchard designed a miniature slide projector to fit on a contact lens, that image then became stabilized on the retina, because whenever the eye moved to track the image being projected onto it, the image moved

**Team #1 - TARGET - Trial #7**
**12/18/74**

*See Appendix A.*

BMS = 5 — SMS = d, cl, w, m, cn

as well. Above, his results show how the image begins to break up for the viewer when the normal tracking process has been interrupted. Only the smaller units of "H," "B," "3" and "4" replace the larger figure of "HB." (27)

The telepathic "eye" cannot track, either. Perhaps it is the memory of the way the eye tracked an image the first time it was seen that is stored and replayed during dreams. Perhaps it is this memory that causes the rapid eye movements (REMs) of dreaming sleep and visualization. It is also possible that it may be the tracking memory which is evoked to embellish the partial image, often described as a flash during telepathic attempts. How does this "flash" occur? That, of course, is the major unanswered question. No matter how intensely the brain has been studied by new technologies in recent years, there is still the Great Mystery of the mind's abilities and the role of intention.

Similar to Pritchard's example, we find that a small detail from the target might be enlarged by the receiver's partial reception into an image that is thought to be complete. Occasionally when the target shows only the head and shoulders of a person, the viewer reports only an ear or an eye. When the whole figure is included in the target, only a part of it might be reported. For example, when the target was a photo of a nude man riding a horse, the receiver of Team #10 reported only "...parts of the body, maybe the knee...." In the illustration below, the receiver of Team #1 reports seeing the knee first, while the body comes underneath, as water is also implied. As she seeks more images, a woman with a flower lei appears. The curly design on the bathtub and/or the leaves behind the bather may have contributed to the idea of a lei. Again, these images are not connected into the one idea. They are

**Team #1 - SENDER - Trial #7**

*(No written comment by sender.)*

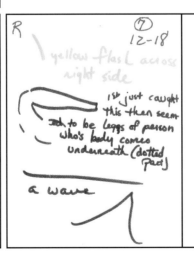

**Team #1 - RECEIVER - Trial #7**

"Yellow **flash** across right side.
1st just caught this, then seems to be **legs of person whose body comes underneath** (dotted part) a wave."

*(the receiver's response is continued on back of her card)*

"Right side of face feels like light but steady pushing
No clear images—no strong ones.
Also flashed on a pineapple and
**woman with short dark hair and a lei.**"

***Team #9 - TARGET - Trial #1***
***11/26/74***
*Painting of Paul Revere for the post office.*

BMS = 0 — SMS = d, s, cn

***Team #9 - SENDER - Trial #1***

*(No written comment by sender.)*

***Team #9 - RECEIVER - Trial #1***

"roundness, but with pointed projections"

received at different moments during the eight-minute session of the trial period (described as brief flashes).

In the illustration above, the receiver of Team #9 draws stars, the head of an animal, and a large shape in the center. These can be matched with those elements in the target, though they were totally missed by all of the judges using blind matching techniques. In this illustration the elements are separate parts, seen at different times during the experimental time period, and are not connected to a whole image.

The viewer can judge the scale of a target fairly accurately in an RV experiment, because the outbound team stands in the environment and provides human scale to everything. But confusion about scale is one major problem encountered in telepathy that uses postcard-sized targets. A picture on a 3" x 5" card, when seen simply as a shape and/or color, provides no hint about the implied size.

The target illustrated at right is from a painting of San Francisco showing the rows of buildings on a hillside, each with many rectangular windows. The drawing from the receiver of Team #1 is certainly similar in shape, but it is reduced to a much smaller scale as she identifies it as a "crate with books." Her drawing of a shape similar to any one of the buildings she describes as a "paper cup turned upside down." Her verbal re-

sponse about something in motion may or may not refer to the sender's drawing of a boat with his verbal response of a "storm at sea." As you can see from the differences below, it is essential to have the simultaneous responses to the target, from both the sender and the receiver, to understand the mental processes involved. In this way more information is provided to assess just what is being sent, what the receiver gets directly from the sender, and what she gets directly from the target.

***Team #1 - TARGET - Trial #5***
***12/18/74***
*A postcard print of San Francisco reproduced from a painting © by Emil White.*

BMS = 0 — SMS = d, s, w, cn

***Team #1 - SENDER - Trial #5***

"Storm at sea"

*This detail of the TARGET picture has been enlarged to show the small **clock** on the tower.*

***Team #1 RECEIVER Trial #5***

"Like mobile. **Paper cup turned upside down. Crate with books, 1/2 round clock.**"
  "1st—flashed on part of Santa again— white trim on jacket.
  2nd—Mobile in motion or something suspended and spinning or revolving."

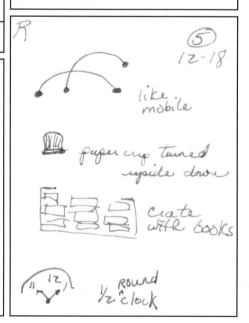

**Team #4
TARGET
Trial #1
2/26/75**

*Magazine photo of a painting.
See Appendix A.*

**BMS = 0
SMS = s, cl,
          w, cn**

*Team #4 - SENDER - Trial #1*

"Soft, Warm, Pleasant,
Majestic.
Generally nice."

*Team #4 - RECEIVER - Trial #1*

"Orange—Brown—Feline—Tiger.
Female in a jungle setting—dark background.
Relaxed tension—Readiness."

In any case, it does seem that the telepathic image is delivered in small bits to the visual cortex and/or visual memory. From there a meaningful whole may then be interpreted. When the receiver returns to the hyperspace for another image, which is again only a small bit, it is usually reported as being a separate image. Several small bits are often identified in the reports and drawings, but they are rarely put together into one image by the receiver unless she has trained herself to do so. Unfortunately, many of our targets have so many images combined that it was very difficult to get complete image responses from them.

The two illustrations here show what happens when the smallest detail is taken for the whole picture and trans-

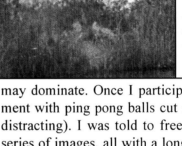

*Enlarged detail of the TARGET picture, which is still quite vague. Yet, to a dedicated cloud watcher it could look like a tiger in a jungle in a dark background.*

may dominate. Once I participated in a Ganzfeld experiment with ping pong balls cut in half over my eyes (very distracting). I was told to free associate, so I reported a series of images, all with a long black object in the center and two "arms" out at each side. All my images matched the shapes in the target—a section of a tree trunk with branches. Since the whole symbolic tree shape was not in the slide, I did not identify any of the shapes as a tree.

lated into a totally different concept than the target implies. Above, the faint impression of an animal in the grass is embellished. In the example on the right, the small details of the target also seem to have been translated by a memory into a personal concept. The lines and dots on the butterfly wing may match the lines and dots of the bingo game, but the original idea about the whole target of a butterfly with spots was lost. The first shape "seen"

**Team #3 - TARGET
Trial #10
11/20/74**

*This is a postcard painting, sent through the mail. Artist is unknown.*

**BMS = 0 — SMS = 0**

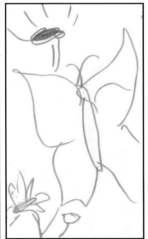

**Team #3 - SENDER
Trial #10**

"Joy & Sun & lightness
Bright fluttering,
stretch to the light.
Warmth & happy
light-heartedness.
Apt. 72."

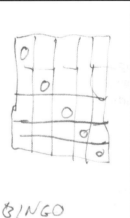

**Team #3 - RECEIVER
Trial #10**

"BINGO
CHANCE
cheating
excitement
breathless
hoping"

*This detail of the TARGET is enlarged to show the five spots between the lines on the butterfly's wing. The spots and lines are in the same arrangement in the receiver's drawing.*

*This set was not matched by any of the judges, but this response and this target are both unique in all of our 400 trials.*

The trials on the next two pages were done in the video studio at Santa Rosa Junior College (SRJC). This session was planned for one sender and two artists who acted as receivers simultaneously. Since from our earliest studies we found that shape similarity to the target or sender's drawings occurred more often than other types of similarities, I hoped to record it while it happened, if possible. The director of the SRJC video studio, Bob Budereaux, could superimpose images from both cameras onto one video tape because they were connected to the mixer in the sound booth. If indeed two people did draw similar shapes at the same time, I wanted to see it in real time, even though these shapes might eventually take on different concepts.

Since both artists, James Dowlen and Tom Byrne, can do automatic drawing in the way some might do automatic writing, they don't have to know what they will draw; they just begin and let the drawing show the way. For many of us, a green blob must become a "leaf" or something else we can verbalize. For these two, it is enough for them to draw what they see in their minds, without having to name anything. Even Major General Thompson reported that artists were the most successful in the remote viewing experiments done by the Department of Defense. (28)

The studio director, Budereaux, acted as the monitor for this experiment. His was the only voice used during the session to announce when to begin, when to wind up the drawings, and when to rest. He had arranged separate areas for each participant so that they could not see each other. He could see Byrne's drawings from the mixing room. The video cameras could be moved to record whatever seemed to be of interest at the time. The camera operators heard Budereaux through earphones, telling them only where to move the cameras from one place to another. Though the 1977 equipment was primitive by today's standards (black and white, reel to reel, ¾" video tape), he was able to superimpose one event of similarities happening in real time. This type of study should be repeated with the technology available today.

We need to remember that the artists were attempting to be telepathic while sitting under hot lights and with camera crews watching. They did experience some dis-

**TV Team - TARGET Trial #6 - 3/25/77**

"15—The Devil"

*Tarot Card*

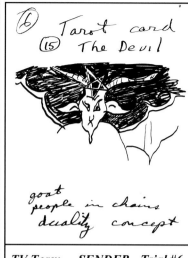

**TV Team - SENDER - Trial #6**

"Tarot card
(15)  The Devil
goat,  people in chains
duality concept"

**TV Team - RECEIVER 1 - Trial #6**

James Dowlen

**TV Team - RECEIVER 2 - Trial #6**

Tom Byrne

comfort, and their first attempts were generally unsuccessful. However, the trial above represents the sixth one in the series, and the results show that both of them gradually began to be somewhat nonattached to the situation, at least long enough to respond with partial images.

Each receiver drew a very different response for the targets during the session. We can see how each one translated that first partial impression differently. Dowlen seems to have looked for several images. One image suggests a person behind a curtain, symbolic of a person who tells fortunes by reading cards (perhaps tarot cards). Dowlen's card has a star on it, and the hand reaches out to show it to us. Then he draws a man with a star over his head. His images ignore the dualities of the archetypes that have appeared in the responses of several other receivers when the symbols for God or the devil became part of the target picture (illustrated in Chapter Two).

Byrne draws a woman. In the target, there is a woman who is chained to a man, and she does have small horns at the top of her head. In Byrne's drawing, the woman has long ears that are similar in size to those of the devil, though the devil's ears extend from the side of his head and are horizontal. It is his horns that grow from the top of his head. Byrne includes a panel showing pyramids and a man on a camel. His archway is not in the style of ancient Egypt, suggesting a blend of cultures. He was unable to explain the symbols in his picture. He said that the images just came to him while he was drawing.

drawn a head with something growing out of the top. It seems also to bend in the same direction as the hair on the head drawn by the sender. Byrne said he had not finished his drawing by the time Budereaux announced that the session had ended.

Often a session recorded on video only shows what the receiver says and draws, and sometimes what the sender says, but rarely what the sender draws at the same time. In the future the simultaneous recording of telepathic sessions could prove useful in the understanding of the actual mental processes involved, during the transference of imagery from one person to another.

It is both a help and a hindrance to be able to hold as many images in mind as these artists do. They can start on a telepathic image and get sidetracked by the many associations of imagery acquired through their years of drawing everything around them. Byrne and Dowlen are disciplined

*TV Team*
*TARGET*
*Trial #7*

*3/25/77*

*A magazine*
*reproduction*
*of a Baroque*
*painting.*

"The Beheading of St. John the Baptist."

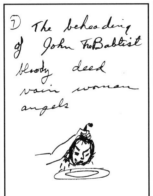

*TV Team - SENDER*
*Trial #7*
Jean Millay

"The beheading of John the Baptist. Bloody deed, vain woman, angels."

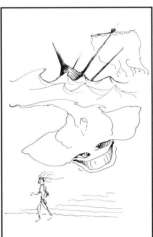

*TV Team - RECEIVER 1*
*Trial #7*

James Dowlen

*TV Team - RECEIVER 2*
*Trial #7*

Tom Byrne

The picture used in Target #7 is from a poor reproduction of the painting of "The Beheading of St. John the Baptist," which had been printed in a magazine and then pasted onto a 3" x 5" card. We have not attempted to improve the quality of the target here (which might be done by obtaining an original slide of the painting). We only want to show the target as it was used in this trial. As the illustration above shows, both artists drew heads with something coming out of the top of them, as in the drawing by the sender. Also, at the top of Dowlen's drawing, there is a mast with a flying sail. Notice the similarities in shapes with the cross and banner that the angel at the top of the target picture is holding. The angle of the mast is similar to the angle of the angel's cross, and the angle of the wand is like the prow of the ship. Byrne has

and focused enough to demonstrate the immense potential intelligence of the visual system.

The ability to be free enough to receive the distant image is essential, but the ability to maintain the focus on the distant image requires a firm discipline. It is important to blend the freedom and the focus to avoid the frequent mind wandering that occurs so often during these exercises. Brainwave biofeedback training has demonstrated that people can learn to increase their ability to sustain a focus of attention. (29) It has even helped those with attention deficit disorder (ADD and ADHD).

**9. The sense of pairs and/or opposites** has often been used in a child's game called "word association." One says "salt," the other says "pepper." We could make a long list of such pairs or opposite words, such as light/dark; sweet/sour; happy/sad; cops/robbers. Some forms of therapy have found it useful to ask a client to respond spontaneously to certain words, in order to reveal pre-conscious information about the client's mental illness.

So it should not be surprising when we find telepathic responses that seem to conform to this word association game. Generally, the judges did not match them. However, when we looked at the whole collection of four hundred trials, we found many which fell into this category. In one ten-trial session, the receiver of Team #3 gave five opposite responses to the sender and the target, which caused their entire score to be well below the level of chance.

For example, one target was the title from *LIFE* magazine with the red background and bold white letters. The sender of Team #3 wrote on the back of her card with large red letters, *"Bold, risk-taking, full, sure, positive vitality, lively!!! Bam Bam!!"*

Her lover responded by writing in very small red letters, *"Gloom, baroness, foreboding, dark, dreary, misty, quiet, solemn."*

When another target of a pink piggy bank became the target, she wrote, *"Funny flowered pink piggy bank. Absurd and winsome—Dumpy and lovable. Happy to be himself. Pleased with his inner treasures. Full of enough, so there!"*

The receiver responded to this with an opposite idea again, *"questioning, leery, hesitating, pondering, confusion, searching."*

When the target was a microscopic view of a snowflake, the sender of Team #1 wrote about the cold. His lover, on the other hand, included these words in her response, *"...feeling warmth..."*

One target for Team #10 was the colorful title word for *MAD* magazine. The sender wrote, *"Mad—crazy."*

Her lover drew only a few unrecognizable lines and wrote, *"I immediately felt peaceful."*

Besides the opposite responses, we also found a few *very obscure* paired responses. They were not matched by the judges, but we did wonder why such images would appear to the receiver in such a situation. I list a few of them here, not to say that they were actually telepathic, but to raise the question about how such responses originate.

One target was the figure of the young boy draped in scarves, which was cut from a photo of the larger Salvador Dali painting, "The Dream of Columbus." The receiver drew a pipe and a potato. Even though we can draw a relationship between the massive impact that tobacco and potatoes had on the Europeans as the result of the voyages of Columbus, this is an odd response for any trial.

One target picture (trimmed to 3" x 5") was part of the famous scene of the white-haired God reaching to touch life into Adam. The head of the reclining Adam is not seen, only part of his body and his hand reaching to receive life. The receiver's drawing shows a profile face looking up. He wrote about a "lying down face...old man." We know that Michelangelo painted the ceiling of the chapel while lying on his back on a scaffolding. He spent years in that position in order to complete this masterpiece.

Another example of an obscure response is illustrated below. The target was a picture of an old etching of Stonehenge. Stonehenge was centuries old before the Celts moved into the area, yet artifacts show a Druid shaman wearing deer antlers on his head during rituals there. Dowlen's drawing of a deer's head is in a setting that suggests mystery and ritual. It is a curious response, whether or not it represents an obscure relationship to Stonehenge.

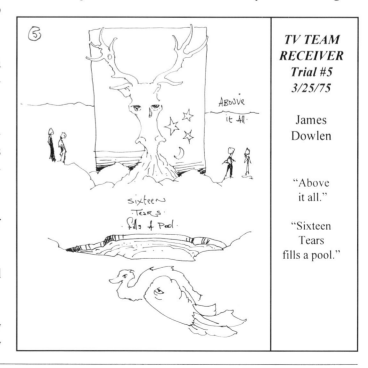

*TV TEAM RECEIVER Trial #5 3/25/75*

James Dowlen

"Above it all."

"Sixteen Tears fills a pool."

**10. The sense of resonance** is so important at any time, and especially during telepathic attempts, that I have devoted Chapter Four to a discussion of various aspects of the subject. In his book *Cosmic Law,* Dean Brown listed at least fifty senses and suggests that there may be many more. We have only illustrated ten here. However, many of the senses he has listed share a common source within the sense of resonance, whether with people, animals, plants, or with the Earth itself. Many of us have felt the comfort of a cat's purr. Generally, the vibration and the sound of the purr is the harmonic of alpha brainwaves of our own relaxation. The resonance of crickets on a summer night can also lull us into relaxation. Music can establish a resonance pattern for all who are in the mood to hear that particular form of rhythm.

Rupert Sheldrake, PhD, has proposed several studies of resonance, including one about whether or not a person is able to detect when another is staring at the back of his head. (30)

Our studies included the attempt to train couples to establish a resonance with the electrical activity of their brainwaves through biofeedback. Some couples who were deeply involved in their romantic relationship were able to become sensitive to each other on that very subtle level of resonance after only three training sessions. They seemed to enjoy the sensations of rapport and believed that the biofeedback tones of *IP Synch* identified a close feeling they already knew. Some of our couples were not able to increase their ability to do this in such a short amount of training time. One couple found that they did not want to be that close, that their differences were too great. The woman called me to say, *"I never want to synchronize my brainwaves with him ever again!"* Their romantic relationship was over after the three training sessions. She was too independent to submit to his ego demands to control her.

In the illustration below, the receiver of Team #11 has not drawn an image that we can recognize, but his comments reveal that he has felt a resonance with his partner and with the essence of the target.

In all of the examples of sensory perception presented in this chapter, we have tried to demonstrate how each of our sensory systems can receive and interpret information from a distance. It seems that a person's dominant cognitive style is also often dominant during telepathic reception. Some people *think* more often in words, some *think* more often in feelings, and some *think* visually, etc. My own dominant thinking processes are visual. People who like to play word games have often laughed at me because I am very slow in processing a word pun.

Telepathic communication is basically no different from ordinary communication in that way. We have our set of memory associations, we have our dominant cognitive styles, and we have our intentions to communicate beyond ourselves. Sometimes we resonate with others so that long explanations are not necessary, and sometimes we are in a totally different mindset and communication does not take place. Many comedy routines have been based on two different "reality" systems using the same words with different meanings for each person. When the audience knows both sides of the joke, they can laugh at the two actors who are talking together from very different mindsets. Each believes that communication is taking place, but neither person has any understanding of what the other is actually saying.

In our telepathy studies, such fundamental differences are stretched out so we can study them. When we resonate with others we have an opportunity to communicate with them on many levels at the same time. When we don't resonate, we may not be communicating at all.

*Team #11*
*TARGET*
*Trial #2*

*11/11/74*

*This photo was cut from one of the magazines listed in Appendix A.*

**BMS = 4**
**SMS = s, cl, m, cn**

*Team #11 - SENDER - Trial #2*

"Illusive, mysterious, in motion..."

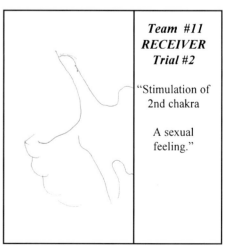

*Team #11*
*RECEIVER*
*Trial #2*

"Stimulation of 2nd chakra

A sexual feeling."

## CHAPTER TWO — MULTIPLE PATHS THROUGH THE MAZE OF MIND

What is meant by multiple paths through the maze of mind? As we explored the processes of thought, studying the results of our telepathic attempts, we found a labyrinth of different kinds of thoughts that surfaced at different times. When receivers are asked to draw what they see during these attempts, usually they close their eyes to seek an image and wait in silence until an image emerges. The first image may be related to the target, but it is often more closely related to the on going mental activity of the individual. This is what most of us expect of any such attempts by ourselves and others who are untrained in psychic activity. In the 50% of responses judged to be only partially correct, we see a few elements of the target material intrinsically blended with a variety of internal mentations. The diagram on page 37 illustrates a possible model of the multiple paths that our various personalities might include. The model is derived from our analysis of the four hundred telepathy trials completed by eighteen different teams between 1974 and 1980, and from the results of different remote viewing experiments between 1975 and 1986.

What we see in these results, and what we experience in ourselves, is that we seem to have more than one personality for different reasons at different times. Our conflicts arise because our various selves have different needs. For example, one of our receivers was so fired by her biological need to have a baby that her young boyfriend, not at all ready for nest-building, broke up their relationship and left her. Her need for the relationship, as well as her desire to

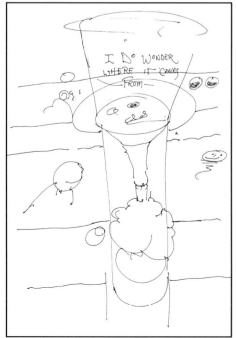

have a baby, were in conflict. At first, this conflict was more apparent in her telepathic responses than any similarities to the targets. During her last telepathic session, she drew an image of her future creative path in life. Years later, she told me that she had happily integrated her different selves in following that path. (See page 65.)

At the International Transpersonal Psychology (ITP) Conference in Prague in 1992, one of the founders, James Fadiman, PhD, spoke about multiple personalities. (31) He reviewed some of the historical theories about personality, such as the idea that we are a single unified being; the idea that there is no self; the idea that we are merely a collection of behaviors; or the idea that we are all multiples. Dr. Fadiman said:

> There is a model of the mind which seems to fit both historical experiences of every early people and seems to fit the experiences of most people I meet (except for psychologically trained professionals). [*Ed. note:There is much laughter from psychology professionals present.*] And the model is that **we are multiples.** Pantheism is a representation of our internal state, and it is not a surprise that psychiatry has used the Greek myths to suggest many aspects of the self because the Greek Pantheon is a more normal representation of who you actually are. So the self, I suggest, does exist. It is not unified. It is a collection of personalities. And the model says that if you work on yourself for many, many years, and take psychedelics, and go to India, etc., etc., that you will become a collection of selves, not unified, but that the collection of selves will be better behaved and you will get into less trouble.... When I listened to Ram Dass's talk, and heard about the demons that used to be large and dark and now are small and friendly, it suggested that as one improves in mental health, one gains a better understanding of the totality of one's multiplicity and is more likely to have the correct Being at the correct time. So there's a slang term in American, not in English, called, *"Who is minding the store?"* That turns out to be the critical question in mental health....
>
> Those who end up in mental institutions do not have appropriate control of the personality, and behave badly at the wrong place and time....

In 1965 Bunny Bonewitz told me that she had compared a shift in eye dominance with a shift in speech patterns of dozens of people. She concluded that there are four verbal personalities and eight nonverbal ones. Bonewitz continued this study for several years and attempted to define each personality by its type of pattern of speech (i.e., feminine, masculine, force of will, and repetitious memory, which she named "nema, animus, will and shadow").

Among the Espiritistas, a multiple personality is assumed to be caused by a discarnate spirit who takes control of a personality, especially if that person continues to hold on to anger, or other negative emotion for a long time.

I visited a clinic of Espiritistas in São Paulo, Brazil, directed by Eliezer Mendes, MD. He hired mediums to exorcise spirits. While I watched, the doctor instantly hypnotized three mediums and the patient by putting one hand in front and the other hand in back of each head in turn. They all lay on the floor with their heads touching in the four cardinal directions. The patient would lie quietly while the three mediums carried on his internal dialog for him (often an intense argument). Gradually, the mediums and the patient came out of trance and discussed what each had experienced. Then the doctor put them all into trance again, telling the patient to be the healer and to restore energy to the mediums through laying-on of hands.

In two hours, I saw the same mediums assume four different personalities for each of four different patients. The patients who were waiting their turns, along with myself and other observers, sat around the edge of the room and watched what happened to those before them. The therapy was apparently very effective. When a spastic man was hypnotized I was amazed to see one of the mediums take on the spastic-type movements, while the spastic lay quietly, free of his spasms, at least while in trance. (31)

Here, however, we are not talking about spirit possession as they do in Brazil. That is a concept which may exist from time to time to create a multiple personality. Over the last twenty years of guiding people into their own mental explorations, I have found only six people who actually needed an exorcism. When a headache is caused by an external spirit, no medicine will relieve it. The exorcism, when needed, relieves the headache instantaneously. Spirits and channeling are discussed in Chapter Five.

It is quite possible that our way of defining multiple personalities may be different from the way Fadiman talks about them. We might not be talking about the same thing. However, we do seem to be in agreement that each of the

> **"So the self, I suggest, does exist.
> It is not unified.
> It is a collection of personalities."**
>
> James Fadiman, PhD

multiples we experience generally arises from ourselves. There are many who have tried to define the different types of personality. There are standardized personality tests from the simplistic (e.g., the Myers-Briggs Personality Inventory) to the complex ones that judge all psychic experiences as "psychotic" (e.g., the MMPI). However recent advances in psychology emphasize the human potential rather than the limits imposed by rigid classifications.

Dean Brown has translated from the Sanskrit sixteen dimensions of intelligence that are defined in the ancient *Aitareyopanishad*. (33) These are: 1) consciousness; 2) instinct; 3) discrimination; 4) intelligence; 5) wisdom; 6) insight; 7) perseverance; 8) reason; 9) genius; 10) impulse; 11) memory; 12) conception; 13) will; 14) vitality; 15) desire; and 16) drive.

Many of these sixteen dimensions are intrinsically involved in the telepathic process, or are part of the drive and perseverance to explore and expand telepathic ability. However, except for memory and desire, they are not illustrated by specific responses in our collection of telepathic trials. We can show fourteen different areas that can interact in a variety of ways. Each of our own multiple personalities may be an expression of a different ranking of dominance among the areas. This list may not include the full classification of possible human dimensions, yet the illustration on the opposite page is a diagram of types of telepathic responses. Our multiple personalities shift according to social needs, personal comfort, or unconscious motivations. There is also a shifting of dominance of types of thought that seep through into awareness from the preconscious during quiet meditation just before a telepathic trial. The pre-conscious information often provides insight about our multiple dimensions that extend into the hyperspace, beyond the limitations of space and time.

The diagram on the opposite page is symbolic of an N-dimensional model. Energies are spiraling out from within the center—spiraling from the source in the state of non-duality. These spirals then pass through the infinite realms of the hyperspace body and whirl around as dualities of the archetypes, adding positive and negative charges to the dance of thoughts. Thoughts about dreams, memories, emotions, intellectual and social concerns, innovative ideas, sexual desires, and survival issues all weave together in different ways to create our multiple personalities. Imagine this idea of energy spiraling in colors of light, shining from our own source of thoughts. Enjoy the experience of being the source of light energy. Becoming the center of the radiance is the true nature of our own reality.

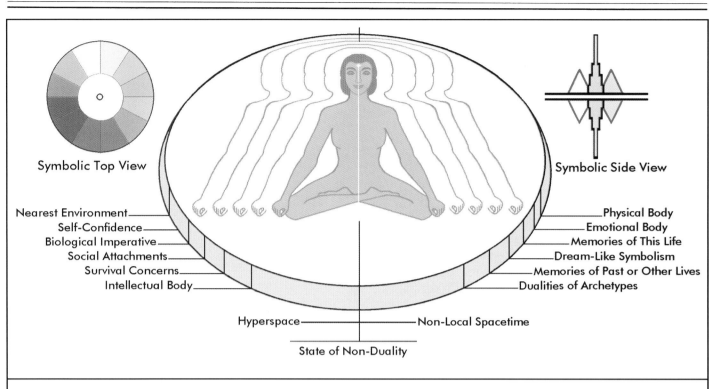

Symbolic Top View

Symbolic Side View

Nearest Environment
Self-Confidence
Biological Imperative
Social Attachments
Survival Concerns
Intellectual Body

Physical Body
Emotional Body
Memories of This Life
Dream-Like Symbolism
Memories of Past or Other Lives
Dualities of Archetypes

Hyperspace —————————— Non-Local Spacetime

State of Non-Duality

The *top view* shows twelve divisions of the mental maze in a circle, with a lighter circle to symbolize the two multidimensional layers. The *side view* shows three layers to include the edge of the center circle of twelve divisions, the hyperspace body, and the state of non-duality. The horizontal center line is the primary connecting core of the creative which touches all other dimensions. This center line represents the power of CREATIVITY to focus attention in any part, and in any dimension. It is the *creative personality* which can SYNTHESIZE any combination of parts into innovative expressions as desired or needed. It is the *creative spirit* which chooses those parts that will dominate to form the basis of the primary personality.

## FOURTEEN CHARACTERISTICS THAT ILLUSTRATE THE MAZE OF MENTAL ACTIVITY:

**Area #1.   The Nearest Environment** — Are there distractions in your immediate space? Sometimes, without knowing it, such distractions invade your imagery. Every afternoon, a train went through the middle of the valley a few miles from where we were conducting the research. We were all so used to it that we ignored it. However, once while it was still far off, the receiver of Team #2 drew a train. By the time the session was over and she saw that her drawing of a train had nothing to do with the target, the sound of the train was quite noticeable. She realized then that her first image was based on the distant sound of the train. It became part of the near environment when it registered in her ear, even though the train itself was still quite faraway.

It is the *nearest environment* of the outbound team that one hopes to see during remote viewing experiments. (34)

**Area #2.   Self-Confidence** — Receivers will often report whether or not they feel confident about their responses.

People who are timid may let images go by (even correct ones) without responding to them. Later, when they see the target, they might say, "I saw that, but I was afraid it wasn't right." A person who is self-assured in lIfe can express any idea that comes to mind (important or not) without worrying about what it might be.

**Area #3.   Biological Imperative** — The biological imperative to reproduce often dominated the thinking of the couples in our teams, either by the desire to do so or by rejection of the idea. These issues created problems about life style, sex, pregnancy, child care, and money. The first eleven teams were mostly students at CSUS. Most were in their mid-twenties, except for one team, a slightly older couple, who were making plans to live together. Another team was married with two children. The five teams who participated in the 1980 study were older. Some of them had already raised families. One team was married. Still, the targets of babies usually evoked responses from the biological imperative, regardless of the age of the teams.

**Area #4.  External and Social Attachments** — The need to find a partner, or the way an ongoing relationship was working out (or not), were important issues. The person's relationship to the community, to special organizations, or to school and its requirements, as well as the ability to organize time for a partner and his/her own personal needs, all imposed words or images onto the response cards of both team members. For young couples, the biological imperative was often at odds with their relationships.

**Area #5.  Survival Concerns** — These fundamental concerns get woven in different ways into all the other parts of the maze. For the student who needs at least a part-time job to stay in school, or who rarely has enough money to fix or to have a car (in an area with poor or no bus service), or who is always hungry, these issues are not far from his/her imagery during these experiments. For that reason, I always had a kettle of soup, stew, or beans and bread and salad for those who came for the session. Many of them took advantage of this, and needed to do so.

**Area #6. The Physical Body** — When the body is uncomfortable, the physical concern may be visualized instead of the target. One way to describe what happens here is to think of dreams. Most of us have experienced a dream about having to go to the bathroom. One part of our multiple selves is reluctant to wake up from sleep, and another one is inhibited from relieving the body pressure while still in bed. The dream may take us on a frustrating trip to find a bathroom, which is closed for repairs when we arrive, or moved farther on. Finally, the dream message reaches through to consciousness, and we awaken. Hunger is another image-maker. During the 1980 study with an older couple, a receiver was hungry and drew pictures of food twice during the first five trials. Both were unrelated to the target pictures. After lunch, three of his trials were hits.

From this study we show illustrations of five types of images from the physical body: 1) Discomfort from tight clothing; 2) Hunger or the opposite feeling of having eaten too much; 3) Discomfort from internal causes, such as illness or pain; 4) Sleepiness, which may prevent direct imagery, or the sleepy person may complain of too many images; 5) Sensations of sexuality and/or sensuality. The experience of flow, when we are focused in sensuality, is so fundamental for telepathy that the chapter on resonance discusses it at length. When two people feel that they are in harmony with each other and/or with nature, there is a resonance within the body, the mind, and the soul. The resonance of prayer can be healing. (35) The resonance of music has the power to bring people together.

**Area #7.  The Emotional Body** — The emotional state of love affairs of either team member was often the source of imagery during the trials. Occasionally their telepathic communication was *only* about their relationship, and neither the sender's nor the receiver's card would have any similarities to the target. When participants were mad, or sad, or glad, images and words relating to these emotions would also be included on the response cards.

> **The experience of flow, when focused in sensory awareness, is fundamental in mind-to-mind communication. When two people feel that they are in harmony with each other and/or in harmony with nature, there is a resonance at some level within the body, the mind, and the soul.**

**Area #8.   The Intellectual Body or Mental Body** — These are the thoughts related to verbalization and reason that engage our focus of attention. Words about books or a study hall appeared more than once just before a midterm or a final exam. Other responses came from other things that might be a focus of the mental realms, whether "intellectual" or not. One couple watched a lot of TV over the holidays, especially the ball games. The husband included several responses for that session (e.g. "...as seen on TV").

**Area #9.   Memories of Experiences During This Lifetime** — All of our childhood memories are part of the maze of memory. Some are not evoked until we are reminded by an association. Some are only evoked during a moment of meditation or profound stillness, when the verbal mind stops talking to itself. The vacuum of *no thought* which then occurs becomes immediately filled with whatever is nearest in the pre-conscious mind and that quickly pops into awareness for interpretation by one of the sensory systems. The deeper memories may need a powerful, spontaneous experience or help from a guided imagery session before they surface. However, all our memories are available, and sometimes they will surface during the quiet period of a telepathic session. Only the receiver can judge this type of associated material. An outside judge may never match it as a "hit." This is where the telepathy attempts serve the participants more than those who wish to *prove* or to *disprove* the existence of psi. The researcher in this case is only a bystander in the integral processes of the participants. While it is true that any picture can evoke a mass of free associations (and this activity has become the subject of parlor games), it is also true that any blind matches made of telepathic trials might be just as far-fetched. However, what the participants feel about their own results can help them in their understanding of themselves and their relationship to each other. Our participants wanted to learn to improve their communication with each other, and they were willing to share their thoughts about it with us. Many of the illustrations in this chapter reveal these inner thoughts more than they demonstrate telepathy from the official targets. Yet, we do see some form of communication taking place and sometimes a conversation.

**Area #10.   Dream-Like Symbolism** — In the dream telepathy studies by Dr. Stanley Krippner and others at the Dream Lab at Maimonides Medical Center in Brooklyn, New York, symbolism was expected to be woven into the telepathic dreams. (36) Though our participants were awake, dream-like symbols were woven into their telepathic drawings also. The visual system *talks* to the mind differently than the verbal system does. The process of creating images that communicate ideas from the hyperspace into awareness must use the existing filters. For example, a young man's response to a photo of a nude man hugging a woman who was semi-nude (but wearing green pants) was "A gun, a football and a Kirlian [fig-shaped] leaf."

**Area #11.   Memories of Past or Other Lives** — Sometimes we might experience what seems to be ourselves, but with a different body in the past or in another life. It is not necessary to believe in a past life, but the information about the experience (whether it is a fantasy or not) usually relates to a present dilemma. (37) When we are willing to explore this cosmic drama, we can apply the lessons learned from it to our current situation, and can gain important insights that can be useful in the future. The experience of dying in a past life can help alleviate anxieties about death. The experience of merging with another can provide helpful information for us and for the other person.

**Area #12.   Basic Dualities of Archetypes** — Gods and demons also play a part in our mental maze, even if we think we do not believe in them. If we are holding unresolved dualities within us (good/evil, right/wrong, beauty/ugliness, etc.), these may manifest in our images as a basic struggle between the archetypes from the timeless realms. Several telepathic responses show these dualities to be paired; for example, a target picture of the devil evoked a response about God. A target picture that mentioned God evoked a response of a devil. Different teams gave the same type of paired or opposite responses, suggesting that certain fundamental dualities lie deep in the cultural psyche, not unique to any one individual.

**Area #13.   The Hyperspace** — Our hyperspatial body is the realm of our multidimensional consciousness, which can be *projected* into the dimensions of our spacetime awareness. Through meditation and nonattachment to the limitations of spacetime, our awareness can be *lifted* into the multidimensional realms of the hyperspace. (See the Sirag illustration on page 12.) It is because of our multidimensional nature that we are able to *see* things at a distance during remote viewing. It is because of our identity with the hyperspace that we can attempt to *find* the message being sent. However, whatever the message might be, it must then be interpreted through the limitations of our spacetime awareness. That may be dominated at the time by areas in the maze that inhibit accurate interpretation.

Responses can be received through any of the brain's interpretive and sensory systems, and can provide concept or mood similarities, or perhaps the same exact words may arise in the mind. The receiver may even identify with the subject of the target and write about similar internal feelings. Most of our response similarities, however, were visual. That is because we asked for a drawing first. The mind reaching out to the target may pick up only a brief sensory impression. If that is an image, it may be received only partially, because the telepathic eye does not track, as the physical eye does. Physicist Saul-Paul Sirag has said, "...the space/time projection provides only a partial view of the hyperspace events." As we gain experience traveling in the hyperspace, we learn to be more at ease among the vast realms available for exploration.

**Area #14.   Interconnectedness of All Beings; Non-Duality, Cosmic Love** — To experience this state of oneness with all things we search for enlightenment. There is no differentiation here; we are all part of all things. This is not the place where telepathy experiments take place. One is not interested in proving such minor events here. Later, in a different state of mind, insights and realizations gained from experiencing this state of wholeness can be discussed. Only the hum of pure vibrations exists in this area of awareness—no words at all, though spiritual healing might begin with this resonance. Here we can experience Earth (Gaia) directly as a conscious entity and all beings as a part of a consciousness that is infinite and eternal.

The dualities of good and evil, war and peace, honesty and corruption have not gone away, but in this state of consciousness, this state of oneness, there is no duality. Ideas about ways that might help alleviate social problems may arise out of our meditation, but while we are focused in the center of ourselves, there is only oneness.

The brain is basically a dual system, with the right and left sides of the cerebral cortex sometimes performing different tasks and sometimes duplicating tasks. But in the very center of the brain there is a place of focus (perhaps in the ventricles) which is beyond words, a place where the sound of AUM exists for all time. When one chooses to become nonattached to words and thoughts, this hum resonates body, brain, and mind, aligning our consciousness so we can pass through the doorway into the hyperspace.

From the *Tao Te Ching,* by Lao-Tzu:
(Stephen Mitchell's English translation) (38)

...The unnameable is the eternally real.
Naming is the origin of all particular things.
Free from desire, you realize the mystery.
Caught in desire, you see only the manifestations.
Yet mystery and manifestations
Arise from the same source.
This source is called darkness.
Darkness within darkness.
The gateway to all understanding.

**All Areas Are Interconnected Through Creativity** — Creativity does not have a number on the list for the mental maze, because creativity is the organizing principle for our experiences and for how we choose to respond to events. The diagram on page 37 shows creativity as the center line connecting all the levels of the labyrinth of mind. The *creative spirit* chooses which levels will be dominant to form the basis of the personality. The *creative personality* can synthesize any combination of its multiple selves to

Students in Marge King's science class explore the changes in their brains' electrical activity, as different types of thoughts cause the mandala patterns to respond with different colors. (39)

Electronics by Scully.    *Brainwave Light Sculpture* by Millay.

achieve innovative solutions to problems. This synthesis often requires a period of quiet contemplation, or sometimes deep sleep. Inventors have reported that solutions to projects have come to them in dreams. (40) When we are actively involved in creating, our attention will be focused on the creative process until the best idea, image, or resolution emerges. The creative fire burns through emotions as well as pain. The creative personality learns to focus all its energy to become one-pointed.

During my many midlife crises, my various multiple personalities were at war with each other. My need for a relationship was at war with my need to care for my children. All these were at war with my interests on the intellectual level, which didn't pay enough for rent and groceries. During a time of reflection about what to do, Tim Scully gave me his new brainwave analyzer to use in designing a feedback system for it. During the hours I spent practicing voluntary control of my own brainwaves in order to find out what feedback would enhance each frequency and not inhibit it, I discovered the benefits of *brainwave synch.* Gradually, my various personalities began to communicate with each other again, instead of maintaining an uneasy and dysfunctional separation. Through synchronizing my brainwaves, a synthesis was taking place among my various selves across the steady hum of the electrical sine waves. Out of that came a powerful creative vision that inspired a new direction for my life and this research. Below left is an illustration of one of the results of that vision, the *Stereo Brainwave Biofeedback Light Sculpture.* The design uses eight layers of edge-lit plexiglass. Each layer has a mandala pattern carved into it that is different, but reciprocal to every other one. Together they create a single radiant energy design. The beta, alpha, and theta signals from both brainwave analyzers light up each layer of plexiglass with a different color as the student's thoughts or emotions change. Layers seven and eight respond to eye blinks and muscle artifacts.

Many students also discovered their own creativity through their participation in the interhemispheric brainwave phase-coherent *(IH synch)* biofeedback training. When the ratio of phase coherence of alpha increased for people during training, invariably they would find an answer to a problem or recall something from memory. Through the nonverbal pure hum of the phase-coherent brainwaves, an integration of verbal and nonverbal information seems to take place. Many students later reported to me that they had learned to use that "synch feeling" in their meditation practice long after the electrodes and brainwave analyzers had been put away.

## AREAS OF THE MAZE THAT FREQUENTLY INFLUENCE TELEPATHIC IMAGERY

**Area #1. The Nearest Environment** — The illustration below shows how a decoration in the subject room had a ringing effect on the images of the receiver after her eyes were closed. She was looking for the image her partner was sending (the mountain), and from that state of mind, she didn't recognize that the image that first appeared to her had a similarity to the four-foot-square, blue velvet tie-dye hanging on the wall behind her. The act of seeing it, apparently, was not conscious, but the after-image remained. It was there when she closed her eyes and she drew it as though it were a telepathic image. Since the next target was an ad for a pack of cigarettes (smoking was not allowed in the subject room), she resisted her urge to smoke and drew the mountain which matched the sender's drawing of the previous target. This was the only time a mountain was drawn with sketchy lines in one color in the four hundred trials. Other mountains from the study were drawn very differently with solid colors. The judges matched Response #4 with Target #3. None of the judges matched any of the targets in this set of five trials.

**Area #2. Self-Confidence Level** — The artist James Dowlen did not feel it necessary to name all his images. He was confident in his drawings, whether or not he knew what he had drawn. This is very important in telepathic activity. Any image, word, feeling, or concept, no matter how bizarre, might be from the target. Targ has referred to the "high strangeness level" of material as being the most likely to be important. (41) When the receiver fearfully passes judgment on his/her images or feelings, there can be too much censorship, and the parts that are most likely to be accurate will not be used in the telepathic response. The receiver of Team #1 did very well for her first three targets. But she started to feel a lack of confidence, and for the next one in that set of five trials, she drew two pictures unrelated to the target and wrote, "...I don't feel very strongly about either impression." She seemed to know when she was wrong, and usually identified her lack of confidence. However, she did get nine fairly good or partial "hits" in the total of twenty trials she attempted.

At SRI, Targ allowed his receivers to pass if they didn't feel confident about their responses. They completed only one trial at a time, with immediate feedback. We completed five in a series before feedback was given, with no passes. Targ's system was better for establishing statistics than ours was. Our method was not designed to *prove* psi. Our participants were free to explore their subtle levels of communication through all their responses and thus to discover their pre-conscious thoughts as well.

| | *Team #5 - TARGET - Trial #3*<br>*3/6/75* |
|---|---|
| | *Photo of mountains and skiers cut from an old magazine listed in Appendix A.* |
| | **BMS = 0 — SMS = color** |
| | *Team #5 - TARGET - Trial #4*<br>*3/6/75* |
| | *This target (not shown) is a photo of a pack of cigarettes from a magazine advertisement listed in Appendix A.* |
| | **BMS = 0 — SMS = 0** |

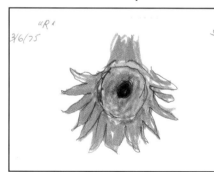

| | **Team #5**<br>**RECEIVER**<br>**Trial #3**<br>"Sunspot or abstract-shaped blob. Like tie-dyed irregular shape almost with pseudopodia or octopus-like." |
|---|---|

**Team #5 — SENDER — Trial #4**
"Cigarette, disgust, *[brand name]*, package."
*(Sender's drawing not shown.)*

| | **Team #5**<br>**SENDER**<br>**Trial #3**<br><br>**"Mountains,**<br>Skiing, Trails, Skier, Snow. The 'Unconscious.' " |
|---|---|

| | **Team #5**<br>**RECEIVER**<br>**Trial #4**<br><br>"Clouds, possibly rain clouds— and maybe **mountains...."** |
|---|---|

**Team #5 - TARGET - Trial #4**
**12/16/74**
*Photo from* LIFE *magazine. See Appendix A.*

BMS = 0 —— SMS = 0

**Team #5 - SENDER - Trial #4**

"Glasses,
birth, baby,
doctors, mother."

**Team #5 - RECEIVER - Trial #4**

"Wooden construction—angular—
weathervane maybe?
**No idea what it is really.**"

**Area #3. Biological Imperative** — There was a time in our culture's history when a couple arrived at the age of sexual maturity (around age fourteen or sixteen), and they were married and raised a family as babies came naturally. Sometimes the parents arranged the marriage, and gave them some goats and a piece of land if they were lucky. Members of some communities would help raise a barn. As part of a family and a community they worked together. Babies were considered a blessing. Today, in spite of the fact that education takes a longer time before a couple can earn enough for marriage and a family, the biological imperative to conceive children at that earlier age is still a very strong internal directive that can create extreme conflicts among the various personalities within the maze. Babies are not considered a blessing for students expected to get a college education first. The responses illustrated here were not matched by the judges, and they seem to be unrelated to their targets. But they reinforced the inner feelings of the couples, and opened the dialog between them about having babies.

Illustrated above is the only target picture of a baby as it is being born. The receiver of Team #5 had a very negative response to it. She and her partner teamed up only for the sake of these experiments. They were just buddies. She had NO intention of getting pregnant while still in college. For her, the large *X* meant that even her unconscious mind was set in that decision, even if she had "no idea" what she had

drawn or why. She laughed when she saw the target, pleased that she had drawn that image from her unconscious. She told us she had been burned at the stake for being a healer in the sixteenth century. She was totally focused on earning her certification to do healing work in this life. Nothing would be allowed to interfere with that.

Below is an example from the older group. When the receiver of Team #14 later compared his response to the target and his partner's response, he told her he would be very proud if she wanted to have his baby, and the peacock hat symbolized that for him. There are other pictures of children among the targets called "baby," but only two pictures of the unborn. One is a fetus in a test tube. The sender of Team #7 expresses an emotional reaction. She writes "...poor baby—doesn't get mother's warmth...in a lifeless tube." Her lover writes, "...Geometric figures or tools...."

**Team #14 - TARGET**
**Trial #8 - 8/15/80**

*This is our rough sketch of the photo.*
*Copyright © 1965 Lennart Nillsson.*

BMS = 1 — SMS = 0

**TARGET #8**
(notes about target)

*Our sketch of the incredible photograph of a fetus by Lennart Nillsson is very rough. We do apologize for that. The actual target used for this trial was a photocopy of one that was published in* LIFE *magazine in 1965. (42) Over the years even the photocopy became so scratched that it could not be reproduced here.*

**Team #14 - SENDER**
**Trial #8**
"The prisoner—
little alien inside me.
Baby in my belly"

**Team #14 - RECEIVER**
**Trial #8**

"Man in Peacockskin hat"

| | |
|---|---|
| ***Team #7 - TARGET - Trial #5***<br>***2/23/75***<br><br>*This target is a color photo of a nude couple in an explicit pose. It was cut from one of the magazines listed in Appendix A. Neither the photographer nor the subjects are known. The camera is actually focused over the man's **left** shoulder. His hand is pushing her breast up as the sender's drawing suggests. They both look bored.*<br><br>**BMS = 3 — SMS = d, s, m, cn** | 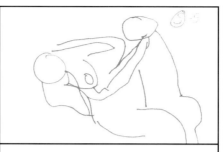<br>***Team #7 - SENDER - Trial #5***<br><br>"SEX Yum Yum<br>Two bodies warm<br>Yum Yum Sex YA! YA!" | <br>***Team #7 - RECEIVER - Trial #5***<br><br>"Dice—<br>Looking over a **man's rt. shoulder**<br>(feel hungry, cigarette)" |

Team #7 had several reactions to the biological imperative, which they did not realize until later. The target above was not a photo of a baby, but of a coupling couple. Several pictures of this same couple in explicit poses were cut from the same unknown magazine. (Two other photos from that series were eventually chosen as targets by different teams and are illustrated on page 59.) Because the source of the photos cannot be found to obtain permission to show them, the sender's drawing will have to do to indicate the pose. The rest must be left for your imagination.

The receiver for Team #7 was a student, but his lady was not. He volunteered her for the study because parapsychology was his major. She enjoyed the telepathy part, but she was the only one who did *not* like brainwave synchronization training. She wrote, "I do not like to be hooked up. I think it is uncomfortable. I don't find any synch...fun, helpful, or educational...." To her the EEG machines were "unnatural." She was very adamant and outspoken that everything should be natural, including the rhythm method for birth control. When her receiver compared his response to the target, he was only puzzled that his vision was "...over a man's *right* shoulder," and the photo was over a

man's *left* shoulder. We talked about how reversals of right and left occur frequently in psi. He did not realize at the time that his sexual activity might be like playing dice, as his pre-conscious mind seemed to be telling him. Within two months his partner became pregnant. He quit school at the end of the semester, got a full-time job and they were married. Their baby was a girl.

**Area #4. Social Attachments** — The same receiver of Team#7 illustrated this area during the same session. He responded to the sun target below with "...marriage (Diamond)." The "...tricycle" in his response implies that his pre-conscious knew a baby was in his future, or perhaps the spirit of the unborn was attempting to contact him.

For Team #10 the symbolism was reversed. Their target was a diamond ring and the receiver responded with a bright sun. Both of these teams were later married after college. Team #8 had the only other target of a diamond ring. They were happy with their relationship and had *no* intention of getting married. They thought a formal wedding was a hollow ritual, and a ring was empty symbolism. His response to the diamond was an empty hardware store.

| | |
|---|---|
| <br>***Team #7 - TARGET - Trial #1***<br>***2/23/75***<br>*A magazine advertisement. See Appendix A.*<br><br>**BMS = 5 — SMS = s, cl, w, cn** | 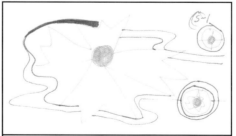<br>***Team #7 - SENDER - Trial #1***<br><br>"Stars & distant galaxies.<br>Could be the place where the star ships<br>are from? Deep space." | 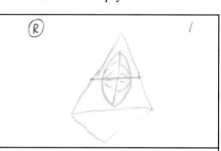<br>***Team #7 - RECEIVER - Trial #1***<br><br>"Maybe bicycle or tricycle<br>**Spinning earth**<br>Marriage (Diamond)" |

Another example of this subject of marriage and social attachments was given by Team #11 when the target photo showed a couple dressed in wedding clothes, standing at a church altar. The sender writes, "Ridiculous, silly, proper." Her lover responds with, "Swinging like a door." They lived together until the following semester, when, after many changes in plans, they separated.

Team #1 began with a string of hits and near hits. During the second session a few weeks later, a picture of a Greek horse statue was the target. The sender really enjoyed this picture, identifying with the horse. He wrote, "Yellow horse that bucked and thrashed in front of... [partner] & then snuggled up with her." She did draw some similar shapes with the right golden color, but she also wrote, "...I felt threatening feeling, overpowering." After being threatened, she did not wait for the snuggling feeling. When he saw her drawing, he acted hurt that he had put so much effort into the sending and she didn't receive it the way he expected. This was, of course, the wrong attitude, and the monitor gently chided him for this. However, he continued the argument after the session was over, and apparently built up some anger as well. Later she called me to say that she never wanted to synchronize her brainwaves with him again. The horse episode came during the last session of their part of the study, just as the semester was over. It was also the end of their relationship.

The members of Team #3 were a bit older than the students. She and her partner were planning to move in together after the first of the year. She had an adolescent daughter from a previous marriage. They seemed quite content with their relationship, but one potential problem was dramatized when a picture of a mother holding the hand of a little girl became the target. She wrote about a "Child's soft warm hand touching mother's. Velvets of cloth and skin. Richness of velvet and love. Safe & secure." He responded with a picture of an upset stomach. I don't know how that relationship worked out. The bottom line for most mothers is the child. Men rarely seem to understand this, and expect their needs to come first. This is a problem in many relationships today as divorce and remarriage rearrange family ties for children.

Are these responses as unrelated as they seemed to be to the outside judges? The answer is yes, when the goal is to reproduce a word, concept, or image that exactly matches the target. However, the intention of these participants was to learn more about their communication with each other, so the answer is more complex. Their honest responses provided them with important insights, and also provided us with information about the way our pre-conscious minds influence our interpersonal communication.

**Area #5.   Survival Concerns** — The problems of survival, of making a living, finishing school, having to take one or two jobs to get by, all can create dreams and images. How many times do we lie awake at night, trying to *imagine* how to get through difficult times? Team #9 started out with a strong telepathy score, but toward the end of the semester when term papers were due, their responses became scattered. She wrote, "Rushed, too much to do." He wrote, "...hard not to think about things...Mind wandering, thinking a lot. Hard to focus on receptive mode."

For the target of death below, the sender of Team #14 found it difficult to send that thought to his lady. She, however, resolved the concept very well. She was a nurse, and death was no stranger in her work at the hospital. Her symbol of it as an "Angel of the Night" was one of the ways that she could do her job well and be nonattached to the inevitable. He was relieved when he saw her response.

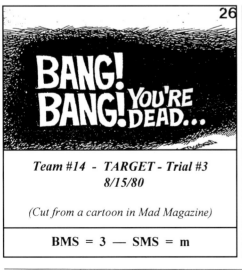

Team #14 - TARGET - Trial #3
8/15/80

*(Cut from a cartoon in Mad Magazine)*

**BMS = 3 — SMS = m**

Team #14 - SENDER - Trial #3

"Bad image.
This is hard to send to...
[partner]"

*Team #14 RECEIVER Trial #3*

"Very Dark.

Angel of the Night.

Couldn't determine gender."

**Area #6.   The Physical Body** — The first on the list of imagery arising from the physical body is that of discomfort from clothing. This is seen at right in the response from Team #7. When the receiver looked for an image, he found long stringy lines, a floating shape, and something white, but for him, these brief images only related to the feeling that his headband (for holding the EEG electrodes) was too tight. He did not identify the content of the target, yet three of the judges did match it. The receiver from Team #12 drew images for the second category of physical response, food, because he was hungry. His responses improved after we fed him. He was one of the older group participating at the Washington Research Institute (WRI), and unlike the earlier study which was conducted with hungry students, I hadn't automatically made food available before the WRI sessions began.

Team #4 provided a response for a third category on the physical level. He seemed to be catching a cold, and his response was a bottle of pills for an illness (see page 57). When receivers expressed the fourth category of physical response, there were no relevant images, but the written responses included complaints about feeling sleepy or very tired. Below is an illustration of the fifth category, but this is the result of a physical response that was received telepathically, not one that began as an internal discomfort. The receiver of Team #14 could feel in his physical body the energies that his partner was sending to him. His response was not from shape or drawing similarities; instead his memory associations found a more familiar representation for the same concept. This is the second time he referred to a Rodin statue in his responses.

The woman receiver of Team #12 wrote this response to a target picture of a nude couple embracing: "Two Ballet Dancers, legs kicking up high." Teams #12 and #14 were in the older group with the 1980 studies, and they were not inhibited about their basic energies, as were some of the younger students. Most students gave dream-like symbolic responses to target pictures with explicit sexual content. The one exception among the students was a response by the receiver of Team #11. He was able to express his physical sensations directly, since he and his lover seemed to resonate well. He drew a sketchy blue line and wrote about "Stimulation of the 2nd Chakra. A sexual feeling." (See page 34.)

*Team #7 - TARGET*
*Trial #3 - 2/23/75*

*cut from wrapping paper.*

BMS = 3 — SMS = s, w

*Team #7*
*SENDER*
*Trial #3*

"Pretty flowers.

I held them out for [*partner*] to smell."

*Team #7 - RECEIVER - Trial #3*

"Headband, hat, tight on forehead.
Ancient wise man
**w / long white** hair & beard."

*Team #14*
*TARGET*
*Trial #3 - 8/9/80*

Yoni-asana
*Painting.*
*Nepal c. 18th*
*century.*
TANTRA ASANA
*by Ajit Mookerjee*
© Copyright 1971
Ravi Kumar

*Below is a quote from the* Tantra Asana *book:*

"...*After perfect control of the senses, one must approach the 'devout woman' by stages and transubstantiate her into a goddess....*" (43)

BMS = 5 — SMS = cl, w, m,  cn

*Team #14 - SENDER*
*Trial #3*

"SEX"

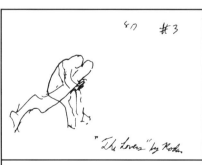

*Team #14 - RECEIVER - Trial #3*

*"The Lovers*
by Rodin."

**Area #7.   The Emotional Body** — The person who attempts to send or to receive a non-emotional telepathic message over a distance must first clear any emotions that are foremost in the mind. I could usually tell when my children were mad, or sad, or glad, but not always why. If they felt guilty about something, I could make up many scenarios about the possible reasons. My interpretations might be much worse than what really happened. When my son was a teenager he said to me, "Mother, you *assume* too much." My response was, "OK, then, tell me what is really going on." A loved one who has a serious need can send a psychic call for help that is very strong, because of the emotions involved. But the receiver needs to be clear and open to receive it accurately.

One extremely emotional time for me and for my daughter Mara provides the background for this story about the need to control emotions in order to establish a clear mind-to-mind communication over distance. Neither the children nor I had seen their father for nine years. He had remarried, had two other sons, and had moved to the Hawaiian Islands. When Mara was twenty-one years old she decided that she wanted to visit them, and had saved some money to do so. Before leaving, she threw the coins for the *I Ching*. (44) The hexagram was *SHOCK*. We couldn't decide whether that meant that he had sobered up finally or was worse than before. Nevertheless, she wanted to find out for herself. He was, as usual, very charming at first, and seemed glad to see her. Within a couple of days, however, he went on a violent binge. His own multiple personalities had become even more widely separated than they had been before. After years of working with a Freudian analyst, he recovered painful memories of childhood abuse by his parents. With that discovery, he became aware of an intense hate for his mother. However, his expensive Freudian therapy was incomplete. It did not include forgiving his mother, so he passed his anger on to me, and then to his daughter. She was shocked by his uncontrolled meanness toward her, his other family, and the animals.

She hastily stuffed necessities into her backpack and left to join friends who were going hiking up the mountain of Haleakala. He called me for the first time in nine years while in this drunken state, and for a moment, his rage energy shook my small apartment. In the maze of my personalities was one called "Mother Tiger defending her young." Another part was the researcher of brainwaves. The *Stereo Brainwave Light Sculpture* was sitting before me. I really wanted to know what rage looked like in the EEG. Many people had come to see how the machines would register different thoughts and moods, but we had never seen the EEG of anyone who was as seriously angry as I was at that moment. When I turned on the feedback, I saw that red patterns of theta (low frequencies, high amplitude) flashed first on the right side and then on the left, alternating. It was time to put the synchronization theory to the test. I practiced *IH synch* for an hour. The experience was both transformative and informative. I learned, for the first time in twenty years, that I no longer feared that man. He was, at that moment, more afraid of me and the inevitable consequences if he harmed our daughter in any physical way. The psychological abuse was now part of her karma, and I could not protect her from that.

Nevertheless, I worried about Mara. She did not call that night, nor the next. I realized that I was beginning to project many fears into the situation. So I drove to my favorite mountain retreat. Usually I would meet friends at the cabin. But this time, there was no one around for miles. In the morning I arose before dawn to purify my thoughts from intense emotion to a quiet nonattachment. Next I began to call up the image of her face, but it continued to turn away for several hours. My need to communicate was great, so my focus of intention was set. Finally, the thought came that to receive a message *from* her, I would have to see her as an honored teacher, not as "my little girl."

At that moment, an image of the inside of a golden tube from my third eye appeared, stretching across the three thousand miles directly connecting to her third eye. The message was brief but very clear, "Pray, don't worry, mother." When a mother worries about her children, she is actually surrounding them with negative energy, because the psychic connection is always naturally present, whether she is conscious of that or not. A prayer, which can be thought of as intentionally surrounding them with love and a golden light, can provide them with extra energy that they might find more useful during their own difficult situation. Mara Mayo had chosen to go to the top of a sacred mountain for the sunrise, as had I, in order to meditate on the problems at hand. Her life took on a very different direction from that experience. I learned that worry is the wrong way to communicate with loved ones. If you have a reason to be concerned, do something useful: send love.

Emotions color all thoughts, all perceptions, all interpretations of "reality." Sometimes the students wrote about their unresolved emotions. For example, a picture of a girl stimulated the sender to write about her friend's interest in other women. He wrote about his concerns for her. Neither one paid any attention to the girl in the target picture.

**Area #8.  The Intellectual Body or Mental Body** — The person who studies quantum mechanics, philosophy, or great literature, is called an intellectual, but the one who watches a lot of TV is not. However, whatever occupies the focus of mental attention is included here, and we find some of it written on the cards of our telepathic responses. During a session that was held when the midterm exams were scheduled two days away, a receiver drew a stack of books as his response to a totally unrelated target of a rain cloud. The same man drew a different picture of a globe and another stack of books just before his final exams. Neither response had any relation to the targets.

*Team #6 - TARGET*
*Trial #6 - 1/10/75*

BMS = 1 - SMS = d, s, cl

*Team #6 - SENDER*
*Trial #6*

"Cold, but rich, quality"

*Team #6 - RECEIVER - Trial #6*

"Woman bathing—
**as in a bath soap ad."**

curved. The same shapes become the down-turned feet of the tub. He writes about a TV commercial, which had been repeated frequently (as they all are) for the purpose of imprinting the memory (which it did).

Examples of the influence of TV came from the receiver of Team #6, who completed the second session after finals were over. The team could be more relaxed for telepathy trials at that time. Many of the shapes and colors the receiver drew were remarkably similar to those his wife had drawn of the target. However, he had been watching a lot of TV during the break (especially ball games), so his similar shapes were transformed into concepts from TV programs, news, and advertisements. One target was a photo of an orange sunset reflected in water. His wife drew long horizontal lines of orange and brown. His response also contained long horizontal lines of orange and brown, but for him it was "a crowded football stadium." His response above shows a person *in* the tub, instead of a painting *on* the tub. The handles on the vase are up-turned and

Illustrated below is another response from Team #6 from watching TV. Violence and graphic pictures of news events do influence our pre-conscious imagery systems. The subject of this target is only cartoon violence, but the images are translated into the latest violent drama that the receiver had seen. He is an adult, but the same violent imagery has an even stronger influence on the minds of children, whether seen on the news, cartoons, or films. Images replay over and over again in daydreams or during sleep. They have a direct effect on thinking. How often do you say the same things over to yourself in imaginary conversation with another? How often do you hear the words of a song repeated in your mind, whether you like the song or not? Neither the images, sounds, nor the words leave the memory. And they do resurface from time to time in the physical body, in the emotional body, and in the intellectual body, and are carried over through the memories of childhood into old age. They can become deeply imbedded into the symbols of thought, becoming part of your reality.

*Team #6 - TARGET - Trial #5*
*2/28/75*

"TROGLODYTES!!" *(1974 Marvel Comics)*

BMS = 5 — SMS = cl, w, m, cn

*Team #6 - SENDER - Trial #5*

"Far out"

*Team #6 - RECEIVER - Trial #5*

"Person shooting others in a
street scene (B & W)—
Sinister, violent, death, hatred."

In the illustrations at right, the concept of a "powerful man...." and the shape of a head with something around the neck was transmitted successfully. However, the concept of size is very different. Such shifts in scale are common when using small pictures as targets. Since the receiver had been reading about the gigantic ancient Egyptian statues that had to be moved because of the Aswan Dam, the idea of power along with the shape in the sender's drawing were both transposed to fit recent mem-

**Team #1 - TARGET
Trial #1 - 11/19/74**
*See Appendix A.*

BMS = 0
SMS = d, s, m, cn

**Team #1 - SENDER
Trial #1**

"Powerful man with ominous overtones....

Don Juan.
Flashes of
Fred Sanford."

**Team #1 - RECEIVER - Trial #1**

"Reminds me of the pyramid thing in Egypt they moved 'cuz of the Aswan Dam.

—green patch of some sort, also...person. Definite feeling of some sort of triangle, sometimes upside down, floating, turning."

ory. The receiver wrote comments on the back of the card as well as on the front all around the drawing. Since they would be too small to read when reduced to the size above, I removed them so the drawing could be seen more clearly.

The monitor related the image to Shakespeare, but that relationship to the target did not occur to either member of the team, even though the man is wearing a costume of the period and is writing in a book. The intellectual level, as we have defined it here, includes the ideas that we have read about, thought about, or have watched on TV remaining in our thoughts as abstract mental concepts. We all think very differently about things according to the experiences imbedded in each part of our maze, and according to which part of our own maze is dominant at the time. The constant overlay of recent memory on the incoming messages is really an essential part of our mental processes.

**Area #9.  Memories of This Life Since Conception —**
Childhood memories and their associations are always with us. We may not be aware of them; they may be locked deep in the unconscious, or close to the surface of awareness in our pre-conscious mind. Those memories in our pre-conscious may appear easily during deep relaxation or meditation. That is why sometimes they surprise us as responses during our telepathic exercises. Both team members are asked to close their eyes, relax, and let the mind float beyond the cares of the day for the first two minutes of each session, just after the target is chosen. The sender is asked to think about the target and the re-

ceiver is asked to clear his/her mind. At the end of two minutes, the monitor announces that the sender will begin drawing. The receiver can do whatever comes to mind. Both are given time to relax and to clear their minds again before the next target is chosen. This quiet time is enough for some of our participants to allow the pre-conscious thoughts to float up to the surface. There they can easily dominate whatever faint impression might have been received from the target or from the sender. A message from the pre-conscious might even be triggered by the concept of the target, the shape or color of it, or the message might be important enough to just push beyond all other thoughts.

The young women's Team #2 provided an early childhood memory in response to a target, which was a photo of a football player in action. Neither of them were interested in football, but the sender made a good drawing of the player and wrote, "tried to see me & [partner] watching a football game, laughing." The receiver drew several scratchy lines on the card and wrote, "Angles, points, stem, shredded wheat magnified." Her earliest memories of football players were those pictured on "Breakfast of Champions" cereal boxes right next to enlarged pictures of wheat. None of the judges matched this one, but everyone thought it was funny. This is a good indication of the lasting impression of first memories. If you close your eyes and ask yourself to remember the first telephone number you ever had to remember, do you see it, or hear it, or dial it? The way you learned it then is the way you remember it now. When the images from early memories influence the responses to telepathy, the receiver is often surprised.

The illustration below is a clear example of the way an early childhood memory can be evoked by a target. A stop sign is an extremely important symbol to be imposed on a child very early. It will be remembered indefinitely.

The judges had no trouble matching this one by blind matching techniques. Team #4 was the young men's team. They were both musicians who had been friends through school. In the first series of studies done in 1974-75, they were the top-scoring team in telepathy as well as in brain-wave phase synchronization, though both telepathy and *IP team synch* scores were measured separately during different sessions. (In Chapter Four we explore the concept of resonance and harmonics in mind-to-mind communication as well as in music.)

When childhood memories are relatively happy, a person may remember them easily, including crawling under chairs and tables, the feel of those first brave steps when learning to walk, and the emotions of that first day of school. In my own work with hypnosis, I have explored the educational benefits of exploring early memories of childhood and birth, as well as before birth. The happy memories can be re-lived to bring fresh happiness into the present. When memories have been traumatic, all of them may be locked into the subconscious. Hypnotherapy can be extremely useful as a tool to find them. When the guide is compassionate and the qual is supportive, even the most terrifying memories can be re-experienced until the emotional body no longer feels the pain, but can keep the memories and be nonattached to them. (These ideas are discussed at length in Chapter Six.)

Yet we do find that memories of the past can be malleable. Old memories can be altered by changing our reactions to them. Old angers can be relieved by the act of forgiveness. Old fears can become strengths by confronting them instead of hiding from them. Old grief can be softened by the realization that consciousness belongs to eternity. Old attitudes can be modified by a realization that most concepts of reality are home-brewed. Re-framing old memories can be encouraged for positive therapeutic use (e.g., forgive a parent who was abusive and explore his/her fears for understanding). When we learn to own all our memories biofeedback can be useful as a way to release our physiological and emotional reactions to them. The actual memories may remain, but our reactions to them can be changed. The future is also changed by the way we make a conscious choice to perceive things.

Each person's memory of a dramatic event may very well become different when everyone compares notes at a later time. Each person projects into the event his/her expectations, hopes and fears. What each one remembers is a combination of reflections from one's projections overlaid on the event itself. As time goes by, each of those projections gets amplified. The actual event was totally different for each person. That is why attempts at telepathy can be so useful. They stretch out that misty edge between the external event and the internal projections that make up our different "reality concepts." We can watch our own shifts take place from the external through the internal maze, instead of just being caught up in our own thoughts on the one side, as though they were the only reality available. Sometimes it is a shock to discover just how differently others think about some issues than we do. For one thing, they may start with a very different set of memories and a very different belief system about the nature of the world. (In Chapter Nine, the way logic is derived from the initial belief system is examined.)

For science to be truly honest in its explorations, these issues must be constantly monitored. Today, we see science conducted to "prove" or to "disprove" things, depending on the politics of the granting agency. We call that "grant proposal consciousness," and the various government and commercial interests may sometimes promote a concept for profit or for political gain. Each scientist should declare a starting belief system because it may color the design of the research. There is no escape from memories influencing an experimenter effect in all research and especially in the field of psychology. We live in a "psychic soup," yet we tend to hide personal projections from memory under the false illusion of objectivity.

*Team #4 - TARGET*
*Trial #5*
*12/12/74*

**BMS = 4 — SMS = cn**

*Team #4 - SENDER*
*Trial #5*

"Stop What?
I'm innocent. Demand."

*Team #4 - RECEIVER - Trial #5*

"Children—
Street—something
(associated with childhood)."

**Area #10.  Dream-Like Symbolism** — One of the best research studies in telepathy was done at the Dream Lab in the Maimonides Medical Center in Brooklyn, New York. (45) Messages were sent to people while they were dreaming. The EEG identified the periods of dreaming, so the sender was informed when to begin. Near the end of the average dream, the patient would be awakened and asked to tell about the dream. This was tape-recorded after every dream during the night, for an average of about four dreams. Dream-like symbolisms were woven into bits and pieces of the messages, and sometimes the messages were indistinguishable from the dreamer's own internal dynamic. Many books are written about the symbols that appear in dreams, beginning with Sigmund Freud and Carl Jung. (46, 47) Joseph Campbell later provided a series of books and videos on myths and their symbols. (48)

While the weaving of symbols between the dreams and the telepathy was expected from the dreamers at the Dream Lab, many of the same types of symbols were also woven into the responses from our telepathy experiments, even though our participants were fully awake. Among our four hundred trials, several common types of symbols appeared in the responses of different teams. The blind-match judges, who saw only one set at a time, did not match them with their targets, nor did they look for or expect such symbolic responses. Each one was counted as a *"miss."* It was only with the additional analysis of the entire set that the scope of the repeated patterns was seen. Since several different teams provided the same types of responses, we studied the symbolism to reconsider the idea that telepathy might actually be taking place on a very different level of consciousness than previously thought.

I. Thirteen people are paired with the sun, moon, or planets in ten separate responses.
   a. Three men are paired with the sun.
   b. Three women are paired with the moon.
   c. Four people are paired with the planets.
   d. A mother holding an infant, and movie star Shirley Temple are paired with sunlight.
II. Eleven people are paired with buildings in ten separate responses.
   a. Five women (semi-nude or as a symbol of sexuality) are paired with a church, temple, or pagoda.
   b. Three men are paired with humble buildings (bunk house, adobe, or vacant building).
   c. One villain is paired with a hospital.
   d. A close-up of a couple kissing is paired with a skyscraper and lots of good feelings.

III. Nude couples in explicit poses are paired with rockets blasting off in two separate responses.

IV. Fourteen people are paired with food or with medicine for illness.

V. Three people are paired with musical instruments in two separate responses.

VI. Opposite responses were also common. For example, if one writes "cowboy," the other writes "Indian"; one writes "happy," the other writes "sad."

VII. Some pairings between targets and responses may or may not be related, though obscure matches can be made. However, if they were actually related, it would give rise to a re-examination of the entire process of mind-to-mind communication.  (See page 33.)

We do not see these repeated pairings of targets and responses by different teams at different times as random events. For example, illustrations of such pairings have been seen in early publications as well as in our own responses. The first edition of *Mind To Mind* by Rene Warcollier in 1948 included illustrations of his telepathic experiments. It was translated into English and republished in 1963. (49) One of his targets was a stylized drawing of a sun with rays extended. The response was a sunset behind a man on horseback. In 1930, Upton Sinclair published accounts of his telepathic experiments in *Mental Radio*. (50) Sinclair referred to the response by his wife (illustrated below) as "A highly humorous sunrise."

**SENDER**

Upton Sinclair

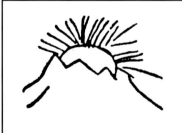

**RECEIVER**

Mary Craig Sinclair

*These illustrations are from* Mental Radio.
*Copyright © Upton Sinclair, 1930.*
*Copyright © Charles C. Thomas, 1962.*
*Published by Collier Books, New York, 1971.*

**Team #8**
**TARGET**
**Trial #9**
**2/28/75**

*From* National Geographic *magazine.* *See Appendix A.*

**BMS = 3**
**SMS = w, m**

**Team #8**
**SENDER**
**Trial #9**

"Gentle man, Rich with life's experiences, good vibes...."

***Team #8  -  RECEIVER  -  Trial #9***

"Sunset on ocean beach— very nice—together feelings"

From our study we see that both Team #8 and Team #11 have responded in a similar way, as illustrated here. In each example, the man's head and the sun are paired, just as in the example by Sinclair nearly seventy years ago and in the example published by Warcollier's research fifty years ago. Some symbols in the human mind do seem to remain the same over time. The idea that our father is the sun, our mother is the Earth, and our grandmother is the moon are ancient symbols as old as recorded history. The Greek god Apollo was thought to drive the sun chariot across the sky every day. His twin sister Artemis was the goddess of the moon. The Romans assigned the names of gods and goddesses to the different planets that we still use today. Saturn represents the "heavy" influence in the charts of astrology. In our study, a target showing a picture of a man with a rope around his neck, about to be hung, was paired with the planet Saturn with a ring around it. In the chart at right, all of the *targets* that were pictures of suns, moons, or planets are listed with their responses. The list of all of the *responses* for suns, moons, or planets that occurred in the study are listed in a chart on the next page. Of those seventeen responses, ten of them include people.

### ALL TARGETS WITH SUNS OR PLANETS

| Target | Response |
|---|---|
| 1. Happy face in the sun.......... (blue drawing) | Blue sky with clouds |
| 2. Faces with planets............... (M. C. Escher etching) | Bright sun (See page 52.) |
| 3. Suns and stars..................... (painting) | Spinning earth...diamond (See page 43.) |
| 4. Sun & ocean (painting)....... | Lighthouse at sea (See page 19.) |
| 5. Solar system diagram.......... | Female with large bosom (décolletage) & many colored balls |
| 6. Sunset reflected in water..... (photo with orange & brown horizontal lines) | Football stadium (drawing with orange & brown horizontal lines) |
| 7. Sunset................................. (photo of orange sky, hills, birds—no sun showing) | Oval shapes (complete miss) |
| 8. Planet Saturn...................... (NASA photo) | Big Bad Wolf (See page 173.) |
| 9. Earth from the moon........... (NASA photo) | World spinning around (See page 18.) |
| 10. Earth in space..................... (NASA photo) | Tail of rocket ship taking off with fire coming out of the end |

In the history of music, there has never been a man like Ludwig van Beethoven.

**BMS = 0  —  SMS = 0**

**Team #11**
**TARGET**
**Trial #6**
**12/19/74**

"In the history of music, there has never been a man like Ludwig van Beethoven."

*(See Appendix A.)*

**Team #11**
**SENDER**
**Trial #6**

"Anger, face genius."

***Team #11  -  RECEIVER  -  Trial #6***

"Sunny, bright."

BMS = 0

SMS = m

*Team #15 - TARGET - Trial #2*
*8/19/80*

*The original target was trimmed from a greeting card to fit our 3" x 5" target format. The title of the M. C. Escher original etching is* Bond of Union. *A rough sketch is provided here to identify the target used (with apologies to M. C. Escher). (51)*

*Team #15 - SENDER - Trial #2*

"Eyes of the world.
Eyes of God.
Galaxies, Space,
Black & White."

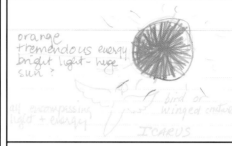

*Team #15 - RECEIVER - Trial #2*

"Orange, **tremendous energy.** Bright light. Huge sun? All-encompassing light & energy. Bird or winged creature. ICARUS."

In the illustration above, the sender of Team #15 projects the idea of the "Eyes of God." His partner receives "tremendous energy" and "bright light." When he writes of the black and white images, she writes about a "winged creature, ICARUS." None of the judges matched this set, yet the spiritual resonance between the couple is evident.

| ALL RESPONSES OF SUN, MOON, AND PLANETS | | | |
|---|---|---|---|
| Response | Target | Response | Target |
| 1. Sunset............................ | Old man with beard (color photo) (See page 51.) | 9. Rays of Sunlight. Cecil B. deMille's picture of God............ | Shirley Temple (b/w photo) (See page 53.) |
| 2. Sunset............................ | Ludwig van Beethoven (painting) (See page 51.) | 10. Trees and sun............... | Dragon with fire (painting) |
| 3. Lunar eclipse of sun...... (See below.) | Man kissing lady's backside (color photo not shown) | 11. Trees and sun............... | Mother and infant son (color photo) |
| 4. Bright light, huge sun, tremendous energy........ | Escher's spiral faces, *Bond of Union.* (Actual target is not shown. See above.) | 12. Moon............................ | Evening city skyline (color photo) |
| | | 13. Witch and moon........... | Parthenon at night (photo) (See page 54.) |
| 5. Sunset............................ | Diamond Ring (color photo) | 14. Moon over mountain... | Girl playing with blocks (b/w photo) |
| 6. Bright sun, explosive energy........... | Rainbow on waterfall (color photo) | 15. Globe of Earth with clouds, oceans............. | Snowflake cracker box (advertisement) |
| 7. Warm sun energy, color of sunlight............ | Yellow roses (color photo) | 16. Planet Saturn............... | Man with hangman's noose around his neck (color photo) |
| 8. Sun energy coming and going into Eye........ | Nuclear blast (photo) (See page 22.) | 17. Planet Saturn............... | Paul Revere (painting) |

(The Saturn response may be precognitive. ·
It was given four trials prior to the only target of the planet
Saturn used in the entire study. See page 172.)

*Team #8 - TARGET #9*
*12/5/74*

*The target is a photo of a man kissing a lady's backside. Both are nude. They are outdoors in the sunshine. Permission to show them is not available. The drawing by the sender shows the way they are posed.*

*This target is from a magazine listed in Appendix A.*

**BMS = 0 — SMS = cl, w, m**

*Team #8*
*SENDER*
*Trial #9*

"Warm, loving, exciting, natural, fresh sweet skin."

Ⓢ
12/5/74
9

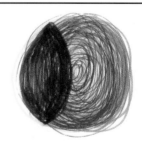

*Team #8 - RECEIVER - Trial #9*

**"Lunar eclipse of sun—**
Sun is really bright. Very clear picture.
Fire feelings—full of energy."

*Team #8*
*TARGET*
*Trial #4*
*12/5/74*

**Shirley**
**Temple—**

*Photo cut from*
*old magazine*
*listed in*
*Appendix A.*

BMS = 1 — SMS = s, m

*Team #8*
*SENDER*
*Trial #4*

5
12/5/74
4

"Sweet,
warm,
cuddly.
Polka dot."

*Team #8 — RECEIVER — Trial #4*

"Rays of sunlight bursting out of
billowing cloud formation.
Feelings of great power therein.
Cecil B. deMille's
picture of God—heaven, etc."

Such examples as the one on the opposite page from Team #15 indicate that a conversation is taking place, rather than just a parroting of imagery or ideas. The judges are looking for the *same* image or concept, and often are unable to match the two parts of a psychic conversation.

Another illustration in which the concept of God appears in the response is shown above. The target is a magazine photo of Shirley Temple. In this response, the couple does not seem to be in a spiritual resonance; rather, the response seems to arise from the realm of the symbolic. Symbolic imagery is often manifested through our preconscious as marvelous humor. We do appreciate it, not only when the receiver of Team #8 responds with a movie mogul's idea of God and heaven, but also when the target shows a man's head being partially eclipsed by a "moon," as in his response on the previous page.

In the illustration below, the movie star's name is not Temple, but the response from the receiver of Team #11 is that of a temple or galaxy. The photo of Sophia Loren is paired with both the symbols of a heavenly body and a holy building. The chart at right lists the ten different responses in which buildings were paired with target pictures of people. The women are paired with places of worship, while the men are generally paired with much smaller buildings. When the whole figure of the man is in the target, some are matched accurately, others are matched with a small part of the body and naturally some are missed all together.

| ALL RESPONSES OF BUILDINGS TO PEOPLE TARGETS | |
|---|---|
| Response | Target |
| 1. Temple, galaxy.................. | Sophia Loren (photo, shown below) |
| 2. Japanese pagoda (red)....... | Cheerleader—red sweater (photo) (See page 55.) |
| 3. Mystical pagoda.............. | Nude woman in ocean (color photo) (See page 55.) |
| 4. Church............................ | Semi-nude woman (color photo) |
| 5. Skyscraper....................... | Couple kissing (close-up color photo) |
| 6. Witch & moon.................. | Parthenon at night (reverse match) (color photo) (See page 54.) |
| 7. Indian adobe..................... | Cowboy on horseback (drawing) |
| 8. Stinky bunk house........... | Saxophone player (line drawing) (See page 56.) |
| 9. Vacant building................. | Tibetan Guru (painting) |
| 10. Hospital hallway.............. | Dread Dormammu (color cartoon) |

*Team #11*
*TARGET*
*Trial #9*
*12/5/74*

**Sophia Loren—**

*Photo cut from*
*magazine listed in*
*Appendix A.*

BMS = 2
SMS = s

*Team #11*
*SENDER*
*Trial #9*

"Voluptuous,
Big."

*Team #11 - RECEIVER - Trial #9*

"Temple, Galaxy."

On the right is one of my favorite drawings of the 1940s by James Thurber. (52) While the house here represents a domineering woman to the frightened little man outside, the buildings our teams drew in response to targets of women were places of worship or contemplation. In the 1940s and 1950s it was common for those in therapy to blame *mother* endlessly for all psychological problems, thanks to a reckless interpretation of Freud's writings. Even the paintings by Wm. DeKooning reflected that thinking. (Today, the concept of mental health includes forgiveness for those who have caused us pain, because unrelieved anger is known to cause even worse problems.)

The symbolic pairing of a woman and a building is illustrated below by the women's Team #2. The sender writes, "Tried to visualize...[partner] as a Greek woman there...." Her partner sees a witch in the full moon. While this temple was dedicated to Athena, the receiver's association is with the Roman goddess of the moon, Diana. Those who follow the cult of Diana, in spite of later Christian dominance, still hold celebrations on full moon nights.

**Home by James Thurber**

*Team #2 - TARGET - Trial #3*
**12/11/74**

*Photo of the ancient Greek Parthenon at night. (From a magazine listed in Appendix A.)*

**BMS = 1 — SMS = cl, w**

*Team #2 - SENDER - Trial #3*

"Tried to visualize building, its antiquity, *[partner]* as a Greek woman there, the constancy of this structure"

*Team #2
RECEIVER
Trial #3*

**"Dark night**— halo around moon. Plaight! Giving up feelings— can't get any flashes of nothing."

After the receiver refers to a "dark night," drawing a moon and a woman with a witch's hat on, she claims she cannot get any *flashes* of imagery. Her visual response seems to have been spontaneous, though her verbal response is mostly unrelated to it. The visual and verbal systems seem to be "thinking" on different levels.

Another photo of the Parthenon was used in the 1980 study. The receiver of Team #12 made sketchy drawings with the orange pen. He identified one of those drawings as the "Jefferson Memorial...." There were fifteen *targets* of buildings used in these studies. Four of them had two or more buildings or cityscapes. Two of the cities were matched and two were missed. There were eight targets with single public buildings, and three with smaller houses. Two of the large buildings, with domes (the Taj Mahal and the Vatican), were paired with bottles (similar shape, wrong scale) by different teams. Five large buildings were matched with shape or color similarities or small accurate details. The eighth one is shown above. Of the three smaller houses, one was matched in shape only and two had concept similarities.

Twenty-five buildings were given as *responses* in this study. Five responses were matched with targets of buildings or with part of their details. Four of the twenty-five building responses had some image or word similarity to their targets, and six were missed completely. Ten responses were given to targets of people.

The frequent pairing of buildings with people does not seem to be a random relationship, even though they were not matched by the judges. This relationship is common in dream-like symbolism. In our study, however, the buildings paired with the female targets are quite different from the buildings paired with the male targets.

Instead of the threatening, dominant woman of the Thurber drawing, the women in our targets are matched with places of contemplation or worship. Perhaps if only one team matched a church, pagoda, or temple with a target of a young woman, we might have dismissed the response as unrelated. But at least five different teams responded in this way. In all but the one response shown on the previous page, some of the lines, colors, and shapes of the buildings and the women are very similar. In the one above at right, notice how the red and green colors are used, and how the upward curve of the red arms of the cheerleader are similar to the upward curve of the red pagoda roof. Notice also how the red stripes in the sender's drawing of the skirt are similar to the red stripes on the base and on the side of the roof of the pagoda. The blue of the sky is seen in the receiver's drawing as the blue in the small pond. Both the senders and receivers were always given packets of the same type of ten colored marking pens, because color can be an important similarity.

If these were random responses, the same concept of a pagoda in response to female targets from different teams would be rare indeed. This same symbolism, repeated by these different teams, does suggest that telepathy is actually occurring, but it does so on a level not yet explored in depth. It deserves much closer examination in the future.

**Team #8 TARGET Trial #7**

**2/28/75**

*See list of magazines in Appendix A.*

BMS = 0
SMS = d, s, cl

**Team #8 SENDER Trial #7**

"Exuberance, energy, light-hearted, All-American."

In the illustration below the receiver of Team #3 has drawn a pagoda for his response as well. In this example, he used only one color that was in the sky of the target photo, unlike the three matching colors in the response seen at right. However, there is a similarity in the use of line. The prominent **"V"** shape in the drawing of the lady is repeated three times in the roof of the pagoda. Among all the words used in the four hundred trials, the word *pagoda* was only used in these two responses.

**Team #8 - RECEIVER - Trial #7**

"Japanese or Chinese garden with **pagoda** —lots of greenery around—small pond"

Another response (not shown here) is a drawing of a "European cathedral." The target is a photo of a semi-nude woman with a long curving necklace. The receiver of Team #8 drew a church with a long curving arch, a cross and a round stained-glass window where the shape of the head would be. The woman's necklace is tied to suggest a cross at the bottom. The sender, however, used the terms "soft, sensual..." The receiver used the terms "...cold stone." He drew buildings for human targets four different times.

**Team #3 - TARGET Trial #2 - 11/20/74**

*This target is a photo of a nude woman who is partly silhouetted against a colorful sunset. She is standing in the ocean with her arms in the air.*

*(See Appendix A.)*

BMS = 0
SMS = s, cl, m

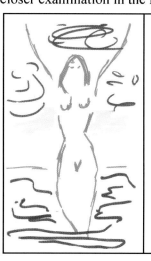

**Team #3 SENDER Trial #2**

"Cool air on wet skin; surge of water, swirling. Naked skin, soft stirring hair."

*Pagoda*

**Team #3 - RECEIVER Trial #2**

"**Pagoda,** Mystical, Serene, Pensive, Enshrouded."

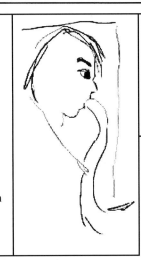

**Team #3**
**SENDER**
**Trial #7**

"Musician—Flutes, clarinets and saxophones, jazz beat. Grooving into the music. Getting lost in it. Eye not seeing—hearing inside the music. Away from me into his music."

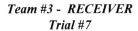

**Team #3 - RECEIVER**
**Trial #7**

"Corral & bunkhouse —stinky, icky, dirty."

**Team #3 - TARGET**
**Trial #7 - 11/20/74**

*Life drawing by Millay.*

BMS = 1 — SMS = s

The buildings that accompanied the targets of the men, however, were generally small and humble, even for a target picture of a painting of "Guru Padma Sambhava," who is surrounded with symbols and a halo. The picture is completed in the precise formality of an ancient Tibetan style. It is also inscribed with prayers for peace in both English and Tibetan, yet the building given in response by the receiver of Team #3 is very small. He does not name the type of building, but writes, "Vacant, solitary, overgrown, quiet, sad memories, old." (One might find an obscure relationship to the sadness of the Tibetan situation.) However, in the illustration above, the same receiver from Team #3 draws a small dirty bunkhouse, though the sender expresses an entirely different mood. She writes that she feels the music she imagines being played. This is the same man who drew a pagoda for the target of a lady in the ocean on page 55.

The receiver of Team #8 draws a one-room building in response to a cowboy on a horse chasing a coyote. He

describes it as follows: "Basic adobe shelter— opened in front—dark. Cliff in back of it (dwarfs its true size). American Indian. Good positive feelings from it. A place of protection." The same receiver describes a hospital when the target is the Dread Dormammu from a Dr. Strange cartoon. Surprisingly, four of the judges actually matched the cowboy with the Indian adobe. No one matched the Dread Dormammu with the hospital.

The illustration below is the only response of a church made by a woman in our study. All the other church-type responses were given by men to target pictures of women. When the sender of Team #13 saw this response by his partner, he was very pleased. The target reminded him of their favorite camping place along a creek in Cazadero (though it is a postcard photo of "The Moss Temple" by Yoshinori Kamikawa). Since they had camped along the creek many times, he named the place when he transmitted the message to her. For them, it was a most spiritual place to be. When the study was over, he insisted that several of us join them one day on a walk along the creek to see it and to feel it for ourselves. We did go with them to spend a lovely day hiking there, and it did look very much like the target photo. It was indeed a special place for peaceful contemplation and a place to seek spiritual revelations.

**Team #13 - TARGET - Trial #2 - 10/2/80**

*Postcard photo from IMPACT, Concord, CA.*
The Moss Temple *by Yoshinori Kamikawa*

(No score. Sender/receiver reversed roles.)

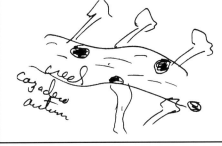

**Team #13 - SENDER - Trial #2**

"Creek— Cazadero—Autumn."

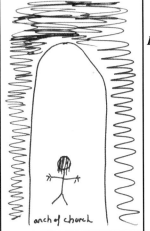

**Team #13**
**RECEIVER**
**Trial #2**

"Arch of Church."

The rest of the targets of nude or semi-nude ladies that did not elicit responses of sex, temples, or churches seemed to be related to food. In the illustration at right, the receiver of Team #8 provides a rather humorous association. In the same set of trials this team matched people with food twice. When a photo of a creamy chocolate cake became the target, the sender draws a very good picture of it and writes, "Creamy, gooey, secure. I was sending the smell of chocolate, too." Her lover writes, "Young man comforting older woman—compassion.

**Team #8 - TARGET Trial #8 - 2/28/75**

*Magazine print of a painting by Goya.*

BMS = 2 — SMS = s, cl

**Team #8 - SENDER Trial #8**

"Antique feeling, sensual, rich."

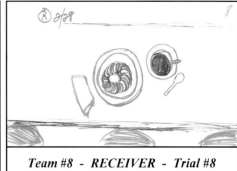

**Team #8 - RECEIVER - Trial #8**

"Coffee & donut on a cafe counter. I'm hungry! Person just got up for a second."

Lots of emotion evoked in picture." Two of the five judges matched the coffee and donut with the lady in the Goya painting, but no one matched the chocolate cake with the young man comforting the older woman.

There are twelve *targets* with pictures of food only. Two more targets featured pictures of a person eating the food. One other was a bottle of whiskey, and another showed a person taking a pill. Of these, five were paired with people, and two were paired with animals. Oddly, three different teams responded to the food targets with drawings of sailboats. Those three were the only sailboat responses in the study. Among the responses to the food

targets, seven have shape and color similarities, but seven others missed the targets altogether.

There are sixteen *responses* that include food, one with rye whiskey, and two with a bottle of pills (one is illustrated below). Nine of the food responses were given to targets of people. One is shown above, and one is on page 43 in which the receiver writes, "...feel hungry, cigarette." That target is a sexually active couple.

The pill bottle responses were given only twice in the four hundred trials. The one below seems to fit into the same concept as the pairing between food and women. The receiver of Team #4 said he was catching a cold. The other response is a bottle of red pills. It may or may not be precognitive, since it was given just two trials before the only pill target in the study. It shows a hand with red fingernails putting a pill in a mouth painted with bright red lipstick.

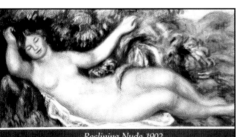

**TEAM #4 - TARGET - Trial #10 12/12/74**

**"Reclining Nude 1902 Pierre Auguste Renoir"**

BMS = 2 — SMS = 0

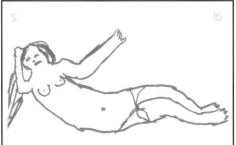

**TEAM #4 - SENDER - Trial #10**

"Carefree—Lush—Joyful. Unknowing & not needing to. Body glow.

Paradise Garden."

**TEAM #4 - RECEIVER - Trial #10**

"Dr. Leary's preparation for quick relief of post-LSD psychosis. Something artificial—Drugs for illness or an illness of self in my eyes. A MEDICINE. Might be me own head...." *(sic)*

**Team #7
TARGET
Trial #7**

*11/26/74*

*Design from an
unknown source.*

*See Appendix A.*

**BMS = 3
SMS = s**

**Team #7
SENDER
Trial #7**

"The Kiss,
Woman/Man
holding heads,
eyes closed."

**Team #7 - RECEIVER - Trial #7**

"1.  Black Piano / Keyboard.
 2.  On Stage."

At least four of the food responses to targets of people were matched in shape and/or color. One had no relationship. The receiver declared after the first session that he was very hungry. He gave a food response to more than one target at that time. All images seemed to arise in his mind, not through resonance with his partner, but through resonance with his body. One target picture of a Christmas box of chocolates elicited this response from the woman receiver of Team #1: "...Didn't get any impression 'til Santa Claus turned sideways with a load on his back."

Two responses to targets that implied sexuality are both musical instruments. Both musical responses are illustrated above and below. For the stylized drawing of a couple kissing, the receiver of Team #7 draws a large grand piano with some curved shapes that are similar to the shapes of the elbows of the kissing couple in the target.

The musical response that the participating team and the monitors enjoyed most is illustrated below. The two people of Team #10 were lovers at the time of this experiment and were later married. He played the guitar from time to time for his own amusement. He was not a profes-

sional musician, nor was he planning to become one. Playing music was an enjoyable experience for him, and the association between his music and his sensuality is unmistakable.

There are only four *targets* in the set of four hundred that include musical instruments. One is a photograph of an ancient Greek statue of a man playing a long flute. The drawing by the receiver of Team #9 matched it in color and shape and with an image of a man, but the receiver's man has a long gun instead of a flute. The second one is the saxophone player (page 56). The third one is a dog playing a gourd drum. The colors are orange and brown, which the receiver also uses, but the response seems to have no other relationship to the target. The fourth one is a line drawing of Saraswati (goddess of music in India) playing a sitar, surrounded by symbolic imagery. The receiver does not draw an image but writes that she is sleepy and "...can't focus in. Get a lot of activity around edges...."

There is one target that implies music, though no musical instruments are seen in it. The target is part of a Grateful Dead poster. The image is a well-known one of the skull surrounded by roses. The receiver of Team #15 draws only swirly lines and hearts in the pink color of the roses.

**Team #10 - TARGET
Trial #10 - 2/25/75**

*This target is a color photo of a nude man, which was cut from a magazine. The actual source and credits are not known. The flesh colors in the photo are similar to those in the receiver's drawing of the guitar. The pose is shown by the sender's drawing.*

**BMS = 3
SMS = s, cl, cn**

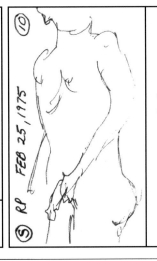

**Team #10
SENDER
Trial #10**

"Naked man
touching his
penis.
I flashed on
seeing
*[partner]*
as the man."

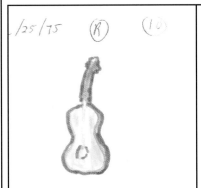

**Team # 10
RECEIVER
Trial # 10**

"Guitar,
Cello
or Bass.

Maybe someone
playing it."

*TARGET - Team #4*
*Trial #3 - 2/26/75*
*&*
*TARGET - Team #6*
*Trial #9 - 2/28/75*

*The same nude couple was photographed in three different explicit poses. Two are used here as targets and the other one is mentioned on page 43. Here, two different teams respond with a similar concept of rockets. One team is the young men's team. The other is a man and wife, with the wife as the sender.*

**BMS = 1 — SMS = 0 (Team #4)**

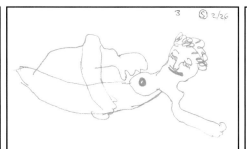

***Team #4 - SENDER - Trial #3***

"AAAHHH Lust, Slurp.
Excitement (or trying to be)
Breast—More (Gimme)
MMMMMMMMM"

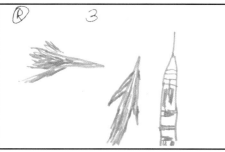

***TEAM #4 - RECEIVER - Trial #3***

"Blue steel—cool gleaming
Swift motion
Artificial—Technological
Angular—Projecting"

The targets of couples involved in explicit sex all elicited interesting responses. Some responses from the older group were directly related to their targets, but most of the responses from the students seemed to arise from the level of symbolism. Team #4 and Team #6 each gave separate but similar responses of rocket ships to targets of the same nude couple in different explicitly sexual poses. These are illustrated above and at right. Both receivers are men. More men chose to be receivers than did women in our study. Only one picture of a nude couple became the target for one of the women receivers, and she responded with, "Two ballet dancers...legs kicking up high." It would be interesting to study the differences between the responses of men and women with a larger group of receivers relative to the subjects of babies, children, and scenes of explicit sex.

There are only two other *responses* of rockets in the entire set of four hundred trials. One is provided by Team #12 when the target is a NASA photo of an astronaut standing on the moon. For that one the receiver draws an image of a standing rocket and writes, "...Missile. Space major image. Mountain—volcano, barren." All five judges matched that trial easily. For the other response, the receiver of Team #1 writes about a "...rocket firing off." The target for that one is also a NASA photo of the Earth from outer space. Three of the five judges matched it.

There were only two other *targets* with different photos of astronauts on the moon. For one of them, Team #2 responded with a drawing of a monkey with a banana and words about whiskey. This was not matched by any of the judges except one. He insisted that the response actually had a relationship to the target, because he had read in

***Team #6 - SENDER - Trial #9***
***2/28/75***

"FAR OUT"

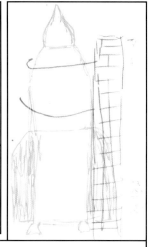

***Team #6 - TARGET***
***Trial #9 - 2/28/75***
*(See description above.)*

**BMS = 1 - SMS = s, cl**

***Team #6 - RECEIVER - Trial #9***

"1st impression - long cylindrical object to
right, of steel.
2nd impression -   space rocket or launch pad."

some tabloid that an astronaut had referred to his space suit as a "monkey suit." He had also read that one of the astronauts had a drinking problem. The receiver of Team #2, who had drawn this response, had no concept of such a relationship. She felt that her response was a miss. Even judges are not immune to the images projected into clouds. Or perhaps this pairing of target with its response could fall into the category of a very obscure relationship.

The receiver of Team #5 responded to the other target photo of astronauts with a drawing of a flying saucer and writes about "UFO or 'flying saucer.' Extraterrestrial intelligence. Uri Geller, blinking lights...Mission Impossible?" This trial is illustrated on page 63. The rest of our UFO collection of responses is illustrated on pages 61 and 64. There were only three of them altogether.

**Area #11.  Memories of Past or Other Lives** — It is rare for a telepathic attempt to evoke something as deep in the psyche as a past-life type of experience. These may come in our dreams, and if we hold a belief system about the world that does not include such ideas, they would be unnoticed. Such evocations may come as a result of a guided deep relaxation experience in which one is encouraged to travel into other time frames. Even there, the experience may seem to be only a dream, or the symbolic experience of a cosmic drama. It is not necessary to believe that you have lived in a past life to experience what it might be like to be someone else. It is possible to experience being another person in another time, or another one in this time. Once a person asked me why she had been able to experience two different lives during the same time period. Logically, she could not imagine herself as having had two past lives in a time frame that overlapped. I told her that for one thing, logic in the timeless realm is not the same as it is in the spacetime frame we usually experience, but for another thing, it is possible to experience what your grandmother felt during her lifetime, as well as what your grandfather felt during the same time. We can feel into the experiences of the bird in the tree above us, or into the health situation of our loved ones. Part of the process of spiritual healing involves feeling into another, before the practice of guiding the healing appropriately begins. Merging minds with a lover is no doubt a familiar feeling for many.

Peru, and there under the influence of a shamanic ceremony and the clear night sky, the resolution of her personal ancient drama was revealed to her. It is not important whether the experience represented an actual past life, or whether the pre-conscious chose to cast a present dilemma into a past time frame, so the plot would seem less threatening and be easier to resolve. The target picture of a Mayan pyramid motivated her to pursue a life-changing journey. This pyramid is not from the civilization in which her experiences were played out, but it triggered the deep memory that she had recovered from within herself.

**Area #12.  Basic Dualities of Archetypes** — Gods and demons are fundamental in the cosmic dramas of the timeless realms. If there were no demons, we would have to create one to balance the dualities. However, there are already many that exist from the stories created by countless civilizations since humans decided to speak to each other in a language. When we encounter a demon in a vision it may be from our own culture, or it may arise out of a culture unknown to us at the time. If we are amazed by its appearance, we are even more amazed to find it a second time, pictured in a book of ancient art.

Images and stories about gods and demons are common throughout history. Modern experiences of them were studied by Carl Jung, who called them the "archetypal ex-

*Team #16 - TARGET - Trial #2*
*8/14/80*

*Photo of a Mayan pyramid. See Appendix A.*

BMS = 0 — SMS = cl, w

*Team #16 - SENDER - Trial #2*

"Solid
Mammoth
Ancient"

*Team #16 - RECEIVER - Trial #2*

"gloom, dark projectiles, war? or sadness,
**heavy,** see mostly **black,** no color.
Feelings at the base of the spine—
**Grounded.**"

However, there was one instance when a receiver felt, after looking at the target, that she had touched into an unresolved past-life experience. She had already received, through dreams and meditation, hints of such a life, and she was still wondering about it. She had felt the concept of death during the session, and then later when she saw the picture of the pyramid, she said there seemed to be a connection to her unresolved "history." Months later, she was able to go on a journey to explore ancient ruins in

periences." He hypothesized that they exist in the "collective unconscious" of all of us. We find such experiences described two thousand years ago. An explanation of the *The Tibetan Book of the Dead* is provided by Evens-Wentz. (53) A very different version of this *Tibetan Book* was published by Leary, Alpert and Metzner in the Sixties. (54) It was read aloud to guide people through experiences that emerged during LSD sessions. All demons and gods are considered to be products of our own minds.

*Team #7 - TARGET - Trial #7*
*2/23/75*

"LIBERTY — IN GOD WE TRUST"

**BMS = 0 — SMS = 0**

*Team #7 - SENDER - Trial #7*

"A COIN—25 ¢.
A wig on George's head.
Liberty
In **GOD** we trust"

*Team #7 - RECEIVER - Trial #7*

"Love & warmth.
**Devil** or pitchforks—**Red**
**White** clouds, fields (plowed), **Blue** sky."

In the illustration above, the receiver of Team #7 demonstrated the relationship between the dualities of the archetypes when he drew a red devil in response to the words "In God we trust." Perhaps, the receiver also included the words "Red...white...and...blue," because the picture on the coin is George Washington. (During a session three months earlier, this team chose the only other target of a coin. That one had the face of Liberty on it instead of Washington. The sender focused on the winged messenger, Mercury. The different way they both responded to that target is illustrated in Chapter Seven.)

Team #1 produced a different illustration of the relationship of the dualities of archetypes (below). The name of the devil is on the target, though the image doesn't show horns or a tail the way it is often pictured. Nevertheless, the receiver first drew the shape of Tom Walker's hat and turns it into a "flying saucer shape—little green men...." The inclusion of a galaxy and the milky way shows that she is experiencing something about the target that is larger than life. At the end she notes, "Flashed on angel." So this relationship is not between God and the devil, but between an angel and the devil. The little green men are sometimes symbolized as representations of the devil by some, and others think that ETs might be angels in disguise that have been around for a long time. It is especially interesting, relative to the pairing of archetypes, to have both the angel and the little green men on the same response. The relationship between devils and flying saucers or UFOs and their little green men have been a part of our symbolism and science fiction films for a long time.

There were only two other targets with a picture of the devil. One was the tarot card on page 31. Dowlen did not respond to it as an archetype but he did draw similar shapes and content. The response to the other devil target was a desert scene. However, this same pairing of dualities was also revealed in the SRI study. (See page 62.)

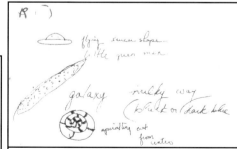

*Team #1 - RECEIVER - Trial #2*

"flying saucer shape—**little green men**—
galaxy—milky way—(black or dark blue)
spiraling out from center.
Seems like something with a nucleus
of some sort with things coming out of it,
possibly revolving. Like Milky Way
with cluster of stars so, brighter—rear center.
Flashed on **angel**."

*Team #1 - TARGET - Trial #2*
*11/19/74*

*John Quidor's*
**"The Devil** and Tom Walker" *(1856)*

**BMS = 2 — SMS = s, w, cn**

*Team #1 - SENDER - Trial #2*

**"The Devil.**
Tom Walker.
Merger."

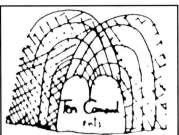

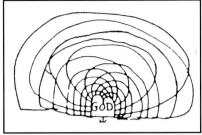

Third Response to Target #3

The **devil** at left is the sender's drawing from the SRI experiments. Above are two details from Uri Geller's responses to this target, in which he writes *"Ten Commandments"* in one and *"GOD"* in the other. The one at right is his third and final drawing for this set, in which he has the tablets of Moses behind the Earth, driving off the pitchforks. He also drew a snake and an apple (below, left).

Uri Geller gave me the first hint of this natural pairing of gods and demons in 1973, when Targ asked me to draw a picture of a farmer with a pitchfork. Targ gave me a very large black marker and a poster-sized pad of paper. Geller, on the other hand, was sitting in a large comfortable chair in an electromagnetically shielded room with a regular pen-sized marker and a letter-sized pad. For me, the drawing was a kind of dance as I covered the paper using large swings of my arms and body. Detail was not possible with such a large marker, and all my drawings were done quickly, as I usually put myself into a light trance state to do them. They were very crude, but simple, since we were mainly focused on the ideas and images to be *"sent"* to Geller, three buildings away. After I saw how crude the "farmer" looked, I spontaneously added the horns and tail without thinking and wrote *"DEVIL"* on the top.

Geller was surprised by his first response. He was used to simple targets without symbolism, such as a boat or a kite. But when he wrote about "God" and "The Ten Commandments," he was puzzled, and expressed this to Hal Puthoff. Geller could speak into a microphone so Puthoff could hear him, though Geller could not hear any of us. Puthoff could relay messages to us by telephone in the other building. When I heard of Geller's puzzlement, I wondered how the devil would be represented to a man from Israel. But of course the Old Testament is essentially similar, and so I spent a moment or two thinking about Adam and Eve with the snake and the apple, without drawing anything. At that point, Geller told Puthoff that his images were changing, and he drew an apple with a worm in it, wrote the word, "apple," and he also drew a snake. Since he had not made any connection between the snake and the target, I again focused on the devil. After that, Geller completed the final drawing seen above right. Before this experiment began, all of us had spent a few moments in meditation together, though in our separate buildings. I felt we had all reached a very peaceful, even spiritual, state. When Geller later compared his responses

America's rise superpower

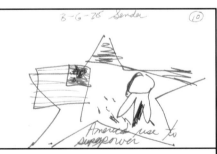

**Team #5**
**TARGET**
**Trial #10**
**3/6/75**

"America's rise superpower"

(*NASA photo cut from an ad for a book about landing on the moon.*)

**BMS = 4**
**SMS = cl, w, m, cn**

*Team #5 - SENDER - Trial #10*

"America's rise to superpower.
Space—Astronaut
U. S. Flag
Footprints
Star"

*Team #5 - RECEIVER - Trial #10*

"UFO or 'flying saucer.'
Extraterrestrial intelligence—Uri Geller.
Little green men (?) Blinking lights.
Creature features—tapes that self-destruct.
Mission Impossible?"

> **"...You are now in the magic theater of heroes and demons.... Do not be afraid of them. They are within you.... Your own creative intellect is the master magician of them all. Recognize the figures as aspects of yourself...."**
>
> *THE PSYCHEDELIC EXPERIENCE:*
> *A Manual Based on The Tibetan Book of the Dead*
>
> by T. Leary, R. Metzner, R. Alpert (54)

with the target, he told me it was against his religion to mention the name of the devil in the temple. He felt that to be the reason why he drew the tablets of Moses as though they were driving the pitchforks away.

In contrast with the SRI studies, the receivers in our studies were not allowed to talk at all until after all five trials had been completed in the series. The sender never knew directly when the receiver was confused, and did not try to change a "sending" strategy, as I tried to do. This example is the second time I tried to add information to the "sending" process while working with Geller. (The first time is described on page 26.) Geller did not attempt to make the connection between the two types of images on either occasion. To do so seems to require a different type of mental activity, such as shifting from scanning the hyperspace to a linear mode of logical thinking. I have tried to tie separate pieces of telepathic imagery logically, and each time, logic has failed to produce the correct response. Only by clearing my mind beyond logic, analysis, and emotion can I receive telepathic messages correctly.

Ever since the stories about little green men from Mars first appeared, humans have been conjuring up such images. In 1974, a respected medical scientist with many inventions for helping people joined a respected Hebraic scholar to announce that there would be a major alien invasion within three years. This was Andrea Puharich, MD, and James Hurtak, PhD (56) They each had a different interpretation about just who these aliens might be. For the scientist, they were people and computers from the future coming back to warn us about our dangerous technology. For the scholar, they were Elijah and other heroes from the Bible coming to save us from evil. Many of us were amazed that prominent men would make an announcement that we thought was ridiculous. Others took the whole idea very seriously and started groups to pray to the ETs so they, too, might be accepted into this new wave of future

perfect beings. Later on, the stories of abductions (after hypnosis) all seemed to describe the aliens as, sure enough, little green humanoids. The famous researcher of UFOs Jacques Vallee, PhD, expressed great concern for this development. He agrees that there is certainly a strange phenomenon that is unknown, but the "non-believers" in the government will not do proper research on the subject, and the star-struck "believers" are now so fixated on the "little gray-green guys," that when a fourteen-foot humanoid emerged from a space craft in full sight of many people in a park in Russia, the event was ignored by both sides. (57)

Some of the students who participated in our experiments in 1974 were impressed by Hurtak when he spoke on campus that year. Three different teams referred to UFOs in their *responses*. The receiver of Team #1 drew a flying saucer for the target of the devil on page 61. The response by Team #5 is on the page opposite and the other is on page 64. There are only two *targets* in that suggest UFOs. One is a triangle-shaped craft behind a closeup of Darth Vader from *Star Wars*. The receiver of Team #12 drew diagonal lines (similar to the triangle craft) and wrote, "Plane or Fence—floating—flying." The other target shows three luminous blue and white saucers hovering near a temple. The receiver of Team #15 drew a pitcher and another blue shape and wrote, "Metallic gold—shiny steel. Glass, metal computers." Both these trials were matched by the judges.

*"It appears to be Siva, manifesting himself as Lord of Destruction, but why he's in Hartsdale on a Thursday night is beyond me."*

**Drawing by Lee Lorenz**

"It appears to be Siva, manifesting himself as Lord of Destruction, but why he's in Hartsdale on a Thursday night is beyond me."

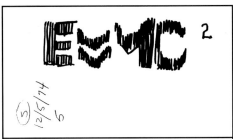

| Team #8 - TARGET - Trial #5 11/20/74 | Team #8 - SENDER - Trial #5 | Team #8 - RECEIVER - Trial #5 |
|---|---|---|
| **"E = MC ²"** *(See Appendix A.)* | "I totally focused on the **number 2**, but I was still aware of the rest." | "Saucer-type craft sailing thru space. Feelings of openness, spaciousness, **lots of speed.**" |

**BMS = 4 — SMS = m, w, cn**

The sender of Team #8 (above) writes that she "totally focused on the number 2...." Since *"C"* represents the speed of light, and *"2"* means the speed of light squared, there is a lot more speed suggested than I can comprehend at this time. Four of the five judges matched this trial. There are no drawing, shape, or color similarities, but word, mood, and concept were matched.

**Area #13.   The Hyperspace** — This area provides the mind of the receiver with basic information from the target, such as shape or mood. Rarely is information pulled so deeply from the consciousness of the sender as in the illustration shown at right. After one series of remote viewing experiments had been completed (described in Chapter Three), I had invited the viewers (Dowlen and Byrne) to my apartment in Petaluma for supper. The experiment was over at 4:30 PM and I expected to serve supper at 6:30 PM. During that time, I felt a need to sleep, though I rarely take a nap in the afternoon. Dowlen continued to draw the images that came to him while in his studio in Santa Rosa. It was as if he were able to pull information from my unconscious. He drew the high windows of my apartment and the round table under them, even though neither he nor Byrne had ever been to my apartment before. He said the table he drew looked like one his mother had. (My table was round, but different.) Because his drawings were so similar, I looked for a letter on the floor as he had drawn it and found just one. It was an announcement about a parapsychology conference in Brazil. It had been sent to the apartment I lived in a year ago and forwarded to a former roommate who had saved it for me. I had not answered it, because I could not afford to go, and it was too late to submit a paper. Nevertheless, because Dowlen wrote that it was there and that it was important, I did respond to that letter. The next year I moved to San Rafael, California. In the spring, a telegram was forwarded to me from my former address in Petaluma. In it was an invitation to present my work at the next conference in Brazil. Had I not answered that letter, the invitation would have been undeliverable. The post office does not keep track of four different addresses over a two-year period. Yet Dowlen's drawing, pulled from the hyperspace the year before, resulted in a free trip to Brazil for me. The story of that trip is discussed in Chapter Five.

*James Dowlen — REMOTE VIEWER — 5/10/76*

*"Mon., May 10—5:00
A letter on the floor...
A letter of importance & opened—on the floor...."*

**Area #14.   Interconnectedness of All Beings; Non-Duality, Cosmic Love** — Non-duality means no differentiation. A person in this state of consciousness is no longer interested in telepathic communication. The feeling of oneness with all life is said to be one manifestation of the state of enlightenment. Through the non-verbal phase-coherent wave forms of a stabilized EEG the brain integrates itself between many of its areas and multiple personalities. This state does not last indefinitely, but the learning that occurs during this state of mind improves the synthesis of our multiple selves. Eventually we come back to the world of differentiation and the apparent separateness of other people and things. But the feeling of inner peace and inner learning that evolves from our time spent in this state may last indefinitely and this can be re-experienced. Finding a spiritual practice that helps us to remember this state reinforces the experience. Taking the time to develop a habit of meditation allows the benefits to become firmly established. The ritual of preparation for the practice is designed to *enhance the focus of attention on the eternal.* The blind adherence to ritual itself can become a distraction from the essential focus. Through the practice of meditation our minds are prepared with the spiritual strength needed to avoid panic when crisis arises. Through meditation on the oneness of all life, we gain the insight and vision to guide us through the forest of our own illusions and through the busy world of people and things.

The receiver of Team #15 was so involved with her meditation practice that she drew the infinity sign as a response to two different and unrelated targets in the same set of trials. Her verbal response to one was "nothing, void, infinity, universe." We have much respect for her advanced state of meditation, but by tapping into this area, she reached beyond the mental state needed for a telepathic experiment. That set of trials was conducted immediately following a brainwave biofeedback session in simultaneous alpha and phase coherence at the UC psychophysiology lab. That was the only telepathy session done while the participants were wearing electrodes so the paired EEG measurements could be recorded. During the telepathy part of the session, the feedback tones were turned off, but not the chart recorder outside the subject room. The charts showed that she maintained a high percentage of *IH synch* during the telepathy trials as well.

**All Areas Are Interconnected Through Creativity** — Creativity is in each of us waiting to blossom. The creative fire can synthesize our multiple personalities, joining them in mutual communication. We are all familiar with stories about creative people who are devoted to their art, music, writing, dance. While some people allow one or more of their personalities to become hostile toward others, many artists devote their art to help needy causes. The creative spirit has fourteen areas to manipulate. Perhaps only a few of them are synthesized to bring out a creative expression, while the other areas might remain undeveloped.

Below is one example of the creative use of the quiet time during our telepathy exercises. At the beginning of our studies, the receiver of the young women's team was recovering from an unhappy love affair. On the margins of several of her cards, she made comments about dancers, always expressing surprise to see what she had written. She knew they were not related to the target. Yet her drawing of the famous dancer Isadora Duncan (below) symbolized a creative inspiration for her. That quiet voice of the intrinsic dancer within her expressed its creativity through integration of her personalities. When I met her years later, she had become a dance therapist. (The response of a nude may or may not also relate to the sender's later report that she was thinking about the time they both had gone "skinny dipping" in Alabama.)

*Team #2 - TARGET - Trial #9*
*2/27/75*
*Photo of a lake, beach, and trees cut from a magazine listed in Appendix A.*

**BMS = 1 — SMS = cl**

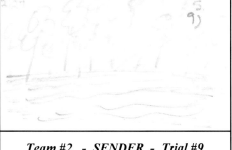

*Team #2 - SENDER - Trial #9*

"tried to send blue, blue water, green green trees, then later tried to envision *[partner]* & me **swimming** in water, going to shore. Reminded me of Alabama."

*Team #2*
*RECEIVER*
*Trial #9*

**"Isadora Duncan.**

**a frog...."**

The concept of our having multiple personalities is actually useful, once we get acquainted with them. The illusion that we are always performing with the same personality is not useful because it can be shown that we are not.

We have seen great comedians perform while everyone laughs, yet for some, their own life situation is not so funny, perhaps even tragic. We have seen presidents handle serious international situations with great self-confidence. Yet their own fears of nuclear war or other potential disasters are as deep for them as for the rest of us. The ability to be the one in charge, the one who is cool under pressure, is a useful part of the multiple personality, even though another part can see the danger and feel the fear.

Sometimes a person who thinks of him/herself as always sweet and kind can be shocked when a violent emotion erupts as the result of righteous anger. My mother encouraged us to acknowledge our anger, and then do something useful with it. She did not allow outbursts of excess anger in our house, but we were not seriously repressed in this way, because she set an example. She would go outside and attack the Bermuda grass with a grubhoe until her own anger had subsided. Then she would decide how the upsetting situation could be handled in a civilized way. She said the Bermuda grass always forgave her and grew back in the wrong places anyway. Later she expressed her finest creativity through her pottery. I have found writing to be one good way to use the adrenalin of anger or irritation.

There are a variety of creative ways we can learn to deal with our emotions. Violent action against others can cause harm to them and to ourselves as well, so it is not useful. Screaming and yelling stirs up a like response until no one is listening to anyone else. This is also useless. Repression of anger causes illness to the self; for some it is like a time bomb planted among the multiple personalities; for others it is more like a slowly leaking toxic waste dump. Eventually, an explosion occurs at an unexpected moment, or a cancer develops in an area unprotected by the immune system. Anger needs to be acknowledged. At the same time a practice must be established to find creative ways to use all the extra energy stirred up with the adrenaline of emotion. Some of humanity's most important advances and inventions have been made because some people were angry enough to create ways to solve dangerous problems.

Creative ideas can arise spontaneously after the quiet time of no thought while integration of the separate personalities is taking place. Allowing the creative to manifest fully involves: opening the mind to expose what fearful repressions may lurk there among the multiple personalities; allowing the senses to develop; forgiveness of self and others so anger doesn't build into madness; finding a positive use for the energy of emotions; learning the techniques of focusing attention; developing a meditative practice to seek the feeling of oneness with all life and the infinite; enjoying the evolution of intelligence and compassion as it develops within you from these practices.

The practice of telepathic communication with your loved ones is a useful way to expose your natural differences in cognitive style, in memory associations, and in symbolic imagery. True love asks, *"Who are you?"* True love does not demand, *"I love you, therefore you must become the one I want you to be."* (Since we are all multiples, that command is impossible to achieve anyway. If enforced it could lead to repression or separation. No one can play the same role at all times.) As you discover your own intrinsic style of symbolizing ideas, you can then explore the unique ways of thinking used by your partner. As you gain understanding of each other's individuality, within the qual of total mutual acceptance, you find that you can blend your combined wealth of symbolic imagery to enhance communication into deeper meanings for your lives.

The demands of our literate society to translate all of our multiple selves into words reduces our inner nonverbal feelings, indescribable visions and fleeting emotions, into near extinction. The richness of this inner life can be released through telepathic exercises. When we allow our various personalities to explore freely what it means to have a multidimensional mind, the creativity of our whole society might then begin to understand what wonders await us all as the next century dawns.

## CHAPTER THREE — REMOTE VIEWING

*Remote viewing* (RV) has a very different protocol from what I have been calling *telepathy*. Both experiences involve mind-to-mind communication, but the set of four hundred trials discussed in the first chapters was done using target pictures pasted on 3" x 5" cards. With one exception, there was only one sender and one receiver. Remote viewing is often done with an *outbound team* consisting of two or more people. The *remote viewer* can be one or more persons located from five miles to several thousand miles from the target site and each other. In one of our studies, there were several people at different locations. The entire environment of the outbound team becomes the target. The first thing for the viewers to decide is whether the outbound team is indoors or outdoors. After that, they will try to "see" the environment in more detail, or to perceive what the outbound team is doing there. The job of the outbound team is to interact with the environment to provide a stronger signal for the viewers. Occasionally the viewers would "see" more things in the environment than the outbound team saw while they were there. Later trips to the site might confirm that the remote viewers were correct.

This chapter is organized into four sections. The first section will show one session done from one side of the Santa Rosa Junior College (SRJC) campus to another. The second section features a series done within a range of five to thirty miles. The area included Santa Rosa, Cotati, Petaluma, and Novato. One pilot session was done across San Francisco, when the outbound team could use a hand-held video camera. The third section includes a series of four sessions done between Hawaii and Northern California. The distance between these areas is nearly 3,000 miles. The fourth section describes only one session stretched across an area of approximately 8,000 miles. It involved groups of people in several places at once: Estes Park, Colorado; Carlin, Nevada; Santa Rosa, California; and Lake Guatavita and Bogotá in Colombia.

As soon as I had discovered the artistic talents of James Dowlen in my psychology class (during the school term of 1974-1975), I was eager to see what he could do as a remote viewer. In August 1975 an opportunity presented itself to explore what might happen between groups in different sites stretching across 8,000 miles. Dowlen sat in his California studio alone to draw whatever came to his mind during the early morning hours planned for that event. His series of drawings provided evidence of "psychic soup" since they included activities at all the distant sites.

***James Dowlen***
***Classroom Notes, 1974-1975***

***Left to right, clockwise:***
***1st — 1974***
"3rd floor Stevenson"
"Occidental Healing Center"
"INSHALLAH"

***2nd — 1975***
*(quoted from tapes played in class recorded by Tim Leary in prison.)*
"Game of Guru!
Uplevel any question asked
& put it in Cosmic Ref."
"The game of Higher Intelligence"
"The purpose of Life...
to evolve beyond life.
Electromagnetic
Where did we come from?
Life was planted on this planet."

***3rd — 1975***
" 'When I pick up the instrument,
I'm pure.'
—Ali Akbar Khan"
"1st World Congress of Sorcery"

## ONE REMOTE VIEWING TRIAL ACROSS THE SANTA ROSA JUNIOR COLLEGE CAMPUS

Since the campus video studio was available for teachers, we decided to do a telepathy session there. Two cameras might be able to capture two similar drawings in real time. Bob Budereaux, the director, wanted to record the artists attempting to do RV as well. As soon as everyone was settled in the studio, I drove around some nearby stores to find a site and finally decided on the biology building on the campus. There is no other building like it. This is the only session that was done when the outbound team was closer than five miles, but the timing was dependent on the availability of the video studio. After I parked the car, I was embarrassed to realize that I had not brought drawing paper. Eventually I found an old envelope in my purse that I could use for sketches (parts of the faded address can still be seen in the photo). Tom Byrne carefully draws the correct building, as illustrated below right.

James Dowlen has a different response, and it is fascinating to watch it evolve. In his first set of drawings, he sees the curved forms, but cannot decide what they are. He writes, "From Bells, to Boobs, to Eggs—." Following the

idea of bells, he thinks of used appliances and draws a person pushing a shopping cart. When he begins another page of drawings (illustrated opposite page), the curves are reversed to be telephone wires with birds on them. Next they become a laundromat. By the time I have gone inside the

### REMOTE VIEWING TARGET SITE
**Biology Building on the SRJC Campus**
**April 15, 1977**

"Bldg. w/curved arch.
(lobster, turtle, fish tank: alive)  Owl (stuffed)
posters: one-celled animals, arthropods, mollusk, flat worms"

*(Sketches made by Millay at the site on both sides of an old envelope.)*

**Tom Byrne — *REMOTE VIEWER* — April 15, 1977**

"TRUCK"

*(Byrne makes a more complete RV drawing of the outside of the biology building than does Millay, who is looking at it.)*

building and begin to draw the live turtle and stuffed owl, Dowlen gives another interpretation to the curves. They are now drawn in a larger scale, becoming architectural. Next he elongates the bell, but he also weaves a large bird into his curved archway. The shape of the outstretched wings of the stuffed owl that I have drawn are translated by Dowlen into hands behind a head. Gradually, some of the actual themes of the remote viewing site are beginning to emerge. In his last drawing, he creates a series of large arches. The evolution of his series of curves can be followed step by step. We are watching remote viewing as it happens. The evidence of the transmission of forms from mind to mind is clearly seen.

There has been an accepted idea for many years that concept precedes percept. Often it does, though it compromises true objectivity. However, here the reverse is true. The perception of the curved lines came first while another mental process hunted for a concept to fit them. I have had this experience myself many times. The form is often given in a clear vision. But the concept that goes with the form is usually created internally. When it is, error in di-

rect transmission can occur at that point. Our projections, colored by our belief systems, can overwhelm subtle messages. Once a vision to solve a math problem came to me, but the teacher told me that if I couldn't put it in words, I couldn't think about it. At first I was crushed, and I allowed my grades in math to drop from an "A" to a "C." It took me a few years, but eventually I recognized that it was he who had limited himself about the concept of thinking. Visions are fundamental. They come before language.

**James Dowlen — REMOTE VIEWER — April 15, 1977**

"USED APPLIANCES — From Bells — to Boobs — to Eggs —"

**James Dowlen — REMOTE VIEWER — April 15, 1977**

*(Above are the second and third pages of Dowlen's drawings.)*

## TWO REMOTE VIEWERS RESPOND TO SITES FROM FIVE TO THIRTY MILES AWAY

In the spring of 1976, we were able to conduct a series of ten sessions that included RV sites in and around Cotati, Petaluma, and Novato, California. Several sites had been chosen for us by another psychology teacher in Santa Rosa. The names and directions to these sites were placed in sealed envelopes and given to a third person (Bunny Bonewitz) in Cotati. Unlike the SRI protocol, where a monitor sits with the viewer and asks him/her questions about the site, Dowlen preferred to stay alone in his own studio, where he was comfortable and would not be distracted from his own light trance state. All participants were volunteers (we had no research funding), and the comfort of each one was important to ensure best results.

The sessions were planned at certain times and coordinated by phone. Byrne agreed to participate from his own art studio, when he had time. Neither artist needed to prove psychic ability. They were just curious about what their own results might be. The outbound team went first to Bonewitz's apartment and threw dice to choose the envelope. Bonewitz produced the right one from a hidden place. The outbound team was not to open the envelope until they had driven some distance away. They would try to arrive at the site at the scheduled hour and spend fifteen to twenty minutes interacting with it. If a session were planned for the second hour, they would take a break before opening the other envelope to find out where to go next.

| | | | | |
|---|---|---|---|---|
| **Target Sites, Number of Pages of Drawings, Number of Correct Matches, and Types of RV Sites** | | | | |
| **Date**<br><br>**1976** | **Remote viewing target site** | **Number of pages of drawings by Dowlen & Byrne** | **Major elements of the site** | **1st & 2nd choices matched correctly by five judges** |
| 4/15 | Petaluma, Cemetery | Dowlen = 3 pages | **Outside** - flag, truck, graves, trees, indoor/outdoor green grass-like carpet | 2 - 1 |
| 4/15 | Petaluma, Smoke Shop | Dowlen = 1 page | **Inside** - flag, candy, smoke, pinball, dog photo, loud music playing, traffic lights by front door | 0 - 1 |
| 4/19 | Cotati, Water Tower | Dowlen = 3 pages | **Outside** - fence, sheep, tower on hill, concept of water (not seen), winding road below the hill, trees | 0 - 0 |
| (While at the water tower, the outbound team reports, *"He is having trouble finding us and he is feeling rushed and distracted."* See Page 169.) | | | | |
| 4/29 | Cotati, Ice Cream Parlor | Dowlen = 2 pages | **Inside** - food, lights, chairs, tables | 2 - 2 |
| 4/29 | Cotati, CSUS Duck Pond | Byrne = 1 page | **Outside** - water, ducks, footbridge, large buildings, trees | 2 - 1 |
| 5/03 | Petaluma, Walnut Park | Dowlen = 2 pages | **Outside** - gazebo, trees, lawn, flowers, children's play ground | 1 - 1 |
| 5/03 | Novato, Small Airport | Byrne = 1 page | **Outside** - small airplanes, cars, control tower, landing lights, gas trucks, gas station, small fire truck | 2 - 2 |
| 5/10 | Petaluma, Savings & Loan | Dowlen = 1 page<br>Byrne = 1 page | **Outside** - office building closed, street, walkway lights, flowers, water fountain | 0 - 1 |
| 5/10 | Petaluma, Old Train Track Hwy. 116, under US 101 | Dowlen = 1 page<br>Byrne = 1 page | **Outside** - train car & tracks under freeway bridge, hill on west side of freeway, creek runs into river | 2 - 3 |
| 5/10 | Petaluma, J. M.'s apt. | Dowlen = 2 pages | **Inside** - high windows, letter on floor under desk, round table, framed sketch of nude on wall | 2 - 1 |
| | | | Total correct choices out of 50 (10 sites / 5 judges) | 13 - 13 |

Chance score = 10%

JD = James Dowlen — completed 15 pages full of drawings
TB = Tom Byrne — completed 4 pages full of drawings

1st choice scores = 26%
2nd choice scores = 26%

The artists would draw whatever came to mind during that time. At the end of all sessions, the list of sites and the entire set of drawings were given to the judges. They were asked to rank their choices from most confident to least confident using numbers from one to four. One of the judges matched only two out of the ten sites correctly in her first choice, and only two others in her second choice. One judge matched three correctly in his first choice and three others in his second. Two of the judges matched four correctly in their first choices but were only able to match one each successfully in their second choices. The fifth judge matched *none* of them correctly for his first choice but he did match five of them correctly for his second choice. This produced a score for the study of 26% for the first choices and 26% for the second choices. Chance expectancy was 10%. These scores are only slightly better than chance, and therefore they are not seen as a strong indication of RV success.

Even though we did our best to follow the protocol established by SRI, it was not always possible for us to do so within the limitations of time that the volunteers had available. The two talented artists could participate only after they had met the deadlines of their contracts for commercial art.

We also found along the way that we had made errors in planning. We did two sessions, one after the other, to take advantage of those times when the artists were available. However, they frequently continued to draw while they were in the mood, without taking the time out between sessions. The images they provided during those times might include scenes which were not part of the official site. Another error in planning involved expecting the entire series of ten sessions to be matched all at once. It was confusing and time-consuming for the judges to keep in mind all ten sites, while comparing them with nineteen pages of drawings. The work of judging was more demanding than the volunteer judges expected. (One wrote that he had matched some sites arbitrarily, because of confusion and lack of time.)

The illustration below demonstrates what happened when Dowlen began drawing before the scheduled time of the session. F.B. and I acted as the outbound team on this occasion. Before opening the envelope, we had stopped at the Loop Center in Cotati to pick up information about a conference on computers. The paper was pulled from an old file cabinet sitting on a rickety desk. Dowlen's drawing of the event was such a remarkable match that I returned to photograph the file and the desk. Since it wasn't the official target site and had not been photographed when we were there before the session started, it is shown here as an anomaly, just to illustrate the difficulties the independent judges had trying to match the official sites with the responses in this series of RV experiments.

However, in spite of our problems with statistics, the wealth of data we do have for our continuing examination is priceless. In studying it all, we find that it is in the unexpected events, and in the errors in timing, that the processes of mind-to-mind communication are revealed to us bit by bit. So much of what actually happens during such exercises in RV is not in the sketches and photographs, nor is it found in the notes, but it *is* in the reality of each participant.

Map of the area used in this series of remote viewing sessions. The distance between Santa Rosa and Novato is approximately thirty miles.

The outbound team stopped at the Loop Center in Cotati to pick up information about a conference to be held at CSUS.
After leaving, they opened the envelope to find that the official target site was the Walnut Park gazebo in Petaluma.

*(Photo by Millay.)*

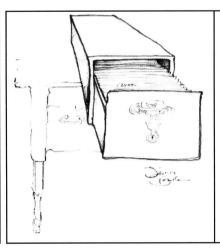

*James Dowlen*
*REMOTE VIEWER*
*May 3, 1976*

Dowlen made this drawing fifteen minutes before the RV session began. It is what the outbound team saw at the time, but it did not relate to the official target site.

Each may have symbolized the message differently, but something comes through on one or more levels of the multiple mind and is translated through some process of the sensory system.

In the first chapter on sensory perception, we demonstrated ten different ways the senses pick up and interpret information from a distance. We don't suggest that these are the only ways this occurs. The ten we have chosen to discuss are the ones we are able to illustrate from our studies at this time. As more research into remote perception develops, using other talented people with different types of dominant cognitive styles and different belief systems, no doubt other ways will be found.

Dowlen and Byrne have trained themselves to see images and each one has a unique way of interpreting similar shapes and forms. Working with them in this more extensive remote viewing series was a privilege. They gave us a wider perspective on what is humanly possible during telepathy and remote sensing.

For the first session, the outbound team opened their envelope after leaving Bonewitz's apartment in Cotati and read these instructions: "Turn on Petaluma Hill Blvd. and drive to the cemetery." There was no indication about whether to turn right or left to go north or south. The directions did not name either a Santa Rosa or a Petaluma cemetery. The team had to find a pay phone, call an intermediary who would call the teacher in Santa Rosa, and wait by the phone for a call back to find out. At 3:45 PM, Dowlen

***REMOTE VIEWING SITE TARGET SITE***
***Petaluma Cemetery***

***April 15, 1976***

Tall gravestones
seen at the target site.

*(Sketch by Millay
on the outbound team.)*

***James Dowlen — REMOTE VIEWER — April 15, 1976***

"Details—of a Switch Box.... 3:45
364 - - -
4:00  Felt a cold wind."

***REMOTE VIEWING TARGET SITE***
***Petaluma Cemetery — April 15, 1976***

*(All three photos on these pages by Millay.)*

**REMOTE VIEWING TARGET SITE**
*Petaluma Cemetery*

*Left* = Truck, trees, monument, cabin (flag not shown).
*Right* = Cement square grave site, indoor-outdoor carpet, gravel, and plants.

**James Dowlen**
**REMOTE VIEWER**

*April 15, 1976*

*Left* = "April 15 4:00"

_____

*Right* = "4:15 - Wool Carpet"

records this confusion (at left) in his first drawing for the April 15 RV session, that was scheduled to begin at 4 PM. Dowlen's picture shows two people pointing in different directions. The image he draws and labels "details of a switch box" could refer to the telephone used at that time, or it could refer to a monument since it is similar to ones that the outbound team drew when they finally arrived at the site, as illustrated. The three numbers were part of the sequence of the telephone number that was called, and the round forms in the creek echo the round gravestones. The drainage ditch that was in back of the cemetery is hardly as decorative as the one Dowlen drew. In any case the outbound team ignored it at the time.

At 4 PM, Dowlen draws a truck parked near a cabin (illustrated above). As one can see, his drawing is quite similar to the truck and the cabin shown in the photograph. They are used by the cemetery workers. Dowlen includes a flag on the truck. There was a flag in back of the cabin, so it is not shown in the photograph above. Unlike Dowlen's design, the flag is an American flag flying on a regular flagpole. At 4:15 PM Dowlen draws another re-markable image. That was the first time I had ever seen indoor-outdoor green grass-style carpet used on a grave site (though it is in common use now), and I commented on

it at the time. However, Dowlen refers to his carpet as a "wool carpet," and elaborates on the idea with a design of strange light and dark animals facing in opposite directions. The plants he draws around his carpet are similar to the ones in the photograph. The frame he draws around the carpet resembles the cement square around the grave plot. Dowlen's images were so specific to this target site that we were eager to see what he might be able to draw next.

The day was sunny and bright, and walking around in this cemetery was quite pleasant. The outbound team did not project the idea of death and sadness. Perhaps if they had been able to generate some of that type of energy, the *concept* of a dreary graveyard might have helped both the artist and the judges to separate this site from other, happier sites. However, two of the judges did match this set correctly as a first choice, and a third judge matched it as a second choice. Dowlen seems to follow form more than concept, and he rarely expresses emotions about the pictures he creates. We previously saw this tendency in his responses in the telepathy series. When several others paired symbolic images of the devil with God or angels, Dowlen simply drew the forms (e.g., a star over a man's head). Often he will embellish these forms. The flag and the wool carpet are examples of this.

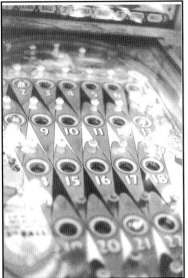

**REMOTE VIEWING
TARGET SITE**
*Petaluma Smoke Shop
April 15, 1976*

Details of the numbers,
bumpers, and holes on a
pinball game machine.

*(All three photos by Millay.)*

**James Dowlen
REMOTE VIEWER**

**April 15, 1976**

"Chasing"

"Snack time?
Berrys
Hungry..."

"School"

"I'm
looking
for
numbers."

"Who's communicating
with who —"

"Armored Car?"
"——> 4:40

— Still Hungry —
For Some Berries —>"

***Interior of the
Petaluma Smoke
Shop***

Pinball game
machines, candy,
stars and stripes, and
a portrait of George
Washington.

**April 15, 1976**

The wooden
"cigar-store
Indian" stood in-
side the smoke
shop. The other
articles were in
the front window.

*(Sketch by Millay.)*

Byrne was not able to participate in the session on April 15, because of a last-minute deadline on his commercial art project. However, Dowlen did so well during the earlier session at the cemetery that his drawings for the smoke shop are surprising. By the time the outbound team had stopped for stoplights, passed the Greyhound bus station, and parked the car, Dowlen was already creating the page of drawings illustrated above. The loud music the manager of the shop was playing could be heard several doors away. There was no one else in the shop. In order to stay there for the duration of the session and make sketches (above right) without distressing the manager, the team bought and ate candy while they played a game of pinball.

In the RV drawings above, Dowlen utilizes a number of different ideas. Even though there is a picture of a dog in the front window, the dog he has drawn looks more like the one on the Greyhound bus station sign, which was down the street from the smoke shop. Dowlen mentions being hungry while the outbound team ate candy, and he writes that he is "looking for numbers" while the outbound team plays pinball. If an armored car drove by, the outbound team was unaware of it. However, the small drawing of an armored car at the bottom of the page inspired one of the judges to match this series of drawings with the Savings and Loan Co. site, based on the conceptual relationship between the two ideas. Because Dowlen mentions being hungry, another judge matched this drawing with the ice cream parlor site.

The smoke shop was a very small one on a main street in Petaluma. In 1976, this area was still quite rural, so only the main streets had stoplights. None of the other RV sites had any that were close by. The early American flag on the wall above the Gilbert Stuart portrait of George Washington may or may not have been the influence for the school sign. Most of us grew up with such images in front of the classroom, although our version of the flag had more stars. This is all just conjecture, because Dowlen himself doesn't know why certain images come to him.

If Dowlen's drawing is a symbolic picture of a pinball game, where "looking for numbers" is part of the game, then the scale of the game in relationship to the people is obviously wrong. If Dowlen is showing street workers underground, the outbound team did not record seeing them. Distortions in scale are not often seen in RV experiments, since the outbound team provides a human reference to the sizes of things found in the environment. However, distortions are common when small pictures are used for targets during telepathy, since they can show any size object.

None of the judges matched this set for first choice, and only one matched it as a second choice. This drawing is judged a miss. The judging process depends as much upon the dominant level of personality that is current at the time as the remote viewing process does. It may even depend upon some synchronistic event while the judges are visiting the site. For example, three of the judges matched the gazebo series of images with the smoke shop and pinball parlor site because they heard loud radio music coming from that site as they approached it. The gazebo site does refer to music. When the hash pipe was seen in the front window, judges matched it with the smoking joint.

Even though this remote viewing seems to follow some of the activity of the outbound team, the added drawings were not helpful to the judges in matching targets to the official sites. While such images seemed to interfere with statistics, they certainly added color and information to the basic process of RV. The outbound team did feel, in those days, that smoking marijuana helped them change their focus from daily problems and shift it to the "here, now" so they could more easily focus their total attention on the randomly selected site. Since they had smoked the joint in the car before the scheduled time of the session, it never occurred to them that the viewer would draw it. Dowlen did not censor his images, and we did not want him to inhibit the results we wanted to study. Since he did automatic drawing then the idea of censorship is totally incompatible with the state of mind that is required to attempt such activity. The outbound team did express shock, however, at seeing that their secretive activity could be seen and recorded by another person nine miles away. Though the artist may not have been inhibited in expressing his images, this drawing did encourage the outbound team to become somewhat inhibited in their activity between sessions.

It is worth noting here that one of the motivations for many college students to participate in research about RV and its possible relationship to brainwave biofeedback was their own use of marijuana. They felt that it improved their sensitivity, though the government reported that it would cause brain damage. Students needed to know for themselves how it affected them. A 1975 study of an effect that marijuana has on brainwaves is discussed in Chapter Four.

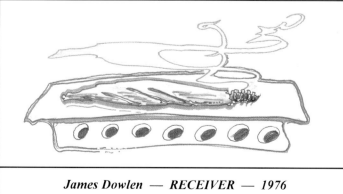

*James Dowlen — RECEIVER — 1976*

*Remote viewing before scheduled time.*

***REMOTE VIEWING TARGET SITE***
***Petaluma Smoke Shop***

***April 15, 1976***

The front window display at the smoke shop shows a water pipe, other miscellaneous items, and part of an American flag. (Another early American flag hangs inside the shop.) A photo of a dog smoking a cigar is taped to the window.

On April 19, 1976, Dowlen reported that he wasn't sure just what time he would be home to participate in an RV session. However, he did agree that he would like to do so. For that reason the outbound team decided to schedule only one site on that day. They all agreed that the team would go there, wherever it was, and stay until sunset, which would be about an hour. That was much longer than any team usually spent at a target site, but that would allow time for Dowlen to fit it into his uncertain schedule. The target site turned out to be a very uninteresting one, a large water storage tower west of the freeway near Cotati.

**James Dowlen**
**REMOTE VIEWER**
**April 19, 1976**

"Sunset Remote Viewing
6:10"

F.B. and I were the outbound team on this occasion. A friend had loaned me a camera to get better pictures, and after parking the car at the bottom of the hill, I took a picture of the tower and then locked the camera in the trunk so I wouldn't have to carry it up the hill. We climbed over the fence and while I walked at my own slow pace, F.B. raced up the hill. I sat on the ground by the tower and made sketches of the sheep, the back road, and a few trees. When Dowlen arrived home and began to look for us, both of us could feel his energies. We knew that he felt rushed, yet his first image was accurate (left).

For myself, the length of time spent there allowed my thoughts to drift away from *sending* images of the site. The area of my greatest concern at that moment was the difficulties my daughter had encountered when her father was drunk and mean. I had not yet gone to the mountain top to try to establish psychic communication with her. The story I have told about that on page 44 had not yet been resolved as I sat brooding at the base of the water tower. The situation for me was still an extreme, unresolved crisis.

Dowlen did not draw the water tower, or even a concept of it. The three pages of drawings that he did make on that day provided some of the most important and fascinating insights for me from this entire series of RV attempts. Dowlen drew images and symbols from my deeper thoughts, rather than from my drawings or photographs made at the site. This psychological exposé of my conflicts and concerns for my daughter during that time created much difficulty for the judges when they attempted to match the drawings with the sites. None of them were able to match the water tower site with any drawings made by either artist. The revelations were for me alone. Things from my past that Dowlen could not have known, as well as some yet to be seen in the future, were elegantly symbolized. His ability to create images from the deep psychological events in another's personal history shows us that we are all connected in mysterious ways and on multidimensional levels. Such images can bring the hidden parts of consciousness into the light, and for me they had a healing effect. It would take another book to demonstrate the connection between my life and those drawings. Chapter Seven includes Dowlen's drawings that were precognitive.

**REMOTE VIEWING TARGET SITE**
**The Duck Pond at California State University at Sonoma**
**April 29, 1976**

*(All four photos of the site by Millay.)*

*James Dowlen — REMOTE VIEWER — April 29, 1976*

*(Dowlen actually drew this at the end of the RV session at the ice cream parlor. While still there, the outbound team opened the envelope to find that the next target site was to be the duck pond.)*

**REMOTE VIEWING TARGET SITE**
*The Duck Pond on the CSUS campus*

*April 29, 1976*

Photographs taken at the site include the pond, the footbridge, and the campus buildings.

The next two sessions were held on April 29. The first RV target site was the ice cream parlor. We happily ate ice cream and discussed the progress and difficulties of this current research project. We also talked about our own personal RV impressions of Mars and the single cells or slime molds that might be found at the bottom of the deepest canyon. Dowlen expected to participate in both sessions that day. For the first one, he drew a picture of a person holding balloons. It seemed unrelated. He drew a person standing at the edge of a canyon. (It also seemed unrelated, except to our discussion of the canyon on Mars.) He drew another that is illustrated in the chapter on precognition. In the center of his page of drawings, he drew the image illustrated on the previous page. It, too, seemed unrelated to the ice cream parlor. However, before we left there, we opened the sealed envelope to find the instructions to the duck pond on the CSUS campus. Dowlen's drawing seemed to match the pond. On the next page he began by drawing a fork and then wrote that he was interrupted by two phone calls, so he did not continue drawing that day.

Byrne's page of drawings (illustrated above right) was the only one for this second session. His images begin at the top corner with the "Flying Hamburger." Byrne told us later that he was puzzled about that at the time, since it seemed to him to come out of nowhere. Byrne's images move from the bridge which resembles the footbridge over the duck pond, to the pointed-roof building, which resembles one of the CSUS buildings. Then Byrne drew a smaller building that might be (according to Byrne) a restaurant run by "Mamacita." The idea of hamburgers is a

*Tom Byrne — REMOTE VIEWER — April 29, 1976*

"Flying Hamburger"
"Rolling Hills" — "Mamacita" — "The Pass"

strong one and that translates into food in general and influences the rest of Byrne's drawings. Before the duck pond session began, the outbound team ate ice cream to interact with that target site, but that did not include hamburgers. Later the mystery may have been solved. One of Dowlen's phone calls was from a friend who asked if he wanted her to pick up some hamburgers before she returned. He agreed. Byrne, in his own studio, is very sensitive to his friend and to the others involved in the session, so when he got an image of "Flying Hamburgers," he included it in his page of drawings, without question. He had no idea why. This is a very good example of "psychic soup." All the participants send thoughts and receive them from each other, not just the official sender to the official receiver. The channel, when open, can include everyone involved in turn as they are in an ordinary conversation.

***Toy near the REMOTE VIEWING SITE**
*May 3, 1976*

This is one of the riding toys at the playground in Walnut Park near the gazebo.

*(Both photos by Millay.)*

***James Dowlen — REMOTE VIEWER**
*May 3, 1976*

RV of Playground Toys at Walnut Park.

On the third of May, the official target site for the sixth session in this series was the gazebo in Walnut Park (illustrated below). F.B. and I were the outbound team for both sessions on this day. We parked the car by the curb on the south side of the park and walked to the gazebo in the center of the park. On the way, we passed the children's playground with its swings and metal animals that can bounce (illustrated above). From his own studio in south Santa Rosa, Dowlen seems to record our activities rather accurately during that time. Unfortunately, the playground was not mentioned in the envelope that listed the site to be visited that day, and only one judge matched it.

The session was scheduled to begin at 4 PM. By then we had passed the playground and had walked inside the gazebo, which is used on special occasions by the city of Petaluma for concerts or gatherings of various sorts. Dowlen draws just one pillar in several colors. The pillars of the gazebo are quite simple in design by comparison, and they are painted white. We have found that his drawings are frequently more elaborate than the targets. That is his style seen also in his design of the playground equipment (above). It is interesting to note Dowlen's comments about time: "At 3:45 my brain switched from clear to spaced— Concern about my—memory— I was almost late for the experiment...." He was, as we have mentioned, fifteen minutes early. Perhaps it was because he thought he was late that he tuned in to the early activities of the outbound team, rather than wait for the exact time at 4 PM. Most of us need to take a few minutes to relax from other concerns in order to attempt to tune in to the mind of another. We cannot expect the necessary shift in consciousness to take place instantaneously. Yet Dowlen writes that his brain switched from clear to spaced at a precise time.

***REMOTE VIEWING TARGET SITE**
*The Gazebo in the Center of Walnut Park, Petaluma, CA*

*May 3, 1976*

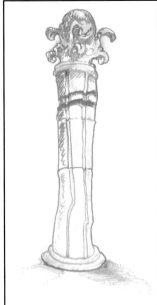

***James Dowlen
REMOTE
VIEWER***

*May 3, 1976*

"At 3:45 my brain switched from clear to spaced — Concern about my — memory — I was almost late for the experiment....

(Solid —> Objects—with stripes....)"

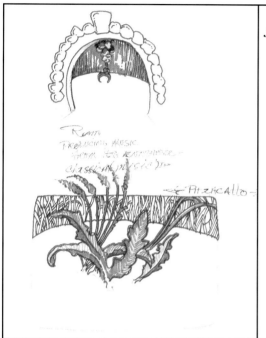

*James Dowlen*
*REMOTE*
*VIEWER*

*May 3, 1976*

"Room
producing
music
from its
entrance —
Classical
Music"


"Pitzacatto"

We attempted to interact with the site this time by dancing around inside the gazebo and singing silly songs. Fortunately, no one was around to hear us. Dowlen's drawings matched the various parts of the setting very well. The drawing (above) looks like an archway and includes comments about a "Room producing music from its entrance. Classical music. Pitzacatto *(sic)*." When the city band plays there, their concerts might very well include classical music. However, classical music was not included in the repertoire of songs we produced from the stage of the gazebo on that day. In Dowlen's illustration one could, perhaps, imagine a row of teeth surrounding the archway with tonsils within.

Once a person has expanded awareness into the dimensions of non-local spacetime, the range of images conveyed is not limited by time. Exact time as we experience it in linear mind may not be relevant. Perhaps only the well-practiced psychic would have control of just what part of time, past or future, might be available to him/her. Had a monitor been there to direct Dowlen to begin only at the scheduled time it may or may not have been useful.

Although we had tried to match the SRI protocol, we constantly encountered a variety of unexpected deviations. Most of them were related to the fact that all our participants were volunteers. They could only spend a certain amount of time doing what we needed to be done. Dowlen chose not to visit each RV site when a session was over, as was the custom at SRI. Since Dowlen had lived in the area for years, he felt he knew the sites and didn't need to take

the extra time to visit them. He had other contracts for art work to complete, and donated all the time he could spare for these experiments. Because of his amazing abilities, we always appreciated whatever time he was willing to devote to this research.

Targ had once suggested that the SRI viewers might be using precognition in their successful responses, since they always visited the sites immediately after each session. However, precognition of the actual site was ruled out in these sessions with Dowlen, except the one he did visit at the end. (That one was my apartment. I had invited all the participants to dinner to celebrate the end of the series.)

In a later set of RV experiments (which we did between California and Hawaii), I chose to take advantage of Dowlen's ability to follow the outbound team from place to place. Since he was usually accurate in drawing the peripheral details as well, we took photographs of everything that we encountered, whether it was important to us or not, and kept a continuous commentary of all events on a tape recorder. This turned out to be very useful and solved some of the difficulties we encountered in this study. It also allowed us a more extensive glimpse into the mysteries of mind during the attempts to explore the dimensions of non-local spacetime. However, that set of experiments brought up many new questions as well. (See pages 86 to 94.)

Once during another RV attempt years later, we did get a monitor to go to Dowlen's studio. The results were almost funny. The monitor (Mark Harris) got lost finding the studio, arrived late, and the distractions were so great that Dowlen turned on his radio hoping that music would help him get back into his own light trance state, nonattached to the presence of another. For myself on that occasion, the randomly chosen envelope listing the official site had to be abandoned. While running across the street for an earlier appointment, my foot slipped off a low platform sandal, and I felt a lot of pain. By the time of the pre-arranged session, the pain had increased and I realized that I must go to the emergency room. There I waited during the entire RV session, until a technician took a few x-rays of my left foot from different angles. A small bone was broken in my foot, so I had to continue to wait for a doctor to make a walking cast. During that time, while listening to his music, Dowlen drew several women who were all pointing their left feet in different directions. He wrote that they were dancing to music.

**REMOTE VIEWING TARGET SITE**
*Novato Airport*
*May 3, 1976*

Left = Gas station
Right = Fire truck

(*Photos by Millay.*)

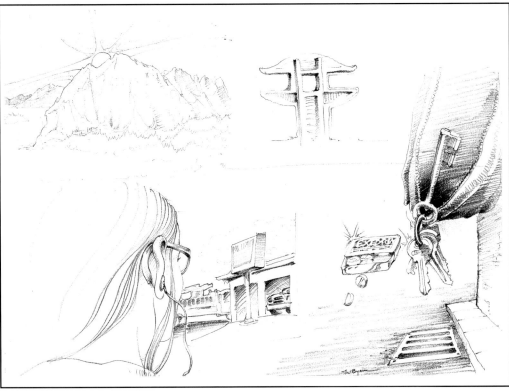

**Tom Byrne**
**REMOTE VIEWER**
*May 3, 1976*

"4:16
Begin — Counter Clockwise
4:18 — Distracted
4:20 — Continue Drawing
5:00 — Stopped"

"NO LIMIT"

"EXCEDRIN"

the top of this series of drawings. It is just south of Petaluma, and it could be seen west of US 101, a few miles north of the airport. However, it was also visible from one of the target sites on May 10th, which was the train tracks under the US 101 overpass.

The next target site on May 3rd was the Marin County Airport in Novato (illustrated above). Only small planes used this airport, so it was easy for the outbound team to wander around it and take photographs. The airport is thirty miles south of Santa Rosa on US 101 and is the farthest target site used during these RV experiments (see map on page 67). All the RV sites in this series are located along that thirty-mile strip. Those on the right or the left of US 101 are only four or five miles from the highway. The area is mostly rural with cows pastured in farmlands. Oak trees are scattered across the rolling hills which are covered in green grass and wildflowers from the first rains in the fall until late May, when the grasses become dry and change color to tan until the next rains in October. All these hills are similar to Byrne's drawings on the opposite page. The one hill that is not like the others is being carved away for road gravel. Most of it is gone, now, but at the time it looked something like the one that Byrne drew at

Byrne wrote that his drawings continue counter clockwise, so the next image in his series included the idea of a gas station and a truck, perhaps a fire truck. There is rarely a need for a person to wear earphones at an ordinary gas station, so perhaps the lady with the earphones could represent a person in the control tower. The large truck seen in the photo above left is actually a Chevron gas truck. There was a fire truck stationed at the airport for emergencies, but it was only a pickup truck (illustrated above).

Byrne's drawing in the lower right corner was confusing to the judges. No one knows who might have dropped some keys and pills down a grate on that day. The drawing is very precise, but we could find no relation between it and the target site. Perhaps someone at the airport dropped them, but the outbound team did not talk with others there

**REMOTE VIEWING TARGET SITE**
*Novato Airport*
*May 3, 1976*

One of the landing lights at the airport.

*(Photo by Millay).*

***Tom Byrne***
**REMOTE VIEWER**

*(This detail of one of Byrne's drawings on the opposite page shows a similarity to the landing light in the photo above.)*

during the session. The last drawing in Byrne's series, in the center of the page at the top, has a strange shape that is similar to one of the landing lights (above). Two judges matched this in their first choices, and two others matched it in their second.

On May 10th, the last of the series, there were two sessions scheduled. The first was to be inside the Savings and Loan Co., but it was closed when we arrived there. The outside of the building had a fountain and a bed of flowers, but not much else there was very interesting. However,

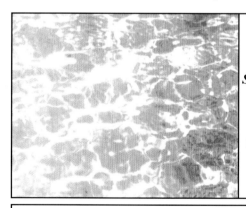

**REMOTE VIEWING TARGET SITE**
***Savings & Loan Co.***
*May 10, 1976*

Millay took several photos of the patterns of water moving in the fountain while at the target site.

*(At left is an enlarged detail of Byrne's flat graphic design.)*

Dowlen drew a nude lying on a couch as though in a framed picture hanging on a brick wall. (See page 84.) Later that day, he would see a less elaborate drawing of a nude, framed and hanging on the wall in my apartment.

In order to interact with the S. & L. environment in some way that might communicate to the viewers, F.B. took off his shoes, rolled up his pants legs, and waded in the fountain, though the water was quite cold. Byrne drew a person with his pants legs rolled up and asked a question, "Stranded on the beach?" Meanwhile, I photographed the flower bed and the patterns of water which are illustrated below left. Byrne drew flat patterns with "serrated edges" and flowers. The flowers are ordinary and might have been seen anywhere, although this is the only site where I photographed them. To us the most important drawing of the

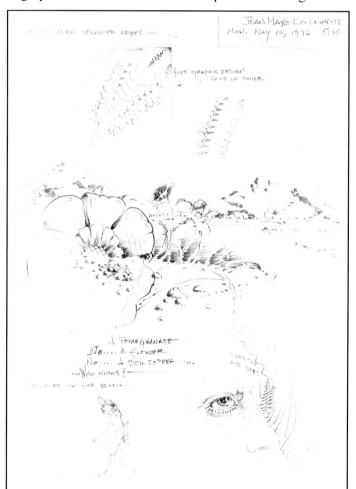

***Tom Byrne — REMOTE VIEWER — May 10, 1976***

"Keep seeing serrated edges. Flat graphic design came up twice. A Pomegranate... No...A flower...No...a Bell pepper... ...Who knows?— — Stranded on the beach. Does the eye see?"

series, however, is the woman's face seen at the bottom of the previous page because it includes the question Byrne writes on her forehead: "Does the eye see?" This is the major question of remote viewing research. Even the viewer doesn't know what it is in him that "sees" ten miles away.

Many have searched for answers to this question. What is it that allows the conscious awareness to create an internal image of a distant event? If I ask you to close your eyes and to visualize a flower, or some other simple thing, most people can do this. As an art teacher I have found only three students over the many years of teaching who were unable to do so. Others just might not have tried, but eventually they could learn to do so with certain exercises that I could teach them. So the images are programmed somewhere, possibly in the visual association areas of the brain, perhaps only in the hyperspace. When you ask yourself for an image (or other sensory input) in relation to another person, it is important that you allow your verbal and emotional minds to become silent. Somewhere the very subtle images come through, but only when the rest of the mind stops talking to itself and allows itself to become receptive. When you are actively putting energy out, it is rare for a message to come in. If you are transmitting, you are rarely receiving. If you are receiving, it is because at that moment you are not transmitting. When two people talk at the same time, very little gets through to either of them. RV works on a similar principle. However, when a few minutes are allowed for each transmission, it is possible for the information to alternate in both directions. During the SRI experiments that I participated in, I could often tell whether Geller received the message, or only part of it, or was not yet confident in his images. That was because his energies would become so charged (i.e., happy when he knew he received it correctly, depressed if he felt he had it wrong) that I could feel his emotions during the session.

**REMOTE VIEWING TARGET SITE**
*The old train and tracks*
*May 10, 1976*

These tracks were located just off Highway 116 after the turn-off from US 101. An American flag is flying over a small building in the background.

*(This area is now a marina on the Petaluma River.)*

**REMOTE VIEWING TARGET SITE**
*The old train and tracks*
*May 10, 1976*

This shows the back of an old rusty boxcar at the site. The wheel, some connections, and a hose are shown here.

*(All photographs on this page and on the one opposite are by Millay.)*

*James Dowlen — REMOTE VIEWER — May 10, 1976*

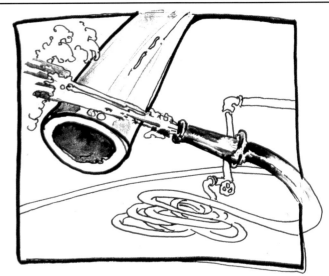

*James Dowlen — REMOTE VIEWER — May 10, 1976*

The second session on May 10th was the old train tracks off Highway 116 and under the bridge of US 101 (a location that now has been turned into a marina for small boats). At the time, the tracks and old trains were rusty and the creek beside them was full of weeds. Dowlen included the tracks and a building, but instead of a flagpole, he drew a streetlight. Next to the creek was the Petaluma River with the US 101 bridge over it. Byrne included a bridge and water. I photographed the train from different angles. F.B. crawled under one of the boxcars to take a picture of the hoses and pipes underneath. Both remote viewers include images of hoses in their responses.

### REMOTE VIEWING TARGET SITE
**The old train tracks**
**May 10, 1976**

The US 101 bridge over the Petaluma River is seen behind the small creek. The hill in the far background was mentioned before. It is being carved away for gravel.

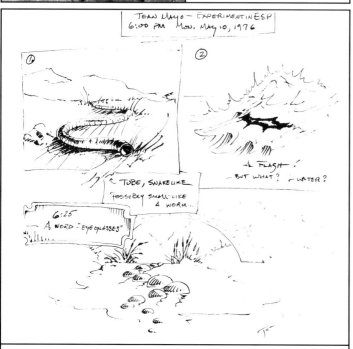

*Tom Byrne — REMOTE VIEWER — May 10, 1976*

"Jean Mayo — Experiment in ESP
6:00 PM  Mon. May 10, 1976
A **Flash!** On What? — Water?
A **TUBE**, Snake-like. Possibly small—like a worm....
6:25 — A word—'Eye glasses'."

The following story illustrates the problem of reception vs. transmission: When my son had been injured in an accident, I was very actively involved in taking part in one of the first coast to coast video conferences on alternative forms of healing. My subject was biofeedback, and I was very busy planning what I would say. Our group of conference participants went to the military establishment in Moffett Field in California. The images and voices were sent via satellite to the other participants at the military center in Bethesda, Maryland, where they responded to us. Satellite communication is now in common use, but in those years, the military, government officials, and major TV networks were the only ones to have such equipment. When the session was over, I planned to drive to Sacramento, because my mother was in the hospital being prepared for an operation. At the same time, another friend was in a hospital in Palo Alto with a broken leg. Afterward, a phone call informed me that my son was also in a hospital in Folsom, near Sacramento. When I arrived to see him, he was distressed, because of past experiences he assumed that I would have known about his accident psychically. Unfortunately my activity precluded receptivity, and any subtle thoughts about a hospital were already logically accounted for by my mother and friend. It was a shock to both of us that I didn't automatically know that he was in trouble. Over the years, I had walked many hospital corridors waiting for him to recover from one thing or another. We had experienced amazing healing through powerful prayers of friends who helped save his life. We both had been able to *see* these friends come to bless him in spirit. This time, my first job was to have him moved to a hospital with better monitoring equipment, request the prayers of family and friends, and sit beside him for a few days, channeling healing energy. Later there would be time to study why my son's accident did not reach my awareness immediately.

During such a crisis, no one took the time to try to prove that dramatic remote viewing and psychic healing might be taking place. The present moment took all of our attention, as it should. It is because of those sacred personal experiences that these RV experiments were designed. We tried to follow *the scientific method* to show others that such mental activity is a vital and intrinsic part of all of our lives and can be used by anyone who is honest enough to sort clarity from internal projection, transmission from reception.

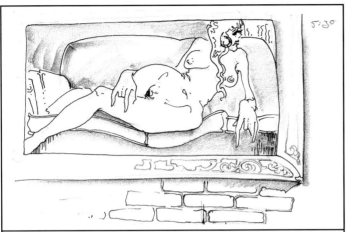

*James Dowlen — REMOTE VIEWER — May 10, 1976*
"5:30"

*(Dowlen completed this sketch while the outbound team was at the Savings and Loan Co. target site. He made no drawings that even resembled that site. The only site he visited at the end of any session was my apartment, where the matching sketch at right was framed and hanging on the wall.)*

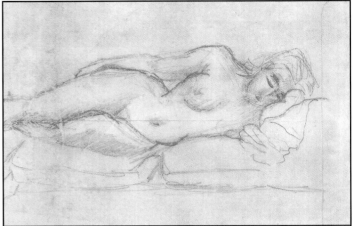

A pencil sketch by the late artist Bill Mayo in 1950.
*(This was only 6" x 9" framed.)*

When the two sessions were over, all participants were to meet in two hours at my small apartment to have dinner. After I arrived home from walking around the old train tracks, I suddenly felt quite sleepy and all I really wanted to do at that moment was to lie down. This feeling surprised me, because I almost never take a nap in the afternoon. My bed was a thick mattress on the floor, surrounded by large cushions, all covered in soft furry fabrics. This bedroom was also my living room. In front of the bed stood the stereo brainwave analyzers, phase comparator, and light sculpture. A small round table stood under high windows. The small pencil sketch by Mayo (illustrated above, right) hung on the wall.

The illustration above was made by Dowlen while we were still at the Savings & Loan Co. He did not visit that site, as usual, nor did he visit the old train track site. He did come to my apartment for dinner later on. This was the only site in the whole study that he not seen before, and did visit. When the session at the train tracks had ended, he did not quit drawing. He continued with a second image of a person lying on a sofa (illustrated at right). His two images of a woman lying down on a sofa seemed to be a remote viewing of the small Mayo sketch on the wall of my apartment. I did not own such a sofa, but when Dowlen arrived for dinner, he noticed in the sketch the same sofa cushions he had seen earlier.

In the foreground of Dowlen's drawing (right) is his

comment about "3 CARDS." This shocked me when I saw it. Krippner had advised me to limit my dissertation to the first three months of research so the results could be contained in a simpler format. I had told him that writing was so difficult that I *never* wanted to write again, and that's why I wanted to include all the experiments in the dissertation. Dowlen's drawings look like books. They revealed to me what I didn't want to know in 1976—that I would eventually write three books (this is the third one). It never occurred to me then that the "3 CARDS" might refer to the telepathy trial cards that I was memorizing in sets of three.

In this same series of drawings, Dowlen drew the one shown on page 64 of a "letter of importance on the floor."

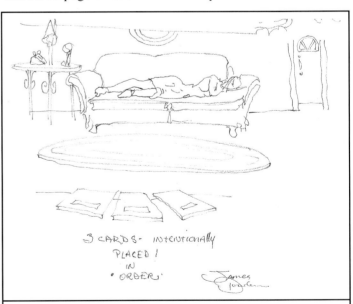

*James Dowlen — REMOTE VIEWER — May 10, 1976*

"3 CARDS — INTENTIONALLY PLACED! IN ORDER...."

## A SHORT PILOT STUDY ACROSS SAN FRANCISCO USING A VIDEO CAMERA

By 1983, the technology for portable, hand-held color video cameras had improved greatly over what was available in black and white in 1977. Henry Dakin generously loaned one to Mark Harris, Sola Smith, and me to use in an RV experiment. The outbound team would use the camera, and the viewer would make sketches and keep track of time. We did not bother with the protocol of using the randomly selected envelope with the secret target site written inside. We were only playing a game of exploration with the equipment. We each took turns being outbound team or viewer, and then discussed the potential and the problems of each experience. Some trials seemed successful, and some were not, but the one worth mentioning here shows the *process* of viewing remotely, which is what we were most interested in at the time.

In this instance, I sat comfortably on the grass in Golden Gate Park in the afternoon sun. It was a lovely day to play games. Harris and Smith decided to go to the Golden Gate Bridge. First Smith used the video camera to show the bridge as they drove across it. Then they turned around and came back to the south end and parked the car. As they walked up to the pedestrian part of the bridge, they passed some flowers planted inside a cement circle. Then they walked on the bridge itself, first looking up at the tallness of it, then pointing the camera to look down at the water far below. As they walked, they also focused on the traffic beside them, and recorded the noise of it going by. When they reached the center of the bridge, Harris decided to use the zoom lens on the skyline of the city, focusing on the point of the Transamerica building.

Meanwhile, back at the park, I "saw" the flowers and the lines going up very high. The first drawing I made is illustrated below. I could hear the noise of the traffic and could feel that cars were close by. The way I have made the drawing suggests the towers of the bridge and the lines around it. But I didn't think of the concept of the bridge. I could feel that they were on concrete or sidewalk, not ground, and that many cars and people were near them.

Then, all of a sudden, I was looking down from a high place. Now logic entered erroneously to explain the sensations. I hadn't experienced them going up in an elevator, so I was confused. I write the questions, "elevator? or shift in camera angle?" The next image I had was the pointed tower of the Transamerica pyramid, and I knew what that was. However, by then I was looking straight across at it, seemingly level with it. Right away, I decided that their location was in the financial district. That accounted for the traffic and the tall lines, which I decided then were buildings. And the flowers, well, logic dictated that there must have been a flower stand on the corner. So I went back to my first drawing and added windows to the other tall lines to make them look more like buildings. All very logical and wrong. These drawings in sequence show the evolution of viewing remotely, and the errors that logic may contribute during the RV process.

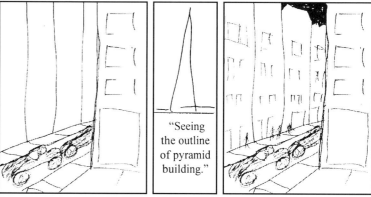

*Jean Millay — REMOTE VIEWER — 1983*

"Tall buildings persist. I have tried to visualize them in outdoor nature places, but the sense of being some place with stuff towering over me is persistent. People passing by and cars. Long vertical lines. Tall masts? No. At 3:59 now changing from up high looking down. Elevator? or shift in camera direction? Seeing the outline of pyramid building. Traffic! Heavy traffic! 4:06 PM—end."

**REMOTE VIEWING TARGET SITE**
*Golden Gate Bridge, 1983*
**Outbound Team — Harris and Smith**

*(This picture was made from a video image recorded by Smith as Harris drove across the Bridge.)*

## REMOTE VIEWING OVER 3,000 MILES BETWEEN HAWAII AND CALIFORNIA

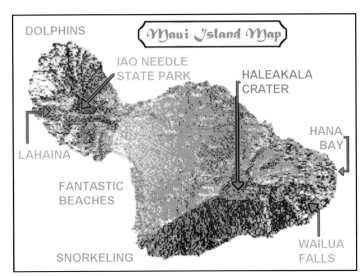

*Maui Island Map*

DOLPHINS

IAO NEEDLE
STATE PARK

HALEAKALA
CRATER

HANA
BAY

LAHAINA

FANTASTIC
BEACHES

SNORKELING

WAILUA
FALLS

The first two Hawaiian sessions were conducted on the island of Maui, and the second two were conducted on the Big Island of Hawaii. The outbound team had decided that the site would be chosen by an unknown person after we arrived on the island, and just before the hour of each session. Six friends agreed to participate as remote viewers. Cheryl and Will Wells would work as a team. James Dowlen, Greg Schelkun, Sola Smith, and Mark Harris would all be in different places in northern California. The days and times were pre-arranged before I left for the islands. Busy schedules during the time from 6:30 PM to 7:30 PM PST prevented some of them from responding to all four sessions. When they could participate, they sent their taped impressions and drawings to Saul-Paul Sirag at the WRI in San Francisco for security until I returned to report where we actually had been. I also sent my tapes and undeveloped film to Sirag after each session. Our Hawaiian study could not be judged in the SRI protocol because neither viewers nor judges could visit the distant sites.

The chart on the opposite page lists the major comments from the viewers in California. Their words that seemed similar to the target sites are printed in bold letters. Responses that are illustrated are also identified.

For the first two sessions on Maui, C.B. had agreed to take the time to participate as the other half of the outbound team. Because of his interest in remote viewing, he had been willing to help fund the study and was also willing to drive the car while I recorded our adventures.

On March 22, 1986, we were directed to an ancient sacred cave facing the ocean, where a royal birth had taken place. I had borrowed a super-8 movie camera, to record in real time all the images, comments and events that occurred during the sending period, as Harris, Smith, and I had done in San Francisco. We took a picnic lunch along for snacks, and settled it all on the top of a grassy cliff.

Dowlen had tuned in late on this occasion, and he looked back in time for a vision. He drew several unrelated images as he gradually moved backward in time to the RV day. The first image he drew for the 22nd of March session was of the feet of a man who lives in different worlds (illustrated below). This is a direct psychic reference to the wide variety of activities and interests that C.B. pursues in his quest for knowledge. These activities make it seem as though he lives in several different worlds. Dowlen had never met C.B., nor had I told him about any other possible members of the outbound team. Dowlen's other page of drawings for this first session are illustrated on page 88.

The sacred cave facing the ocean was located down a short trail lined with ironwood trees. At the top of the trail was an unusual tree that had a tangle of roots showing above ground. I took several still photographs of the area. As I approached the cave using the borrowed movie camera, it stopped functioning, and for the rest of the sessions I had to depend upon my small, portable, audio tape recorder for keeping track of the sequence of events of each session.

Wells reports seeing "...historical site..." near the ocean on a grassy area. Harris reports "...Shot of tree at top

*REMOTE VIEWING TARGET SITE*
*March 22, 84*

Millay attempts to film the waves and the birth cave historical site.
*(Photo by C.B.)*

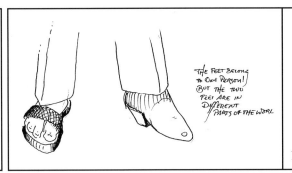

THE FEET BELONG
TO ONE PERSON!
BUT THE TWO
FEET ARE IN
DIFFERENT
PARTS OF THE WORLD

*James Dowlen*
*REMOTE*
*VIEWER*

"The feet belong to one person! But the two feet are in different parts of the world!"

| REMOTE VIEWERS IN CALIFORNIA | March 22, 1984 TARGET SITE ANCIENT BIRTH CAVE NEAR OCEAN | March 23, 1984 TARGET SITE WAILUA FALLS to HANA BAY |
| --- | --- | --- |
| James Dowlen | One full page of drawings **illustrated on page 88.** Drawing of feet, **illustrated on page 86.** | One full page of drawings and comments, **illustrated on page 89.** |
| Gregory Schelkun | Drawing of mountain and box. Comments: "Rocks, mountain, volcano with metal box." | One full page of drawings with labels, **illustrated on page 89.** |
| Sola Patricia Smith | "Seven Sacred Pools, bridges, **ocean.**" | "Lots of sand. Beige. Jean in blue dress & large white necklace. Very happy." |
| Cheryl & Will Wells | **"Feeling of being up high on edge of hill overlooking green and ocean.** Modern building behind. Botanical preserve or **historical site."** | (No response by Wells team for this session) |
| Mark Harris | "General impression of...**green meadow turf sloping down from dirt parking lot to ocean. Trail** across meadow **ending up at a small gorge** with pool and stream and waterfall.... **Ocean breaks** on sandy beach. **Shot of a tree at top of trail**...goes down to 7 sacred pools." | "Impressions: **Green abundant plant life thru camera. Jungle passing thru in car.** Gardens, both **flowers** & vegetable. Maybe a grove... Also red to black lava rocks near beach. My impression would be red sands beach-cove in **Hana. Lava rock cliffs.** ...sunny with intermittent clouds." |
| | March 28, 1984 TARGET SITE HOME in KEAAU, OLAA DISTRICT | March 29, 1984 TARGET SITE CITY OF REFUGE, SOUTH OF KONA |
| James Dowlen | One full page of drawings and comments, **illustrated on page 91.** | One full page of drawings and comments, **illustrated on page 92.** |
| Gregory Schelkun | Drawing and comments of an erupting volcano, **illustrated on page 90.** | (No response by Schelkun for this session) |
| Sola Patricia Smith | "Main idea: volcano" | Drawing of volcano **illustrated on page 90.** "Jungle w/green and lots of **flowers. Gardens. Jean in long blue dress. House on stilts** with an aluminum roof." |
| Cheryl & Will Wells | **"Eastern side.** Lagoon beach. **Sunset. Macaws eating fruit  (mangos?)"** | **"I get a feeling of heavy climbing.** Jean trying to catch her breath climbing up. **The color 'red.'** Along a ravine in the jungle. **No one there. "** |
| Mark Harris | "...**Sort of flat there,** cane fields and taro patch.... **Red hibiscus. A house...on stilts** with rusty **tin roof.... Smoke from volcano is visible...as well as red glow...closer to OLAA forest** reserve on way to Hawaiian volcanoes." | "Impressions thru the lens—Long stretch of beach with a point at right end...**waves breaking farther out over rock** or reef... **In parking lot, car is white** compact. **I think area is Kona** between Captain Cook and Kahaluu." |

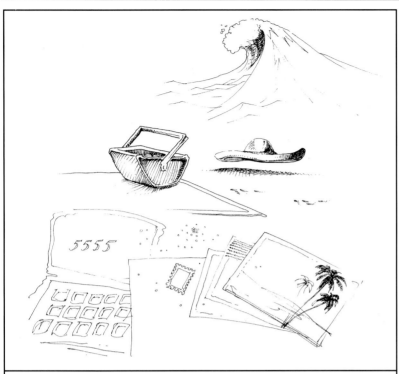

**James Dowlen -- REMOTE VIEWER -- March 22, 1984**

*(Dowlen is in California viewing J.M. and C.B. in Maui, Hawaii.)*

relate to us both are the picnic basket and the ocean wave. I did photograph ocean waves, but neither of us wore a hat like that.

For the second session, a stranger recommended that we visit the Seven Sacred Pools, but warned us about the narrow road. C.B. decided to take a chance on the difficult drive from Hana to the Wailua Falls (the official name of the pools). We spent the whole afternoon of March 23 there. Then about fifteen minutes after the hour of sending had begun, we began to walk down to the car from the highest waterfall, where we had taken several photographs (one is illustrated on the page opposite). C.B. drove back to Hana Bay. The road is so narrow and he had to honk the horn before crossing a bridge or approaching a blind curve to warn any cars that might be coming from the opposite direction. The trees over the road were so tall that they were woven together high above us. One of my running comments recorded on the audio tape was this: "The trees are so thick in some places here, it seems as though we are driving through a tunnel." Every canyon had a waterfall and flowers, every outside curve was a blind curve. To get an idea of the problems of that road it is best to see it from the air. The picture reproduced below is from a postcard we bought when we arrived in Hana.

The remote viewing drawing illustrated on the page opposite was done by artist and spiritual healer Greg Schelkun. He correctly drew and labeled a waterfall, flowers, Hana Bay, and a tunnel (which does not exist in those locations, except as I describe the tall trees on the tape). Schelkun had completed his drawings in the first half-hour.

of trail...." However, none of our participants reported seeing a cave. Both Harris and Smith (in different places) had written that we were at the Seven Sacred Pools (the Wailua Falls) this first session. The same responses by Smith and Harris may have been simultaneous guessing on both their parts (as participants in our psychic soup circle), or they could have been tuned in to each other more than they were to us, or they could have had a precognition about the next day's session. We don't know enough about the process at this time to determine the most reasonable explanation. Might there be a way to tell if a response was a good guess or a real remote viewing? This question had come up from past sessions as well. For that reason I hoped we would be able to find out what our viewers might actually "see" if we started at a special site and then traveled away from it.

Meanwhile, back at the cave, my attention was directed to the struggle I was having with the camera. C.B., who had never participated in a serious interaction with an RV site, decided to try out his new portable laptop computer and to write a few postcards to his friends. Dowlen continued to explore the man with feet in two worlds. His additional page of drawings (illustrated above) included the postcards and C.B.'s computer. These pictures could refer only to him, not to me, nor to our official target. Among this set of Dowlen's drawings, the only ones that

Postcard photo of the Hana Highway as seen from the air.
*(Photo by George Bacon. Distributed by Movie Supply of Hawaii, Honolulu. Printed in Australia by Colorscans.)*

**REMOTE VIEWING TARGET SITE**
*Wailua Falls (Seven Sacred Pools)*

*March 23, 1984*

*(Photo by C.B.)*

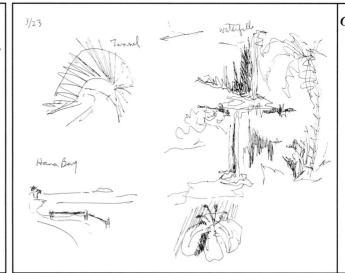

*Greg Schelkun*
**REMOTE VIEWER**

*March 23, 1984*

"3/23

Waterfall
←
Tunnel
Hana Bay"

Certain that his response was correct, he mailed it to Sirag.

We continued to focus on sending, because the experimental hour was not yet over. C.B. insisted on stopping at the small store that we saw by the road to get some snacks and cat food after we arrived in Hana. I went into the store for just a moment to remind him to get suntan lotion also. However, since we were still in the sending period, I told him, **"I won't stay here.** I'm going back to the car to continue focusing on the receivers." At that time, I took a picture of the store (below, left). Since it was getting dark, the photo is not very clear. The small store in Hana and the cat (illustrated on page 3) were definitely not what one would expect to see in scenic Hawaii. Our experiment to test what might result if we traveled from place to place was resolved in the responses of these two artists. The drawings by Dowlen (right) show the building with the high windows, the food, the bugs, the bottle of suntan lotion, and he has even written my comments, **"I won't stay."** Since we spent part of the sending period driving, Dowlen's image of the car is also relevant. His comments may be a clue to the mental processes involved, especially this one: "This seems like a dream, but like all deep, deep dreams, it is hard to know for sure"

**The Small Grocery Store in Hana, Hawaii.**
We stopped here before the end of the second remote viewing experiment in Maui. The high windows that match those drawn by Dowlen can be seen over the top of the open doors.

*(Photo by Millay on March 23, 1984.)*

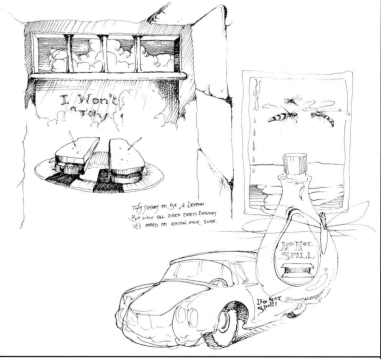

*James Dowlen — REMOTE VIEWER — March, 23, 1984*

"I won't stay — "
"This seems like a dream, but like all
deep, deep dreams, it is hard to know for sure.
Do not spill. Do not spill."

Hawaii Island Map

Waipio
Mauna Kea
Elev. 13796
Akaka Falls
Kailua-Kona
Hilo Bay
Keaau
Captain Cook
City of Refuge
Kilauea
Active Volcano
Kau Desert
Mauna Loa
South Point
Elev. 13680   Active Volcano

Both of the active volcanoes, Mauna Loa and Kilauea, are identified on the map on the left. The lava from Mauna Loa was flowing northeast, toward Hilo. The lava from Kilauea was flowing south, and would continue to do so intermittently for more than fifteen years.

The Hawaiian newspaper *The Tribune-Herald* published this picture of the Kilauea volcano erupting on March 30, 1984. (58)
*(Photo by Larry Kadooka.)*

After the first two sessions on the island of Maui had been completed, C.B. returned to one of his other worlds. Sessions three and four were to be held somewhere on the Big Island of Hawaii (a map is illustrated above).

When I arrived in Hilo on March 27, the Mauna Loa volcano had been erupting for two days and the lava was flowing toward the outskirts of town. It had not erupted for many years, and the residents of Hilo were quite worried. On March 29, Kilauea began to erupt as well. It was the first time in more than 116 years that both volcanoes had erupted at the same time. Their rivers of lava were flowing in opposite directions, and the reddish haze in the sky could be seen nearly everywhere. All the major TV stations covered the event for the world news. I expected this to compromise the RV sessions we planned to do. Smith, Harris, and Schelkun each mentioned the volcano in their responses for the third session. For the fourth session, Smith gave two pages of drawings. One was of the volcano (below) and the other page included a flower garden, and a

house on stilts, etc. (these comments are listed on pages 87 and 93). I still have the descriptions of the day-by-day volcanic events which the Hawaiian newspaper (*The Tribune-Herald*) had printed after the eruptions ceased on April 15. However, that paper had listed the date of the beginning of the Kilauea eruption as March 30. This is in error, since we saw it on March 29 and even our remote viewer, Smith, refers to "2 volcanoes" on that day.

Since my daughter Mara lives near Keaau, in the OLAA district, this RV experiment allowed me the opportunity to visit her for a few days. I asked her if she would choose the location for the third and fourth sessions, and she agreed. For the session on March 28, she decided that her own house and garden would be as good a target site as any on the island, and it would be easier for her than driving me around. For years, she has cultivated all the flowers and fruit trees that will grow in her climate. Now her yard is like a park. She has also built several aviaries under the trees to raise cockatoos, macaws, and other exotic birds.

*Greg Schelkun*
*REMOTE VIEWER*
*March 28, 1984*

"Sand & sky
flowers—pinks
verdant forest
Volcano Fear"

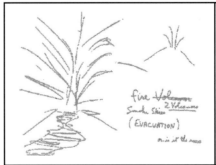

*Sola Smith*
*REMOTE VIEWER*
*March 29, 1984*

"Fire ~~Volcano~~
2 Volcanoes
Smoke Skies
(Evacuation)
Or is it the news"

I agreed with her choice of target site, since Smith was the only one of the receivers who had ever visited Mara's place. During the session, I photographed her birds, flowers, fruit trees, the sun with the glow of the volcano, and Mara and her children. After dinner, she invited several of her friends over for the evening to meet me. These were people who had an interest in remote viewing. They told me about their own personal psi experiences, and asked me many questions.

Dowlen's drawings suggest the evening gathering, with a group standing and sitting near a tall lamp. He features "a young lady with very beautiful long hair..." and puts her on a pedestal. Dowlen has never met Mara, but as you can see from the photograph (above right), she does have long blond hair. Dowlen's image of the old crone tossing bones or coins could have related to me. At least I can identify with the image, considering the role I played when Mara's guests arrived.

Dowlen describes "the golden display of sunset..." and draws it reflecting in the ocean (illustrated at right). We didn't see it that way on the eastern side of the island. This is the only time that two viewers mentioned a sunset, and while that does not seem to be at all remarkable during an RV session, this is the only time during my entire stay on either island that I photographed the sun. Actually, it was too early for the sun to set during our session period, but the sun attracted our attention, as it was glowing reddish through the volcanic debris and mist (illustrated below).

Harris describes the house "...on stilts with...tin roof ...." and places us correctly in the OLAA district.

*REMOTE VIEWING TARGET SITE*
*Keaau, Hawaii — March 28, 1984*

Mara Mayo holding
three newly hatched baby birds
from her aviary.

*REMOTE VIEWING*
*TARGET SITE*
*March 28, 1984*
Macaws in Aviary

*C. & W. Wells*
*REMOTE VIEWERS*

"**Macaws eating fruit**
(mangos?)"

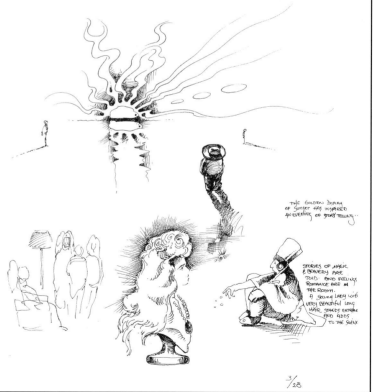

*James Dowlen  — REMOTE VIEWER — March 28, 1984*

"The golden display of sunset has inspired an evening of story telling.... Stories of magic & bravery are told. And feelings of romance are in the room. A young lady with very beautiful long hair stands entranced and adds to the scene."

*REMOTE VIEWING TARGET SITE*
*Keaau, Hawaii — March 28, 1984*
Sun glowing through smoke and mist above volcano.

*(Three photos on this page by Millay.)*

**James Dowlen — REMOTE VIEWER — March 29, 1984**

"An ivory ball on a golden chain & three walnut shells."
"¿ Is it Luck or is it Skill ?"
"Indecision        3/29/84"

*March 29, 1984.*

Granddaughter Tylea wanted me to play this game with her, but we had to leave for the Kona side of the island to get back before dark.

*(Photo by Millay.)*

For the fourth and last of our RV sessions, Mara decided that she would choose a target site on the Kona side (western side) of the island, since she had to go there to do some shopping anyway. She would wait until the very last minute to see where we were, then she would decide exactly where the best target site might be.

The Big Island is approximately 150 miles across, and there are only three major roads from one side to the other, as you can see on the map on page 90. One is the Saddle Road, a windswept, partly desolate pass between the 13,796-ft. summit of Mauna Kea and the 13,680-ft. summit of Mauna Loa. That road might have been closed by then, because the lava flow from Mauna Loa was approaching dangerously near it. The second road is Volcano Road, which rises rapidly up to the pass between Mauna Loa and Kilauea. The third road across the island is a scenic, winding, narrow road along the cliffs looking down on the bright blue ocean on one side. On the other side the

deep green of tangled jungle rises endlessly, and from time to time there are glimpses of rainbows shimmering off cascading waterfalls from every canyon. The annual rainfall along that side of the island is approximately 130 inches per year, so it is usually wet or at least misty. Mara's first errands of the day were in Hilo so she decided to take the coast road, since it is the nearest road out of Hilo.

When her shopping in Kailua-Kona was completed, and as the time arrived to return home, Mara wondered whether or not to drive back the long way along the coast, or to drive over the road between the two erupting volcanoes. She finally decided to take the Volcano Road. The City of Refuge would be on the way, so she chose it to be the RV site. This was our last session in this series of RV attempts, and it was the most dramatic.

The City of Refuge is a protected National Park. There was an old Hawaiian law that if a condemned person could swim across shark-infested water and arrive there safely, the gods meant for him to be saved. There are several temples on stilts to resist the occasional high tides, and the roof of one of these can be seen above a high protective fence in the photo on the opposite page. There are many tall wooden statues inside the fences and around the temples.

As soon as we arrived at the City of Refuge, my granddaughter Kahili went off to gather shells to show me (see opposite page). She thought it was very strange to see her grandma wandering around talking into a tape recorder to no one in particular. I looked at all her pretty shells very carefully, but I did have to explain to her that she couldn't take any of them home with her from this place since it is a protected area.

When this last session was over, the ride home between two erupting volcanoes was extraordinary, and the view was spectacular. Mara's car was a small truck with a motor not much larger than a motorcycle motor. The truck was now full of the supplies she purchased in Kailua-Kona, and the children were sleeping in the back under the canopy. With the extra weight, including myself, she was concerned that the car might get overheated and develop a vapor lock going over the mountain pass. The red-hot glow from the two volcanoes shimmered in the heavy mist that their heat had pulled from the ocean, yet we couldn't stop to gaze at it or to take pictures as the overloaded car might not start up again. So I hung my head out the window part of the way. The view was awesome. It was a grand and fearsome ride between the two volcanos that I will never forget. When the car did come to a stop, we had reached the other side of the pass, out from under the misty rain. Actually, we were very lucky then because a telephone was only one block away where Mara could call for help.

From this session, the Wells team writes, "I get a feeling of heavy climbing. Jean trying to catch her breath climbing up. The color 'red.' Along a ravine in the jungle. No one there." The color around us was indeed red, the adventure and the view were breath taking, and the little car did struggle with heavy climbing over the volcano pass. We did not see any other cars up there. Part of the road goes through some jungle, but most of it is scrub brush and ohia trees on lava.

Dowlen is the only one who seemed to ignore the news of the erupting volcano, and he continued to look for where we actually were or had been. He drew images of the things I paid attention to and photographed. For example, before we left for Kona, my granddaughter Tylea wanted me to play a game with her. Since her mother needed to leave for the other side of the island right away, we didn't

**REMOTE VIEWING TARGET SITE**
*The City of Refuge*
*March 29, 1984*

Kahili brings the shells she found along the rocky shore to show her grandmother. In the background, one of the ancient temples is being repaired.

*(Photo by Mara Mayo.)*

*Sola Smith*
***REMOTE VIEWER***

"Jungle w/green and lots of **flowers...Jean in long blue dress. House on stilts** with aluminum roof."
*(The flowers were near the visitor center parking lot.)*

have time to play the game. Nevertheless, I photographed her with the game (illustrated on the previous page). Dowlen draws a very similar image of the game and asks if it takes luck or skill. (My visit was so short, Tylea and I never did play the game, so I didn't have the opportunity to find that out.) Dowlen then draws several seashells, as I had paid close attention to those Kahili had collected also.

Dowlen draws a very unusual face (below). The City of Refuge is full of statues of the gods of the ancient Hawaiians. Their faces are sometimes fierce and sometimes sad. Dowlen's face could represent one of those, or

**REMOTE VIEWING TARGET SITE**
*The City of Refuge* — *March 29, 1984*

Some of the many carved wooden statues to be seen at the City of Refuge site.
*(Three photos by Millay.)*

INDECISION

**James Dowlen -- REMOTE VIEWER**
**March 29, 1984**

"INDECISION"
*(Enlarged to show detail)*

it could represent Mara's indecision about the target site, or which route to take to the other side of the island.

Harris writes that we were on the west side of the island, which was correct, but he said that we were just above Captain Cook, which is actually a few miles north of the City of Refuge (see map on page 90).

That was the last of this series of RV experiments that we had scheduled. However, it was not to be the last of my own experiences in RV on this journey. On my way back to California to see what had been received by the viewers in California, I first flew from Hilo to Honolulu, Oahu. While there I learned about another form of remote viewing from a very different belief system. I had an opportunity to spend a couple of days visiting my dear friend Shelby Parker. Since Shelby saw that I was very tired she wanted me to meet a friend of hers who claimed to be a *kahuna* and spiritual healer, named Morna Simeona.

This kahuna was a short, gentle, middle-aged woman who did a "clearing" process for me with her assistants, Stan Haleakala and Kamile. They asked me to lie on a table on my stomach with my eyes closed, while they sat around me and looked at me very intently. They did not touch me, but soon energies filled my body. Apparently, when I had guided friends to explore their inner visions before coming to Hawaii, I had taken some of their sadness into myself and had not totally released it. Now it was being released. After that, as the process continued, I experienced a series of images that felt like past lives passing by. The first ones I recognized, and then there were many that passed through my imagery in rapid succession. I had never seen or felt anything like that before. When I arose from the table, I felt highly energized. They offered no explanations whatsoever for what they did. I could not explain what I felt. I just accepted the experience. However, I was reminded of a line in Ken Kesey's book, *Sometimes a Great Notion,* in which he wrote, "So help me it's all true, even if it never happened." (59) I felt great!

After that, the kahuna was willing to answer a few questions. She seemed very sweet and unassuming, but full of knowledge about the multiple realms of the hyperspace that I had only barely touched upon in my research. She talked about speaking directly to Pele, the goddess of the volcano, her reasons for doing so, and the answers she received. (60) The volcanic flow was nearing the outskirts of Hilo, and there was much concern among all the people. Those who lived in Hilo were afraid that the volcano would flow over them. Many might have to evacuate their homes and farms before they burned in the lava. There was a stand-by order for such an evacuation if the eruption continued. Some people were urging the governor to order bombs to be dropped on the flow to try to divert it from Hilo. In the past, this had been done. However, one eruption had stopped at about the same time, so no one knew whether the bombs had helped or not. Now there was considerable debate about whether or not it would be useful this time. Since the land and the volcano are sacred to the Native Hawaiians, they argued against the bombs.

That is why the kahuna had evoked the spirit of Pele and had spoken directly to her. Pele had promised her that Hilo would be spared. *"Pele no hurt Hilo,"* she told me. Simeona called the governor to tell him of Pele's promise so that he would not order the bombs to be dropped.

Whether the governor of the state of Hawaii believed the kahuna or not, or followed his own instincts, the flow from Mauna Loa stopped by itself within four miles of the outskirts of Hilo. But the eruption was not over. Pele began another flow nearly parallel to the first one, and it, too, stopped before any houses were touched. The Mauna Loa eruption finally ended on April 15. Kilauea also stopped, started again later, and kept erupting intermittently and is still going, 15 years later (1999). In its path, it destroyed the marvelous warm swimming place called "the queen's bath," the visitor center, and the Royal Gardens community of houses. The flow of lava has added much hot real estate to the south end of the island as it pours into the sea, raising boiling clouds of steam.

Local people reported seeing a fireball which appeared as a flash of white light moving from one volcano to another. Hawaiian legend calls that a *"popoahi."* This is described as the way Pele travels from one place to another. Perhaps the light was ball lightning between the two streams of molten iron. No one really knows just what it might have been. Since it has an ancient Hawaiian name, it may be a common occurrence during volcanic eruptions.

Persinger (61) suggested that the heavy pressure of Earth when it is grinding together just before an earthquake can cause a ball of light to appear above the area which is most affected. In February of 1998, such a light was seen over Reno, Nevada. UFO devotees were quick to claim it as an extra-terrestrial vehicle. The talk shows were full of UFO lore and "government cover-ups." A few days later, a 4.3 earthquake shook the area just north of Reno. The radio buffs never mentioned that possible relationship. Each person chooses to believe in a favorite "reality."

## A REMOTE VIEWING EXPERIENCE THAT SPANNED 8,000 MILES AND SEVERAL SITES

The First World Congress of Sorcery was to be held in Bogotá, Colombia, in August 1975. At that same time the Association for Humanistic Psychology (AHP) would be holding its annual conference in Estes Park, Colorado. Because of my research with the *Stereo Brainwave Biofeedback Light Sculpture and the Phase Comparator*, I was invited to Bogotá to make a presentation with it at the Congress. (62) This seemed like a perfect opportunity to attempt a long-distance RV experience, since Geller also had been invited to the Congress. Stanley Krippner, PhD, Bunny Bonewitz, Suzy Engleman, PhD, Alberto Villoldo, PhD, my sister Marge King and others would participate from the conference in Estes Park. Walter Houston Clark, PhD, led the meditation for the eighteen people who joined the sunrise circle there. Rolling Thunder would be holding his own sunrise ceremony around a fire in Carlin, Nevada, as usual. The plan for those in Estes Park was to go up on a mountain at sunrise, build a fire, hold hands in a circle, and tune in to each other. Then while tuning in to the Earth and giving thanks to the Great Mother, they would attempt to tune in to us in Colombia. They would each throw a coin for the *I Ching* to create the randomly selected message to transmit to us in Bogotá. The sun rose first in Colombia, since it is the eastern most of all the sites, then in Colorado, and a short time later in Nevada. Since Dowlen was in California, he agreed to get up at 3 AM and draw whatever images came to mind. There were several parts to this prearranged experiment, and only some of it could be carried out as planned because of much last-minute confusion.

1) We all hoped to be able to tune our brainwaves, as much as possible, into the *ionosphere-earth waveguide frequency* at the same time (see page 105). This is a standing wave between the Earth and the ionosphere, caused in part by continuous lightning storms around the Earth, especially in the rain forests of the equatorial zones. The consistent frequency of this standing wave (7.8 Hz) coincides with our brainwaves of the lower alpha/upper theta ranges. The length of this standing wave is the circumference of the Earth. While I can't measure the frequency of a brainwave beyond direct contact with the scalp, theoretically we might be able to establish a harmonic with that frequency, and be able to resonate with each other and with the Earth.

In 1975, Lee Sannella, MD, and Itzhak Bentov had reported, "When a situation exists where there are two oscillators vibrating at frequencies close to each other, the oscillator which is operating at a higher frequency will usually lock into step the slower oscillator. This is rhythm entrainment. When in the state of deep meditation, a person goes into sine wave oscillation at approximately seven cycles per second, there is a tendency for him or her to lock into the frequency of the planet." (63)

2) Geller still wondered about his possible relationship with UFOs and aliens at this time. The announcement by Puharich and Hurtak about an alien invasion in three years was still a hot topic for some. Timothy Leary, PhD, had published (from his jail cell) a list of questions to ask, just in case anyone ever did meet an alien with a higher intelligence. Below is a copy of part of the announcement that I gave to those who were interested (it includes eleven of Leary's original questions). My idea was that if we could triangulate the planet with mind energy that resonated with the higher energy source of the Earth itself, we might be able to ask, "Who goes there, friend or foe?"

---

On August 27, 1975

At dawn (between 5:20 a.m. and 7:00 a.m. Mountain Daylight Time) we will meditate on our relationship to Higher Intelligence, and attempt telepathic communication. As an aid to the exploration of cognitive differences and similarities, please draw a picture or write... verbalize as much as you can, about your impressions after the dawn meditation between Estes Park and Bogotá. This should be...separate from your answers to the...Leary questions below, since they will go to different places.... Your name and address should be included....

Many thanks, peace, love,
signed, Jean Mayo [now Millay]

---

PROBE FOR HIGHER INTELLIGENCE
Extended answers to these exploratory questions are invited.

Timothy Leary          May 14, 1975

1.  Do you believe the concept of Higher Intelligence is a useful concept?
2.  How would you define Higher Intelligence?
3.  How would you define intelligence?
4.  It has been said the human brain is an instrument which humanity does not understand how to use. Comment please. (questions 5, 6, 7, 8, 12, 17, 18 are not included here)
9.  Do you think that a level of intelligence exists that is as superior to the human as the human is to the ape?
10. If so, in what form does it exist?
11. Do you think Higher Intelligence exists on other star systems in the galaxy?
13. Do you consider DNA as an intelligent entity? Why?
14. Do you consider the nucleus of the atom as an intelligent entity? Why?
15. Do you believe that humanity will evolve to a higher level of intelligence?
16. If so, what form will this take? (64)

The first problem became apparent as soon as I met Geller at the Congress of Sorcery. He was surrounded by bodyguards with very heavy and very negative energies. We both decided that it would not be a good idea for him to participate in our sunrise circle, because we did **not** want to subject the other groups to that much negativity during a peaceful meditation. Now I urgently needed to develop a Plan B. For me the whole atmosphere of the conference, along with the energies of some of the people I had met, seemed extremely weird. The commercialization of the conference bordered on the hysterical. I finally relaxed somewhat when I identified my problem. The event had some similarities to a Kool-Aid acid test. Well, I consoled myself, "I survived one of those, I should be able to float through this one as well." After that, I threw the *I Ching* for advice and this was useful: *"...look for other helpers...."*

A Native American medicine man (called a *mamu*) from an isolated mountain range in northern Colombia (the Sierra Nevada de Santa Maria) had been brought to the conference to participate in the opening ceremonies. His name was Seucucui (see the photo below). When I met him, I could see that his energies were clear, his aura was radiant, and I felt that he had great spiritual power. In order for me to speak to him two interpreters were required (English to Spanish to his native language). When I told him about our plan he agreed to lead the meditation, because he said that he had a dream before coming to Bogotá

about opening new doors of communication. He was especially interested that another Native American, Rolling Thunder, would participate. (65) He wanted the meditation to be held at Lake Guatavita, not in the busy city. The lake had always been a sacred place for them and for their ancestors (the Muiscas). The conference organizers agreed to provide transportation to the lake before dawn.

I didn't try to communicate any of these last-minute changes of plan to those in the US (poor phone service). Nor had Dowlen been told the *I Ching* would be used as a message. King decided this just before I flew to Colombia.

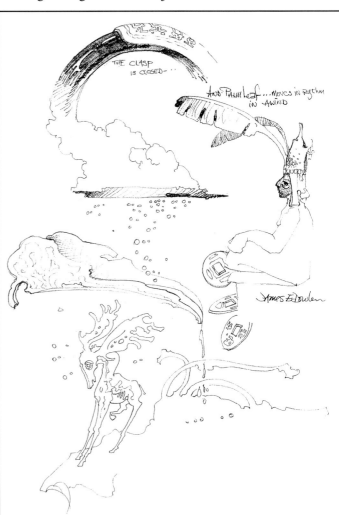

***James Dowlen — REMOTE VIEWER — August 27, 1975***
*(Page one of two pages of drawings)*

**"The clasp is closed.
And palm leaf...moves in rhythm in a wind."**

*(The I Ching coins and the ring with a clasp were in very different locations from each other. The deer spirit is used by some Native Americans to carry messages through the hyperspace.)*

3) The night before the event, Geller did agree to tune in to the Colorado group from his hotel early in the morning. However, during our discussion I discovered that he had never heard of the *I Ching*. So I loaned him my own copy of the book, along with the three Chinese coins tucked inside the pocket of the leather cover. Even after an explanation, I was not overly confident that he would be able to figure out how a message would be transmitted through the tossing of coins in Colorado. Whatever happens is what happens, and we would see.

4) Rain poured on us during the pre-dawn hours of August 27. What else can go wrong? The promised buses were not available, so the organizers had arranged for a series of taxi cabs to drive us to Lake Guatavita. After a long drive through the rain, we arrived at the lake just as the rain stopped, and I remembered that Rolling Thunder always expected a light rain to clear the air before a sacred ceremony. The morning light showed us that much of the lake-front area had been fenced for private property and houses. We continued to drive until we found an open space for our circle. By then the sun was rising. Fortunately, the sun would not rise in Colorado until after we were organized. The ground was still damp from the rain, but we sat on it anyway.

There were perhaps twenty people from different countries who had agreed to participate at that hour. The only two I had met before were from the USA—Lee Sannella, MD, and Andrew Weil, MD. Weil later published a semi-humorous account of the event in *Rolling Stone,* titled *"A Bunch of the Brujos Were Whooping It Up."* (66) Among our group was a dramatic Venezuelan priestess named Beatriz. She embraced me (surrounding me with all her feathers) and declared to all that I was a cosmic sister reincarnated from the Aztecs. Still holding the attention of the others, she pulled out a cigar, demanded fire, and then offered the smoke to the four sacred directions. Eventually, we all settled into a circle, including the cab drivers, who seemed not to have a clue about what we were up to. Since I don't speak Spanish, I could not explain it to them.

Seucucui, his brother, and the woman who interpreted for them sat above our circle. When we were all quiet, the mamu stood, barefoot, radiant in his tall hat and homespun dress, and offered a handful of coca leaves to the four sacred directions. His voice energized all of us. Here in the clear air at Lake Guatavita, the mamu's chant established the circle of communication and closed the loop that connected us all across continents. The energy thus established was magical and memorable. (A tape recording of this

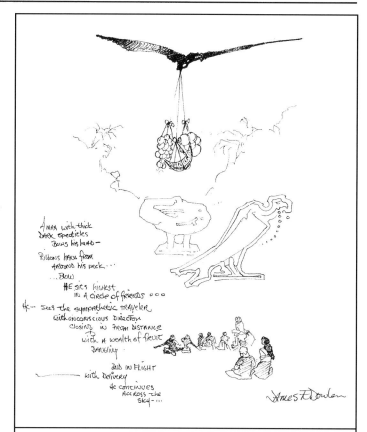

**James Dowlen — REMOTE VIEWER — August 27, 1975**
*(Page two of two pages of drawings)*

"A man with thick dark spectacles bows his head...
Ribbons from around his neck...bow...
**He sits highest in a circle of friends...**
He sees the sympathetic **traveler with uncertain direction**
closing in from distance with a wealth of fruit dangling....
And in flight—with delivery he continues across the sky...."

chant was made on a poor-quality tape recorder, but I still have a copy, and it still has the power to evoke a special feeling.) After the mamu had finished, we began our silent meditation. It was exciting to feel the Earth turning toward the sunrise, and to feel the changes in energy as its rays warmed each meditation circle in turn. Several members of our group later wrote about their visions of people on the hillside in Colorado. When the sun rose in Nevada, the added energy of the Native Americans there was clearly felt by many in our circle, and that high-energy field crossed all language barriers. Rolling Thunder would offer prayers and tobacco smoke to the four sacred directions as Seucucui had offered his coca leaves and the priestess had offered her cigar smoke. His powerful personal symbol of the eagle was "seen" by people in all locations. Two members of our circle reported "seeing" Native Americans around a fire in a desert setting—some wearing blankets.

In the first page of drawings made by Dowlen (on page 96), he symbolized the closed loop with an image of a ring clasped, exactly like one that a woman demonstrated for me at lunch the day before. I had examined it closely then, because I had never seen one like it. Even though Dowlen expected to find Geller as the receiver, he makes no drawings of him. Dowlen does include the *I Ching* coins, the idea of rain, an elaborate image of a deer, and a native (with a more elaborate and taller hat than that of our mamu). It was months before I learned that some Native Americans of Central and South America use a deer spirit to carry messages across time and space. In Dowlen's second page of drawing, he draws and writes that the leader "...sits highest in a circle of friends..." as Seucucui, his brother, and the woman who translated from Indian to Spanish had chosen to do. Dowlen draws a large eagle and writes about "A man with thick dark spectacles bows his head..." One man who fit that description had joined us hoping the mamu might find his kidnapped son.

Meanwhile, in Estes Park, a group of interested people walked to the hill nearest the conference center, built a fire, and held hands in a circle. As the sun rose, Dr. Walter Houston Clark led a deeply moving meditation. The coins for the *I Ching* were passed around so that each person threw only one coin. The lower trigram that emerged from this was the mountain; the upper trigram was fire. Those

***Estes Park, Colorado, August 27, 1975***

A group gathers around the fire at dawn in Estes Park, Colorado. They are preparing to throw the coins of the *I Ching* as the randomly selected message to "transmit" to Geller and me in Bogotá, Colombia. When the sunrise caused the distant hill to a shine in a golden light, three participants referred to it in their responses as a pyramid. Geller drew three pyramids.

*Photo by Marge King*

two together form hexagram #56, *"The Wanderer."* In Colombia, the only participants who had any familiarity with the *I Ching* were Sannella and me. After our circle broke up, he told me that his vision was the trigram for fire. Later the trigram for the creative came to him, but it was in a shadow. My vision was the trigram for mountain, and I also saw the trigram for the creative in a shadow. What should we make of this? I did ask the group in Colorado to begin by building a fire on a mountain, after all.

First I will offer a brief explanation so you can see the problems we had in deciding the response. The Chinese coins of the *I Ching* are counted as heads or tails. Heads represents the Yang principle of actions and tails represents the Yin principle of receptiveness. The Yang line is straight, the Yin line is broken. The eight trigrams in pairs make up sixty-four hexagrams, each with a name and suggestions for how the superior person might respond to the question at hand. Below is an example of six of the eight trigrams.

| Creative | Receptive | Fire | Mountain | Wind | Water |
| Heaven | Earth | | | | |

As you can see, only the bottom line is different between fire and mountain. This could have been considered a changing line, that is, fire over the creative changing to mountain over the creative. The first would have been hexagram #14, *"Possession in Great Measure."* Mountain over the creative would have been hexagram #26, *"The Taming Power of the Great."* The actual hexagram sent to us was #56, fire over the mountain with no changing lines. The synchronicity of the symbols together should have told me the answer. But I tried to work it out logically to include the shadowy creative. While I felt very much like a wanderer in a foreign land, there are several other interesting synchronicities that seem related to this message. For example, Dowlen's comment about the *"...traveler with uncertain direction..."* could be related to the *I Ching* hexagram of the wanderer.

Our visions had enough accurate elements in them to be considered good enough for most RV, but my logical interpretation of the trigrams was incorrect. This really taught me how part of what we get telepathically is subject to our *creative* interpretations from within. The presence of the trigram for the creative in shadow in both of our images suggests that more than mere viewing is happening. We are also being given an instruction from the superconscious about the pitfalls inherent in the process of remote viewing.

Additional information was provided as the session came to a close. Seucucui chanted again to disconnect us from the other dimensions. Then he spoke about our relationship to the Earth. Without my telling him anything about our previous plan to attempt to communicate with a higher intelligence that could operate a high energy vehicle from another planet, he said, "If you are looking for higher intelligence, you should look first to the animals, because they don't destroy the beautiful things of nature." We had gone to find a higher intelligence, and we found a man from a culture that has survived in these hills for uncounted centuries. His culture was considered primitive, yet his knowledge of the hyperspace clearly represented a high form of intelligence. Since then, I have become more interested in the idea of ultra-terrestrials than extra-terrestrials. Ultra-terrestrials are those spirits, angels, and guides that have always co-existed with us on other dimensions, and cross over from time to time to provide important information. Extra-terrestrials will have had to travel for hundreds of light years to get here and bring their hardware with them. For some reason, our materialistic culture finds the idea of spirits impossible to comprehend, but space travel is acceptable. In any case, I no longer pursued the quest for that form of higher intelligence. Even Geller became more interested in developing his own mind power than waiting for an unknown alien to give it to him. His recently published *Mind Power Kit* makes that very clear. (67) You can contact his web site for additional information about using more of your own higher intelligence (www.urigeller.com).

After we left Lake Guatavita and returned to Bogotá, I went up to the 28th floor of the Bogotá Hilton where Geller stayed. He forgot to wake up at dawn, but when he did, he said he found one of the *I Ching* coins stuck to his forehead. He returned my book to me so I could decipher the trigrams we had visualized. I read to him the instructions for the hexagram *"Possession in Great Measure."* The message of that hexagram pleased him greatly (since then he has become quite wealthy finding gold mines and oil for mining companies). During that reading, we both saw a flash and heard something which seemed to drop from the ceiling over by the large corner windows of his room. There was no one else there at the time. The street could be seen twenty-eight floors below, but only if one were to stand very close to the windows.

Geller went over to see what had dropped and to try to

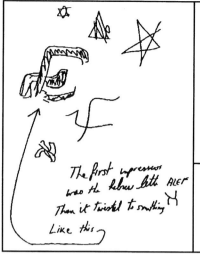

*Uri Geller*
**REMOTE VIEWER**
*Bogotá, Colombia*
*August 27, 1975*

"The first impression was the Hebrew letter ALEF. Then it twisted to something like this...."

*(Perhaps Geller was trying to draw a Chinese character, though the one for the wanderer is much more complex than this drawing.)*

figure out where it had come from. He came back with a very curious look on his face. He said it was a candle that a friend had made for him in New York, and that he hadn't brought it with him. He felt that it had been teleported here by unknown psychic means. I have to admit that I was skeptical about his explanation and quite unimpressed. I was still miffed that he hadn't bothered to wake up in time for our morning RV session, as he had promised. Then as I looked at him, his energy (his aura) changed into radiant light. It was clear that *he believed* what he told me about the candle being teleported, even

*Brenda Smiley*
**REMOTE VIEWER**
*Lake Guatavita*
*August 27, 1975*

if I didn't. At that moment, he sat down and drew the pictures illustrated at the top, right. As he began drawing the first image, he described to me what he was seeing: "I saw a star—no, not a star of David, a five pointed star." He started to draw, crossed it out and tried again. Next he drew an Alef (a Hebrew letter), and wrote that it twisted into some other shape he couldn't draw or identify.

In Estes Park, Shalom Neuman drew an Alef, along with Hebrew prayers, across a large sheet of paper, and wrote, "...I found myself wanting to make it easy for Uri— because his success, even in the easiest situation would convince me that ESP is possible." At Lake Guatavita, Brenda Smiley also received the Alef symbol and drew the image illustrated above, right. The 1975 *AHP Newsletter* printed this RV story. (68)

In Estes Park, Alberto Villoldo meditated on a morning star and drew a *five-pointed star*. With his drawing he wrote, "Impressions of a sunrise ceremony & Rolling

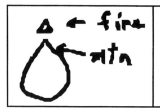

*Bunny Bonewitz SENDER Estes Park, Colorado*

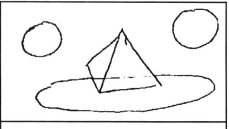

**REMOTE VIEWER**
*L. K. mailed this response from Oregon*

Thunder saluting the four directions. Mountains with mist. Fire. Reverence. The EAST morning star." Among the responses were several images of stars and pyramids. Fernando, the tourist guide from La Rana, reported that his main image was a bright star. The star was such a transcendental image for the priestess from Venezuela (Beatriz) that during our session she cried out that she had seen the star of her life. Her loud voice distracted several people in our circle from their meditative focus. They complained about it in their written reports.

Three people in Estes Park wrote that the sunrise on the mountain looked like a golden pyramid. The triangular fire above left is from Bonewitz. The pyramid below that is from L.K., a receiver in Oregon. There might be no limit on how far our brew of psychic soup could expand.

On Geller's second page of drawings that morning (illustrated below), he included three pyramids and an image of an eagle, as Dowlen, in California, had done, and as

Tall Blond person
DOG BIG
Green one EARTHquake
NOV
DEC
eagle

*Uri Geller*
**REMOTE VIEWER**
*Bogotá, Colombia*
*August 27, 1975*

"Tall Blond person. Dog, green. Earthquake, Nov. Dec. Big one. **eagle.**"

*(Geller's drawings of three pyramids, an eagle, and four cans were matched to sender activity. We were not able to match his responses of the tall blond person, the dog, or the color green, to anything. There have been big earthquakes in Nov. and Dec., but he didn't give place or year.)*

John Sack had done in LA. While some of Geller's responses were too indefinite to be useful, he also drew four round cans with round center lids. This intrigued me, because it was very specific. I knew that one participant had spent some time rolling marijuana joints before going to the conference in Colorado especially for use during the remote viewing event. They were put in four round cans that formerly held tobacco, and they had center lids as Geller had drawn them. These joints were to be passed around at the sunrise meditation to anyone who felt that such chemistry might add to the energy being sent. Previous anecdotal reports and our brainwave research had suggested that it could be extremely useful for those who wished to improve their focus of attention in the hyperspace. I have no idea who smoked them on this occasion, but I do know that the cans came home empty.

(In those days, the cost of that much grass was not as prohibitive as it is now. The costly political "war on drugs" has caused an ounce of grass to be more expensive today than an ounce of gold. A person in those days could actually afford to take that much to share with others, especially if it had been home grown. This was before the Justice Department chose to allow the confiscation of the property of those who grow it, even though such action could be considered technically unconstitutional.)

Before we left Lake Guatavita, Seucucui told me that this event was only the public part of the session, and that if I wanted to know more, I was invited to come to his village. (69) Naturally, I decided to accept such a gracious personal invitation. Fernando, who spoke both Spanish and English, was willing to arrange the trip to the remote village near San Sebastian, and to accompany me there. Another young woman S.G. insisted that she be able to come with us. (She claimed to be a newspaper reporter, but no report of our excursion was ever made that I know of.) However, she did help translate and that was very useful.

The first part of our journey was on a small plane to a small town. From there we were to catch a bus for the next part of the journey. Fortunately, the bus was not to leave for two hours. The meat pie that had been served on the plane had begun to cause my intestines great pain. Fernando knew of a place, a sort of restaurant, where I could rest and order some tea. He was also able to find some local cannabis, which was strong enough to help. He explained my pain to the plump, friendly woman who owned the home restaurant. She showed me a bed to lie on, and though we had no common speaking language, she looked and acted compassionately and reminded my of my grandmother. Then she offered me a different kind of tea, which I was grateful to drink. She prepared meals for customers on a large open-fire stove, outside under an awning. Fernando was concerned that I might not be able to continue, since the rest of the journey would be somewhat difficult. I told him that if Rolling Thunder could process the bite of a rattlesnake as part of his ritual of becoming a medicine man, I should be able to process a little food poisoning before meeting Seucucui. So with the herbal tea and the soothing smoke as allies, I lay down on the bed and spent an intense time mentally "encouraging" the poison to pass through my intestines. By the time the pain had developed, it was already too late to throw up. Fortunately, all the poison and its pain was removed from my system before the bus left town. We walked as rapidly as possible and arrived at the station just as it was ready to go. I saw a stall with hats for sale, and knew I needed one, but now it was too late to buy one. Our "bus" turned out to be a cattle truck with boards for seats. People climbed in with their packages and live chickens under their arms or in baskets. We crowded together for a long bumpy ride. Once we passed by a person leading a burro. It seemed to have many sticks with strange branches tied to each side. However, when we were closer, I could see that the "sticks" wiggled around. The "branches" were actually the feet and tails of large iguanas being taken to market alive as fresh meat. Eventually, the bus stopped at an even smaller village, and we all climbed off, glad to stretch and to be released from those hard board seats.

From this village, the only way to our destination was by mule or jeep. We took the commercial jeep which could hold six passengers. It wound around the hills on rutted roads made of decomposed granite that had been scraped from the same hills. I had spent part of my childhood in the arid Great Basin on the eastern side of the Sierra Nevada mountains. One encounters a lot of decomposed granite there as well, yet I wondered how they could be the same range. I would have to look it up in an atlas later. The jeep climbed up and down several times until it reached nearly 6,500 ft. elevation, and then down again a few hundred feet, until we arrived at a place with mud huts with thatched roofs, two concrete block buildings, and a couple of small cabins up on the hill, apart from the village, that were used for tourists. S.G. and I were directed to stay in one of those. Now I needed a hat more than ever. My hair is thin, so the top of my head felt quite unprotected from the direct rays of the equatorial sun at that altitude.

We were introduced that evening to a large group of natives, most of whom were wearing their traditional long dresses. They were holding some sort of regular town meeting in one of the larger mud structures. After we were briefly introduced, the meeting continued. We sat on benches and watched without benefit of translations from the native language. However, they reminded me of P.T.A. meetings that I had attended with my parents as a school girl. I recognized the actors in the play by their voices and postures—the men who wanted to talk and be noticed, the women standing in the back holding babies to keep them from crying, the semi-heated discussion about some issue that eventually seemed to be resolved. Later we were told that each person in the village shared the work load. Seucucui felt that it took so much time for him to gather and prepare the healing herbs that he should have less of the regular chores to do. Some compromise was achieved at the meeting. As mamu, he has walked over the entire area barefoot, and he knows every plant and how to make use of it for healing. He was concerned because the younger generation did not have enough interest to learn what was needed to keep the knowledge alive.

The next morning we were introduced to a group of children in front of another large mud hut. We remained outside in the sunshine and did not go into this one. I was told that the Catholics kept the medicine men separate from each other because they were afraid of their power. Also, one of their most sacred temples had been destroyed by the Catholics who built a concrete block house on the same site for the Catholic school. Suddenly, I had a brief vision of an army of Catholic crosses over the many years all attempting to overwhelm this small village. Seucucui told me the Spanish called them the Arahuacos, but they called themselves the Abinticua. He said that they are our elder brothers on this land. They all walked barefoot to stay in contact with the Earth. The youngest children did not wear clothes. A brown-bodied two-year-old stood proudly with his arms in the air, facing the sun. Then he came and sat on my lap as I sat on the ground. He was named after his father, Seucucui, which I learned means *"bearer of the light."* Another brief vision came to me that he was Seucucui's own great-grandfather, reincarnated to continue to bear the light.

The children gathered around me as I drew pictures for them of other Native American dwellings, such as teepees, cliff dwellings, and igloos. Adults and children alike were eager to see what other Native American cultures might be like. I encouraged the children to draw pictures for me as I drew some for them. Some of these are discussed at greater length in Chapter Six. I did wish I had a camera or a tape recorder, but alas, I had to settle for my own rough sketches. Most of those that I drew were left with the children, but some of the sketches I made are illustrated below. This is all I could do on scraps of newsprint-type paper and with a light blue pencil that was provided for the occasion. (I could not have reproduced them here without the benefit of the computer, scanner, and a good graphic program.)

When I was standing again, I began to realize that I was taller than the women, and I was also taller than many of the men, even though I am only five feet four inches in height. It was a strange feeling for me, since I am used to being considered a shorty at home. Once a group of women, very shyly and hesitantly, came up behind me to touch my thin, light hair. Their hair is thick and black. They pulled back instantly and giggled. It was though they had not seen any like it before, though I know that visitors do come to their village. There were three other people in our jeep, though they were not in this group, because it was a meeting especially organized for us. One woman brought out a spindle that was used to spin the wool by hand to make the hats and coca bags used by the men. She offered

to show me how it was done, and when I did it poorly, we all laughed. They said that the men must weave their own dresses. The stripes and geometric patterns are made with the natural light and dark colors of the wool.

Apparently only the men chew the coca leaves. The women gather it and the mamu blesses it. The sharing of coca leaves seems to be a standard way for men to greet each other. As one arrives at a meeting, he exchanges a few coca leaves with all the other men present. When he departs, they exchange leaves again. The leaves are carried in the special handmade bags along with a gourd and a stick. The gourd is full of crushed seashells. With the stick, the shell powder is mixed in the mouth with the juice of the chewed coca leaves to create an important chemical combination. After a time, the sticky greenish substance is removed from the mouth and rubbed on the gourd to form a ring. As the supply of shells diminishes, the ring gets larger. Since they walk barefoot over steep hills at an elevation of 6,000 feet, they seem to get stamina from the coca. (There was a great need for a good dentist among the

*Sketch by Jean (Mayo) Millay*
*Seucucui, Mamu of the Abinticua*

Seucucui is holding a gourd of crushed shells to mix with the coca leaves. The wad of leaves can be seen as a lump in his cheek.

*(This sketch was made during the meeting in the mud hut temple as he sat on a very old, hand carved, sacred bench.)*

**Sketches of the Abinticua by Millay**

"I made many sketches on scraps of paper provided for me by the local people and gave most of them to the children. Two small drawings made by the children (above right) are in the upper corner of my sketch of one of the elders."

*(Other drawings by the children are illustrated in Chapter Six.)*

Left = the woman who spun wool. Right = one of the elders.

group that I saw. I suspect the shells wear down the teeth, even though there is no intention to chew them as well.)

Later that day, I was invited to a special temple (mud hut) for a meeting with the elders. Fernando would translate from Spanish to English. A young man, who was a teacher from the Catholic school, acted as translator from the Indian to Spanish. The path to the temple wound through a scattered stand of tall maize. It was not planted in rows, but seemingly grew up haphazardly. Beyond that and other garden plants, we arrived at the temple doorway. Our guide motioned for me to step inside first. As I did so, Seucucui stood up to greet me. His hat hit a small, gold-painted plastic crucifix and knocked it to the floor. It had been hanging on a nail at the edge of a small wooden shelf, which was molded into the mud walls of the hut. My response was an immediate and cheerful, "Oh! How cosmic!" Our eyes were locked in a very brief moment of intense mind-to-mind communication. Then I added, "We don't need that, I'm not Catholic" and shrugged my shoulders. Another brief moment of direct eye contact, and he swooped down, picked up the crucifix, and tossed it irreverently onto the shelf. "Good," I said, and we both smiled. The Catholic school teacher did not smile. Actually, his jaw dropped for a brief moment. It was clear to me that the crucifix had been put there at the last minute for his or perhaps for my benefit. Our first communication had been established on a positive note.

The mud hut was round and quite tall. The only other decoration on the walls was a black and white block print poster. The image was a fist in the air, and the large type at the top read, *"INDIGENOUS ENCUENTRO."* I didn't need a translator for that, either. The artwork was done in the heavy block-print style of communist posters from Eastern Europe. The life style of indigenous tribes is communal. They understand that way of thinking about social organizations. However, communism to them is not the same as it was then in the USSR.

Along one side of the temple was a high bench with a long table in front of it. It was here that the translators, one of the elders and I were asked to sit. When all were settled, Seucucui told me how the worst diseases of our civilization are caused: we have schizophrenia because we have paved the ground with cement and have separated our children from the Earth, the great mother; we have heart trouble because we have lost our love for the great mother; and we have cancer because our whole civilization has grown to be a cancer on the planet. Different races have different jobs on this Earth. Theirs is to pray to the Earth to keep the

balance, but we, their younger brothers and sisters, are unbalancing it very rapidly with our arrogance about our technology and the way we use it. The group of men began to be very angry and their comments seemed to be directed to me personally as a member of that civilization. I had to point out that I was only a poor school teacher, and I could do very little to change the system. The two translators helped me to explain that I was very sympathetic to their situation and I deeply appreciated that we had this chance to meet. We all settled down again, peacefully. At that time a large cup of tea—made from local herbs—was brought in and served to all of us to share. (Gradually as the meeting progressed, I was reminded of a story my uncle told me long ago about visiting a Paiute camp and sharing some kind of "tea" with them. He said in his Western drawl, "After a while, my head came up out of my collar and I could *see* for a lo-o-ng ways." I was beginning to feel that this tea was also pleasantly mind altering.)

We were all quite mellow as they asked more questions about northern Native American tribes. I drew more pictures and told them about the blankets and the pottery of the tribes in the southwest, but when I spoke about the turquoise and silver jewelry made by the Zunis and Navajos, they became very agitated among themselves. Finally it was explained to me that they understood why the Navajos lost their power. It was because they were willing to sell their magic rocks. This was considered to be a very bad omen to those present. Their own magic rocks were agates. Seucucui showed me his set of stones. He said he could even heal bones with them when the moon was waxing. The magic rocks must always be kept very sacred.

As the meeting came to a close, I promised to send them some books about the northern tribes (which I did, though I never knew whether the Abinticua people ever received them). I chose books with many beautiful pictures. Since I knew of no postal delivery to San Sebastian, I could only send them to Fernando to deliver. He wrote that it would take him a long time to translate them. Later, he wrote that he planned to give up being a travel agent and go back to school to study anthropology.

Seucucui asked me to stay longer, because other people would be walking over from another remote village. He wanted them to meet me. However, my reservations to fly home could not be changed without additional money, which I did not have. So when the jeep left the village, we were on it. Partway up the first hill, the jeep stopped for some reason. We all had to get out while it was being fixed. Fernando and I stepped behind a small hill just off the road and smoked the rest of the cannabis. When we came back, we saw a dewy fresh flower in the middle of the road. How very strange! It is quite arid there with no such flowers, or any other plants, in the immediate area. Naturally, I picked it up, and when we got back into the jeep, I put it on the dashboard, since I was in the front seat. Having learned that everything in the village seemed to have a spirit, I thought to myself, "This is for the car spirit." Immediately, Seucucui's face was a powerful vision in front of me. *"You put your magic into the machine, and you have used the machine against the land and the people,"* he said. *"We put our magic into the land, and the land will win."* At exactly that moment, the jeep stopped. This time it had water in the carburetor. We all piled out again, and were told that, since the car was overheating, we would all have to walk up the next steep hill. I laughed at the appropriate synchronicity of the apparent power of the land (and water) over the machine.

However, I still had no hat, and with the equatorial sun singeing the top of my head at that elevation, I was quite uncomfortable. I put my jacket over my head for the walk, but it was heavy and hot. I walked slowly while my "psychic conversation" with the mamu continued. He wanted me to walk so I might become somewhat acquainted with the land. He kept asking me to stop and look at certain things. The nearly empty jeep, which by now had been fixed, chugged by us and the driver waited at the top of the hill for us to arrive. I was the last one to climb into it, and the impatient unknown others made snotty comments about me being slow because I was overweight. Since I had been involved in a deeper psychic conversation, I could ignore them easily. This time, the front seat was taken, so I sat in the center section. Just as I was seated, Seucucui's face was before me again to continue our conversation. I closed my eyes and said to him, "Please, your magic is greater than mine, I just need to catch an airplane." At that moment he laughed, and his image popped out of my vision like a pin-pricked balloon. I had to laugh, too. The jeep had no more problems with vapor lock or anything else, even though some of the hills were just as steep as the first one. We were able to complete our journey with no further problems. I always wished I had been able to return, but that has not been possible. I gave Seucucui's photograph to Rolling Thunder, so they might communicate directly.

No matter how loudly some scientists, with a certain mindset, complain that parapsychology is a pseudoscience, the facts remain that mind-to-mind communication, remote viewing, resonance, and contact with the dimensions of spirits, ancestors, and guardian angels are valid realms of human consciousness. They are practiced by millions of people from a variety of cultures around the world. Only some of the highly trained scientists of Western civilization still continue to choose to ignore the reality that our minds are truly multidimensional. The success of remote viewing can provide that eventual realization.

## CHAPTER FOUR — RESONANCE

*Webster's New World Dictionary* has a long paragraph of definitions for the word *"resonance."* (70) These definitions include its use in chemistry, physics, medicine, sound, electricity, and phonetics. The definitions we use here most often include 1) sound, *"reinforcement and prolongation of a sound or musical tone by reflection or by sympathetic vibration of other bodies, or by increasing the intensity of sounds by sympathetic vibration"*; and 2) electricity, *"the current or voltage is in phase respectively with the applied current or voltage, or the natural frequency of the circuit is the same as that of the incoming signal."*

Illustrated below and on subsequent pages are charts of resonant frequencies from 1000 seconds per cycle, measured as .001 Hertz (Hz), to many thousands of cycles per second, such as $10^{17}$ Megahertz (MHz). These frequencies include the electromagnetic energies from the sun, from other galaxies, from the Earth, and the various types of radiations produced by humans. The chart also includes the frequencies of sound waves. The different types of frequencies are identified in the key below. At the bottom of the charts the numbers indicate the frequencies of the waves in Hertz (Hz). At the top of the charts the numbers indicate the length of the waves in meters, microns, and angstroms. Since the frequencies of visible light, for example, are very fast and are measured around $10^9$ MHz, the length of the waves of these frequencies is quite short and measured not in meters, but in angstroms (see page 107). In contrast, the electrical activity of the brain (below) has been measured between 4 Hz to 40 Hz or more, and though it can only be measured if electrodes are firmly placed on the scalp, the length of the wave is theoretically as long as the circumference of the Earth. The Earth itself has a resonance in this extreme low frequency (ELF) range called the *"Ionosphere-Earth Waveguide Frequency."* It is the result of the continuous flashes of lightning, especially around the equator. The height of the wave is determined by the distance between the Earth and the ionosphere, producing a standing wave at 7.8 Hz. This frequency corresponds with brainwaves measured at the lower alpha range and the upper end of the theta range. It is possible to establish a phase-coherent brainwave resonance with this Earth frequency, through meditation in nature, away from the 60-Hz power lines and loud traffic sounds. In silence one can directly experience the Earth as a conscious entity.

In this chapter we examine various forms of resonances that affect brainwaves and consciousness, such as light, sound, other humans, animals, plants, and the Earth. Resonance is the basis for the experiences we enjoy in the multidimensional realms of sensuality. Our internal reaction to sensual resonance might evolve toward the peaks of ecstasy, accompanied by the high-amplitude, slower brainwaves of emotion. Certain frequencies seem to accompany specific types of focus of attention; whether emotions cause a shift in brainwave frequencies or whether the brainwaves cause the emotions is an interesting question.

We have seen that each person's brainwaves can be as unique as the details of personal handwriting. Yet within each frequency category, there are some general types of similarities. The frequencies from 13 Hz to 25 Hz and above are called the beta range. These are often associated with activity and concentration or nervous tension and anxiety. The most common range for simple relaxation is called the alpha range, from 8 Hz to 12 Hz. Joe Kamiya, PhD, developed feedback sounds and found that subjects could learn voluntary control of these frequencies. (71) The high-amplitude alpha is also associated with deep meditation. The brain frequencies from 4 Hz to 8 Hz are called the theta range. Low-amplitude, irregular theta waves are identified with inattention or drowsiness. At the Menninger Foundation, Elmer Green, PhD, and his wife Alyce Green trained people in both alpha and theta biofeedback for meditation. (72) The frequencies of 4 Hz and below are called the delta range. A normally healthy person may produce delta during deep sleep. Delta may identify an area of brain damage in an injured person.

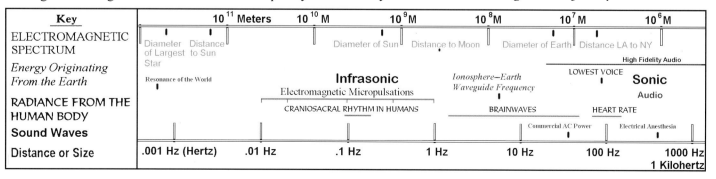

## ENTRAINMENT OF BRAINWAVES
## WITH BRAIN BIOFEEDBACK

The frequencies of the alpha range are more likely to be seen in the EEG as simple sine waves that can be synchronized. The system we used in our study was designed by R. Timothy Scully, PhD. (See page 10.) A sketch of it is illustrated at right. Two brainwave analyzers sent signals to a phase comparator that determined when both signals were in phase. Les Fehmi, PhD, trained clients in alpha synchronization in a program that he called "open focus." (73) His system was different from Scully's system, since it averaged the frequencies instead of comparing them.

Since many people produce more alpha rhythms from the occipital areas when their eyes are closed, we used sound as well as the *Light Sculpture* for feedback. One AUM tone was heard when the two signals were both in the alpha range. A second tone, harmonic with the first one, was heard when the two signals were not only in the alpha range simultaneously, but were also phase-coherent (i.e., in the same frequency with a slightly varying phase angle). We found it important to avoid using earphones for feedback. The earphones were too close to the ears when practicing interhemispheric alpha phase coherence, and the rapid on/off shifts at the start of the practice could be distracting. For most of our participants, the mellow feedback tones needed to be across the room, so that the individual could hear it and either allow the sound to be in the center of his/her head, or become nonattached to the sound and just stop thinking for a while. Paying attention to the sound or to the stream of images during alpha practice would automatically shift the frequencies and turn the sound off.

We used a slightly expanded range for alpha feedback, from 7 Hz to 13 Hz. That range provided only a small keyhole for looking at the potential relationships between thoughts and the EEG, but it did give us some important information. In preliminary explorations with feedback for other frequencies, we found that emotions such as anger and fear often accompany brief bursts of high-amplitude

**Stereo Brainwave Biofeedback Light Sculpture**
**Designed in 1972 by Scully and Millay**

*(Not shown is the phase comparator machine designed by Scully in 1974 especially for our study. Illustrations of two of the eight mandala patterns are shown in color on page 10. A pair of four differently colored lighted panels respond to the different brainwave categories as sorted through each brainwave analyzer independently.)*

theta first on one side of the brain and then on the other, in an asymmetrical pattern. It seems that learning voluntary control of brainwaves, can help one to learn to use emotions creatively. Theta can accompany other emotions such as orgasm as well . We also found that some people could synchronize their beta rhythms, especially when both eyes are exactly focused on one point. This proved to be valuable for some students who learned to increase their ability to focus attention. From that ability they were able to make more efficient use of their natural intelligence.

The illustration above shows one experience that was common to our participants and to us. Thinking in words, or being analytical, was associated with brainwave signals that were often different from side to side—that is, asymmetrical. Not thinking, or meditating, was associated with increased simultaneity of frequencies from both brainwave signals. Most of the participants in our biofeedback training program did learn to identify the mental processes associated with the tones and many learned to extend the as-

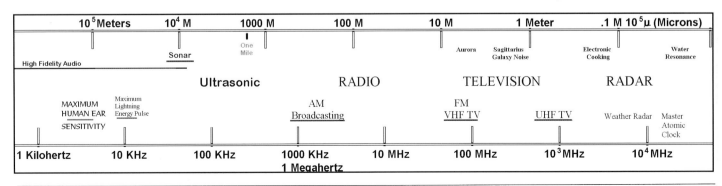

sociated frequencies from within. Those who did learn to do this reported that they found the practice to be useful.

What we called *IH synch* (inter-hemispheric synch) was measured from symmetrical places on both sides of the occipital region. When the ratio between an individual's simultaneous alpha score *(IH relative sync)* and his/her phase-coherent score *(IH absolute sync)* jumped dramatically, from 50% to 80%, s/he would invariably say, "Oh, I just remembered...," or "I just figured out the problem," or some other spontaneous comment about an important insight just realized. Perhaps a problem might be solved by *not* thinking about it for a short time. It may be that through the pure wave form of phase-coherent brainwaves, the nonverbal and verbal areas of the brain communicate with each other to bring information into awareness. Many of those who practiced synch were able to remember the feeling of it long after they ceased using the machines. Some later reported that in a crisis, they could remain calm by remembering the feedback tones used in the training.

Participants in our study were asked to write about the strategies they used to keep the alpha phase-coherent feedback tones on or off. A few comments are as follows:

1. *There is a centeredness (literal) to experience. Imagery is framed with a predominance of mandala patterning. Awareness is acute.*

2. *First time—after—felt clear headed all day.*

3. *When I'm in Sync I feel nice and relaxed. When I'd start registering on the sound too much...I'd go out of Sync. I reminded myself to relax and would find my mind wandering. As long as I allowed the thoughts to flow, I seemed to remain in Sync. When becoming    aware of a thought I didn't like, I went out of Sync.*

4. *Sustained focus in nonverbal sensuality.... The tone is on when words are absent; as soon as I tell myself about it, the tone stops.*

5. *When in Sync with myself, I have no thoughts in my head. The Synch tone is very calming and I seem to blend with it. A very complete feeling.*

6. *Sustained Sync elicits a feeling of being grasped in a beam of cosmic rays, an immobilization, an electric shock of energy, like being center stage in a spotlight.*

7. *Extremely calming and centering....*

The experience of resonance is fundamental to the realms of sensuality. The pure vibrations of light and the pure hum of sound or synchronous brainwaves eliminate words and overpower verbalization, for that moment.

Musicians live in that place of sound. To be in tune and in time with the rhythms are fundamental concepts in music. Someone once asked Louis Armstrong what jazz was all about. His famous response is a classic description of the realm of sensuality: *"If you gotta ask, you'll never know."* Knowing implies that one experiences the pure hum where words do not exist. Ustad Ali Akbar Khan is a famous musician from an entirely different musical form than jazz and from a very different culture. He is a master of North Indian classical music. He once played music for us that had never been written down, but had been passed down from teacher to student from the time of Akbar the Great in the 16th century. He said this: *"Music is training for the ears, not for the eyes."* (74)

Since each of the sensory systems learns different things, the habit of modern education—of insisting that everything be verbalized—has resulted in the near-loss of some traditions such as early folk music, the ability to visualize in three dimensions, and mind-to-mind communication through space and time. In the 20th century all things had to be proved in mathematical terms, in words, through measurement by machines, or by double-blind research. The concept that we all live in a "psychic soup" of interacting mental and physical resonating systems has

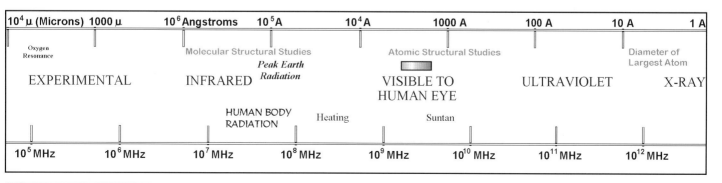

been ignored by such thinking. So the mind vibrations of the researcher have never been measured, even though s/he is considered to be "objective," that is, external to the observed. Now, of course, it can be demonstrated that we are all connected in the energy field.

Biofeedback training in *IH* phase coherence was only a preliminary part of our study, though it proved to be extremely valuable for those who practiced it. What I was most interested in was the possibility that two people might be able to synchronize their brainwaves with each other, and perhaps that would improve their telepathic attempts. As we developed the protocol for this research, we were concerned that the brainwaves of the monitor might exert an influence on those of the teams who were practicing alpha rhythms with biofeedback. Since the monitors could alter the outcome of such subtle research by being in an anxiety state, they were the first to practice biofeedback for *IH synch,* prior to measuring the EEG for any of the participants. Once they had experienced for themselves just how easily they could be distracted by sounds or movements during a brainwave biofeedback session, they were more sensitive to the needs of the other participants.

Creating a seemingly casual environment was the next priority. We were not in a lab setting with white coats. We were in an apartment with floor cushions, happy colors, and food available for hungry students. We provided mandalas for the participants to color to help them make the transition from school anxieties to the relaxed state that would be useful for their practice of *IH synch.*

Volunteers chose their own partners. The time for learning alpha synchronization was limited to one semester, so we needed to work with those who had already established some rapport. The first meeting was spent explaining the equipment and trying some preliminary telepathy trials, so the teams could decide for themselves who would play the roles of *sender* and *receiver.* That relationship remained the same throughout that first study. They did ten telepathy trials on their second session. Following

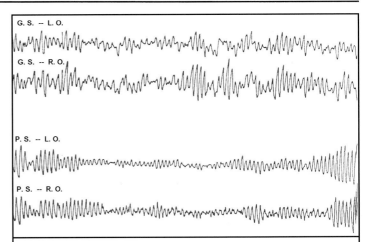

**Brainwaves can be as different as personal handwriting.**
The top two EEG signals are from the left and right occiput of one man. The bottom two EEG signals are from the left and right occiput of his wife. Their alpha rhythms have different shapes and different amplitudes.

that, there were three brainwave training sessions. Each person first practiced *IH synch* before the team practiced *IP team sync* together. After that, they did another ten telepathy trials to see if the training helped their scores. None of our original questions were answered. Many other questions surfaced, and some intriguing statistics emerged, which demanded more study. The statistical relationship between *IP team synch* and telepathy is on page 110.

Even though individual EEG records can be very different, as we have said, some couples were able to identify the percent time of their *IP team synch* and then to increase it using the biofeedback tones. Some were not able to learn this in the short time allowed. Comments made by those who were able to increase the scores of their *IP team synch* revealed the ways in which members of each team related to each other. The lovers related their experiences of synchrony to love, the musicians related their synchrony to music, and those who hoped to improve their communication and to enhance their relationship felt that biofeedback helped them to understand each other better. All participants wrote a few words about how they felt after each of the training sessions. Some of their statements are quoted here.

The young men's team were musicians who had known each other since grade school. The receiver reported:

*Relative* [simultaneous alpha in IP Synch] *is like both of us nailing our alpha level at 100%. Then it's a matter of*

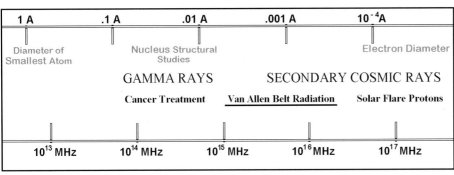

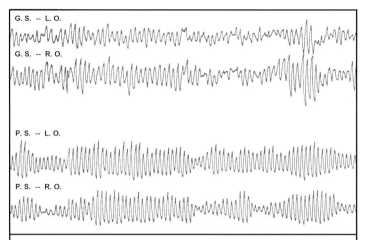

G. S. -- L. O.

G. S. -- R. O.

P. S. -- L. O.

P. S. -- R. O.

This shows the brainwaves of the same couple after they have practiced *IP* alpha phase coherence biofeedback for about twenty minutes. The amplitude of all four signals has increased and the shapes of both sets of alpha rhythms now show more similarity.

*attuning—fine-tuning—microvoltages and wave amplitudes. Experientially, once I get where we're both doing 100% alpha, then I get that he's higher or lower than I am. Then I can consciously do things like relax, deep breathe, and "be" there and raise or lower my level. I'm not clear always on what I can "do" to do absolute* [IP team synch in phase-coherent alpha]. *I am clear that efforting, trying, or working does not work to get into absolute.*

The comments above and below are from the partners of Team #4. For them the brainwave biofeedback *synch* training was similar to exploring the resonances while playing music. They approached the training as if it were a game to play, not at all like a serious experiment. Their scores, in both telepathy and *IP team synch*, were the highest of the first eleven teams. The sender of that same team gave this humorous report:

*Absolute Sync—where it is and how to get there. First, drain your mind. Then decide on a place to meet and be there. When we get together it's like perfect communion, comfortable, just exceedingly nice. It's powerful and safe. When we open our eyes we look at each other and say, "Yep." We just both got something far-out. When we are connected we can travel together, play psychic tag, and hide and go sikh* [sic].

Several teammates declared that they were deeply involved with each other romantically. For them, the *synch* experience was similar to making love. The gentleman of

one of those teams wrote this response:

*Together—feelings of love emotions and togetherness (a lot), heavy, then to light and euphoric. After-feeling was somewhat like that after love-making—calm, streaming. Good place to be.*

His partner's response added to our understanding of their methods of keeping the tones on:

*I felt really good while we were in Relative Sync* [simultaneous alpha]. *It's easy—just focus on my own balance. When we did Absolute* [phase coherence], *it felt good, too, except when I was unsure where* [partner] *was putting his focus. When we agreed on what we'd focus on, it was easier.... When he rubbed my foot and kept the sensation moving from place to place, the tone stayed on longer. Our focuses kept following the same point of touch.*

The gentleman from another loving couple said he felt the experience was:

*...similar to an Aikido exercise, projecting energy out of the forehead...appreciation for the opportunity to explore deeper levels of communication together....*

The husband from the older married couple in the 1980 study wrote that he experienced:

*...Intense focus at the heart level.... Afterwards it seems that maybe we converse more—or is it our differing opinions don't clash so much....*

The wife from the younger married couple of the 1974 study reported:

*I felt a heightened feeling of euphoria, like being able to see exactly where my relationship is—being sure of it.... A new awareness and appreciation of biofeedback.*

Some couples told us that the *synch* training had helped them learn to become more aware of each other's needs. Such experiences carried over to other aspects of their relationships. The lady of one happy team wrote about how they both felt:

*The experiment has put us in a good place together. Able to give each other our own space. I've gotten into paying more attention to my own various states. Been really good for both of us.*

When the attempt to synchronize was not successful, the reports that day would include such comments as:

*...I couldn't synchronize well with* [partner], *probably because of an interpersonal problem, now resolved.*

*Hurried. Too many things to do before Christmas. About to move.*

*My mind went wandering....*

*...I think I had too many expectations and wasn't allowing the flow.*

*My thoughts jump around in my head.*

From sixteen participants, there were only three negative reports about the *synch* training. Two people complained of headaches after long sessions, because the primitive headbands we used then were too tight. The monitors had been instructed to double-check all headbands, but on these two occasions, the participants did not complain until the session was over. One woman participated in the biofeedback training only to please her boyfriend, but she complained all the time. She said she did not like it, because it was "unnatural" to use machines to measure mental activity. However, the idea of just allowing the flow

---

Another experience of resonance between people is one of discomfort. If one person has a headache, others who are near him for any length of time may pick it up. Once I had been invited to demonstrate the *Light Sculpture* to a small group at the National Institute on Drug Abuse (NIDA). Among the group were two men who came together. One had a cold. When the other volunteered to be hooked up to the brainwave machine, I could see from his asymmetrical patterns that he had acquired a headache from his friend. I asked him if he had a headache, and he said he did, though he seemed surprised that I would know. I asked him if he would like me to take it away for him, and he smiled with great cynicism, and said, "Sure." So after removing the electrodes, I put my hands on his head to break the resonance he had with his friend. His headache went away. He looked amazed and spoke to those present, "She put her hands on my head, and my headache went away!" His belief system did not include the idea that it wasn't his to begin with, or that anyone else could change his patterns of energy. He was unprepared to hold conflicting opinions about reality, or to question his old beliefs. Later he said to me, "You really do have something *else* in mind for education, don't you?" I said, "Yes, I do." He and his friend walked away, shaking their heads from side to side indicating no comprehension.

---

was mentioned by several of the participants as being the most useful, especially those who had studied Aikido or meditation. Only the feeling of pure vibration helped keep the phase-coherent tone on. Words or analytical thinking turned off the feedback tones for individuals and for the teams.

The student monitors administered a Myers-Briggs Type Indicator to all participants of the first study (including themselves and me). (75) Several interesting synchronicities suggested unconscious experimenter influence, though the final scores were not known until the end of the semester. For example, my scores were as follows:

Sensation   = 3 —— Intuition   = 19
Judgmental = 6 —— Perceptive = 22
Thinking    = 7 —— Feeling    = 13
Extrovert   = 13 —— Introvert  = 12

Among the twenty-two people who volunteered for this study a majority of them had dominant scores similar to my own. Seventeen people were dominant in *intuition* and *perceptive*, and only five were dominant in *sensation* and *judgmental*; nineteen were dominant in *feeling* and only three were dominant in *thinking*. My scores were evenly divided in the *introvert/extrovert* scale, and eleven of the students were introverts and eleven were extroverts. (So that was the only score that the student monitors could use for their statistics class. Their results showed that those whose scores were highest in *IH relative synch* were more likely to be extroverts, and those whose scores were highest in *IH absolute synch* were more likely to be introverts.)

At the end of all sessions, we compared the average of both relative and absolute *IH synch* scores for each individual, the average relative and absolute *IP team synch* scores, and each team's telepathy scores. When we later compared the team synch scores, we found that the occurrence of simultaneous alpha rhythms for each team was random when compared with their telepathy scores. However, the overall percent time scores of alpha phase coherence between each couple showed a strong correlation with their telepathy scores. (The graphs are illustrated on the opposite page.) This was surprising since the mean of all the telepathy scores for that first study was only 23%. This could not be considered significant, because the expected score for chance alone was automatically set at 20%. (That is because five independent outside judges attempted to match the receiver's responses to the sender's responses and targets by blind matching in sets of five trials each.) The major question then was, if the telepathy results were not considered significant, why is there such a strong correlation with each team's EEG scores in phase coherence?

A more careful look at both results was needed. First James Johnston compared the *ratio* of the phase-coherent scores with the simultaneous alpha scores and found an even closer correlation. That is, instead of using the total score of phase coherence, he took *only the percent of simultaneous alpha that was in phase.* If a team has 60% alpha, and only 10% of that is in phase, then it is not as significant as if a team has 50% alpha but 20% of that is in phase. For example, the members of Team #3 were simultaneously in alpha 93% of the time, but only 11% of that was in phase. Their telepathy score was 11% below chance. The members of Team #4 were simultaneously in alpha 92% of the time and 27% of that was in phase. Their telepathy score was 36%, which is 13% above chance. The higher telepathy scores of the 1980 teams raised the average from 23% for the first eleven teams to a combined average of 25.8% for the sixteen teams. The average alpha phase-coherent ratio (APCR) for all was 18.7%. The 1974 and 1980 scores, seen together, produced a correlation coefficient of p < .001, which is statistically significant. (76)

With the equipment that we had in those years, it was not useful to measure both telepathy and *IP team sync* at the same time. The electrodes distracted the participants who were trying to receive, and the attempts to draw pictures created many artifacts in the EEG signals. We did try to take measurements during the two minutes of silent meditation, after the target was chosen and before the drawing began. However, this attempt proved futile as a means of answering any of the questions about simultaneous EEG during telepathy. Synchronizing and visualizing both seem to require an ability to focus attention intensely. It is likely that each mental process requires different patterns of focusing. The strong correlation between the two activities may be just two different ways of observing how loving couples are able to pay close attention to each other. Intention and ability to focus attention may be the only link to both events. Even with less invasive modern equipment we may never be able to pinpoint any particular frequency related to the reception of a telepathic image, because it may be received seconds before the mind brings it into awareness. Also, one receiver may become aware of hearing part of the message, another may feel a body sensation, and another may see it. Each of those perceptions are indicated in a different place in the brain. According to the reports of our participants, the experience of *IP team synch* seems to be related to touching, sensuality, music, loving feelings, Aikido. No one mentioned imaging as being associated with the biofeedback tones used for phase coherence. During telepathy receivers refer to a sudden flash, whether it is an image or another type of sensation. Perhaps it is received so rapidly that we wouldn't recognize it if we saw it in the EEG anyway.

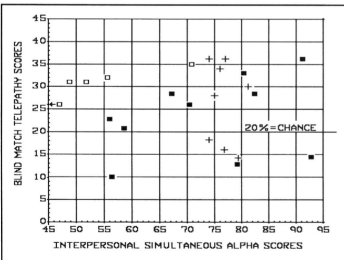 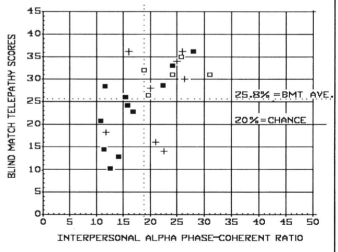

**The average blind match telepathy scores (BMT) for all 24 teams is 25.8%.   This includes 355 trials in 71 sets of 5 trials.**

| The average interpersonal simultaneous alpha scores *(IP relative)* are only random when compared with the blind match telepathy scores. (Graph above left) | The average interpersonal alpha phase-coherent ratio is 18.7% (APCR). The APCR compared with the BMT for 1974 and 1980 produced a correlation coefficient of 0.74 (P > .001), N=16. When the 1975 scores for the eight teams (distracted by EEG measurements) were added, the correlation coefficient was 0.60 ( P > .002). (Graph above right) |
|---|---|

KEY
- ■ = Teams 1 to 11, 1974
- + = Teams 4 to 10, and 2, w/EEG electrodes, 1975
- □ = Teams 12 to 16, 1980

## ENTRAINMENT WITH LIGHT

Entrainment of brainwaves means that light and/or sound in a steady rhythm can cause the brainwaves of a person to produce the same or harmonic rhythm. Our equipment was not programmed at that time to record the possibility of harmonics between people, though I had observed some events that would be interesting to explore further. One person might be producing 20 Hz and the teammate is actually producing 10 Hz, while they subjectively feel in perfect harmony with each other.

There were machines being developed then which advertised that they would drive the alpha rhythm, and therefore they could put people into a state of relaxation. For example: A machine that used blinking lights and sounds was being demonstrated and sold (at a very inflated price), because the seller made many claims about the healing effects related to reduction of stress due to the entrainment of the user's alpha rhythm. There was no point to the seller's attempt to prove the effects of the machine on me, because I could produce alpha rhythms at any time, and under almost any circumstances. I could even block the effects of the light, through years of having practiced my ability to focus attention in different ways. So Johnston, who had programmed the Langley Porter EEG equipment to run our 1980 study, agreed to meet me at the Washington Research Institute after work to check it out. To get there he drove from Palo Alto to San Francisco. When he arrived, after more than an hour of maneuvering through Bay Area rush hour traffic, the expensive machine did ***not*** put him into alpha, as advertised. Since we were able to measure the actual effects of the blinking lights on his brainwaves with our equipment at the same time, we could see the differences. His brainwaves were in the fast beta range (around 19 Hz, as one would expect after a rush-hour drive), even though the lights were flashing in his eyes at 10 Hz. There was also a shooshing sound that was auto-matically set to produce the same rhythm as the lights. However, when I adjusted the frequency of the lights and sounds to synchronize with Johnston's own frequencies, his brainwaves suddenly dropped into half the speed (into the alpha range at 9.5 Hz), even though the flashing lights were still set in the faster frequencies. That experience strongly suggests that the brainwaves of two people might also lock into a harmonic resonance.

When you use a machine to induce your alpha brainwaves rather than finding your own natural resting frequency through biofeedback, you can encounter several problems with certain frequencies and certain colors of blinking lights. Those highly touted instruments which assume that you will be relaxed or that your visual system will be stimulated to project many colorful hallucinations may or may not perform as advertised. The assumption does not always hold true, because they don't start out by matching your own particular resting frequency. Most of the machines attempt to drive the EEG into one of their own predetermined set frequencies. Barbara Brown, PhD, observed sudden shifts in the EEG patterns of a subject as a response to a flashing light when the color of the light was changed. (77) She reported that one person's EEG was twice the flashing frequency of a green light. When the light was changed to red, the brainwaves immediately began following the light at the same rate. She also recorded the brainwaves of another subject, "whose brainwaves following a flashing blue light were better in the right cerebral hemisphere, but when the flashing light was red, the brainwaves of the left cerebral hemisphere followed the flashing frequency more accurately."

We were interested in just what people saw when a light was flashed, in brainwave range, on their closed eyelids. Not wanting to hurt anyone's eyes, I chose to use an 8-mm. variable-speed movie projector rather than a strobe light. The strobe light is a cold light, intensely bright, and it is off more than it is on when it is flashing. The old movie projector has a warm light, and it is on more than it is off when it is running (we used only the light and did not run any movies during this experiment). [The old movies were shown at 18 frames per second (FPS) which was

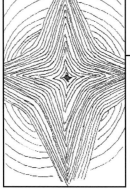

At left is a drawing by Rich Miller in response to 14 FPS. This suggests the interference wave form pattern that is common with this frequency.

On the left is a drawing by B. Crisp Kinemitsu in response to 12 FPS.

On the right is a drawing by Allan Roshlind in response to 10 FPS. He writes, "Patterns are moving constantly. Impossible to draw."

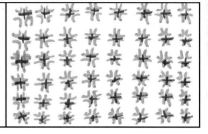

barely fast enough to give the sensation of movement to the individual still frames. When a sound track was added to the edge of the film, the speed was increased to 24 FPS.] The lines on a TV screen move very rapidly to create an image, but the whole picture changes at the rate of 30 FPS. This causes the brainwaves of some people to become entrained. They can be hypnotized into becoming addicted to TV. The results of this type of resonance are discussed further in Chapter Six.

Over a period of a few years, I found one hundred students willing to volunteer for this project. Using the old movie projector, I asked them to tell me when they "saw" something and to draw whatever that was, as well as they could. The results of that study demonstrated that many people do respond in similar ways to certain frequency ranges. From my collection of drawings over the years, a pattern of vision emerged. Even though each drawing was unique, certain types of patterns were relatively common:

1) When the flicker rate was in the slower, lower theta, delta range (between 1 and 5 FPS), the patterns seemed to be large masses of red against large masses of dark blue or green. Both masses seemed to be amorphous shapes.

2) When the flicker rate was in the beta range (between 13 and 16 FPS), the patterns were drawn with only one color, either red or black. They looked like interference waveform patterns (see opposite page). By 18 FPS the patterns disappeared into a light that seemed almost steady.

3) When the flicker rate was in the alpha, upper theta range (between 6 and 12 FPS), mandala-like patterns would be drawn. Descriptions of moving reciprocal dots, going from dark to light, were provided (illustrated below). This range was the one most students identified when asked to "tell me when you see something." So most of my examples are from that frequency range. The drawings were made with colored marking pens on 5" x 7" cards in a classroom setting. There was only time for students to make quick sketches, just to indicate the type of imagery. I have included a typical example of student's drawings from each range of FPS. (below).

Even though occasionally another image from other mental processes (e.g., a cup of coffee and a donut) might be superimposed over the typical drawing of the mandala, the similarities of drawings in response to flashes of light in the brainwave range of the resting pattern of the eye suggests to me that the eye might be looking at its own structure. We may be projecting what we are looking **at** from the structure we are looking **with**, just as when you close down the lens of a slide projector, the filament of the bulb can be seen on the wall. The rods and cones of the eye may be responding in turn to the on/off cycle of the flashing light. Forms similar to the designs from the flashing lights are seen in religious designs around the world. The symmetrical mandala is widely used. No doubt we respond to such patterns because they resonate with the matrix of our own vision. Other remarkable examples come from the work of M. C. Escher. (78) He has integrated equal patterns of light and dark in his etchings to represent people and animals. One especially remarkable mandala of his is the working of devils and angels together. On first look, some people see only the white angels, and others see only the black devils. Eventually, they find that the two images are blended together in one design. Perhaps that is another example of how such images are paired as we have seen them in our telepathic responses.

In a report in the *Association for Humanistic Psychology: Perspective,* Raymond Gottlieb, PhD, OD, describes how light can be used in healing. (79) He claims that the breakthroughs in science, technology, and medicine in the 21st century will be about light. His own research using diffuse light on the eyes and coherent light on the body of his patients demonstrated positive physiological effects. Following are a few excerpts from this excellent article:

The emergence of colored light therapy is just around the corner.... Light's impact on biology and medicine has been conjectured for centuries, but photochemistry has taken a back seat to physical chemistry except in the obvious area of botany.... But over the last three decades discoveries in nonlinear quantum photobiology have been occurring at an increasing rate—self-targeting, self-tunneling,

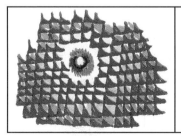

On the left is part of a series of drawings by Mike Mulhaney. This one is in response to 8 FPS. He writes: "I can't come close to reproducing what I saw. One recurring pattern was like this."

On the left is a drawing by Larissa Vilenskaya in response to 6 FPS. The sense of the light/dark reciprocal patterns seen here was the most frequent response to the FPS range between 9 and 6.

soliton sound/light waves, DNA as a coherent light source, the cell as a light computer, electromagnetic vibrations as the primary signal for inter-cellular communication. There are even optical models of the brain that meld spirit and matter....

In Russia, light therapy has been found to dramatically improve healing and reduce side effects in life-threatening diseases. Gottlieb reports on the Russian research as well:

> Ultraviolet light injected into the lungs using needles and fiber optics has been found to be twice as effective as drug therapy in curing pulmonary tuberculosis, without side effects, if treated early. The same results for diphtheria using red laser light shined into blood vessels. Red light was found to heal intractable lesions such as stomach ulcers over 95% of the time without the use of antibiotics or other drugs....

Gottlieb is the Dean of the College of Syntonic Optometry, a pioneering group promoting light therapy in the United States. Syntonic optometrists will prescribe a formula of colored filters for each patient. These are placed in a phototherapy device, and the patient is asked to look into it for twenty-minute periods several times a week, usually for about six weeks. I personally watched Gottlieb work with a young boy whose vision improved dramatically. Gottlieb describes some of the results of this light therapy:

> Behavioral optometrists using syntonic phototherapy (the optometric equivalent of humanistic psychologists) successfully treat children and adults with learning, reading and attention disabilities, people suffering the effects of head trauma and stroke, retinal diseases, cross eyes, headaches and senility. Syntonists could supply thousands of examples of successful case histories. I have included two dramatic ones here from my practice:
>
> A 78-year-old woman patient came to me for double vision. Her eyes suddenly went crossed eight weeks earlier. In addition, she was mentally confused and emotionally distraught and had been since the death of her husband ten months before. After twelve 20-minute treatments, her eyes had straightened and she regained mental/emotional balance and coherence. When I asked her what she thought had helped her get better, she said, "...Every time I watched the green light I could feel things changing inside my head until one time there was a kind of pop and everything became clear."

> Another patient, a six-year-old girl, was on the verge of being kicked out of her school into a special school because she could not learn and was disrupting her class. She was diagnosed as autistic and retarded from an early age and was so hyperactive that I could not even examine her eyes. Her history included a toxic pregnancy, cord wrapped around her neck at birth, and her father was run down and killed in a crosswalk a few feet in front of her when she was two. We started her immediately on syntonic color therapy using yellow-green filters to eliminate any toxemia that might have remained from the pregnancy. The results were astounding. In five treatments she had become a calm, cooperative and communicative little girl who could learn and participate in her normal first-grade class....

> Psychotherapeutic application of light has gone far beyond using bright white light for treating winter depression.... Texas psychotherapist Dr. Steven Vasquez has pioneered an approach he calls *Brief Strobic Phototherapy.* He uses flashing colored light along with therapeutic dialogue and reports dramatic success with depression, panic attacks, rage, dependent behavior, grief, anxiety, post trauma, shame, guilt, obsessive thoughts and MPD. He chooses the initial color based on his patients' presenting symptoms and then applies other colors and strobe rates as patients express unresolved issues during the therapy. Vasquez finds that the effects of colored lights linger for days after therapy sessions and that the strobe puts the patients into trance states....

Trance states can be used as an important part of healing today, just as they were thousands of years ago, when the medicine man wore deer antlers instead of a white coat. In some tribes, the clan mothers performed the medicine ceremonies to induce trance states. In Chapter Five, we discuss various forms of trance and the information that trance makes available. It may come to us in metaphor, and so we need to learn how to interpret our own symbols, our own internal metaphors.

The Native American shaman Joseph Rael said, "Everything is metaphor and is a resonating energy of the Great Spirit." (80) This also suggests that our minds are forms of light energy. The concept of light includes not only the visible spectrum, but the entire electromagnetic spectrum that comes from the sun, the reflections from water and air, the heat from the Earth, and the forms of radiant energy that we produce. These are all forms of light.

We found we could introduce students directly to their own resonating energy of light using *The Stereo Brainwave Biofeedback Light Sculpture* and various other biofeedback devices. They could see immediately that the electrical activity of their thoughts and emotions not only changed the color of the lights, but also affected their muscles, changed the level of their skin conductance, and raised or lowered their skin temperature. Scully adapted biofeedback of EMG to the early Atari video pong game. One student with an attention deficit problem was able to focus attention on the pong game for longer periods of time each class period, "because I want to see if my right eyebrow can beat my left hand." Another feedback machine controlled the forward or backward movement of an electric train when skin temperature was raised or lowered.

From my own experiences teaching various levels of students, I believe that the fifth grade is the best place to start with biofeedback using the "self-discovery model" (rather than the "get-well model" used by doctors and therapists). The students already know the problems associated with grades. The ones at the lower end of the grade point average begin to feel inferior and lose self-confidence, or worse, give up on school altogether. When they begin to establish their self-esteem on the basis of their ability to cause social problems instead of on their ability to learn how to become good citizens, then the educational system has already lost them to the welfare or corrections departments. This is more costly to the community than it would have been to provide a good education earlier. The issue of the importance of self-esteem has been criticized on this difference in interpretation. The importance of establishing a child's self-esteem as a productive, creative citizen of the community cannot begin too early in life.

One winter I had an opportunity to serve as a substitute teacher in a fifth-grade classroom. I was delighted and brought several types of biofeedback instruments with me, including the *Light Sculpture*. (81) Here is a story about a fifth-grade boy from that class:

Gary was a hyperactive child who was wonderful at kickball. He created a constant distraction during class, as though he were always on stage. Many of the children laughed at his pranks; others were annoyed. His reading ability was nearly third-grade level. When I took the class to the library to choose a book for a report, the only book Gary would consider was a story about a sports hero (in large type). When I suggested another story, he refused, saying, "No! Sports have to be my life. If I'm not picked up by the majors by the time I'm out of school, I'm going

to commit suicide." His self-esteem about sports hid his fear about his lack of academic ability. He felt he had been branded as dumb, and that his only chance of success in life would be as an athlete. When I announced that book reports were due on Friday, Gary complained that he absolutely needed two weeks to finish his book and to write a report. (I knew his parents were getting a divorce and that his home was not a peaceful place to study at this time.) Nevertheless, I insisted that reports were due on Friday.

After lunch the same day, it was Gary's turn to see his brainwaves in the *Light Sculpture*. As soon as he was properly connected to the electrodes, I sat beside him and softly suggested to him, "If you could learn to focus your attention, you could become a genius. Do you believe that?" He shook his head. It was obvious he didn't believe that. I pointed to one of the dials on the brainwave analyzer (which was continuously fluctuating widely, as one might expect of the EEG of a hyperactive child). I tuned the machine to provide a feedback tone in the beta rhythm (13 Hz to 20 Hz). The percentage of beta rhythms showing was about 30%. I said, "See if you can raise the number on this dial by focusing a lot of attention on it." Gary managed to raise his percentage of beta to 60%, and the next day he came to me with great personal pride and excitement. "Dr. Millay! Dr. Millay! I finished the book in two hours!" For the first time in his life he discovered that he could gain voluntary control over his mind. No one could ever convince him again that he was just born dumb and that there was nothing more he could do about it.

By the time children leave the security of a one-teacher classroom and move into junior high school, they are already classified into higher or lower groups according to their test scores. However I have seen that good students, through biofeedback training, can move into the gifted classes, average students can begin to make the honor roll, and hyperactive students discover that they can learn to focus and improve their performances. Once children learn to raise and lower their skin temperatures, relax tense muscles, gain voluntary control over skin conductance and brainwaves, no one can convince them they are stupid. Another benefit is that biofeedback will introduce students to their electromagnetic dimensions which may or may not be a "wiggle on the fifth dimension" (as one prominent physicist reportedly called it), but as we gain voluntary control, we will have learned something about our multidimensional minds. Biofeedback can help us identify ourselves as radiant light energy beings, shining in a radiant light energy universe. It is amazing how knowing this raises our real self-esteem.

## ENTRAINMENT WITH SOUND

Sound waves are not electromagnetic, though they can be converted into light and back again into sound. (Consider the soundtrack on a strip of movie film, or the digitized picture of sound that can be manipulated through the computer.) Sound has a very powerful effect on consciousness, because we can be entrained by it. Plato said that music is the organizing function of the mind. Recent research has shown that classical music (especially Mozart) played for infants has a positive effect on the development of intelligence. (82) A continuous drum beat has been used for uncounted centuries to create trance states. Drums and rattles are major tools of ancient and contemporary shamans and are used for healing ceremonies. On the negative side, when junior high students were allowed to play records on the last day of school, two ethnic groups disagreed over the kind of music that would be played and became violent. A third group, who preferred songs about peace and love, climbed out the window to avoid being hit by flying chairs.

In his book *Planet Drum,* Mickey Hart, drummer with the Grateful Dead, gives us the following: (83)

> Rhythm is anything that repeats itself in time: the moon cycling around the Earth, the sap rising in the spring, the pulsing of arteries in the body.
> Science knows one big thing about rhythm, something it calls the law of entrainment. Discovered by the Dutch scientist Christian Huygens in 1665, the law of entrainment holds that if two rhythms are nearly the same and their sources are in close proximity, they will always lock up, fall into synchrony, entrain. Why? The best theory is that nature is efficient and it takes less energy to pulse together than in opposition.
> Because we are a part of nature, it is likely that we are entrained with the larger planetary and universal rhythms that surround us.
> Our word *religion* comes from the Latin and means *"to bind together."* A successful religion is one that binds together all the fundamental rhythms that each of us experiences: The personal rhythm of the human body, the larger social rhythm of the family, tribe, or nation, and the enveloping cosmic rhythms of the planet and universe. If a religion "works," its followers are rewarded by a new dimension of rhythm and time—the sacred....
> In ancient China, Confucius said that music is basic to human nature. In Africa today they say that a village without music is a dead place. In most

Western popular music, spontaneity has been lost in favor of preprogrammed offerings. World music—and the percussive impulse that drives it—reaches past the need of the marketplace to sell, into emotional and spiritual dialogue with older oral traditions.

What we call *world music* really is all the world's music. It's a reflection of our dreams, our lives, and it represents every fiber of our beings. It's an aural soundscape, a language of the deepest emotions; it's what we sound like as a people. The excitement that we feel when we hear it tells us that the door into the realm of the spirit is opening. It's a romance of the ear. It's our musical skeleton key.

Underneath the world's extraordinary musical diversity is another, deeper realm in which there is no better or worse, no modern or primitive, no art music versus folk music, no distinctions at all, but rather an almost organic compulsion to translate the emotional fact of being alive into sound, into rhythm, into something you can dance to....

Ustad Ali Akbar Khan, master of North Indian classical music, told us that in ancient times in India, the doctor would cure people by giving herbal tea, singing and playing ragas to evoke a spiritual state of mind. The ragas (musical scales) and talas (rhythm cycles) are tuned to six different times of year (e.g., monsoon season, spring, etc.) and to four times of day (morning, afternoon, evening, and late night). "The tones of the ragas change according to the earth movement, and also according to the mind and body and soul.... Sound is tuned to the universal harmonies of your mind and body and soul—that's pure vibration. It is the language of God." (84)

However, while the ancient system of North Indian classical music has determined which rhythms and musical scales are appropriate to universal harmonies for healing and meditation, there are some rhythms that are considered to be destructive and inharmonious. I had an opportunity to learn about this in 1967. Ravi Shankar, Alla Rakha, and Amiya das Gupta had given a magnificent afternoon performance at the Monterey Pop Festival. The whole audience felt the sense of spiritual oneness. Later, when the musicians were watching the evening's performances, Jimi Hendrix set fire to his guitar. This was shocking to many of us, and even more so for those who respect their instruments as being sacred so they will help produce sacred music. When The Who began to play, the musicians from India looked at each other and expressed grave concern. They tapped out the rhythm on their knees and spoke rapidly in Hindi. I asked what was the problem. Amiya das Gupta said, "These are *very destructive rhythms.* They could ruin a whole generation of young people."(85) Soon after that, The Who deliberately broke their instruments on the stage. As a group, the Indians stood up and walked out. Deep shock and horror was expressed on all their faces.

Osteopathic physicians Cheri Quincy and Joel Alter have provided us with a medical model of the brain and bone conduction of sound to explain how sound influences trance states. Shamans, medicine men or women, and other healers through the ages used the drum, rattle, gong, bell as sonic drivers to heal their patients. Quincy and Alter write about sonic resonance and its interactions with the dynamics of cerebral spinal fluid in relation to focus of attention and altered states of consciousness. Their paper was published in the *Proceedings of the Third International Conference on the Study of Shamanism and Alternate Modes of Healing.* (86) Following are excerpts from that article:

> We propose that the dynamic responses to sonic (mechanical) resonances by the structures of the cranium, brain, and cerebrospinal fluid have a significant and profound effect on individual states of consciousness and our ability to "tune" or focus attention.
>
> The predictable and reproducible subjective effects of some sounds may be mediated through their mechanical, vibratory and/or resonant actions on the structures of the human body. In particular, certain states of consciousness may be elicited or "permitted," according to the resonant qualities of the cranial bones, and spine, and the vibrations of the intracranial membranes.
>
> Since the cranial bones have been noted to be in a state of oscillation with a period of 6-12 cycles per minute, the interaction between this pulsatile, low pressure, irregularly shaped elastic balloon, within a flexible bony chamber, and external mechanical/sonic vibratory stimuli must be complex. The resulting effects of intersecting waves depend on many factors which include angle of interaction, medium, energy, relative wave lengths, time, etc., but account for phenomena from holography to polarized lenses and rainbows....
>
> *The cranial concept* was first described by Dr. William Garner Sutherland (1873-1954), an osteopathic physician. He observed and studied the bones of the skull. The edges of the bones were beveled or designed like hinges and pivots, indicating to him that they were formed to permit slight movement. This led to the observation of five physiological phenomena:
>
> 1. The inherent motility of the brain and spinal cord,
> 2. the fluctuation (tidal flow of movement) of the cerebrospinal fluid,
> 3. the mobility of the reciprocal tension membrane *(dura mater)* within the skull and spine,
> 4. the articular mobility of the cranial bones, and
> 5. the involuntary mobility of the sacrum between the *ilia.*
>
> It is the harmonious function of all of these units of the Primary Respiratory Mechanism which can be characterized as system in motion that maintains health. The craniosacral system is characterized by rhythmic, mobile activity, which persists through life. The craniosacral motion occurs in humans, other primates, canines, felines and probably all other vertebrates. It is distinctly different from the physiological motions which are related to breathing and cardiovascular activity....
>
> The normal rate of craniosacral rhythm in humans is between 6 and 12 cycles per minute....

(Author's note: This is not to be confused with the alpha rhythm from the brain, which has a range between 8 and 12 cycles per second.) Quincy and Alter also relate this craniosacral rhythm to mental health:

> Changes in frequency have been noted to correlate with psychiatric syndromes and normalization with improvement or cure. Various practitioners have reported changes in speed and amplitude with varying states of physical and mental health. For example, hyperkinetic children have been observed to have abnormally rapid craniosacral rhythmic rates, as have patients suffering from acute illnesses and fever. Moribund and brain-damaged patients will often have abnormally low rates. As the clinical condition improves, the rhythmic rates move toward the normal range. Under normal circumstances, the rate of the craniosacral motion is quite stable. It does not fluctuate with cardiovascular or respiratory rates (e.g., in response to exercise)....
>
> We believe that the effects of such stimuli are not mediated by the neuro-auditory apparatus alone, but profoundly affect the entire neuro-phys-

iological milieu directly through their effects on the craniosacral mechanism, the reciprocal tension membrane, and the tide and flow of the cerebrospinal fluid (csf). The production of interference patterns or the redirection of fluid flow, and perhaps the production of new harmonics or resonances, can be hypothesized to contribute to the profound effects of sound on the state of consciousness of the individual receiving it. Awareness of these effects is apparent in the phrase *"sonic driving,"* used to describe the effects of shamanistic drumming or rattling on trance subjects....

We propose that sonic driving interacts with the craniosacral mechanism in a mechanical, vibratory way to produce its effects.... Other external sonic or oscillation fields may interact with this primary neuro-physiological mechanism as well. Research has yet to explain the mechanism by which electromagnetic fields affect biological systems or how geologic frequencies interact with human behavior. Perhaps the interaction between the external vibratory environment and the internal resonant environment, mediated by the flexibility and structure of the antenna (our bodies), may help to explain the production of naturally occurring "altered states."...

We believe that the combination of cranial osteopathy—subtle adjustment and balancing of the craniosacral mechanism—affects the rhythm played by the reciprocal tension membrane, in the way that frets tune a guitar. The synchronistic application of structural tuning and a clear carrier wave achieved through sonic driving can be beneficial when applied to individuals who are in various states of health. One can change one's response to stress, discharge energy or amplify it, can tune to frequencies of vibrations not yet heard (i.e., overtones), and may allow states of consciousness, restricted previously, resulting in healing....

The Quincy/Alter descriptions of the dura mater in the brain and how it and cerebrospinal fluid respond to sound provide a scientific basis for exploring brain resonance with sound in your own way. For myself, once the *Light Sculpture* had been created, I had a chance to play with it for some time. It had been designed to find a possible synchronization between the alpha rhythms of two people. But long before the phase comparator was developed to do that, I explored the variations in frequency between both sides of my own head in 1973. One evening, while listening to a record of Ravi Shankar and Alla Rakha, I was practicing alpha feedback with the direct warbling tones,

rather than with the already analyzed, and categorized, steady tones. I felt that I had moved into a deeper state and suddenly realized that both warbling tones were in the exact frequency of the tabla (drum) rhythm (fast teental) that Alla Rakha was playing. It was around 8 Hz. The fingers of both his hands were moving on those two drums as rapidly as eight times per second. And each beat was distinct. From that moment on, I was determined to research synchronization because of the extraordinary state of mind which accompanied it.

On one occasion, we were offering a group meditation at the Glide Memorial Church in San Francisco, on an evening when the church could be rented. Wavy Gravy agreed to be master of ceremonies. Four musicians from the Ali Akbar Khan College of Music agreed to play for us. Rolling Thunder, the shaman from Nevada, led the meditation when the concert finished. We originally planned to send a telepathic message to Krippner's group at the AHP conference in Hawaii, but too many unexpected things went wrong. However, one opportunity for research still presented itself. Don Kantor agreed to be hooked up to the *Stereo Brainwave Biofeedback Light Sculpture* while sitting on the stage, in yoga position, during the concert. The audience could see the colored mandala patterns of his brainwaves. The blue lights of the alpha patterns predominated as he meditated. Then the red lights of the theta rhythms began to appear as brief flashes. Since Kantor was facing the audience, with his eyes closed most of the time, he did not see the *Light Sculpture,* which was behind him, and so he was not receiving the light or the sound feedback. While the blue of the alpha rhythm was still dominant, some dimension of his brain was keeping time to the music. His brainwaves were not matching every note of the tabla, as I had observed my alpha rhythms to do: This was a larger-amplitude, lower-frequency (theta) flash which occurred only with the downbeat of the drum, and simultaneously with it. Both the blue alpha patterns and half of the red theta pattern that appeared during the concert as Kantor's brain anticipated the rhythm of the music are illustrated on page 10.

We resonate with the rhythm of each different type of music and each different type of group activity. For those of us who are old enough to remember, resonance also has its dark side. It was frightening to watch the thousands of soldiers and citizens all shouting in unison, "Heil Hitler!" We have seen the thousands of Chinese children waving their red flags, innocently cheering the murderous Red Guard. We have seen crowds of people, who may have originally gathered for a peaceful protest, brutalized by uniformed squads. They then turned into a raging mob, throwing rocks and bottles, breaking windows, turning over automobiles and burning them. Rioters and others who choose violence also have their resonance.

It is fairly easy to meditate when you have a comfortable and quiet space to do this. When you live in a tenement, surrounded by screaming, sometimes hungry people, dealers of dangerous drugs, and their addicted customers, anger and fear may naturally give rise to the music of anger and violence—the dark side of creative expression. It, in turn, provides a resonance to encourage more of those feelings among the young people. The destructive rhythms that Ravi Shankar (from his lifetime of study) knew could ruin a whole generation of young people began to take their toll. The music and lyrics that often shock adults in their comfortable environments are statements about the dangerous imbalance that grows between the rich and the poor, and the rage that such imbalance engenders. Real education among all social classes about multidimensional consciousness is long overdue.

However, concepts about consciousness are growing in the West since the Sixties as the interest in meditation has encouraged a form of music to resonate with peaceful contemplation. In the Seventies, a meditation teacher, Harish Johari, produced "The Song of Breath." It was distributed only through his ashrams in Berkeley, West Germany, and Upper Pradesh in India. Gradually other musicians, such as Deuter (Germany), Himekami (Japan), Oser, Raphael, Howell with Megabrain (US), and others developed a genre that came to be called "New Age music."

The influence of meditation music from India, especially, has been profound. At first the blend was uncomfortable, with guitars trying to play ragas, and sitars or tablas added to rock. But after thirty years of international interaction among musicians, we are approaching what could be called a Golden Age of world sound, not limited to any one civilization. The late Jerry Garcia, one of the world's finest guitar players devoted to rock and roll and country music, recorded his last tapes with Sunjay Mishra in a marvelous blend of the musical cultures—an expression of world music. Garcia, of course, was well-loved by the numerous fans of the Grateful Dead. When the Dead played concerts for 30,000 people or more, everyone moved in time to the music. This was a social phenomenon of resonance that no machine could measure. So much love from the audience poured out to the band and to Garcia, who channeled it all back to them, that just being one among 30,000 people was enough to feel the power of the

charismatic presence. When Garcia graduated from Earth school, people all over the world mourned his passing. His music touched all generations, all social classes—from the White House to the homeless. Those who have identified themselves as "Deadheads" still feel like a special family.

Rock and roll music swept across the world, and along with it the black market for blue jeans infiltrated the communist countries long before the Cold War ended. While James Hickman was able to visit the USSR, he found underground rock groups playing in Moscow. When Gorbachev introduced glasnost, Hickman helped organize one of the very first satellite connections between that rock band in Moscow and an outdoor rock concert in Southern California. The Moscow band was willing to play at midnight, so the audience at a concert in LA could dance to their music, broadcast on an extra-large TV screen. When the satellite moved around again, the group in Moscow could dance to the music from LA. Hickman invited astronauts and cosmonauts to talk to each other about their shared experiences in outer space. Very little of this was covered by the media. One hundred thousand people had attended the US Festival in 1982. What did the media mention? A couple of drunks got into a fight outside the gate. It was the fight that the press covered. The international talks about peace, the opportunity to share music on both sides of the planet, the technology which allowed teachers and students to share ideas and experiences directly were ignored by the media. The event promoted peace between the two most powerful nations, yet it was still politically incorrect, apparently, to show such a peaceful interaction on national TV. Since it had been only a short time before that the President of the United States had called that nation "The Evil Empire," only PBS was willing to show a much shortened video tape of the event afterwards.

By the 1996 Olympics in Atlanta, Mickey Hart (of Grateful Dead fame) joined forces with Zakir Hussain (son of Alla Rakha, master of North Indian classical rhythms). Together they produced an event that included famous drummers from around the world. It was a stirring performance. Every region was represented, including Japan, China, Pacific Islands, India, Europe, the US, several nations of the Middle East, several nations of South America, and tribes of Native Americans.

It is the resonance of world music that can bring people from all cultures together, and entrain them into moments of shared reality. And it is the ethnic music of each culture that helps maintain the range of individual identity. Both types of resonance are essential to humanity.

## ENTRAINMENT WITH OTHER TYPES
## OF RESONANCES

In the 1970s Bob Beck designed a magnetic field device that could be regulated to produce different frequencies. He also designed his own brainwave monitors, but in a different way than Scully had designed the analyzers that we used in our research. Beck's machine averaged the signal, rather than compare two separate signals. Beck also had a frequency detector that could read out the exact frequency being produced, such as 9.4 Hz, or 10.3 Hz. When I had established my dominant alpha holding pattern, he adjusted his magnetic field device to the same frequency, and then slowly turned his magnetic frequency generator to lower frequencies until it reached 8 Hz. My own brainwaves followed that, and I could feel the shift in my level of awareness, even though I was not watching what he had done. The sound Beck used for brainwave biofeedback was also different from the warbling tones that Scully used. Beck's machine produced continuous tones that gradually moved lower in relationship to the slower brain frequencies, and higher for the faster ones. In this way, I was able to pinpoint my own trance state when my alpha rhythms shifted from the louder (high-amplitude), lower (slow), steady tones and slid into the softer (low-amplitude), higher (fast frequency) tones as I moved into trance. (Once fully in trance, I paid no attention to the feedback, but since I had already identified the state with the shift in frequency, I could use biofeedback to attain that state again.) Trance will be discussed in more detail in the next chapter.

Later at the WRI, we planned to study the effects that a stronger magnetic field might have on the electrical activity of the brain. We used a device which could vary the frequencies of the magnetic pulsations, and planned to measure the brainwaves as this occurred. However, the frequencies of the magnetic pulsations drove the responses of the brainwave analyzers directly through the electrodes, whether they were attached to the scalp or not. Therefore, it was impossible to tell how the electrical activity of the brain itself might be forcibly changed by the magnetic field. Ideally, new equipment and better shielding will make it possible for such a study to be done.

We also wondered if spirits might be able to interact with magnetic material. This type of research is, of course, extremely controversial, yet there has been anecdotal evidence that suggests this might be a possibility. One séance was done in the presence of a large magnetometer. When the medium and those present seemed to experience the arrival of the spirit, the pen on the magnetometer moved so

vigorously by itself that it was thrown off the scale. The man who was monitoring the magnetometer did not want to break the focus of the group to reset the pen, so they did not obtain a measure of just how much magnetic disturbance had occurred on that occasion. This was, of course, disappointing, but in such experiences it is always difficult to judge when too much focus on the measuring devices might or might not prevent the event that one is trying to measure. It has happened. On this occasion, the answers given through the medium were enough to convince those present that it was indeed the spirit of their friend. The man had died suddenly and wanted so much to speak to his friends that he had "haunted" the medium for several days. Though the medium had met the man earlier, she was not among his close friends. She was just the one who was open enough to receive the information, and had therefore called the people he really wanted to communicate with to a meeting so they could help put his spirit to rest. This did seem to occur, and she was no longer haunted by him.

Once, Espiritista Joaquim Posé attempted to channel a drawing on a computer from an artist spirit; however, during the save operation, the magnetic floppy disk was totally scrambled. I had to turn off the computer, restart it, and re-format the disk. After all that, the spirit told us that he had scrambled the disk because he did not like the way the drawing looked on the computer, and he did not wish to participate further. At that time, a different spirit introduced himself and told me that I should write a book for children about the spirit world. Part of it was dictated right then and written on the newly formatted disk. The book, however, was never finished.

John Klimo, PhD, has reported on a process called EVP (electronic voice phenomena). (87) This is an attempt to capture the voice of spirits on magnetic audio tape. I find some of the sounds purportedly recorded in this way extremely difficult to understand, but others are clear.

Janet Penrose, a resident of Santa Barbara, California, sent me a tape recording made on her answering machine after her friend Louise had died. Her story is as follows:

She and Louise shared a similar nerve degeneration disease. They often talked to each other for hours on the phone, never answering with the usual "Hello," when they knew who the caller would be, but with a short "Ah huh." As Louise became ill with other complications as well, she was moved to a hospital at UCLA Medical Center, hoping to get a liver transplant. Since that was not possible, Louise was dying. Janet went to the hospital and stayed by her friend throughout her final hours. Louise's parents and other relatives came as well, so Janet went out to her car to take a nap. She felt she was awakened out of a sound sleep by her friend telling her that she had died. When she went back into the hospital some of the life support machines were already disconnected. Nevertheless, Janet chose to lay in the bed beside Louise for about an hour to hold her and talk to her. Even though Louise could no longer speak, Janet talked to her in loving tones until the nurse came in to pull the rest of the plugs. However, Janet continued to talk while tears rolled down her face. And then even the nurse could see that tears were rolling down Louise's face, as well. The hospital staff delayed releasing the body to Louise's father because of their concern about the tears she had shed after she had been pronounced dead. The grieving Janet drove home to Santa Barbara, knowing that she had done all she could do for her friend. She returned to find messages on her answering machine. One message was the *very faint, "Ah huh"* that Janet identified as from Louise. The concept that an answering machine could register a message being sent by Louise is more amazing than the message, if indeed that is what it was. The next message on the tape was Janet's voice telling her niece that she would be home soon. One other message was from someone at the ICU unit at UCLA wanting to find Louise's parents so they could finally release the body to the funeral home.

It is a common experience among humans that our dying loved ones want to let us know, even though we might be far away. My first such experience was when my grandfather died in a hospital in Reno, and I felt his presence in San Francisco. This event happened over forty years ago, and I didn't know how to just relax and let his spirit talk to me. Now, however, I can allow and welcome a conversation with a friend who has graduated from Earth school. At that time, however, I felt an urgent need to talk to my grandfather so strongly that I put in a long-distance phone call immediately to his home in Wabuska, Nevada. There was no answer, but a cousin came on the party line to tell me that he had been taken to a hospital in Reno. I made two person-to-person calls to both hospitals and finally found where he was. The hospital operator said, "He just expired, but his daughter is here if you want to speak to her." I had not yet been told that grandpa had a heart attack, or that my mother had gone to his side. Mother came to the phone and her first words were, "How did you know to call right at this time?" In those days, I was reluctant to say, "Grandpa told me." But this experience was the beginning of a life-long study of such events. The next day, I drove to Reno to be with the family at such a time. Since then, many have spoken to me within hours or days of their departure.

People in various civilizations all over the world are free to speak to the spirits of their ancestors. They can invite them to family events, and include them in their family decisions. Somewhere along the line during the past centuries it had become politically, scientifically, and religiously incorrect to do so in so-called enlightened scientific societies. For those of us who have no problems talking to grandfathers and grandmothers, it is time to come out of the closet. Some ancestors have gone "into the light" and may not care about the current generation, but many are quite curious about the evolution or devolution and the different ways of life their progeny choose to take, and how they manage the events that confront them.

The electrical activity (light) of the brain is judged to be the legal sign of life. When the brainwave stops, the light of life is assumed to be gone from the body. When the heart stops, it can sometimes be shocked into starting again. Some people who have lived through near-death experiences (when either their heart or their brainwaves have stopped for a time) describe having seen a bright light. Does consciousness continue as some form of light?

In 1972, Krippner and Hickman were invited to a psychology conference in the USSR for the first time. While there, they met with other scientists and were given the plans to build a Kirlian device. The device had been named after its inventor, who was quite willing to share his information with them. Essentially, Kirlian photography (also known as high-voltage photography), as defined by Henry Dakin, "is a technique for making photographic prints or visual observations of electrically conductive objects with no light source other than that produced by a luminous corona discharge at the surface of an object in a high-voltage, high-frequency electric field." (88) On returning from the USSR, Hickman built such a high-voltage device and shared his information with those interested in it in this country. Many beautiful images were then made of leaves, flowers, fingertips, or whatever could fit on a small piece of cut film. Dakin built an improved version that could regulate the exact exposure time to 1/30th of a second, so it would be possible to compare the strength of corona discharges from one print to another, and not be confused by different lengths of exposure time.

While Geller was working at SRI, he saw some of the beautiful Kirlian photographs of hands that Hickman had made and Geller wanted such a photo of his own hand. The experiment took place in Palo Alto, California, on the evening of the winter solstice, 1973. Hickman, Dakin, W. Westerbeke, S. Kenny, and I were present. Since the hotel

**The experimental procedure was as follows:**
1) The experimenter asked one of the observers to turn off the lights and he placed a sheet of 4" x 5" film on the glass plate insulator, emulsion side up; 2) the experimenter guided the tip of the subject's right forefinger to the film surface, while feeling carefully for any foreign material that might influence the image; 3) the control exposure was taken (at left); 4) the experimenter moved the subject's fingertip to another film (at right), again feeling for foreign material, and keeping his own hands near the subject's hands to be able to detect any movement. Each exposure is only 1/30th of a second.

*(This is a remarkable set of images from an experiment that was not reproduced, since Geller left shortly afterward.)*

room was small, we all sat fairly close to each other. I was sitting on the floor. When Dakin made the first attempt to photograph Geller's whole hand, the energy interaction was so strong that Geller received a shock. Since I happened to be touching his foot, I also felt the shock.

When Dakin began to put the equipment away, Geller asked why. Dakin said the transformer was no longer working after the shock. Geller asked Dakin to show him the transformer so he could put his hand over it and focus his mental energy. Soon the transformer was working again. Several Kirlian pictures were taken after that, including those above.

The numbers were scratched on the film in the dark to keep track of the sequences. The first image of this series is marked with a large **3.** A watch with a luminous dial was used, so the hands of the watch could be photographed as well. The dial is seen directly under the **3.** The large bright square to the right is part of the wrist band. At the bottom is Geller's fingertip. (The first picture is taken for control to show what everything looks like when no mental energy is being sent to the watch.) The next image is marked with a large **4.** A streak of energy is seen coming from Geller's fingertip at the bottom of the image, as he intends to affect the watch. The watch has now lost ten minutes. Each image was 1/30th of a second, and the watch was handled only by the monitor. Dakin placed Geller's finger where he wanted it on the film. This one-time study cannot be called definitive research, since it was not repeated.

However, it is suggestive that some aspects of our mental and physical energy might be classified as light. There are other aspects of our experiential energy that we call "light" which may not be measurable at all. The Parker photographs of Brown, illustrated on page 8, may be an example of such light emanating from the body at certain

times of high mental, physical, or spiritual energy. Other photographs have captured events that seem to show that. The intention behind taking those pictures of Brown was simply to record a friend working on an exciting new project. When Parker saw the light around his friend, he thought the camera was faulty. There was no attempt to "fool" anyone. We would like to see a serious study using film that "sees" farther into infra-red and ultraviolet in the hope of capturing such an event in the future.

I have seen auras from time to time radiating around people involved in high energy states. Many of the people who claim to see them actually see them differently, yet they may diagnose the same problem. I may see infra-red rising from your shirt covering your shoulder, and tell you that you have an inflammation there. Another may see green sparks shooting off your shoulder and tell you about your inflammation and the mental and/or physical problem that caused it. For those who do see the aura, it is always a combination of the energy of the person you are seeing and the symbolic ways in which your vision interprets the information. Spiritual healer Greg Schelkun allows his eyes to go out of focus, and in that fuzzy space, all the information about the health of the patient, from any source, visual or not, can be symbolized. Though his ability to heal people is not 100%, nor is anyone's, Schelkun's remarkable track record of healing has been well documented. (89)

However, there are self-styled "psychics" who charge money to "read" your aura. One may take your picture with a Polaroid camera, and hold the photo over a lamp while it is developing. The heat and light of the lamp cause a blur of colored light to surround the portrait which is then "read" as though it were *your* aura. Another "psychic" puts a bright light behind a person so an edge of high contrast causes the eyes to track back and forth. The resultant after-images seem as though an aura came from that person.

## ENTRAINMENT WITH CHEMISTRY

Entrainment with chemistry is common to every civilization, even though those are not the terms usually used for such activity. The word "companionship" is derived from the words for sharing bread with one another.

Think of a happy family Thanksgiving dinner. Aunts and uncles bring the salad, sisters and brothers bring the pies. Then the turkey is brought out of the oven to the admiring group, and all eat, talk, share stories, and eat some more, until the resonance of chemistry is complete.

Another example of entrainment with chemistry might be a pizza and beer party for a group watching a ball game. They might have gathered for a tailgate party or at someone's home to watch the game on TV. Sharing food and drinks is a time-honored tradition for friends and families, whether at a wake, a wedding, or any holiday event.

From hieroglyphics, we find that the Egyptians made beer in ancient times. Even today, natives in the South Pacific create their own style of "jungle juice" for social gatherings. Russians felt that vodka was essential to manhood. In the Middle East, the use of strong coffee is one major ritual in the community, and the sharing of some form of cannabis from a large water pipe is another. In Japan, the way tea is served is a sacred ritual. The bread and wine communion (Eucharist) of Christianity is another sacred ceremony with deep ritual and symbolic connotations. The Tarahumara Indians of northern Mexico use marijuana as a sacrament in religious ceremonies. It takes a place in their culture similar to that of peyote in the Native American church ceremonies.

At the office, the group who gathers for a coffee break might share ideas and feelings while they warm their hands on their cups and sip. When coffee is not available, some will carry on their friendly conversation and settle for tea or just hot water in their cups. However, some who are addicted to the coffee may experience a headache from caffeine withdrawal when the coffee is not available, thereby becoming grumpy, not friendly. Those who now have to go outside to smoke a cigarette seem to gather in conversation groups as well. In the past, they could drink coffee and smoke at the same time in the same room as their co-workers. Now, the smokers seek others who are also addicted. They will forego the "coffee break" conversations they used to have with those who drink coffee, but do not smoke. As social patterns change, so do the folks we choose to become entrained with. The chemistry of entrainment may dominate our social life more often than we care to realize.

For centuries the ritual chemistry of diplomacy has been alcohol. It has been credited with breaking down, or at least softening, the barriers of cultural differences. Drinking together could create a resonance of friendship. When treaties were signed, there was always a toast for mutual success. An intellectual (and idealistic) college friend of mine wanted to do something in international affairs. He took a job with the diplomatic corps and was sent to a foreign country. However, the continuous pressure to drink with others was more than he could handle. He was fast becoming an alcoholic, and there was no way to quit or to remove himself from the constant need to share that diplomatic toast. Before long, he was back home where he could be sober again.

Early wars could not be fought unless the volunteer soldiers were promised a measure of grog as part of their pay. The constant demand for rum financed the disgraceful sugar-rum-slave trade that began the population growth of the Americas with Europeans and Africans. Some peoples, among the mix of races that made up the gold rush crowd from 1849 on, felt that whiskey was the measure of a man. He had to be able to hold his liquor. Such a large majority of people in France and Italy still enjoy drinking wine that the making of fine wines has become a well-honored art form. Use of it in moderation can keep relationships generally friendly. Even though every city has its collection of destitute winos who sleep on the streets, this is not a reason to banish the practice from the millions of others who find a glass of wine to be a healthy alternative to stress. Unfortunately, there have always been some who have addictive personalities and will overdo anything.

For many people in all cultures, alcoholism does take a grave toll of human activity. There are others of us who just can't handle the social requirements and are not able to participate in a society which has at times demanded that we all take the social drink. A drink of alcohol causes me to throw up or to fall asleep. That classified me as a social disaster as a young woman. During WWII, movies pushed alcohol and cigarettes as *the way* sophisticated men and women behaved. Rarely was a person in film seen to become friendly, fall in love, or get rescued without a cigarette and a drink. As for me, my throat will not allow cigarette smoke to pass through it. Other young women could approach a handsome man and ask him to light her cigarette. I never had that excuse. I insulted several people before I learned that to refuse a drink was considered an insult. Eventually, I hid my disability at a cocktail party by walking around with a drink in my hand, pretending to drink. Now that I'm older, and my friends like me anyway, that pretense is no longer necessary. Times have changed.

The peer pressure will always be strong to push entrainment with whatever chemical is currently popular. Across the country there is a war of mind chemistry among children in the junior and senior high schools. A wide range of available drugs is commonly used, though few students have any real knowledge of them. Most young people don't know the difference between a higher state of consciousness and just feeling dizzy or silly. They will try what their favorite pop stars use, especially if it is forbidden. The social groups of the schools have become strictly divided among those entrained to enjoy the different types of mind-altering chemistry. Those who choose to stay "clean" and not smoke, drink, or use drugs do not associate with those who do. The pot smokers do not associate with the speed freaks, etc. Information about consciousness is not available, so there is ignorance mixed with foolhardy exploration. Those who *abuse* several kinds of drugs simultaneously will probably suffer health problems. Many of those who choose to take pot and booze at the same time may fall by the wayside of personal accomplishment. Yes, there are those who lose track of their minds while trying to keep up with their social groups.

Yet the use of marijuana promoted an open-minded approach to world events for college students. As the use of marijuana increased in the Sixties, the silent generation became active in the cause of social issues. But casual use of any substance for relaxation and abuse of it are very different things. People who enjoy sharing a special wine with dinner are just as offended as nondrinkers are when an alcoholic becomes obnoxious and spoils the qual of a social group or a family gathering. The drunk who insists on driving a car can cause death and destruction. People who enjoy sharing marijuana are just as offended as nonsmokers are when the "pot head" who abuses it becomes a dependent. But the abuser of marijuana is rarely a danger to others in the way that a drunk can be.

Use of marijuana and LSD tends to produce bonds of camaraderie among people who use them together, to a degree that exceeds the temporary hail-fellow-well-met conviviality of alcohol. This can be true for rowdy gangs as well as for those who meditate together or share lofty conversation over soft music. When this chemically enhanced bond is applied to a group creative activity, participants describe it as "getting inside each other's heads."

## 1. A Brief Observation of the EEG of One Subject Before and After He Smoked Official Government Grown *Cannabis Sativa at* Saint Elizabeth's Hospital in Washington, DC.

*(The names of the people involved in this incident have been changed.)*

In 1976, I was invited to demonstrate the *Light Sculpture* for a small group of administrators from Health, Education and Welfare (HEW), the National Institutes of Health (NIH), and the National Institute on Drug Abuse (NIDA). I had planned to create a video tape to demonstrate how biofeedback could help students learn to focus attention and to help them prevent the *abuse* of drugs. To do this, I needed a grant. The gentleman who had invited me, Jim Henderson, PhD, also offered to be my translator during my presentation. His daughter was a student at CSUS and so he was familiar with the cultural differences that existed between Northern California and the halls of government offices in Washington, DC. He was concerned that my use of language would be so very different from their use of language, that he insisted I print up a copy of the outline of my talk and include in it the definitions of biofeedback and other technical terms. Henderson even went over the talk with me in advance, so he could help during the question and answer period. When the equipment had been set up and the people had gathered, the outline paper was passed around to all present. The presentation was politely received, and eventually I did get a small grant from NIDA to complete the video tape project. However, because of complications during the production in California, as well as changes at the offices of NIDA, I doubt if anyone ever saw the video. It was to be part of a larger film project. However, after we had completed it and sent it, the sponsor of the tape, Henderson, was away from his office for an extended period with an eye operation. When he returned, the tape could not be found. I sent a copy, but my dream of getting the government interested in biofeedback in education had ended.

It was during the 1976 presentation at NIDA that the incident of relieving the headache occurred (see page 110). Among those present were two young men who were involved in legal marijuana research, Ralph Scudder, PhD, and Scott Romer, PhD. I asked them if they were using EEG as part of their study. They said no, but they would be interested. I, of course, was also extremely interested, especially in seeing what questions government researchers of marijuana would be asking. Naturally, I volunteered to take the equipment to their research center. This turned out to be a small area on the fifth floor of Saint Elizabeth's Hospital. Henderson was willing to deliver me and my eighty kilos of electronic equipment to that place, but he was not able to stay and translate.

We put the equipment in a wide place in the hall where the coffee machine was also placed. It was inadequate for a demonstration, but it was the only place large enough to set it up. Unused chairs and tables had been piled back into one corner, though one table could be cleaned off for my equipment. Then I was escorted to their small office where they described their research. They were studying reaction times of right and left hands to images shown to the right or left visual fields. They would take a baseline of reactions, and then provide alcohol to the subject and test reaction time again. At a different time, they would provide the subject some *Cannabis sativa* for another test of reaction time. A wall chart of their findings indicated that the reaction times from alcohol were slower for both hands, but the reaction times from *Cannabis sativa* caused the right hand to slow down to become equal to the reaction times of the left hand. The reaction time of both hands became balanced. Scudder and Romer said they weren't sure what to make of it, but the government wanted to be able to show that a person's driving would be impaired after smoking marijuana. The research had been designed to demonstrate that, and it would be interpreted as having done so.

After that we moved back to the hall, where I hooked up the equipment and tested it, explaining the parts and how it worked as I did so. There was some external electrical disturbance there, but at the moment it was not critical. I offered to test the marijuana myself, since I had already established a long baseline of voluntary control of my brainwaves. It would form an easy comparison with any gain or loss of control caused by smoking their marijuana. However, they told me that women were *never* used in this research. Romer explained that the rules were designed to prevent problems with pregnancy. I assured them that at my age this would not be a problem. Nevertheless Romer told me that only a ruling from the attorney general himself would change the current law. The government didn't want to know what effects marijuana had on women.

A young man I shall call Tom appeared and was willing to be hooked up to the brainwave machine. He was ostensibly a naive subject who had never had marijuana before. The young researchers behind us sat on the backs of the jumble of chairs with their feet on the seats, so they could see the *Light Sculpture*. As we began to find what the subject's baseline scores in the different frequency cate-

gories might be, the researchers were talking loudly. I had to suggest to them that it was inappropriate during brainwave biofeedback. During our explorations and recording of brainwave percent times in three frequency categories, I noticed that Tom had a shift in one hemisphere. He told me that he had a lazy right eye. When I spoke to Scudder and Romer about this, they said it didn't matter. (I kept these judgmental thoughts to myself: *"How can it not matter when their research involves right and left visual fields?"*) Finally I had a record of Tom's range of brainwave frequencies at the time (not really long enough in one short session to call it a baseline).

Scudder brought out a government jar of joints with the THC count neatly written on the outside. Tom was told he could smoke about three-fourths of one joint. He went off into the other jumbled corner, found a chair, and smoked by himself. There was no music, no candles, no camaraderie. The others continued to talk and/or ask me questions. After Tom had smoked the joint down to the line they had marked on it, he gave the rest back to Scudder and came over to be hooked up again to the equipment. We went through the same process as I asked him to focus on the dial, or to close his eyes and take a deep breath, or to remain silent. Eventually, I had another list of numbers about beta, alpha, theta, and synch to share, and I disconnected Tom from his electrodes. I used my best Washington language to report the results. Tom's ability to produce alpha phase coherence had increased, but his ability to produce beta rhythms had been diminished.

At that point, both government researchers asked me, "What does it all mean?"

Losing my Washington formality, I replied, "It means that you are using low-quality dope."

Jaws dropped around the room, and a slightly stammered reply was, "But, but, this is official government marijuana, grown in Mississippi. It has the THC count listed on the side." (In Mississippi the government farmers mix the blossoms with the lower leaves to keep the THC count consistent. Of course that means the mixture also includes more of the sleep component.)

I remained calm but persistent. "But don't you have the ability to use other kinds of marijuana, such as Colombian Red, Acapulco Gold, or Seedless Purple?"

Scudder had now taken charge of this conversation. He was still patient with me in his explanations. "Technically, I suppose we do, but there is an enormous amount of paperwork. It is far too extensive, and takes too much time. The government wants us to use what they grow, so our results will be consistent."

My shock and amazement at what constitutes this form of government research was beginning to show. I responded with some surprise. "But every student who makes grass available for his friends in order to support his own college education knows that price and quality are related. How is it that the government can ignore such important information—that there is more than one kind of marijuana?"

By now both Scudder and Romer were becoming emotional, as well. "Why, if the government ever found out there was more than one kind of marijuana it would invalidate all our research."

He said it himself. It was followed by a moment of stunned silence. I just looked at him and shrugged, I had become unpopular in that environment.

Romer had wanted me to hook up his girlfriend so he could see her brainwaves. She had just arrived and was a little nervous as the electrode paste was smeared into her hairdo, though I tried to calm her. Just then an additional motor of some kind created so much static in the subtle brainwaves that I could not get a signal that was meaningful. (It was even much worse than trying to measure brainwaves by sitting next to the refrigerator at home.) The researchers were both relieved. To them, it meant that my equipment was faulty. The whole demonstration could be dismissed as though it never happened.

We were all relieved that Henderson arrived just at that time. The usual formal greeting took place and he and Scudder helped pack the equipment in their special boxes so I could leave peacefully. No one was happy, especially the lady with electrode paste in her hair.

By the time all eighty kilos of electronics were carefully loaded into the car, I felt drained. Henderson took me to lunch and I told him what I thought had happened. He asked for a written report, which I prepared. It was sad to see that style of government research. The bureaucracy, established during alcohol prohibition, used deliberate scare tactics about marijuana to save their government jobs even though prohibition had ended. To this day the legal issues around marijuana are based on politics, not facts. (90) Such research is designed to keep it that way.

## 2. Pilot Studies on the Effects That Smoking *Cannabis Sativa* Have on the EEG of Volunteers

It was clear that the government was not going to conduct the kind of research needed for those who found smoking marijuana useful for their lives. The only EEG equipment available for research at that time was very large, very expensive, and therefore limited to politically approved institutions that could receive large grants. Even they would have to follow government guidelines to get the grants (one researcher published positive results and was fired). Institutions that wanted to stay in the mental health business in 1976 had to develop "grant proposal consciousness." They had to know what was politically acceptable and write their research plans to support that point of view. Their results also had to conform to that preconceived notion of what the desired results should be. Perhaps things have improved in the last twenty years. I certainly hope so.

Another problem with government research was the rigid idea that THC (Tetra-hydro-cannabinol) was the only active ingredient in cannabis. It was well known elsewhere that there are strong variations among different types of marijuana grown in different parts of the world. In the Sixties, one of the underground labs had done a basic alumina chromatography study on a kilo of Acapulco Gold. This lab found that there were at least twelve bands, each one producing a different mental or physical effect (e.g., one band made them sleepy, another had visual effects with no physical sensations, another seemed to enhance feelings of sensuality, etc.). The dominance of these components seem to vary in percentage from one plant to another, from one type of growing condition to another. In the book *Marihuana, The Forbidden Medicine,* published in 1997, (91) Lester Grinspoon, MD, and James B. Bakalar state the following:

> The marihuana plant contains more than 460 known compounds, of which more than 60 have the 21-carbon structure typical of cannabinoids. The only cannabinoid that is both highly psychoactive and present in large amounts...is delta-9-THC.... A few other tetrahydrocannabinols are about as potent as THC, but are present in only a few varieties of cannabis....
>
> A native of central Asia, cannabis may have been cultivated as much as ten thousand years ago. It was...cultivated in China by 4000 BC and in Turkestan by 3000 BC. It has long been used as a medicine in India, China, the Middle East, South-

east Asia, South Africa, and South America....

The cannabis preparations used in India often serve as a folk standard of potency. The three varieties are known as *bhang, ganja,* and *charas.* The least potent and cheapest preparation, bhang, is produced from the dried and crushed leaves, seeds, and stems. Ghanja, prepared from the flowering tops of cultivated female plants, is two or three times as strong as bhang; the difference is somewhat akin to the difference between beer and fine Scotch. Charas is the pure resin, also known as hashish in the Middle East. Any of these preparations can be smoked, eaten, or mixed in drinks. The marihuana used in the United States is equivalent to bhang or, increasingly in the past two decades, to ganja.

In Northern California spiritual botanists cultivated varieties of cannabis for their different mental and physical properties. Eight people wanted to find out what effects smoking a cannabis that was as strong as ganja would have on their brainwaves. Each of the them wanted to know if smoking actually caused any changes in their ability to exert voluntary control over their brainwaves. The organizer of the group had obtained some high-quality cannabis, and the same lot would be used for everyone throughout this experiment. They asked me if I would lend them the brainwave analyzer equipment to the cause of such research. When our 1975 synch and telepathy studies had been completed, I agreed to make the equipment available, as long as they kept good notes and shared them with me afterward. First, each of the four pairs of people practiced with the biofeedback equipment to establish some voluntary control of their brainwaves. The average scores from their first practice sessions were recorded for each team (for individual *IH synch* and for *IP team synch).* After two additional practice sessions, their average baselines were also recorded. A comparison with these scores was made with the results of their average scores after smoking cannabis. The graphs for the *IH synch* scores are shown at right and the *IP team synch* scores are on page 128.

As you can see, after smoking the material obtained for the study, all of the participants showed an increase over baseline in amplitude and percent-time of *IH synch,* both in *relative* (**R**) which indicates simultaneous alpha, and in *absolute* (**A**) which indicates phase-coherent alpha. All of the teams also produced *IP team synch* (**R**) scores at rates above their baseline scores. The latter increase might be considered to be the automatic mathematical result of the first, but, quite significantly, the scores for *IP team synch* (**A**) failed to show the same direct relationship to the

increase in the other scores, as one might expect. This strongly suggests that the intention and ability to sustain a focus of attention on each other played a larger role in their final *IP synch* scores than did their use of cannabis alone. Some couples are very comfortable together while they freely follow their own separate thoughts. At the same time, they still feel quite close, even though they are not specifically focused on each other.

The *IP team phase coherence* scores were higher for **Teams A** and **B** than their previously recorded averages. Both of these couples reported having focused their attention directly on each other during the precise moment in time identified by the biofeedback tones. They were also able to associate the phase-coherent tones with moments when their feelings of rapport and their sense of touch were

| Brainwave Biofeedback (BFB) *IH synch* Sessions | #1 Average *IH synch* score of first BFB practice session | #2 Average *IH synch* score of two BFB sessions used as baselines | #3 Average *IH synch* score from one session after smoking |
|---|---|---|---|
| Team A A-1 (M) | R = 59,  A = 34 APCR = 57 | R = 78,  A = 48 APCR = 61 | R = 98,  A = 75 APCR = 76 |
| Team A A-2 (F) | R = 82,  A = 45 APCR = 54 | R = 89,  A = 55 APCR = 61 | R = 92,  A = 78 APCR = 84 |
| Team B B-1 (M) | R = 42,  A = 23 APCR = 54 | R = 62,  A = 33 APCR = 53 | R = 89,  A = 63 APCR = 70 |
| Team B B-2 (F) | R = 68,  A = 36 APCR = 52 | R = 72,  A = 38 APCR = 52 | R = 95,  A = 70 APCR = 73 |
| Team C C-1 (M) | R = 37,  A = 12 APCR = 32 | R = 58,  A = 19 APCR = 32 | R = 73,  A = 40 APCR = 54 |
| Team C C-2 (F) | R = 59,  A = 33 APCR = 55 | R = 64,  A = 36 APCR = 56 | R = 89,  A = 57 APCR = 64 |
| Team D D-1 (M) | R = 75,  A = 35 APCR = 46 | R = 85,  A = 40 APCR = 47 | R = 97,  A = 57 APCR = 58 |
| Team D D-2 (F) | R = 79,  A = 41 APCR = 51 | R = 88,  A = 46 APCR = 52 | R = 95,  A = 63 APCR = 66 |

**Interhemispheric alpha phase coherence *(IH synch)* scores**

The average biofeedback percent-time scores show an increase in *IH synch* for all individual team members (**M**) male and (**F**) female after smoking cannabis.

The **R** score = *Relative* (simultaneous alpha).
The **A** score = *Absolute* (phase-coherent alpha).
The **APCR** score = *Alpha Phase-Coherent Ratio.*

| Brainwave Biofeedback (BFB) *IP Team Synch* Sessions | #1 Average *IP synch* score of first BFB practice session | #2 Average *IP synch* score of two BFB sessions used as baselines | #3 Average *IP synch* score from one session after smoking |
|---|---|---|---|
| **Team A** (Lovers living together) | R = 58, A = 10 APCR = 17 | R = 75, A = 14 APCR = 20 | R = 90, A = 25 APCR = 27 |
| **Team B** (Planning to live together) | R = 39, A = 8 APCR = 20 | R = 59, A = 14 APCR = 24 | R = 80, A = 24 APCR = 30 |
| **Team C** (Friends for a long time) | R = 36, A = 6 APCR = 16 | R = 56, A = 11 APCR = 19 | R = 75, A = 10 APCR = 13 |
| **Team D** (Married with one child) | R = 70, A = 13 APCR = 18 | R = 82, A = 15 APCR = 18 | R = 92, A = 13 APCR = 14 |

**Interpersonal alpha phase coherence *(IP synch)* scores**

This chart shows the average biofeedback percent-time scores for each team before and after smoking cannabis. The scores of two teams increase afterward; the others decrease.
The **R** score = *Relative* (simultaneous alpha).
The **A** score = *Absolute* (phase-coherent alpha).
The **APCR** score = *Alpha Phase-Coherent Ratio.*

most intense. **Teams C** and **D** found the opposite result. The individual members of these two teams reported that they had allowed their minds to drift to other times and places (i.e., they spaced out).

For example, both members of **Team C** had drifted off into thoughts about private projects. Afterward, the man declared that he had received a major insight about an important project he was working on. The woman found a way to resolve an interpersonal problem she was having with a co-worker at her job. They were not synchronizing their brainwaves with each other, even though they were both in high-amplitude alpha *IH synch* at the time. Nevertheless, they were both very happy with the results of the experiment.

The wife of **Team D** began thinking about her child and how pleased she was with the creative relationship the young girl had with her sitter. Both the girl and the sitter planned to paint pictures this evening. The husband of **Team D** drifted off to a pleasant time when he was fishing in a warm river. This subjective evidence, like the statistical results of all other studies, supports the conclusion that the production of *IP team phase coherence* is an inten-

tional act distinct from the production of *IH synch,* and beyond the simple mathematical relationship of both signals.

In this cannabis study done in 1976, the individual *(IH relative* and *absolute)* and the team *(IP relative* and *absolute)* scores were separately averaged over the whole session. In a later study done in 1982 with different participants, *IH synch* and *IP synch* scores were measured in another way. For that study, a new counter had been provided, which produced a numerical score for each sixty-second epoch. This allowed us to compare the results as they changed during each session, rather than average the scores for the entire session. Again the new supply of high-grade cannabis was used the same way by all six participants. After a practice period with the biofeedback tones, baseline scores for *IH synch* in both *relative* (**R**) and *absolute* (**A**) were established. After the participants began to smoke the cannabis, the average alpha scores showed an increase over the baseline scores for all of them. Since each epoch was only sixty seconds, fewer of them drifted off into their separate fantasies in that short period of time than in the previous study. The new measurement method provided immediate feedback for couples as well so they could more easily explore the ways they focused attention on each other during *IP team synch.*

The scores for **Team K/A** are illustrated in the first graph at right. Epoch #1 represents the initial hook up, before the couple had settled into an internal resonance with the biofeedback tones. After an introductory period of practice with the biofeedback, epochs #2 and #3 represent the typical baseline scores achieved. Epoch #4 shows the results immediately following the first few puffs of smoke. The *IP team synch* scores for both relative (**R**) and absolute (**A**) rise substantially. Epochs numbered #5 through #9 were taken at random periods during the next twenty minutes. Gradually, the team's phase coherence dropped, and after thirty minutes, the scores seemed to level out, with the **A** scores remaining above the original baseline. If the couple chose to smoke again, the pattern of rising and then falling somewhat was repeated. The total effect of smoking did not seem to last more than an hour or two at the most. All volunteers reported positive experiences that ranged from mildly pleasant to euphoric.

The brainwaves of a person after drinking a glass of wine is somewhat similar to those of a person after smoking a marijuana cigarette. Most people become more relaxed and their alpha rhythms are usually increased. The continued use of alcohol, however, seems to cause the *IH phase coherence* to become reduced, and asynchrony to be

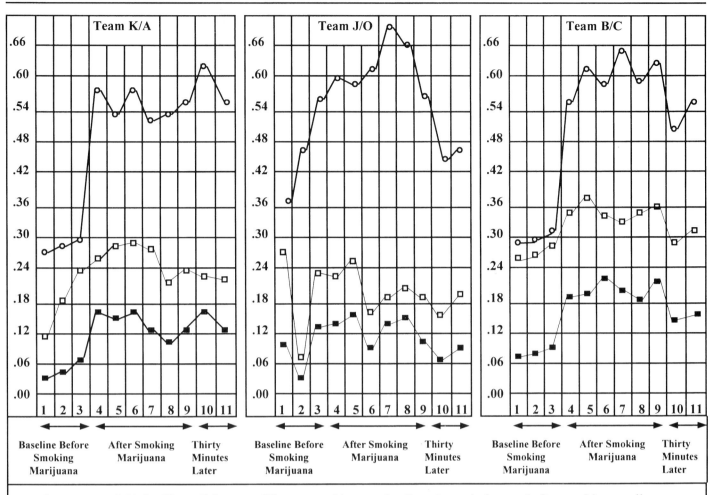

**Interpersonal Alpha Phase Coherence *(IP team synch)* scores for three teams before and after smoking marijuana**

Percent times are along the left side of each graph. Epoch numbers are along the bottom. Each epoch is sixty seconds. After smoking marijuana, the *IP team synch* scores increased significantly for all participants. As the first effects of the smoke wear off, the **R** scores seem to stay fairly high, but the **A** scores seem to level out slightly higher than baseline.

- o    The circles represent *IP team synch* **(R)** scores = *Relative* (simultaneous alpha).
- ■    The dark rectangle represent the *IP team synch* **(A)** scores = *Absolute* (alpha phase coherence).
- □    The open squares represent the ratio between the two scores. **(APCR)** = *Alpha Phase-Coherent Ratio*

increased. That is when the drinker begins to lose ability to focus attention or when his/her muscle coordination begins to become unbalanced. With marijuana, however, continued use does not seem to decrease synchrony for the people we have observed. Eventually the person becomes sleepy, as the faster brainwaves gradually decrease. Some people find some types of marijuana to be useful for sleep.

The issue here is not whether a substance is harmful. Anything used to excess is by definition harmful. The issue is that in our fast-paced society, stress is harmful. The medical community now preaches the health advantages of stress management and pharmaceutical companies advertise expensive pills to reduce stress. Small amounts of alcohol or marijuana are commonly used for relaxation. Our

studies here involved only the moderate user. To my knowledge, none of them ever became addicted.

Don Douglas wrote, "The nice thing about alcohol is the way it slows down mental activity" (i.e., after a very busy day when a lot of thoughts are still whirling around your head, and you do not have to drive anywhere, slowing down can be helpful). "The nice thing about marijuana is the way it speeds up thinking and ideas." (This happens for many reasons, one of the principal ones being that marijuana increases enjoyment of music, comedy, visual art, and other entertainment. Enjoyment of sensuality seems to be greatly increased and the exploration of creative ideas is another.) (92) Some people have claimed that intense focus in sensuality is the essence of Tantric sexuality.

Casual observations over time revealed that the bio-feedback equipment could help run quality control on the substances used for alteration of consciousness. The rule of thumb was this: If the substance decreased voluntary control of the brainwaves, then the user would eventually lose something in his/her thought process or ability; if the substance increased voluntary control of the brainwaves, than it might be classified as having the potential (when properly used) for becoming mind-expanding.

In March 1998, the TV special *Moyers on Addiction: Close to Home* reported that only a small percentage of people who drink become addicted, and an even smaller percentage of people who smoke marijuana become addicted. (93) These addictions are largely due to genetics, though environment also plays a part. A person who comes from a family of alcoholics is 40% to 60% more likely to become an addictive personality. The addictive disease could take the form of addiction to coffee, cigarettes, chocolate, or some other substance including alcohol that might increase the release of dopamine in the brain. (There is a long list of hard drugs in this category, but we are not discussing those here.) When too much dopamine is released, there is a current assumption that the remaining supply in the brain becomes diminished, and the brain's ability to produce it naturally is impaired. This condition is declared to be one of the root causes of addiction, and it seems to occur more often in families. People who use a lot of the low-grade marijuana that has more of the sleep component in it could lose voluntary control of some of their faster beta brainwaves. Though they may have felt that their occasional insights and new ideas came as the result of smoking, they gradually lost the motivation to act on them anymore. If they were in school, their grades would fall off. Like the man on the streets who abuses cheap wine, the abuser of low-grade grass has to smoke more of it to get any effect at all, and then has too few fast-frequency brainwaves to put his/her ideas into good use.

However, the moderate use of high-grade marijuana by millions of people who are not addictive personalities allows creative ideas to flow (partly because of the increased ability to focus attention beyond spacetime). The results of that creativity grace our bookshelves, our films, our CD music collections, stage plays, and art galleries, winning for their creators countless honors. Even top athletes who were able to compete in the Winter Olympics in 1998 were not slowed down by their casual use of high-grade marijuana. Many term papers and dissertations have been inspired by its use, and completed successfully because the high-grade material did not diminish the faster

frequencies of the brainwaves. I am not claiming that all creative people use marijuana, or any other mind-altering chemical. I am saying that many creative people do use it with good results.

In *Marijuana, the Forbidden Medicine* (see page 126), Grinspoon and Bakalar have outlined the history of the laws against the use of cannabis which were based on a major propaganda campaign began in 1937 by the director of the Federal Bureau of Narcotics. Those policies are continued by the DEA even though some courts have declared that marijuana should be reclassified, and several states have voted to make it available. The authors list over thirty medical illnesses where cannabis has been used to prevent discomfort. Among them are: depression, AIDS, cancer chemotherapy, multiple sclerosis, chronic pain, migraine, glaucoma, adult attention deficit disorder, and insomnia. In addition to the lengthy descriptions of these illnesses and how they have been alleviated by the use of cannabis, the authors also mention other uses:

> There is no longer any doubt that cannabis has useful properties than cannot be described as medical. It can be an intellectual stimulant, helping users to penetrate conceptual boundaries, achieve fluidity of associations, and enhance insight and creativity. Some find it so useful in gaining new perspectives...that they smoke it in preparation for intellectual or creative work. Other nonmedical uses of cannabis have less to do with learning. It can enhance appreciation of food, sexual activity, natural beauty, and other sensual experiences, and it can bring a new dimension to the understanding of music and visual arts. Under the right conditions and in the right settings, it can promote emotional intimacy. For almost everyone it has the capacity to highlight the comical in life....
>
> The full potential of this remarkable substance including its full medical potential, will be realized only when we end that regime of prohibition established two generations ago.

"...Using that *[government report]* as a guide... Americans are producing marijuana *[that is worth]* somewhere between 20 to 40 billion dollars every year. We're talking about what may be the largest cash crop in America."

**Peter Jennings reporting on *"POT OF GOLD"* ABC News Saturday Night** (94)

## EXPERIMENTS IN GROUP RESONANCE WITH LIGHTS, SOUNDS AND CHEMISTRY

"Some people have said that the aggressiveness that alcohol stimulates (and that certainly is a characteristic of alcohol) is consistent with Western values and Western culture. Whereas, for example, the more introspective, meditative, reverie kind of state that marijuana... produces seems more consistent with some of the Eastern cultures than with Western cultures. Maybe some of our discomfort with... *[that drug]* has to do with the feeling that this is culturally out of sync with us."

Andrew Weil, MD  (95)

Loud rock concerts with light shows became intrinsic to the "drug culture." These highly publicized events for large audiences had been going on for ten years by 1974, when I had an opportunity to do a light show for an experiment in resonance with a small group. Gurumukh (a psychology student, apprentice shaman and musician) planned a winter solstice harmony festival. He was the director, composer and a performer in the band *Rhythm and Bliss.* They played spiritual songs for local dances, and had become quite popular in the surrounding communities. They reserved a small hall for this event on the CSUS campus on December 21. Another musician Francisco Lupico arrived from LA with *The Cosmic Beam.* This amazing musical instrument, which he had created, was a twelve-foot steel beam with attached musical strings and electronic amplification. (Today, electronic computers might be able to generate such a sound without the heavy steel beam.) Nevertheless, its deep resonating vibration was worth the trip then. All performers volunteered so the tickets could be inexpensive just to defray the cost of transporting the beam on a large flatbed truck the five hundred miles from LA to Cotati. The chemistry for this event, however, would not be alcohol, LSD, or other drugs. Here the participants would supply for themselves the much milder marijuana.

It was the last day of the college semester. The university administration, fearing a rowdy beer bust, required the hiring of two security officers to keep order. Little did the administrators know that on this occasion, neither beer, nor any other type of alcohol, would be the drug of choice. Participants knew what to expect from *The Cosmic Beam Experience,* and would smoke marijuana before they came.

When all was ready, the flute player led everyone into the darkened hall in single file, accompanied by several people bearing candles. They were directed to form a cir-

cle, where they held hands and chanted together. Then as the band started to play, colored lights and patterns changed in time to the music, and the hall filled with happily moving bodies. Later, after a short break, and an additional smoke outside, everyone sat on the dance floor. Most students at this event already knew about chakras (the seven energy centers in the body) and they had read about how the Kundalini could move from the spine up through these chakras, energizing them. (96) When Lupico began to play the *Cosmic Beam*, the dynamic vibrations were not only heard but felt by all the people sitting on the floor. As the resonance filled the room, the entrainment experience for the group was profound.

The security guards had nothing to do. They watched in wonderment as the group held hands in a circle and chanted. There were no fights, no one was stumbling around drunk. There was no beer, no beer cans tossed about the field or the hall. It was definitely not the usual end-of-semester college bash. At the close of the evening, there were hugs all around. Everyone cooperated in cleaning up. The hall and the grounds were left spotless. Those with cars offered rides home to those without them. No one was left behind. The energy was loving and gentle.

In the Sixties, group resonance events (with lights, sounds and strong chemistry) were much less controlled. The dramatic impact of them on the culture has been written about in many ways since then, though perhaps in different terms. When some researchers had predicted in 1959 that guided LSD experiences might increase awareness (and/or intelligence) it was accepted by many prominent adult intellectuals and college students. Its use led inevitably to the increased use of marijuana over alcohol as the drug of choice, not because it was addicting, but because it encouraged a more peaceful state of mind. Again moderation in the use of marijuana, and the rare use of the more powerful LSD, often created a close-knit bond among those who chose to use those chemicals creatively.

Then dramatic recreational use of LSD began. Early episodes of resonance with LSD and music evoked a dimension of group coherence that deserves some mention here. LSD was still legal before 1966, and friends of the musicians would pass out cards announcing when and where there would be a dance. On the back side of the card was the old WWI recruitment picture of Uncle Sam pointing at the observer. The caption had been changed from *"Uncle Sam wants YOU"* to *"Can YOU pass the acid test?"* Participants attended the dance dressed in weird costumes with weirder face paint. If you could drink the

Kool-Aid (laced with LSD) and see past the weirdness of others into the divinity in each person, you passed the test. When everyone felt mentally linked, the power of resonant energy could be transcendental. After one such trip, Phil Lesh, the bass player for the Grateful Dead, was heard to exclaim, "That's the most evolutionary experience I ever had since I first breathed air!" Tim Scully wrote the following about those experiences in a letter to me: (97)

> Psychedelic drugs such as LSD often amplify resonances. One of the most common experiences most people report after taking psychedelics is a sense of oneness with the universe. It is common for couples to feel a telepathic linkage when high.
>
> In early 1966, the Grateful Dead and the Merry Pranksters were traveling together, holding parties from time to time which they called *Acid Tests.* An intense gestalt consciousness often formed during these gatherings, where everyone took LSD, many danced and all were immersed in the music, light show and other rhythms of the party.
>
> We sometimes talked about Theodore Sturgeon's book, *More Than Human,* a science fiction story describing a gestalt formed by a small group of paranormally talented youngsters who spent much of the story looking for "missing" members of the gestalt. When they finally met the missing members and linked with them, a more mature and powerful entity resulted. One idea behind the Acid Tests was to get high with new potential members of the psychedelic gestalt resonance that sometimes formed.
>
> My most powerful experience of this psychedelic resonance happened between Acid Tests, on a day when the Dead extended family got very stoned and traveled to the beach in Venice. We often couldn't tell which body was taking a particular action, because it felt as though our mutual consciousness was pooled to form a single new being whose point of view moved from body to body among the family.

What only a few understood in the early days of LSD was that mind chemistry could shove a person, totally unprepared, into the multiple dimensions of the hyperspace. Nothing in our Western science of mind, psychology, or education had prepared us for what might be found in those other dimensions of consciousness. That era of the Sixties brought a great deal of creative energy into the volatile mix of politics, war, civil rights, and drugs. For those who could be guided into the hyperspace, it was transcendental.

For those who found themselves reliving early childhood abusive experiences with no preparation or anyone to guide them, it could be hell itself.

A fundamental guidebook was provided by psychologists Leary, Metzner, and Alpert. They based it on the results of their years of research and from guiding hundreds of people on LSD trips. They adapted the ancient *Tibetan Book of the Dead* for such trips and called it *The Psychedelic Experience.* Leary provided an introduction to a short movie of the same name. In it he speaks very slowly, recognizing that those who watch the film and/or hear him might very well be in an altered state of consciousness already: (98)

> Psychedelic means mind expanding. A psychedelic experience is a voyage inside—a trip into the countless galaxies of your own nervous system. For thousands of years philosophers and poets have told mankind that there is more inside, that the reality of the external world is only one of millions of realities within the human nervous system. For thousands of years too, men have studied methods of consciousness expansion, techniques for going out of your mind beyond your routine ways of experiencing. Chemicals, such as LSD, are perhaps the most effective method, because the language of the body, the language of the nervous system is itself biochemical. Another form of direct energy which can produce the psychedelic experience is music. Energy vibrations, carefully selected and artfully energized, can take us into new dimensions of space, time and identity.

When guides were not available, volunteers who were familiar with the book came forward. Tom Wolfe described such an event in *The Electric Kool-Aid Acid Test.* (99) One woman drank the Kool-Aid without knowing it was laced with LSD. Unaware that there was a test to be passed, she got caught up in her own projections of weirdness, as though they were "real." Wavy Gravy and his "Hog Farm family" quickly recognized the need to help such people, and at each dance they arranged a quiet area for taking care of any who were caught up in a cosmic drama or were "freaking out." The Hog Farm method was to talk them through their confusion until the people had a greater understanding of their own mental processes. The medical method was to give sedative drugs to a person who was in the middle of a cosmic drama. The drugs often caused that person to remain mentally unbalanced for an extended time, because no resolution of the drama had been achieved. Eventually, the *Rock Medicine* group took over that job of assisting those who became confused. Rock Medicine volunteers have continued to serve at all rock concerts in the San Francisco Bay Area for more than twenty years.

As the police action (undeclared war) accelerated many people knew at deep, and as yet unacknowledged, psychic levels that something was wrong. The military-industrial complex that Eisenhower had warned us about had become politically dominant. The emergence of LSD was the right medicine at the right time and was provided free at many peace marches. It was therefore considered subversive by those who felt that true patriots must support the war in Vietnam. LSD was too strong for some who were unprepared for it, yet it was transcendental for others who passed the acid test. Nevertheless, within only a few years a million or more people had experienced LSD personally, and they began to speak up, questioning old ideas.

One peaceful experiment in group resonance was planned after George Harrison announced that he was studying music with North Indian classical sitarist Ravi Shankar. Those who followed everything the Beatles were doing wanted to know more about it. Shankar and his people were invited to perform at the Monterey Pop Festival in 1967. Many performers, especially those who lived close by in California, agreed to play for free. Shankar, however, was paid a nominal fee, for he had to bring four people all the way from India, and pay full-fare tickets for "Mr. Tabla" and "Mrs. Sitar." (As mentioned, their instruments are sacred to them, and they traveled on the seats beside them at all times for safety.)

Some who heard recordings of sitar music for the first time complained that it was like *"cats wailing on a tin roof."* This is because they were projecting what they expected: a Western-type melody in four/four rhythm. North Indian classical music is based on very different principles, and when one hears it directly without the projections, the music stimulates the nervous system into a profound meditative state. Prior to the festival there were serious questions about how young people, ready for a rock concert, might respond to sounds that were so very different and from a totally foreign cultural tradition.

In those days there was an alchemist, dedicated to providing an important entheogen, or sacrament, and he made it available for free to all who wanted to take it. His name was Owsley. He and his group worked to produce LSD in the highest level of purity. (One report stated that tests showed it to be more pure than that produced by Sandoz

> **"The usual dosage was 300 micrograms, an amount Albert Hoffman later described as an 'over-dose.' Perhaps it was, on retrospect, but it made for one hell of a nice ride, and opened the Veil of Maya."**
> **Owsley**

Pharmaceutical Co.) Owsley wrote, "The amount of Monterey Purple tablets we took to the Pop Festival was about 14,000, and we gave most of them away. We commenced distributing the tabs in the morning of the very first day, and continued throughout all three days...." (100)

There were 2,000 or more free doses of acid distributed an hour before the Shankar afternoon concert, with the hope that the rock and roll fans could then hear the Indian music as it was intended, rather than as a projection from their own Western musical mindset. Few people had ever met the performers from India, but nine local women decided to surround them (three to each player) with loving psychic energy to protect them from any unexpected freak-outs in the audience. The women arranged themselves in different parts of the pavilion, so their energy would be projected from all directions. Other volunteers had spent hours arranging strings of flowers around the stage so the musicians would feel welcome and more at home. The musicians from India had never played at a rock and roll concert. Rock and roll fans had never heard them play. It would be a new experience for everyone.

The audience had heard that these were spiritual people, so when Shankar sat down on the stage and took the microphone and said, "Let's all pray," there was an expectancy of something esoteric to follow. But he continued with, "and hope that it doesn't rain." Since everyone hoped the same thing on this gray day, his down-to-earth comments were well received. The event was off to a good start. Shankar's beginning meditative solo caused many to look at each other in bewilderment. Then an airplane flew over with its loud raucous sound, distracting everyone. (This is a common occurrence there, as the pavilion is very close to the airport.) Most musicians playing set music that had been carefully rehearsed would have tried to ignore it, or just play louder. But Shankar instantly imitated the irritating sound of the airplane on his sitar, blending it in spontaneously, and then continued with his meditation music. There was a momentous reaction from the crowd. With that act, they realized that this was not set music, but music that included all the resonances around, and their responses as well. Shankar, by acknowledging the sound (rather than trying to drown it out, rock and roll style) had recaptured the attention of the audience distracted by it. By then, everyone was with him and the concert continued in high gear. When Alla Rakha joined in with the tabla rhythm, great enthusiasm developed. When he tuned his drums by tightening the heads with a hammer without missing a beat of the fast rhythm, the crowd responded again with great enthusiasm. The concert was truly transcendental for everyone. The crowd rose to their feet in a rousing applause at the end. When the tapes were being prepared for the record and the movie, the airplane and the sitar response were eliminated for their lack of aesthetics, but at the time, that was the glue that joined both cultures in resonance during this major cross-cultural event.

Afterward, Shankar leaned back in his chair backstage with much satisfaction, "Ah! I felt the presence of God today." Alla Rakha and Amiya das Gupta agreed. They were later told that thousands of rock fans in the audience had taken LSD, and that helped them to *hear* the music and respond to it directly. During the performance, one man stood on his head in the middle of the aisle, and Shankar assumed the bizarre behavior was the result of the LSD. He said, "Oh, that didn't bother me at all, there were so many nice people." Alla Rakha commented in his broken English that the audience seemed to be "gentle people. They like us very much. Standing claps, also." The glow of warm feelings from everyone for everyone was radiant and beautiful. The resonance was profound and it lingered for some time.

However, the feeling of oneness eventually would be shattered by each participant's different belief system about what oneness meant. Shankar is a Brahmin of the Hindu priest class. When he played music with such a transcendental effect, his students and others would come to him and touch his feet. He would put his hands on each head and bless them in return. North Indian classical music has Islamic roots, and Alla Rakha is a Muslim. That a Hindu and a Muslim played music together as brothers was important to the government of India, since that country had experienced so much bloodshed as a result of those different belief systems. Owsley believed that his acid had helped the rock fans come together in this situation and to feel that we are all one. He came up to Shankar and put his arm around him, as though they had become brothers, and offered to build any electronic instruments that Shankar might want. It was a warm and generous offer from his heart, to show how much he appreciated the music. But from Shankar's culture, such familiarity couldn't be accepted in that way, and he was actually offended. Owsley

> ### "These are very destructive rhythms! They could ruin a whole generation of young people."
>
> ### Amiya das Gupta (85)
> ### Tampura player with Ravi Shankar
>
> (Comments about the rhythms played by The Who just before they smashed their instruments on the stage at the Monterey Pop Festival.)

also envisioned that a free concert in Golden Gate Park by Shankar would be a transformative event for the whole Sixties scene, which he was helping to choreograph.

Later in the evening, after The Who had broken their instruments and damaged the stage (see pages 116 and 117), the oneness feeling was all over. Shankar never wanted to speak to Owsley again. Shankar's agent refused to allow them to play for free in Golden Gate Park. As world travelers and informal ambassadors, that would be totally inappropriate. Neither the Indian government nor the US government wanted Shankar associating with acid heads. (Though eventually, Alla Rakha did give permission to his son, Zakir Hussain, to play with Mickey Hart.)

Owsley wrote about his response to the festival: (100)

I was appalled at the vibes of The Who and their destruction, but when Jimi burned his guitar, I didn't have anything like the same feeling. The Who used cheap instruments they bought for the purpose and did the destruction bit every time they played....After Jimi's performance at Monterey, he was left without a guitar for the all-night jams in the long shed. I helped him to set up a borrowed guitar with the reversed string scheme he needed to play as a left-hander. I remember the jams as being the absolute peak of the Festival. Both of the two nights between the three days, there were the world's top rock musicians, stoned on acid, gathering to play and jam with constantly varying combos lasting until the morning of the following day. Absolutely nothing before or since has come anywhere close. We loved the days, but lived for the nights.

After the excitement of the Monterey Pop Festival, Ravi Shankar and Alla Rakha played in major concert halls across the country, including the Lincoln Center in New

York, and with Yehudi Menuhin at the United Nations to celebrate its twenty-fifth anniversary. Now their large audiences were well-dressed in New York concert hall style, and most of them were not on LSD. But the intention was already established to really listen to these musicians, who had been famous in India for years. It would take many years before the blend of music from India, Japan, Europe, and America would resonate together as a world sound, but in 1967 that inevitable blend began to be felt. The ancient instruments and the music of India have provided a creative influence on many types of modern Western music.

Popular music branched out along with the different instruments and the different types of chemistry being used. Kantor, who has volunteered with the Rock Medicine group for many years, said that different types of problems are typical at different musical events, depending on the drug of choice. When LSD and marijuana are resonant with the music, those who need help are generally just spaced out, and not a real threat to anyone. When alcohol is the drug of choice, those who need help are sick, dizzy, very drunk; they fall asleep or may become violent. When speed is the type of chemistry that resonates with the musicians, there is much more aggression among the users. Speed is often taken with alcohol, and then the potential for violence is significantly greater. The music that appeals to speed freaks is fast, loud, and the lyrics often express anger. (When such music was played on the radio, I told my teenage granddaughter that I couldn't understand the words. She said, "That's all right, grandma, you don't want to know, they're nasty." She felt the need to *protect me* from obscenities that were commonly heard in her social group, though she knew they were avoided by mine.)

What always alarms conservative adults is the recreational use of psychedelics by young people. In the nineties instead of going to an acid test and drinking the Kool-Aid, young people would go to a rave and buy the high-priced MDMA. Often the dancers develop a warm feeling of friendly connection to the others who are pre-

> **"...there were the world's top rock musicians, stoned on acid, gathering to play and jam with constantly varying combos, lasting until the morning of the following day. Absolutely nothing before or since has come anywhere close. We loved the days, but lived for the nights."**
>
> **Owsley**

> **"...For thousands of years philosophers and poets have told mankind that there is more inside, that the reality of the external world is only one of millions of realities within the human nervous system. For thousands of years too, men have studied methods of consciousness expansion, techniques for going out of your mind beyond your routine ways of experiencing...."**
>
> **Timothy Leary, PhD**

sent. Those who abuse it and mix it with other drugs make fools of themselves as do drunks at legal events. The distinction between the wino and the connoisseur of fine wines was made long ago. Now it is time to make the distinction between those who *abuse* drugs (legal or not) and those who understand the creative and therapeutic use of good psychedelics. However, the usual politics of scare tactics prevailed again until MDMA and all of its potential analogs were made illegal in 1986.

From our own observations over the years, we consider a drug to be abused when it is taken too frequently, with no time taken to integrate the mind. The confusion associated with *drug abusers* may result from a lack of information about the reality of the hyperspace and the necessity of integrating mental processes. Without integration, our multiple selves can become quite separated, and we become exhausted using the energy of one of our selves to suppress the energy of another self. The effort to maintain compartmentalization of multiple selves can lead to chronic depression. When a person begins to drink or to take drugs to solve problems, the initial alteration of consciousness often allows new insights about them. But when this is continued too frequently without a guide, eventually there are not enough drugs around to solve the problems caused by drunkenness or by mixing too many drugs together. Then vitamins and a cleansing process provide a way out and an understanding therapist may be needed.

For many people who felt isolated by the habits of modern society, rock and roll concerts became popular because they provided a sense of community. In the hope of increasing this sense of community, dedicated chemists have made various types of psychedelics available through underground channels around the planet. Psychedelics and rock and roll music played a larger role in bringing about an end to the Cold War than most people know.

## GROUP RESONANCE ACROSS CONTINENTS WITH AND WITHOUT CHEMISTRY

While the interhemispheric synchronization of brainwaves seems to facilitate meditation, and point the way to the exploration of the hyperspace, it is important to acknowledge that the electromagnetism of the brain (in itself) does not seem to be the carrier wave of mind-to-mind communication. Research of remote viewing under water and into electromagnetically shielded rooms has attempted to clarify that issue. Even though a time of heavy sun spot activity may interfere with psychic activity just as it does with radio waves, we believe that an interference with brainwaves can disrupt focus of attention. It is by establishing a steady resonance of focus that the mind can more easily travel freely in the hyperspace where psychic information may be revealed. The steady resonance of focus allows one to become nonattached to the personalites that are locked into space and time, and to move beyond them.

Since our first intercontinental telepathic experiment twenty-four years ago to tune in to the Earth-ionosphere waveguide frequencies to resonate with each other (see page 95), several events have been scheduled to link people psychically across continents. Shortly before glasnost was put into effect in the Soviet Union in 1981, two meditation groups conducted a long-range telepathic experiment. One group was led by Suzy Westerbeke in Sausalito, California, and the other one was located in Tbilisi, Georgia, in the USSR. The project was organized to demonstrate that ordinary people wanted to be peaceful, in spite of the Cold War waged by the military types. Greg Schelkun, who participated in this experience, reported that cultural differences about *how* to conduct such an experiment showed up right away, but that did not dull the loving energy between the two groups. For our side, the idea that the targets should not be known by anyone in advance meant that unknown targets would be pulled randomly from a target pool. Larissa Vilenskaya, LHD, volunteered as the outside observer who would chose a substantial variety of potential targets from my large collection in San Francisco, and to keep them secret.

The Russian group had asked an artist well-known in Tbilisi to prepare beautiful targets. Everyone who participated there had approved the loving and symbolic content of them in advance. When they gathered at the pre-arranged time to transmit one of the messages to the Westerbeke group in Sausalito, the content was received very well. However, when it was time to transmit a message back to Tbilisi, the random selection from the target pool

turned out to be a picture of the puppet Kermit the Frog. The Westerbeke group was shocked. They did not want to send a message representing such a flippant idea. They, too, would rather have had a spiritual and loving image of some sort to send. They were not focused on the frog, and the Russian group did not receive it. The next target was also a disappointment to the California group. It was a picture of Buffalo Bill, carrying a gun. This represented an old violent way of life, and again, they were not united in their intention or desire to transmit such a message.

The Tbilisi group, however, had a tradition of wonderful stories about Buffalo Bill, since he had taken a Russian prince on a hunting trip into parts of the western US. He had also visited Russia and went hunting with the prince there. (In the Buffalo Bill Museum in Cody, Wyoming, there is a marvelous blanket made of furs of different colors from various Russian animals that the prince had presented to Buffalo Bill as a "thank you" gift.) Old Bill was something of a hero in the USSR. Most of the members of the Tbilisi group received that message telepathically as though it were a statue of a hero, while one of them received the idea of violence.

Our tradition of keeping all targets totally secret from the *sender* in advance grew out of the constant attack by skeptics attempting to find all possible avenues of fraud in all psi experiments. It never occurred to the participants in this intercontinental attempt to communicate to deviate from the accepted protocol. However, for this one, skeptics had nothing to do with it. Cheating during this experience was never the issue. This was a spiritual mission. The intention was to be loving, friendly, and to attempt to contact each other in spite of differences in education, ideologies, politics, and a distance of 10,000 miles. Later, when some of Westerbeke's group went to the USSR to meet the other group, they were able to discuss these issues. Friendship was strengthened and that friendship continued. Believing that the regular practice of meditation is primary to the understanding of non-local mind, the Westerbeke group had met regularly to meditate together and to establish rapport before they attempted to transmit messages to the Tbilisi group. I was told that psychedelics were definitely *not* used for that experience.

Other types of very large group resonances were revealed when US astronauts walked on the moon that first time in 1969. Millions of people watched that live television broadcast simultaneously. A profound sense of national pride was deeply felt by all. We were thrilled to think of our men walking on the moon, and watching it while it happened was a memorable experience.

From that event we began to realize that great numbers of people in different parts of the country and the world could be stimulated to think about the same things at the same time. Itzhak Bentov thought that such energy could be used in some way. He suggested that people in a variety of locations might focus their minds together to prevent a very heavy Russian satellite from falling on a populated area. It was already doomed to fall back to Earth and could cause great devastation. Bentov suggested that we use PK simultaneously to lift the object to a higher orbit, or to send it to the ocean. Buryl Payne took up the suggestion and mailed letters to a large group of people, listing the exact time for the experiment in a variety of time zones. He also announced the project on radio and TV. As the time approached for the group to focus their combined mind energy on the space object, Bentov boarded a plane from the Chicago O'Hare Airport. He was scheduled to give a workshop about his research in LA. Then at the exact time the group began to focus on the attempt to raise the Russian object to a higher orbit, one of the engines of the plane Bentov was on dropped from the sky. The plane crashed and all on board were killed. The tragic synchronicity of both events was shocking to all of us. Sannella flew to LA to conduct the workshop in memory of his friend. Yet as sad as he was at the loss of his friend, he felt that even Bentov would understand the karmic humor of both events and might have laughed all the way down to the crash site.

Years later, a massive group meditation was planned to coincide with the Harmonic Convergence of planets. Participants reported feeling the power of love, friendship and gratitude that was generated by so many people meditating at the same time. Today the advancing technology that allows so many people to link up on web sites across the world has generated new experiences in group consciousness, and this promises to grow exponentially.

Following the PK experiments with random-number generators (RNGs) in Princeton, (101) Dean Radin, PhD, designed a way to measure the effects of resonance of large groups of people. On March 3, 1995, he set up several RNGs in different places to look for deviations in randomness while one billion people in 120 countries were watching the live TV broadcast of the Sixty-seventh Annual Academy Awards. He also used RNGs when three billion people around the world watched the opening ceremonies of the centennial Olympic Games in July 1996. He found strong statistically significant shifts away from randomness during the times of the highest interest during both broadcasts. (102) He stated that this variation from randomness implies "...the field-consciousness effect was nonlocal..." and there is "...a fundamental connectedness among all things, including individual and 'mass minds'."

The observed shifts in randomness of a carefully crafted RNG machine (previously tested to be mathematically random) must be taken into account when considering the fundamental organization of the universe, the structure of life and the nature of consciousness. Albert Einstein once declared, "God *does not* play dice with the universe"—yet many leading scientists today disagree with him because they are convinced that chance does rule events. Many cannot believe that precognition is possible, because there are too many variables in the chance of chaos. On the other hand many others have experienced precognitive events that changed their lives. This argument about whether our existence and our world has come about through "chance or design" has raged for generations. Now with the definitive RNG experiments by Radin, it is clear that consciousness can and does affect chance. The old argument has been expanded to show that there is chance **and** design. Consciousness can re-design chaos into order. No "scientific" description of the universe can be complete without including the fundamental organizing principle which is consciousness.

Successful gamblers have always counted on their ability to influence the roll of the dice. Those who practice psychokinesis (PK), spiritual healing, or have learned to believe in prayer and positive thinking use the principles of focused intention. Whether belief is rooted in religion or in the intervention of saints, spirit guides, angels, or lucky charms, the intention to affect the outcome of events has been practiced with varying degrees of success for uncounted centuries by people of all races and classes.

Now we can see the power of the resonance of consciousness over the mathematical purity of the concept of randomness. It would be fun to test this in a different way. Suppose while a billion people are still focused on one TV show, the broadcasting station were to announce that the station would turn off the signal for one minute (or perhaps raging sunspots block the signal). How would the RNGs respond to that? Suppose a billion, or even a million, people who were watching the same show could be convinced to turn off their own sets for one minute simultaneously. In addition to the effect that might have on the RNGs, the sudden shift in the variety of electromagnetic frequencies produced by TV might cause those people to go into an altered state of consciousness.

## DO PSYCHEDELICS HELP OR HINDER INTELLIGENCE OR REMOTE VIEWING?

"...We have entered into the dialog of myth, tapped into that ancient current of passionate hope and risky belief that mankind can evolve into a higher wisdom....The seeds of the sixties have taken root underground. Their blossoming is to come."

Timothy Leary, 1974
*Seeds of the Sixties* (103)

(Written while he was in prison for possession of less than half an ounce of marijuana.)

In this prison paper, Leary outlined the solid scientific research using LSD that he was hired to do at Harvard as a behavioral psychologist, beginning in January 1960. He describes the amazing results they achieved to effect behavior change, and the persecution that followed. After leaving Harvard, he and his colleagues started centers for training in consciousness expansion and a scientific journal for communicating the results of their research.

That blossoming he predicted can be seen today as a few intellectual leaders have been willing to admit that their honored innovations in botany, biology and computer technology, were revealed to them during LSD trips. (104) In October 1996, Nobel laureate in chemistry Kary B. Mullis, PhD, told the audience at the Third International Conference on Entheobotany, "I was at Berkeley and taking acid every week. That's what people did for entertainment: drink beer *or* go out into Tilden Park and take 500 micrograms of LSD and sit all day thinking about the universe, time going backward and forward...."

For a while, there was a fruitless hope that LSD might remain legal. Later there was another fruitless hope that MDMA might remain legal. Its use seemed to open the hearts of people, allowing them to forgive past insults and to show love more easily. It is powerful when used in psychotherapy; for those dying of cancer, AIDS, or other diseases (to help alleviate fear of the unknown); and among philosophers discussing ideas openly and without ego competition. Several books have been written about actual transformative experiences using MDMA (often called *Adam* or *ecstasy*) and some of its analogs. A collection of accounts from people who had experienced MDMA or other empathogenic substances was published in the book

*Through The Gateway Of The Heart.* (105) The following is from one report after a guided therapeutic session:

"...I found that if the mind is focused on an inquiry or is open to some truth, insights concerning the issue are revealed, consistently. One thing that I am most impressed with is that the insights about my life and about the lives of others are so profound that I am motivated to immediately take action. This has turned out to be very effective in my daily life....

I suspect that Adam experiences are quite unique and custom-made to the individual. Motivation, integrity, and the degree one has prepared one's life for true insights... make a lot of difference in the kind of experience that one has. I feel that I have no need for repeated sessions, at least for the present, for the clairvoyance and a sense of open truth in expression that it has helped to open continue for me as a sustained way of life."

MDMA and many of its analogs are thoroughly documented by Shulgin in *Pihkal*. One of them is designated as 2-CD. (106) This is a quote from a person who ingested it in a small dose (about 10 mg): "There is something going on, but it is subtle. I find that I can just slightly redirect my attention so that it applies more exactly to what I am doing. I feel that I can learn faster. This is a 'smart' pill!"

Here is a different report about the testing of the "smart" pill: "The ranges from 10 to 20 mg produced a state of mild intoxication with increased sensory enhancement....From 5 to 10 mg it produced calm states wherein one could read, study, or listen with excelled concentration and...with much better than normal retention."   .

One woman reported an improved ability to play her piano by ear after ingesting one smart pill. She also reported that her increased ability remained when she was no longer under its chemical influence. A man claimed that he was able to challenge and pass his foreign language exam with a high grade after cramming for only two weeks with the help of these smart pills. The answer to one question is that yes, certain psychedelics can enhance intelligence in many ways if used properly.

The word *psychedelic* means mind manifesting or mind expanding. The word is not defined by flashing lights, bright swirling colors, or tie-dye tee shirts, as advertisers would like to have you think. Whether or not the use of psychedelic chemicals can enhance telepathy has been one of my own major questions since 1963. There are several answers to that question which we have explored over the years, and the results are mixed. The first questions to ask are: Have you learned to use psychedelics to expand your ability to focus attention? Have you learned to explore your own projections and emotional attachments? Have you learned how to keep your projections out of the RV exercise as much as is possible? When the answers to these questions are "yes," the use of psychedelics to do remote viewing has a good chance of being successful. Many of us have used them in that way for years. If the answers are "no" you might not find psychedelics useful for RV.

For those who are easily distracted, or who suddenly find themselves involved in an unresolved cosmic drama, then the answer is definitely "no." Here is an example: A young man, we shall call Ed, settled down comfortably to enjoy an evening with friends, all of whom have ingested a similar psychedelic substance. They planned this as a telepathic session with another group of friends in another setting, who have also ingested the same substance. Suddenly, Ed feels like a small child in a bed at his grandmother's house. He hadn't thought about that bed for many years. But now he can hardly breathe, and he is afraid he might die. He asks a friend for help. His friend tells him to go ahead and explore his feelings fully. (The ego-death experience and the vision of the radiant light of pure consciousness is a major goal when taking psychedelics.) However, his breathing becomes even more difficult, and he is immersed in fear. Now the entire group surrounds him, speaks softly, and encourages him to go deeper into his feelings. One friend guides him into the center of the light in his mind, and then out of his body into light. Finally, feeling free of his body, he can breathe easily. The fear was transformed into a transcendental experience. He now feels wonderful! After a long meditation, he returned to the present spacetime and could talk to his friends again. He had pneumonia when he was four years old, and couldn't breathe. He was afraid that he might die then. Over the years he forgot the incident, but the fear was with him ever since. He frequently felt some unreasonable fear whenever he was in a tight situation. Finally he understood why. Having resolved that fear with friends to guide him, he could now breathe better than ever before. Even the recurrent attacks of asthma that he had in the past eventually diminished. The cosmic drama of life and death had been more important than anything else he might have done. Once the drama starts, it must be completed. Any attempt to play other games, such as RV, is definitely not advised, nor would any likely be successful. One has to wait for clarity to be restored before taking on anything external.

> "...I was at Berkeley and taking acid every week. That's what people did for entertainment: drink beer *or* go out into Tilden Park and take 500 micrograms of LSD and sit all day thinking about the universe, time going backward and forward...."
>
> **Kary B. Mullis, PhD**
> **Nobel Laureate in Chemistry**

Such a life and death drama is not the fault of the psychedelic, which is only the catalyst for that particular manifestation of mind. I have seen the same type of life/death drama evoked after only one puff of marijuana. The drama is within, and it can be evoked in any number of ways, such as a fall, an injury, a stay in the hospital, a frightening situation. When such a drama has been evoked and the person becomes afraid and is without a helper who understands, or is in an unsupportive setting, s/he may remain afraid long after the psychedelic (or other catalyst) is gone from the physical system or the environment.

Once I was asked by a medical clinic to work with a young man who had become a hypochondriac. He was sure his heart would stop at any time. He frequently went to the doctor with many complaints, though the doctor found no physical reasons for his fears. We discovered during our session that his fears began during an LSD trip several years before. He feared then he was going to die, and no one told him it was OK to leave the body temporarily. No one knew to tell him to identify with the pure light of consciousness. I encouraged him to relive that fear, even though his screams echoed throughout the clinic for a short time. Finally he was able to experience what it was like to leave his body, and to watch himself scream. Once he did that, the fear of several years was over. It did not return. His doctor reported to me that he no longer complained of heart trouble. Since we were in a medical clinic at the time, and since the patient was afraid of psychedelics, none were used. The whole drama welled up within him using only guided imagery, but it was the same fundamental fear-of-death cosmic drama that we may all face at some time, with or without drugs.

Here is an example of another type of experience in which an attempt to do remote viewing can be badly distorted: A sixteen year old boy just got his driver's license. His mother allowed him to borrow the family car to visit friends, but he was late getting home. As she began to worry about him, she started to project her own worst fears. While she was still crying as she visualized him lying on the ground and bleeding from a terrible accident, he walked in the door, perfectly healthy, and told her about the heavy traffic jam that delayed him. Some people can project all kinds of negativity on their children even without psychedelics. This is not a healthy thing to do, for parents or for children. Even without the use of drugs, people can project their own fears into the unknown, and amplify them. This is a common error with some parents —they worry too much. It may not be easy to establish nonattachment to your children, but it is the best way to achieve clarity about them. (The word *detachment* implies not caring, *nonattachment* is the best form of caring, because it allows clarity of vision without projection.) Whether we know it or not, our thoughts, and especially our emotions, have energy. The emotions of worry, anger and fear communicate to our children in a powerful way both consciously and subconsciously wherever they are. My daughter's psychic advice to me when I was upset is useful in many situations. "Pray, don't worry, mother." Develop the habit of surrounding your loved ones with light, no matter what you think their problems might be. This is the best use of your innate psychic ability. Light is useful to them, fear is not.

A more distant remote viewing example is illustrated by this true story: Tom went to visit various places in Europe. His friend Bill was planning a trip to Europe and was eager to find Tom while they were both there. I agreed to try to make a telepathic contact. After taking LSD, the first two hours were spent clearing my mind, and the next five hours were spent visualizing his face. Each time I "saw" him, he turned his head away, which meant he had not yet noticed that I was trying to contact him. Eventually, as I visualized his face, he looked me in the eye, which is a sign that I can deliver a short message. The message was, "Call me, Bill wants to find you." In the morning Tom called long-distance from Europe to ask me for Bill's phone number. He said he had awakened in the morning with the strong idea that he wanted to communicate with him. By then, I was exhausted, but the experiment was successful.

In the Sixties and Seventies, some of us thought that we needed LSD or psilocybin mushrooms for long-distance telepathy, or for a séance. However, we learned much from their use, and as the years went by, we also learned to operate in the hyperspace more efficiently. The use of the strong psychedelic was no longer necessary. Marijuana worked just as well, and so did meditation. It is much easier to end a session when you want to than to keep

feeling "stoned" for six to twelve hours. It is easier to guide a person, using hypnosis, into the hyperspace and back in two hours than to guide him/her through the many hours that LSD takes. LSD really needs three days for optimum use; one day to prepare the psyche; one to take the substance; the next day to rest the body, and to contemplate and integrate the insights. When using various mind-altering chemicals, we must remember that the body is burning its energy at faster rates than normal. This means that it is essential to replace that energy with rest and nutrients. Owsley once said, "Old heads take vitamins." The implication was that an acid head (a person who chooses to burn life's energy faster than normal for the *high* feeling it provides) would not live long enough to become an "old head" without replacing the vital nutrients the body needs. I know a number of senior citizens (old heads) who followed this advice and can still take an occasional "trip into the countless galaxies of their own nervous systems" just for fun, for increased psychic communication and sensuality, and for the lifelong learning the adventure provides.

Other important questions to ask about using psychedelics for psi activity are which substance used how, where, in what setting, and for what purpose? The setting is important. For good remote viewing work, it is essential that the setting be protected from intrusion, that the qual be supportive, and that the mental attitude be devoted to the task at hand. Once you hold the concept that your consciousness has access to the hyperspace, you are free to explore the multiple dimensions.

Marijuana can be very useful as an aid to hypnosis. A small puff of marijuana can help one to relax and to focus his/her attention on releasing the emotions of old traumatic events which had been locked up in the memory since childhood. Memories of the day we were born can be part of those old memories evoked by hypnosis. Whether or not the hippocampus has been formed, memories of body sensations before language, before birth, are imprinted into

> **There is no doubt that psychedelics, properly used, can help some people develop the mindset necessary for successful telepathy and remote viewing. There is also no doubt that some well-known psychics never needed or used psychedelics. The multidimensional mind is naturally able to travel in the hyperspace, when the limits of personality are put aside. The regular practice of meditation is essential.**

consciousness. (107) Here the resonance of the hypnotist and the client may be improved by the use of small amounts of marijuana, so that the mentations of the client are more easily transmitted to the hypnotist to facilitate healing and release of traumatic material.

Proper use of marijuana can provide spiritual comfort and creative inspiration. Integration of our mental activities is the key to the understanding of our multiple selves. Integration is what all the schools of meditation strive to teach. Without integration, mind-to-mind communication with another is greatly compromised. Our research suggested that the use of high-grade marijuana can increase the interhemispheric phase coherence of brainwaves. This coherence can facilitate the integration of mental functions. The daily practice of meditation is also a way for mental functions to become integrated. When the practice becomes a habit, that effort helps integration to become firmly established.

On the negative side, the billion dollar war on drugs has changed things, so that more tax money is now spent on prisons than on colleges. The prisons are full of those charged with victimless crimes, such as smoking marijuana, or simply growing a plant for home use, while people who need cannabis for medical reasons cannot get it. The prohibition has created crime syndicates and corruption, reminiscent of the years of alcohol prohibition. The price of an ounce of high-grade marijuana is now greater than the price of an ounce of gold. This costly war has not prevented the cheaper low-grade marijuana (containing the sleep component) from being readily available on every school campus. Those government bureaucracies that have disseminated propaganda against marijuana for such a long time have come to believe their own fantasies about it.

On the positive side, the resonance between the chemistry and the music as it developed in the Sixties also changed many things. Countless people learned that the power to make the leap into the hyperspace and into non-local spacetime is intrinsic within each of us. If we don't know how to evoke that potential of the psyche, psychedelics may help us discover it. It is also possible to learn to develop and to expand that personal power without them, though it may take longer. However, through psychedelics our understanding of the multidimensional world is changing—our understanding of ourselves can grow exponentially. The 21st century will not be drug free, no matter how long the war on drugs lasts, though perhaps some of the more dangerous legal and illegal drugs may give way to the use of natural herbs.

> **Dean Radin found strong statistically significant shifts away from randomness during the times when billions of people watched live TV broadcasts. He stated that this variation from randomness implies "...the field-consciousness effect was nonlocal..." and there is "...a fundamental connectedness among all things, including individual and 'mass minds'."**

There is no doubt in my mind that psychedelics, properly used, can help a person develop the mindset necessary to do telepathy and remote viewing successfully. There is also no doubt that some well-known psychics never needed or used psychedelics. The multidimensional mind is naturally able to travel in the hyperspace, when the limits of personality are put aside. I once met Pat Price at SRI. He was one of the very best remote viewers that the SRI parapsychology team had employed in its early research in the Seventies. He was an ex-police officer who had successfully used remote viewing many times to solve crimes. From his years in law enforcement, he totally disapproved of the use of drugs for any reason. He disapproved of my suggestion that they could be used successfully. However, since he was no longer a police officer, we could discuss the issues openly.

The present political scene needs to hold fair and open discussions on these issues as well. Even though not everyone responds to mind chemistry the same way, it is time to drop the false information that leads to hysteria, and face the real situation. Beyond the well-publicized examples of abuse, there are the marvelous uses for creativity. A recent conference on the use of psychedelics as an aid to creativity was held in Hawaii. It was organized by botanist and author Terence McKenna and others. Most of the participants were well-known artists, writers and musicians willing finally to discuss these issues openly, though it was still risky to do so, considering the unsettled legal and political climate in the late Nineties.

Marijuana has been used for healing among millions of people around the world. Many societies have regarded it as a sacred herb and used it as a sacrament since the dawn of human existence. It was found buried with ancient mummies in Asia. Cannabis grows in some variety everywhere on Earth that plants can grow. It can be helpful in mind-to-mind communication, in management of stress, in healing and for integration of the multiple areas of mind.

## EXPERIMENTER EFFECT

Since we co-exist in a rich brew of psychic soup, there is no way to be totally "objective," especially when we study our multidimensional minds in bits and pieces only. The problems begin with the belief system of the observer, the stated goals of the research project and the way the questions are asked, which set the format for the answers expected. The only hope of finding relevant information comes from the need to know. When the research project sets out to prove or to disprove a preconceived idea, it is possible for the observations that are made to be skewed.

**1. Source of Research Funding May Prejudice the Outcome of Results** — If enough money is riding on the outcome, the researcher who is hired to prove or to disprove the value of a product, for example, may be expected to come up with the "right" answer or be fired, or the "wrong" results might be disregarded. Though very little money was available, a battle of belief systems has brewed for many years between skeptics and parapsychologists (pages 201 to 206). A more expensive battle is now brewing between those who were educated in allopathic medicine and those who have studied herbal medicine and stress management. A broken leg needs a good surgeon, but a run-down immune system may need healthy food and protective herbs. An allopathic doctor might prescribe anti-biotics while ignoring diet, exercise and vitamins. The medical research reports show widely conflicting results depending on whether they were generated by pharmaceutical companies, by insurance companies, by doctors involved in "traditional medicine," or by doctors involved in the various forms of "alternative medicine." The general public can become confused.

**2. Resonance or Static Between Observer and Observed Can Make a Difference in Results** — The most subtle level of experimenter effect that we were able to experience directly is in the use of various types of physiological feedback, especially brainwave biofeedback. When I am producing simultaneous alpha, images and feelings roll past continuously. If I find one that interests me more than the rest, my brainwaves change as I pay attention to it. If there is a strange sound, and I listen to it, my brainwaves change. Every shift in focus of attention is accompanied by a shift in the frequencies of the brainwaves. If the monitor studies the equipment in a certain way, I may shift my attention to him/her for a moment. All of this shifting of attention is recorded in terms of the measured percent time of the frequencies being studied. Going deeper, if my phase-coherent alpha increases significantly and the ratio

between that and the simultaneous alpha increases, I am simply experiencing the vibration of the feedback sound, or focusing on the light in the center of my brain. I am not thinking in words or images, but if I say to myself, "Oh, now I'm in synch," the sound turns off. The observer in me and the one being in synch do not operate in the same frequency. A nervous or judgmental experimenter can affect the one being observed, especially if s/he is attempting to do something as subtle as telepathy or EEG biofeedback.

Since there is no real objectivity in subtle mind research, those who pretend that there is may be indulging in hypocrisy. Honesty demands that the researcher state a belief system in advance and how s/he will use the experimenter effect. We tried to create a situation in which brainwave synchronization and telepathy were more likely to happen, since it is rare. We surrounded our participants in a physically and emotionally supportive environment in which our mutually harmonic resonances could encourage the necessary openness to explore what might be possible.

**3. Experimenter Effect Can Be Compared to the Interactions Between Teachers and Students** — A teacher or parent who is frequently judgmental may seriously discourage open mindedness in a child and his/her tender creative efforts. Positive reinforcement of creativity can improve overall intelligence and interest in the world. Raising children might be called an experiment, since babies don't come with instructions. Static in a family makes a difference in the karma of children by the choices each one makes in response to disharmony. One child may develop a feeling of being inferior to others. Another may become rebellious. Harmonic resonance in a family can encourage an openness to explore the array of potential intelligences of all their multidimensional minds.

Cartoon © copyright by Gahan Wilson, 1978.  (108)

# CHAPTER FIVE — TRANCE

## FIVE TYPES OF TRANCE STATES ARE EXPERIENCED IN DIFFERENT WAYS

Since many writers use the term *"trance"* in different ways, this word must be defined before it can be used to communicate the particular meanings intended here. *Webster's New World Dictionary* states that the original meaning is from the Latin *("transire, to die, literally to go across")* We also find some closely related words such as, *"entranced," "transfixed" and "transcend,"* that are also used in discussions of altered states of consciousness. These are all derived from the same root, *"trans."* Among the several definitions of *"trance"* in the dictionary are these five types which are described in more detail in this chapter:

1. *Trance as induced by religious fervor or mysticism*
2. *Trance as a condition of great mental concentration*
3. *Trance as used in hypnosis*
4. *Trance as a result of a stunned condition, as in a daze or stupor*
5. *Trance as used to receive communication from spirits*

Anthropologist Ruth-Inge Heinze, PhD, has traveled extensively in Asia and has lived with and studied the trances of more than 120 shamans. She has provided the diagram below, which includes all types of trance. Her diagram clearly illustrates the important differences between them; loss of awareness vs. increased awareness; mind expansion vs. dissociation. These different types of trance states can range from stupor to great mental concentration.

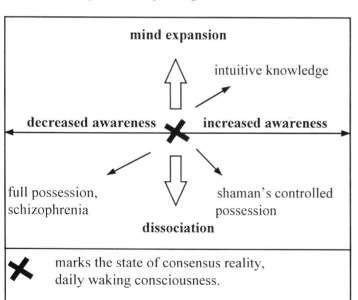

marks the state of consensus reality, daily waking consciousness.

The first type is one that is *induced by religious fervor or mysticism.* This is described at length by Dr. Heinze, in her book, *Shamans of Twentieth Century.* (109) The second type, that is *a condition of great mental concentration,* can be achieved when one is totally focused in the center of the brain where thoughts give way to pure vibration. The brainwaves of one such self-induced trance state are illustrated on page 144. The third type which is *used in hypnosis* is discussed in terms of the beneficial uses of hypnotherapy. The fourth type that occurs *as a result of a stunned condition, as in a daze or stupor* is explored here as it relates to some effects of watching television for long periods of time. (Other causes of this type, such as serious shock or illness, are not discussed here.) The fifth type *used to receive communication from spirits* of discarnate or ultra-dimensional entities is illustrated by the trance paintings of Luis Gasparetto on pages 149 and 150. He is a well known artist in Brazil. He was raised in an Espiritista family, and he claims to channel various famous artists who are deceased. The dramatic shift in his EEG which occurred while he was channeling two spirits simultaneously is shown on page 151.

**1. Trance as Induced by Religious Fervor or Mysticism** — Among the societies in the southern US and in Haiti who practice this type of trance are those who follow Voodooism. The entire group dances to drums and music to reach the trance state that can provide them with visions or until they become possessed by the special spirit or protective deity they seek. Other societies in Africa and South America use a similar process of dancing, drumming and music to achieve this type of trance state.

From her wealth of experiences among the various shamans of Asia, Dr. Heinze writes:

> The shamans I studied in Asia and elsewhere are expected to have access to information not obtainable with our five senses. (Incidentally, in Asia, there are six senses, because the mind counts as one, too.) Shamans in Asia use a wide range of different states of consciousness which can be distinguished by using the working model (left).
>
> The development occurs on the diagonal, i.e., toward mind expansion with increased control over the respective state or toward possession with decreased control over the respective state. Each state distinguishes itself from any other by its state-specific qualities.

All the shamans I worked with told me that they either use sonic driving (chanting and drumming) to call a deity into their body (possession state) or meditation for a mind-expanding state. One of the shamans in Singapore allowed a spirit to use her body while her soul was visiting the heavens. She had no recall of what occurred during possession trance but talked at length about her visits to other realms. Her main work was done by the spirit when she experienced possession trance (the spirit was definitely the actor). In Asia, the people want to come into the "presence of the Divine." They want to look the god into his or her face. They want to talk to the god directly. In most cases, however, it is the god who talks to them. The god knows their problems already without being told.

Generally, when such trance states are deliberately induced in a religious ceremony, there are also those who are designated to help and to protect the ones who become possessed and are no longer able to control the actions of their bodies. When the ceremony has been completed, the participants share their visions and insights with the group.

**2. Trance as a Condition of Great Mental Concentration** — A trance state is for some a key component in the transition from ordinary awareness to the ability to access information from the hyperspace. The ability to maintain a steady focus of attention (or to be driven into it) can trigger the trance state. Since we have observed the brainwaves of various types of trance states of different people over the years, we believe that interhemispheric phase coherence *(IH synch),* no matter how brief, may precede trance as a doorway into non-local spacetime. Trance states are important in the explorations of the potential of mental activity. They should not be hidden, or assumed that they are used only by shamans of primitive cultures. Conscious use of trance states can be educational for everyone.

One of the potential outcomes of sustaining a focus in *IH synch* is a gradual or sudden shift into a state of trance, though this is not always an automatic response. If the individual is focused on the intention to move into trance,

then it is likely to occur. If a person is unaware of the possibility and watches TV (or other flickering light) for a long time, or gets involved with simultaneous group activity which include dancing, clapping, and/or chanting in rhythm, s/he may enter into trance unexpectedly. Anyone can find him/herself in a state of trance and feel that the experience was transcendental. However, without prior knowledge of the state and not expecting it to occur, one can become distressed, feel that something is wrong, feel like a robot, or become afraid. It is important to discuss openly the issues that surround trance states. It is especially important to discuss them with children who watch many hours of TV, as well as with all those who are likely to experiment with various mind-altering substances.

As with other states of consciousness, each person's EEG of the trance state is unique. The illustration below is a recording of my own brainwaves as I entered a trance state. With mental concentration, I can center all thought into a light or a hum without words, I can then move my focus past the spacetime concerns of the cortex and shift it up to the crown chakra (vertex) and beyond. Beginning at this level, several altered states are possible. Part of the job of the cortex and other brain centers is to maintain the personality's relationship to time and space. When my focus of attention is totally centered in the brain, I can become nonattached to present time and space. When I transcend my attachment to words, and to the demands of the dominant personality, I can begin to identify with the pure light of the brain's electrical energy. I can choose to leave the body to see events from a different perspective, or to channel energy in through the crown chakra, or to explore the various realms among the multiple dimensions of mind.

All of us can learn to take advantage of trance states. We can travel in space without leaving the house—to visit friends or to do remote viewing. We can explore parts of our internal body and carry on a discussion with each part about what it needs to be healthy. We can channel energy for ourselves or to share with others. We can travel backwards in time, to childhood memories long forgotten, even to the day we were born (and some believe into past lives, as well). We can travel forward in time, usually only if the

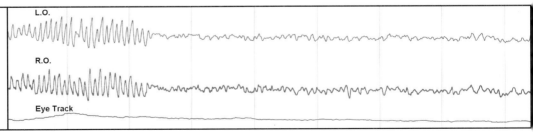

This EEG tracing shows my left and right occiput as I shift my attention from meditation in a phase-coherent alpha to a deeper trance state which has a lower amplitude and a variety of frequencies.

L.O.

R.O.

Eye Track

information is not critical to our desire or emotional attachments. Once a person learns a method of self-induced trance, the intention to know something at a distance is an exercise worth practicing.

**3. Trance as used in Hypnosis** — The third definition of trance suggests the use of therapeutic hypnosis. As you can now discern, the state of mind that is possible through hypnotic induction is not sleep-like as the word implies. It does involve the deep relaxation of the body, however. When the body becomes totally relaxed, the mind can become keenly aware of other dimensions. So the word "hypnosis" is not really accurate, though it is the one most commonly used. The "hypnotist" is one who knows how to guide a person into a trance state, and who can direct a person through the doorway into the hyperspace. I prefer to refer to the hypnotherapist as the *guide*; to the the client as the *traveler*; and to the state one achieves, which encourages open exploration into pre-conscious or even subconscious memories, as *guided trance.* In any case a good guide uses trance as a positive way to help people become re-connected to their own individual realities. (110) A variety of methods has been devised over the years by different practitioners to facilitate this state. A person who is willing can be guided by the voice of one he trusts to become deeply relaxed. This is the first step. The next step is to become nonattached to present time and space. At that point the travel in other dimensions can begin. The guide might suggest that the traveler look around and describe what is seen, or simply answer the question, *"What are you experiencing now?"* If visions appear from the traveler's pre-conscious mind spontaneously while the eyes are still closed, the session has begun successfully. These images can be used therapeutically and expanded to yield creative insights. However the guide must be clear. Since the traveler has allowed him/herself to become open to suggestion, this relationship between the two is a sacred trust which must be maintained to allow the traveler to explore his/her internal processes and not be forced to take on the guide's own personal limitations and belief system.

One useful guided relaxation method involves using the chakras—the seven basic energy centers in the body (e.g., survival, sexuality, power, compassion, self-expression, intellect and spirit). Suggestions are very carefully provided to help us (the travelers) become nonattached to all previous thoughts relating to each of the energy centers until we can *focus all our attention in the center of our brains,* and become nonattached to present time and space. This is the moment that the trip "into the countless galaxies of our own nervous systems" can begin. Memories of

events long forgotten come to life. Our ability to take on the personality of someone else in the past gives rise to the belief among some of us that we actually might be experiencing a past life. We may be, but consensus has not yet been established about just what we are able to experience and how it might be interpreted. The Tibetans believe that the Dalai Lama has been reincarnated fourteen times as the same soul. When he was still a child he even remembered where his former self, the thirteenth Dalai Lama, left his false teeth. This is a very compelling story to support the idea that we have experienced different lives in different times. In any case when a guide can help us feel what it is like to be a different person who is caught up in a different drama, we gain some flexibility in our reality structures. When a guide helps us experience the death of that different person, and the birth back into our present body, we may lose some of our fear of death and gain insight into the existence of consciousness as it shines independently from any particular personality.

Trance can also occur spontaneously in other ways without the suggestions of a guide. We must realize that many things in our world can cause trance-like states. Performances of music, dance, and drama in a darkened theater are designed to take us away from ordinary life events and *transport* us into another world. Appreciation of a great painting can also bring on a state of awe as we become *entranced.* Nature itself may be the guide. A glorious sunrise, the vast distances we can see from a mountain top, or the first radiant flower blooming as the snow melts in spring might very well inspire a memorable *transcendental* experience.

**4. Trance as a Result of a Stunned Condition, as in a Daze or Stupor** — Trance can be a double-edged sword. Used with care it can help cut across years of self-defeating, negative thinking about ourselves (if we have suffered from that). It can show us our potential abilities, opening our minds to our own true multidimensional natures. (111) It can help us find access to non-local space-time (112), and it can put us in direct contact with our ancestors. (113) It can help us blend with nature, for greater spiritual understanding of our proper relationship with the Earth, the source of our life. On the other edge of the sword, it can be used by the greedy on the unsuspecting and uneducated to create desires for things and experiences that are expensive and useless. Fortunes are made and elections are won by those who understand the way human nature responds to repeated suggestions from the media, and the way in which sound bites can be manipulated to influence consumers and voters.

On a sliding scale between the third and fourth types of trance—from simple suggestibility to daze—we find the type of trance that comes with television. The flickering lights and sound can cause entrainment. Underneath all the drama and color is the fact that the TV image is drawn line by line very rapidly (about 530 lines per second), and then the whole picture changes at a rate of thirty frames per second (30 FPS). People who are susceptible to being induced into a trance state at this rate (which is harmonic with either 10 Hz or 15 Hz brainwaves) may very well be stuck with unwanted memories for the rest of their lives. Bio-feedback can help release the physiological and emotional reactions to it, but the memory itself will still be there.

Indeed TV has produced truly great performances, excellent educational programs, live broadcasts of important events wherever in the world they occur, fascinating nature studies using telephoto or magnifying lenses, time-lapsed photography and slow motion that show us things we could never see without them. Nevertheless, among the magnificent programs, we also find the worst of the negative effects of this type of trance. Most are produced by TV advertisers, often using trance states for the deliberate seduction of children. Advertisements for children's toys are the most flagrant in implanting hypnotic suggestions. The children's favorite program will be interrupted every few minutes with very colorful, fast-moving ads, which are repeated every day. By the time the program is over, the children may have an uneasy feeling. If their parents don't buy that toy for them, their friends will make fun of them, and they might be rejected socially. (114) This is what the Christmas season has been turned into. The trance states possible with TV can become addicting, especially for the addictive personality.

One time-honored practice, which has always disturbed me, is the advertising which usually accompanies the evening news around dinner time. The news is dramatized to increase anxiety, so if people develop an upset stomach because of the mixture of food and anxiety, one of the ads will be for medicine to cure acid indigestion. Literally billions of dollars are spent by advertisers to encourage the addiction to TV and to the way their repeated flashing light suggestions can be guided for profit. (115) Almost no research has been conducted by the state or federal governments or by educational institutions to study the effects of trance states on young children. The subject of trance has been sadly neglected in our educational systems, and it should be explored in depth for the sake of understanding the development of memory and the full nature of multidimensional consciousness.

> **The commercial success of movie and television programs which emphasize sex and violence has placed our civilization in a giant feedback loop with the dark side.**

Cartoons are particularly violent, and many children seem to have become desensitized to the violence they see there. Of course some violence has a time-honored presence in children's stories; after all, the wolf did eat Red Riding Hood's grandmother. But a story can be visualized from each child's own imagination. The graphic depiction of blood and guts on TV leaves very little to anyone's imagination, and the memory of those bloody images may have a life-long influence. It is difficult to prevent children from watching such violence on TV. Such movies earn money for the producers because so many people watch them. People are drawn into watching them because sex and violence naturally stimulate the most basic aspects of their multiple personalities. The commercial success of movie and TV programs emphasizing sex and violence places our civilization in a giant feedback loop with the dark side. Since freedom of speech is protected, as it should be, I do wonder what will come forth that will be strong enough to break that feedback loop before our society spirals down into a violence that is uncontrollable. As a society we are unconsciously allowing images of sex and violence to be deeply imbedded in our children's thought patterns as though they were socially acceptable.

It has been only a few decades since there was a public outcry against obscene language used in movies (in 1939, Clark Gable was allowed to say on screen, "Frankly, my dear, I don't give a damn!"). But by 1998, the desensitization was so complete that even the private sexual activity of the President of the US was broadcast daily for many months. Such an attack on the office of President was unheard of even fifteen years before then. This pandering to the public's prurient appetite effectively covered up the fundamental source of corruption that threatens democracy itself. Two of the major 1996 election issues were campaign finance reform and corporate welfare. The decision to table both issues so that the 1998 elections could be heavily financed as usual by interested corporations received only a small report in the media. Had the media decided to take up those issues every day instead of continually hammering away at the President's private indiscretions, the public might have been aroused to demand action against this continuing corrupting influence which exerts pressure on all elected officials. While congress focused on sex to feed the media frenzy, the public watched in outrage; some were upset about the immorality of infidelity and the lies to hide it; others were disgusted about the immorality of the flagrant invasion of personal privacy which could be applied to any of us as well, whether we have anything to hide or not.

Hidden behind the daily hypnotic TV sex report was the ongoing political scramble to raise the money to stay in office. The price tag to run for congressional office jumped from a rough average of eighty thousand dollars in 1976 to millions of dollars in 1996. (116) Because of such high costs, there is a strong feeling that politicians are in the corporate stew pot, no matter who is elected, even though some may actually be dedicated public servants. Bubbling out of that same stew pot, and financed by taxes, comes corporate welfare, some for corporations who avoid paying taxes themselves. (117) The need of candidates to use television hypnosis for repetitious political slogans during elections years is very profitable for the few large corporations who own the television industry. Since it is the federal government who grants the licenses to broadcast initially, this is the one of the first places where the major re-organization of campaign financing might begin.

Yet even during election campaigns, more of us are interested in being hypnotized by fantasy than by politics. Billions of dollars are spent every year to create fantasies for films, television, and theme parks. However as film and computer fantasies become more realistic, the line between actual events and imagination fades. What is the "real" news? How is it skewed politically and by whom? What is only fantasy? How can the average person tell the difference? When actual film images were used to make it seem that President Kennedy said and did things that he did not do or say in life, I was alarmed by the concept. Though the film that did this won honors for using the advanced technology in that way, and many thought it was funny, I feel that the First Amendment should protect the free speech and actual images recorded by the original person, dead or alive. No one should be allowed to digitize or to re-arrange actual footage of a real person to betray his own life. Anyone else has the right of free speech to say whatever he wants about that person, but let him do it with actors, not digitized actual footage. Hollywood has borrowed dramas from historical events and characters to create fiction since the beginning of motion pictures, but at least it is presented as fiction. TV hypnosis has the power not only to change history, but to create it in its own image.

However, we know that television, trance inducing or not, is here to stay. It has changed our world in all of its manifestations—both good and bad. Some people turn on the TV and instantly become dazed so they will watch anything that the flickering lights display without regard to the potential entrainment of memory. Such people seem to use TV to avoid conversation with family members. Others, not so ensnared, use the advertising time to walk away, turn the sound off, or to continue a conversation.

Besides TV, other aspects of the fourth definition of trance also fit into the negative potential resulting from *a stunned condition, as in a daze or stupor.* Fence posts or trees evenly spaced along the highway have been known to cause a driver, going at a certain speed, to go into trance, and perhaps cause an accident. Gambling casinos are carefully designed to cause customers to lose track of ordinary awareness, so they will also lose track of their money. The loud clatter of coins dropping into slot machine trays stir up the hope and greed of each gambler to think that everyone can win. Flashing lights surround the gamblers and reflecting mirrors everywhere. Actual money is exchanged for chips before one starts to gamble (so what is spent doesn't seem like real money), and in Las Vegas, one can put a credit card into the slot and lose everything before awareness returns. These can be serious problems for the unwary and the drunk. Scantily clad ladies make the rounds of the gambling halls to make sure that alcohol can be purchased easily everywhere in the casino. The Nevada state economy depends upon the billions of dollars taken from tourists in this way every year. These profits come from blatantly encouraging the daze-type of trance state in the gambling casinos. Special rooms are created right next to the casino for children to play computer games on look-alike slot machines. The children's environment is also hypnotic. Only the alcohol is missing as the law requires.

> "...If you want to right a wrong
> write your congressman, honey,
> but if you want him to read it
> you'd better send money.
> Write a few zeros out behind the one,
> 'cause that's the way the government
> gets things done.
>
> "And that fat cat rule remains the same.
> Said that fat cat rule ain't it due for change?"
>
> FAT CAT RULE
> copyright © 1989 Donald R. Douglas (118)

**5. Trance as Used to Receive Communication from Spirits** — While the daze-type of trance is used frequently for fun and profit, there are still those among the profit takers who will declare that trance states do not exist. Especially condemned is the fifth definition of trance that is evoked *to receive communication from spirits*. The idea that our ancestors, angels or spirit guides can transmit information to us is anathema to most institutions of Western science today.

The concept expressed by Heinze from her years of studying Asian shamans (that the spirit already knows whatever problems exist) is similar in the traditions of other cultures. For example the children of Native Hawaiians grow up expecting their ancestors to advise them, to offer suggestions, or to complete an unfinished thought. For them there is no need for a séance to call the spirit into the circle. Mahealani Kuamoó-Henry is a Ho'opono pono counselor in Pahoa, Hawaii. She told me that spirits of their ancestors accompany them throughout life and beyond, so it is not necessary to enter a trance state to hear what they have to say. (119) Within the Hawaiian language is found the prescription for the balanced health and life and family harmony. *"Ho'opono pono"* means setting relationships in balance. *"Aloha"* is a key word. *"Alo"* means *to share,* and *"ha"* means the same thing that it does in Sanskrit—*breath,* the essence of spirit and light, that connection which the life force rides upon. (In Greek, the word *"psychein"* means *to breathe* and so the word *"psyche"* became the word for *soul* or *spirit*.) In Hawaiian, the greeting *"aloha"* is not just *"hello"* or *"goodbye"* as the tourists have assumed. Aloha is love. To say *"aloha"* is to stand in the presence of the breath, spirit, and light and to acknowledge and recognize this in the other. This concept of love is based on *"akahai"* which is gentle and caring behavior. In contrast, the Hawaiian word for the white invaders is *"haole."* It literally means *"without breath"* or *"breathless,"* hence without connection to spirit. A major cause of anxiety with *haole* life is the disconnection with ourselves (our multiple personalities), with the Earth, and with those around us. The *haole* are seen as being disconnected also from their ancestors, and from the whole wealth of the spirit world. (120)

Many civilizations choose to honor the spirits of their ancestors and naturally included them in all family gatherings. In our society, some of us quietly feel the presence of grandmothers and grandfathers, and others have been conditioned to assume they are not there. Among my uncles were those who made fun of anyone who claimed that ancestral spirits were present. So I learned to keep my con-

Amelia Rose Garcia was convinced at the time that the painting (right) by Gasparetto was a portrait of her late mother. She sent me this photocopy of an old portrait of her mother (who was also named Amelia Garcia). Her mother was 27 years old when this picture was taken in 1928.

versations with the spirits of our grandparents to myself, except to share this secret with my children. That closed mindedness which unfortunately is widespread throughout Western civilizations, has given rise to the "professional psychic." This is one who will hold a séance for a fee to request the presence of a spirit to talk to the supplicant relatives. The relatives are rarely told that they can receive a communication directly from their own ancestors if they learn to be respectful to them and are open to receive it.

When I was invited to visit the Espiritista Clinic in São Paulo, Brazil, the director Dr. Eliezer Mendes employed three Espiritista mediums to work with his patients. He was able to put each one into trance very quickly, one at a time, by placing one hand in the center of the forehead and one in the center of back of the skull, like a sudden slap. This brought the medium's focus of attention instantly to the center of her head, and that was enough to put her into trance at once. There was, of course, an expectancy and a habit of doing so (a ritual, perhaps), which no doubt aided the onset of trance. During the two hours that we observed this process, each of the three mediums was put into trance four times, and each time they assumed different personalities that related to the different patients with whom they worked. The most amazing patient I observed was the spastic. He never stopped his jerky body movements until he also was put into trance. Then he lay very quietly, while the medium's body began to twitch in the way the spastic's body had done before he went into trance. When the session was over, the patient resumed his twitching, and the medium was free of it. Mendes told us that the spastic had done bad things in a past life and he was gradually beginning to understand what he had done so he would know what to do for penance and seek to be forgiven for his sins. Mendes also told us that if a patient had been subject to shock treatments in the past, that shock would show up in

*LUIS*
*GASPARETTO*

*TRANCE*
*PAINTINGS*
**October 4, 1980**

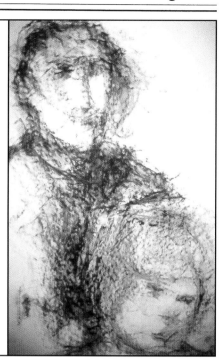

Gasparetto signed the acrylic painting on the left as though it had been channeled by Manet. He rubbed the paint on his hands and completed it in only eight minutes in various purple tones, adding a soft peach accent on the face.

Gasparetto claimed that two spirits controlled each hand separately when he did the pastel portraits on the right. Both hands did seem to work independently and simultaneously as I watched. He signed the lower one by Renoir. If there is another signature for the upper portrait, it is illegible.

the body of the medium during the healing experience. Why? Because while in trance, the medium would establish a resonance with the body of the patient, in order to clear the remnants of past pain and emotional scars. Mendes also claimed success in treating schizophrenia as well as epilepsy. A seizure was assumed to be caused by a spirit guide attempting to communicate with the patient. As the patient learned to channel the guide, instead of blocking the communication, he recovered from epilepsy.

Espiritista Luis Gasparetto came to San Francisco in 1980 to demonstrate his alleged ability to channel famous artists. Gasparetto comes from a family of Espiritistas, and he grew up with the idea that communicating with people who had died was natural. Parapsychologist Jeffrey Mishlove arranged to hold a demonstration session at the Washington Research Institute (WRI), so it could be video taped by Arthur Bloch. Amelia Rose Garcia agreed to play her electric piano during the session, because Gasparetto insisted that he would need music to help keep him in his trance state. He also declared that at an earlier time he had requested famous (but deceased) artists to be present at this session, and that they had agreed to participate.

About fifteen people arrived and settled themselves around on the floor cushions at the WRI. Gasparetto told us about his background and what he would do. Then he took all the paper covers off a whole set of oil pastels and arranged his paint tubes around him on a work table. Mishlove agreed to hand him a clean sheet of good-quality 22" x 30" illustration board and to remove the one that had

just been completed. After all was arranged, Gasparetto went into trance and asked the spirits to approach. He used the pastels for some pictures or rubbed paint on his hands to paint the others. He did one painting with his feet, after he rubbed paint on them. Each picture was allegedly from artists such as Renoir, Rembrandt, Manet, Van Gogh, Picasso. As he finished each one, he signed it with that artist's signature. Each painting rarely took more than eight minutes. After the trance session was over, he signed his own name on the back of each one with the date.

He completed twenty paintings during that time, some better than others. Gasparetto usually worked best in the dark, but he did agree to work in the light for the benefit of the video camera. Nevertheless, he seemed to keep his eyes closed, and often turned his head to the side. On one occasion, he declared that there would be two spirits, one controlling each hand, and he did two portraits simultaneously (top, right). Garcia claimed that the two figures looked just like her husband and her son. Later, she showed some emotion as she expressed her feelings that the Manet portrait (top, left) looked like old photos of her mother, who was deceased (opposite page). The one I liked best is the "Rembrandt" pastel, illustrated on page 150. It hung on the wall at the WRI for years, because so many people enjoyed its calming influence.

One of the paintings done in only five minutes was a very ugly, mostly black, painting. Gasparetto claimed that he had channeled it from Picasso. The music became uncomfortable during this time, and Garcia felt her music

**LUIS GASPARETTO**
TRANCE PAINTING
*October 4, 1980*

Gasparetto signed Rembrandt's name on this pastel portrait, and his own name on the back.

The colors are soft greens with a touch of black in the eyes, hair, and beard. All who saw this could feel the calming influence it provided.

was being channeled as well. When that painting had been completed there was a brief, but very welcome, pause for a change in the music, a change in the energy, and a change in the tape in the video camera.

Sitting behind me during this session was a scientist who was *very* skeptical! His energy was filled with unexpressed criticism of the whole event. I felt as though my own energies were being contained in a sandwich between the curious, the true believers, and this skeptic. Nevertheless, I did want to know for myself what might be happening here, so I became nonattached to the people around me and put myself into a light trance to see what I might find out. Suddenly I felt a very heavy feeling in my body. It was quite uncomfortable. Then a message came to me from a spirit who claimed to be Picasso. *"He"* said to me, *"I will tell you what art is. See all you can and express all you know about seeing."* At that point, the discomfort left my body as suddenly as it had come, but the message remained. Later I asked Gasparetto about his psychic encounter with Picasso. He said that Picasso's spirit was very difficult. It was uncomfortable to channel him. He was also known to be very hard on the women in his life. Gasparetto told me that the ugly black painting that I didn't like was intended to be a portrait of me. I was both disgusted and interested. After all, I had been wearing black clothes, and *"Picasso"* had given me a message that would be important to examine as I continued my research.

Gasparetto agreed to come to the Langley Porter Psychophysiology Lab the following day, so we could study

his EEG before, during, and after his trance state. When he was settled in the subject room and finally hooked up to all the electrodes, he meditated for a while, then asked the spirits to approach. He had a switch to press to indicate when his mind had shifted from one state to another. Since his EEG was rather complex, the PDP-15 computer at the lab was not programmed at the time to analyze all of it. From what we could see just looking at the chart, the record did not seem to change substantially from his unique meditation period to what he identified as his trance state. After he began channeling a spirit, whom he claimed was Toulouse-Lautrec, Gasparetto's own Brazilian accent (Portuguese) seemed to change to a French accent. We asked questions about how spirits interact with the brain and tape-recorded the answers. Unfortunately, some of the words on that tape were indistinct. For that reason, I have added a question mark (?) for those and a dash (—) to show where words are totally indistinguishable. There was no attempt to edit this, since the method of delivery is just as important as the information. The following is an unedited excerpt from that audio tape: (121)

*Millay: How do spirits interact with the brain?

*Gasparetto (allegedly speaking as Toulouse-Lautrec): My special interaction is the pineal condyle, acting directly in the gland. Putting my energy (?) to talk direct with Luis. (—) Putting my energy (?) in the talk of the head of Luis (—) and I concentrate myself 'till I feel that the aura changes color. When it changes color, I feel inspired to start the communication. When the vibration is very very right, I just think all my thinks, yes, transformed, in waves.

The waves go in the pineal condyle. The pineal condyle activates the cortex, and the cortex reads the waves. But I am dealing with his energy. When it is very low frequency, we don't deal with the pineal condyle: we deal with the hypophysis. *[author's note: old name for pituitary gland.]* Hypophysis is responsible to receive open energies and low energies and perhaps this is where the transformations like the (—), the aura (?) happens. For me, the cortex is just a place to represent, in words, my waves.

As Luis is conscious, the pineal gland cannot be controlled totally for me and what I transmit, not caring about Luis, perfectly while I think. The cortex interpreted my thoughts as I have a lot of affinity with Luis. This kind of disturbance is not too much. But when it's not the entity, who has no affinity, it is too difficult (?) to speak. Another

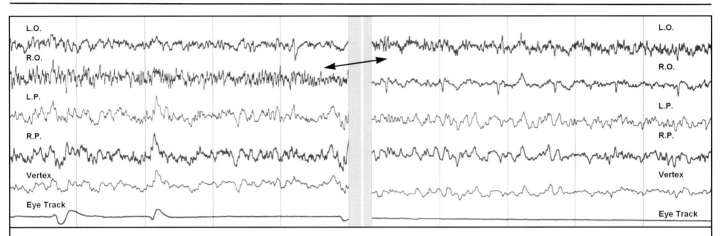

Johnston placed electrodes at five sites on Gasparetto's scalp: left and right occipital (**L.O.** / **R.O.**); the **vertex** (also known as the crown chakra); and left and right parietal (**L.P.** / **R.P.**). One extra site was used to track the movement of the eyes. Eye signals are stronger than brainwaves and can disrupt the accuracy of the EEG measurement. When Gasparetto asked the two different spirits to change sides from where they were, a change can be seen in his EEG between his right and left occipital signals. This is identified with the arrow above. The gray strip between the two graphs indicates that several seconds were left out of the illustration during the change. This is only one example, so it cannot be said to be definitive. Studies of trance states with modern equipment is needed.

thing, my thoughts are in French. As there is yet another (—) in me. To facilitate this communication, I'd like to learn some English and I try to think in English to have more affinity. Unless, if I think in French and Luis transmits in English, it will be a lot of difference in what I say.

The problem is not whether the pineal gland catches what I think, my waves. The problem is the interpretation of the cortex. The cortex is full of information, unnecessary in a conscious trance, and sometimes so tense and so full of energy (these thoughts), it is impossible for us to communicate or let the message pass through all these barriers.

The point where change—the point where all the sensations become perceptions is the pineal condyle. The pineal condyle has a most important function in all these states of consciousness, because the spirit, the soul, has the contact and the terminus of the physical body through this condyle.

But if I want to use Luis as a machine for drawing, I have to use more energy and concentrate also in the cerebral, through the pineal to the muscle (?) and (—) (—) have the electricity—the control of the electricity, which is easier than talk. There is less interference. And with less it is easier than the arms because there is less program—behavioral program—in the legs. Less behavioral program in the legs, easier then to talk, easier to move, easier to express themselves.

Because of Gasparetto's claim that he could channel two spirits at the same time, and because of his demonstra-

tion of drawing the two portraits at the same time (illustrated on page 149), we asked him to channel two spirits while he was on the EEG machine in the lab. When Gasparetto indicated that two spirits were present, a noticeable difference appeared in his EEG between the left and right occipital measurements. I asked him if the spirits could show us other differences, so Gasparetto asked the two different spirits to shift sides. The signals from the right and left occipital electrodes seemed to shift as well. The illustration of this apparent shift in Gasparetto's EEG record appears above. (The time it takes for the shift to occur was eliminated from the graph for space.) These are observations from one session in the lab. We don't know if these EEG patterns would be the same from one day to the next. Research in this area requires more systematic study with the much-improved type of EEG equipment now available.

From time to time we had the opportunity to observe other people in trance states in an informal way. Each person seemed to have a unique EEG trance signature. However, this type of research has been the subject of atheistic taboo for so long that formal studies are rarely funded. Some EEG measurements have been taken from people diagnosed as having multiple personalities. When one personality gave way to another, the report noted that the EEG changed dramatically. It would be difficult to say whether the natural multiple personalities were completely out of communication with each other, or whether the person was possessed by an alien spirit. This question has yet to be answered, because few scientists who have the modern technology, multiple EEG channels and computer analysis available to explore these questions ever dare to ask them.

In our own meditation circle at home, I had experienced the *feeling of the presence of light*. I thought it might be just the result of the combined group energy. To explore this, I hooked myself up to the brainwave *Light Sculpture*. When I achieved a light trance state, the others in the group could see the lights go out as the frequency and amplitude changed. A light being we called "Ronak" spoke through me, or at least it seemed that the information came from beyond myself. (I was never quite sure what it was in those days, not really, since we were not raised to believe in such things.) Each of us, in our circle, always wondered about the source. We continued to meet, however, because whatever it was, it always seemed to uplevel the conversation. We met in the evening, lit candles, burned a little sage to "purify the air," sat in a circle on cushions on the floor, and held hands to keep our energy focused and together. When the lights went out on the *Light Sculpture,* indicating I had reached a trance state (with my eyes closed), questions to "Ronak" were asked by individuals from the group. Information was given to me while the lights were still out, but the blue lights of the mandala patterns turned on again before the answers were expressed aloud. (One group member recorded the session on tape, because I didn't always remember what had been said during the trance state.)

I received the most information about channeling when I was invited to an Espiritista séance in Brazil. And this invitation came about because of Dowlen's RV response when he included "a letter of importance on the floor" during our 1976 series of experiments. (See page 64.) Because I answered the letter that had fallen on the floor, the following year I received a paid invitation to give a presentation at a parapsychology conference in Brazil. The trip to Brazil put me in contact with the belief systems of some in that culture who accept the "reality" of communication with spirits from other dimensions. Even after my experience of channeling, I did not understand them, nor could I discuss them with anyone knowledgeable at home. In Brazil, I met friendly, well-educated Espiritistas who were eager to show me how they interacted freely with hyperdimensional beings who do coexist with us, and will transmit messages. These meetings were most important to me, and I deeply appreciated the people who helped.

One séance was held in a large private living room in São Paulo. Mediums, doctors, and psychiatrists met every Saturday morning. They sat in a circle in straight-back chairs without holding hands. Instead of sage smoke, they placed bouquets of roses in every corner of the room to purify the air, so only good spirits would come to visit them. Then a prayer was offered to Jesus Christ to help them contact a spirit for a message of inspiration. After a period of silent meditation, I suddenly felt the presence of *two* distinct beams of light, not just one, which I might have believed was due to group energy alone. These two spirits insisted that I speak aloud and give a message to the group in Portuguese. I resisted. I was not self-confident enough to try to speak a language I don't understand, especially since I was surrounded by Portuguese speaking strangers. I would have to go unconscious to do that, and I had come as a guest, allowed to observe Espiritistas in action, not to make a fool of myself. I spent the whole meditation period silently protesting this issue with the spirits.

Later, each person in turn spoke about his/her experiences during the séance. When it came to my turn, I was uncertain about what to say. Did spirits actually speak to me? Did I only imagine that they did? I finally mumbled that I had experienced a lot of light. Then the doctor who brought me to this séance spoke to me in English. "Jean, I saw two spirits bow before you. These are important things to us. Why didn't you mention it?"

Without knowing my questions, he had confirmed my experience. It wasn't only my imagination; he had seen two spirits as well. I replied, "They wanted me to speak in Portuguese, and since I don't speak that language, I was afraid to open my mouth. Where I come from, it's socially unacceptable to acknowledge that spirits talk to me."

When he translated that to the others in the circle, I could feel that they felt sorry for me to have come from a culture where such important things are limited by prejudice. (This was a weird contrast, since my *Light Sculpture* with its electronics had been totally misinterpreted there.) Nevertheless, I was encouraged to say, "Since you have recognized them, they have told me that they will give the message to you."

We all resumed our silent meditation, and the doctor gave a very long message to the appreciative group. I was surprised that the message was also given to me simultaneously in the language I do understand. The whole experience was quite exhilarating. Essentially, the message was this: *"The mind is actually a form of light energy that has been radiating for billions of years. We need to acknowledge the many dimensions of our minds, and to learn to use more of them to evolve our intelligence."*

Several times the presence of my spirit guides was made known to me as I traveled to different places in Brazil. They always seemed to me to be formless beams of light. However, even though I didn't talk about my experiences, different people would tell me that they saw one or two spirits around me, at the exact time that I was experiencing them myself. Each one would describe "him" differently. One described a Native American medicine man, another saw a Chinese philosopher, and at the séance, the two spirits were described as a Sikh with a turban and a Frenchman with a plumed hat, who removed his hat and bowed in front of me with a flourish. No one described any women among them.

Once when talking to a well-known Espiritista, I asked about spirit guides, describing "Ronak" as an energy field who had never been a living person, only a being of light. The Espiritista became very haughty and used an insulting tone, saying that I was not advanced enough to have such a high being as a guide. I suppose one of the difficulties of

Once I was called upon to do a séance for a group of tourists visiting a San Francisco hotel and bar that was said to be haunted by a man from the time of prohibition. Several of the employees had reported seeing a ghost over the years, and named him Lester. The tourists included a few believers and the simply curious. They had been wined and dined ahead of time, which was *not* the way I chose to conduct a session, but I was also curious. We arranged the chairs so we could sit in a circle in the empty party room, lit the sage and the candles, played my favorite tape of meditation music, and I began to guide them into a deep relaxation. (Two of the tourists promptly fell asleep, as expected.) When the spirit arrived, he was insulted, saying, "My name is *not* Lester, it's Terry O'Reilly, and this ain't my kind of music!" It seems that he had been an entertainer, who loved the lights and the dancing (especially, the Charleston) and had no intention of *going into the light* as one tourist solemnly suggested to him. He later gave me an obscene version of a popular song of his time called *My Blue Heaven*. The original words to the song were about a married couple; *Just Molly and Me, and baby makes three.* His version referred to his favorite whorehouse down the street. His death came at the hands of someone who was jealous, and was not unexpected. He enjoyed his life then and his continued presence at the club now. He had no interest in "heaven" or "hell," nor had he any intention of going anywhere else. The whole alleged "conversation" with this "ghost" was totally unexpected. I never encountered one like it before or since.

following a formal belief system about spirits is that the belief helps form, as well as limit, the experience to the established rules. Just as our culture refuses to admit the existence of the spirit world, theirs can only accept it in terms of their teachings about it. I feel that when we encounter an energy that is unknown and alien to us, we can only "see" it in terms of our own projections from our previously developed concepts about such energy. That is one of the problems of spirit communication. One person can only imagine an angel, one can only imagine an extraterrestrial, another can only imagine a discarnate being from somewhere else. Others may just feel a tinge of fear at the thought or feeling that a dead relative may be still around after the funeral, even though the deceased may only want to communicate love.

We do expect and usually receive an uplifting message when we ask a spirit guide or guardian angel for advice. When we find ourselves receiving a communication from an ancestor, we also expect some important advice. My grandmother told me about a time living out on the ranch when she was particularly sad. She went outside one night and saw that a golden light surrounded her. Her mother was sending this light to comfort her. She was thrilled with the communication and was able to bear with the difficult times of the depression more peacefully. However, spirits of the dead are not always comforting or more informed than we are. They could be stuck in hateful or racist ideas that were popular in their older generation, or still be fighting the war that killed them. When angry spirits want to involve you in their anger, you may want to try to help them into the light of your own understanding. If they refuse to respond positively, then an exorcism may be needed. Spirit possession by a hostile entity needs to be dealt with. Once I thought I needed an exorcism. The shaman Rolling Thunder helped me to understand it. When he performed the exorcism, using his eagle feather, I felt clear headed immediately.

Sometimes our ancestors may need our advice as well. One of my grandfathers had been born in the South just as the Civil War had ended. So many of his relatives had died in the war, or soon after, that he came West as a young man to seek a new life, but he carried his racial prejudices with him. He came to me in a vivid dream, arriving in a white boat across a dark ocean (this is one of the types of arrival of a spirit of the dead, often reported in the past). An unknown voice spoke in my ear, "Your grandfather wishes to speak to you." By then I was listening intently, though still dreaming. Grandpa told me that he didn't approve of what I was doing. At that time in the late Sixties, I was working for the LA County Museum of Art and helping with their Black Culture Festival. However, in my dream I was able to explain to him gently that times were different, and what I was doing was the right thing to do. He did not object after that. We reaffirmed our mutual love and affection and he disappeared from my dream.

Sometimes the spirit may try to communicate with loved ones, because he died suddenly and is still confused. A woman asked me to do a séance because she was afraid her house was haunted. Whenever she started to relax in the dark or with only a candle glowing, she felt a creepy presence. Ten years before, her younger brother tried to steal something. He was only a teenager, but in the dark he looked large enough to be an adult and was shot by police as he was trying to run away. He felt very guilty about this, and needed to apologize to his family. He really wanted to ask them to forgive him. Whenever they rested quietly enough to be aware of a presence, they became afraid. During our séance, he was able to ask and receive forgiveness, and after that he and they could rest more easily. Fear of the unknown is natural. Since communication with the spirits of the dead is also natural, there is no need for that experience to remain fearful or among the realms of the unknown.

What can we know about the realms of multidimensionality from within the limited dimensions of spacetime? We see that each civilization creates its own concepts of the unknowable to live by. In the last century scientists have fought bravely to find a "real" reality that our civilization can trust. The major revelations of the electromagnetic spectrum, the periodic chart of the atoms, the motion of the planets in our own solar system, for example, are things that are real for everyone, no matter how far their belief systems have wandered into fantasy. Trance states expose that very fuzzy edge between what is actually "out there" and the way we interpret that through our individual reflections from what is constantly being projected from within our minds and memories.

Here, I have only touched upon the aspects of trance that I have had the opportunity to examine with the EEG, and through my own years of trance experiences, as well as performing an occasional exorcism, or acting as a trance or trip guide. Beyond my own experiences, however, there are a number of excellent books on trance states by authors who have a more extensive knowledge and write about trance states in more detail. (122, 123) My meetings with Espiritistas, medicine people, shamans, and kahunas have helped me to understand my own spirit guides and have led to more meaningful conversations with deceased friends and honored ancestors.

But trance states are not absolutely necessary to find yourself in conversation with those who have already graduated from Earth school. Some important information may come to you while you are staring off into space with no particular thoughts in mind. (See pages 120 and 121.) And as we have seen, some will come in a dream.

One very special "song" was given to me in a series of dreams that I would like to share with you. It may or may not be true that the one who transmitted this to me was Jerry Garcia, the late famous guitar player from the Grateful Dead. However, shortly after he graduated from Earth school I was instructed by a spirit so identified to get up and write down the words I was given. Every morning before dawn, *"he"* would wake me up and tell me some of the words. While half asleep, I would think, "Why me? After all, I hadn't spoken to him for a long time before he passed on, and it has been many more years since I did a light show for him." However, I finally wrote the words and mailed them to the Grateful Dead office. After that, I was no longer awakened before dawn, and was allowed to sleep as usual. I wasn't sure of the chorus, though, thinking it had something to do with "fa, la, la, la, la." Later when I was reciting the rest to a friend, the real chorus was given to me before dawn the next day. I guess "feel the love" sort of sounds like "fa, la, la," but obviously I had it wrong at first. Later I realized that the chorus can be used to let your own ancestor or spirit guide know that you are ready to listen. Just repeat it a few times, remembering to focus attention at the top of your head, and then remain very still and quiet until the presence of the spirit manifests.

*Can you feel my soul*
*through the folks who make this song?*
*I have gone away you know,*
*but not for very long.*
*We all go away,*
*blood, flesh and bones all turn to dust.*
*Yet we know there is*
*Eternal Love we all can trust.*

(chorus)
*Feel the love, feel the love, feel the love all around*
*Riding on every vibration of sound.*
*Feel the love pour in through the top of your head,*
*Let it flow from one who is gratefully dead.*

# CHAPTER SIX
# THE DEVELOPMENT OF MEMORY AND INTELLIGENCE

Eighty years ago, neuropsychologist Karl Lashley conducted a search for memory, expecting to find it stored in a certain place in the brain. After spending forty years looking for specialized cells that could be called the seat of memory, he theorized that memory was not located in any one region of the brain, nor was it linked throughout by any specific physical structure. He theorized that it must be located with equal power at all points in the brain. (124) Around the same time, neurosurgeon Wilder Penfield used an electric probe to stimulate the exposed brains of his epileptic patients. (125) He used this while the patient was awake in order to attempt to create a map of the brain's mechanism. He also hoped to find specific memory cells in the brain. When he probed a region of one of the temporal lobes, one patient heard a voice singing, another heard an orchestra playing, and a boy heard his mother talking on the telephone. Penfield also used a probe on the verbal areas of the brain in the left hemisphere while he asked a patient to identify a picture of a butterfly. The patient was unable to do so until the electrical stimulation ended. Then he reported that since he couldn't say the word "butterfly," he tried to say the other word, "moth," but couldn't do that either. His visual memory remembered both and knew there were two words; it was only the verbal expression of the memory that was blocked.

Penfield's results were among those which have paved the way for advances in mapping the brain. Since that time, great advances in the technology of brain mapping included computerized axial tomography (CAT) scanners, positron emission transaxial tomography (PETT) scanners, magnetic resonance imaging (MRI), and of course, desktop computers which are able to analyze twenty or more signals from the EEG simultaneously in real time. (The old PDP-15 computer we used to measure EEG took up a whole room and had only about 16K memory.) Yet in spite of all the improvements in technology, no exact location has been found in the brain for memory storage.

There are many wonderful books written on the research into memory, about the neuronal connections, the chemistry of their interaction, the short-term and the long-term memories. Our very brief look at the development of memory is not intended to ignore any of those careful studies of the material brain. The discussion presented here simply aims to stimulate thought about the extent of memory from different perspectives.

## THE POTENTIAL ABILITIES OF MATERIAL AND MULTIDIMENSIONAL MEMORIES

Memory is both material and multidimensional. Our ability to *express* the information pulled from memory is translated through the material brain. However, we can "remember" events before we were born. We can "remember" events that have not yet happened, as in precognition. We may twist our memories of events to fit a particular personality we choose to identify with. We can change our *reactions* to memories of the past if they are not useful to us in the present. These are aspects of the hyperspatial quality of memory. When we are limited in our ability to express our memories, this may depend upon the chemistry and activity of the actual neurons in the brain. Memory and consciousness are intrinsic to both brain and hyperspace.

As we have seen in our telepathic responses, memories can be expressed through any of the sensory systems. Also we have seen through biofeedback training that a specific train of memory might be evoked by a sore muscle, for example. When the person focuses total attention on the muscle and is encouraged to "go to the source of the pain," the memory of what caused the muscle to go into spasm can be stirred back into awareness. Sometimes the source is actually very old and has been "forgotten." The muscle, not the intellectual or verbal mind, remembered it. A recent event, perhaps not as severe as the one long ago, reawakened the muscle to the "memory" of the first event. Often the emotional attachment to that first event must be released in order to relieve the present spasm, as well.

Since brain research has revealed that the hippocampus is involved in the formation of memory, there has been an assumption that infants do not form memories until that part of the brain is fully developed. However, we have seen over and over again that people can remember the day they were born, the feelings of being in the womb before they were born, and some have even described the moment of conception. (126) So we will look at memory in this chapter as an entity of consciousness with access to the hyperspace. Obviously, the brain's sensory systems, verbal abilities, visualization abilities, motor abilities and all, are needed to express their separate memories. Yet memories can arise also from resonance with others, human or animal, living or dead, or from the energy of special places of power. (127)

**1. Cell Memory, Soul Memory, Creating the Myths of Memories and Reframing Memories** — Paul Pearsall, PhD, reported in an April 1998 article in *Natural Health* magazine, that patients who received heart transplants also received the memories of their donors. (128) Some assumed new habits that were similar to those of the donor, and others started eating foods they did not like before. One especially touching story was of an eight-year-old girl who had received a heart transplant from a ten-year-old girl who had been murdered. Pearsall describes a meeting in which a psychiatrist told this story about the girl:

> Her mother brought her to me when she started screaming at night about her dreams of the man who had murdered her donor. She said her daughter knew who it was. After several sessions, I could not deny the reality of what this child was telling me. Her mother and I finally decided to call the police and, using the description from the little girl, they found the murderer. He was easily convicted with evidence my patient provided. The time, weapon, place, clothes he wore, what the little girl he killed had said to him...everything the little heart transplant recipient reported was completely accurate....
>
> Not only did this girl's—her heart's—memory come up through her dreams, where certainly there is no mental effort involved in summoning the memory, but I maintain that the scientists in the room felt the energetic connection among all of us and they knew that it was something that extended outside the boundaries of current rational understanding.
>
> Our bodies are made up of around 75 trillion cells, which is about 15,000 times the number of people living on the planet. I propose that each of these cells is an energy and information center, that each cell stores "info-energy" that is the heart's code, a code that is not only passed on with a transplanted heart but is available to anyone....

Pearsall makes a good case for the heart's code and the heart's cell memory. He also presents many other examples of heart transplant patients who have adopted different eating habits and personality traits, allegedly from the donor of the heart. While I can confirm cell memory to some extent from our biofeedback training, I could suggest another model to consider that might also explain Pearsall's case studies. The spirit of the girl who was murdered was not at peace. The girl who received the heart is also young and impressionable. This is a perfect case for spirit possession. The girl dreams about the murder and is given the facts of the event so the police can arrest the murderer. Pearsall's story did not continue to say whether that was enough for the spirit, so that she could enter the realm of light, or whether the heart recipient continued to carry on dream conversations with the donor of the heart. He does say that when the story was told at the meeting, "...the scientists...felt the energetic connection...was...outside the boundaries of current rational understanding." My own experience with spirit communication tells me that when the story was told to the group, that was enough to call the spirit of the murdered girl into the presence of the audience, and that it may have been *her* energetic connection from the hyperspace that they all felt.

Pearsall does offer this additional idea to support his model that cell memory may be conscious:

> You may remember looking at cells under a microscope in high school biology class. If we were lucky, we got to look at living cells. That every living cell seems able to somehow "remember" what it is supposed to do and when, where, and with which other cells it is supposed to do it is one of the still largely unexplained miracles of life.
>
> I remember looking at the single-cell paramecium—a complete living thing in one tiny package. The paramecium has no brain, neurons, or synapses, yet every one of them seems to have retained some level of its paramecium heritage. They all remember how to swim, hunt for food, identify and escape their predators, court a mate, and even engage in a rudimentary type of sex. All without a brain....

Paramecia may not be able to remember in the way we usually think about memory, but it is possible that they and all living cells have a form of memory which originates in the hyperspace and projects down into their own particular manifestation in spacetime.

Humans may have access to the memories of all of that, including what it "feels" like to be a single-celled organism. A person can learn, through biofeedback, to control the firing of a single muscle cell. Human memory of what it "feels" like to be a fetus in the mother may depend upon cell memory. The feelings can be re-experienced and described when a person is older. The vibrations of sounds can be felt, and some recommend playing soft music for the fetus. The sage Vamadeva tells a story in the *Aitareyopanishad* about his full cognition about life and the essence of birth while he was still in the womb. (129)

The whole potential of memory as an essential part of consciousness must therefore be multidimensional. It is clear that the old idea of a child being born as a clear slate *(tabula rasa)* is far too simplistic. When each child is born s/he brings into this life a uniquely different way to acquire memories and intelligence. This one cries continuously, that one sleeps peacefully all night. This one boldly takes his first step and then runs, that one is timid and hangs on to things as long as possible. This one eats everything in sight, including things s/he shouldn't, that one is finicky or allergic to many things, including mother's milk. This one is nervous and fearful, that one takes on the world with hearty enthusiasm.

Children can and do choose the events that will evolve into life's mythologies in their memories. Consider this example from two relatively happy households. Both mothers are basically gentle and truly care about the health and happiness of their children. One day, the first mother is overwhelmed with work that must be done before visitors arrive. The five-year-old girl and her younger brother begin fighting. With this the mother reaches her limit of patience. She tells them to stop and when they continue, she gives them both a short swat on their bottoms, and sends them to their rooms for a time out. The girl is annoyed with this, carries this myth into adulthood, and years later tells her therapist, "Since mother didn't spank me very often, I couldn't trust her because I never knew when she would blow up like that again." Perhaps the event only happened a half dozen times in a dozen years, but once the choice to view punishment this way had been made, the projection of the "reality" of mistrust was set.

The second mother is also overwhelmed with some work that must be done by a certain time. Her five-year-old boy fights with his younger sister. She tells them to stop and when they continue, she gives them both a short swat on their bottoms, and sends them to their rooms for a time out. After a while, the boy peeks around the corner of the kitchen door and asks, "Mommy, do you need a hug?" Of course she responds to this and stops for a hug. Then he asks, "Now, do you feel better?" The point of these two actual accounts of observed behavior is that one child *chooses* to be the victim and the other *chooses* to be the healer.

Neither child in the example just mentioned was ever abused. However, the child who *is abused* psychologically and/or physically may have less choice about his/her memory of that abuse. Once when I was discussing the vindictive and mean behavior of one man (who was not present)

with others in our meditation circle, I said, "Well, maybe it was because he was beaten by a drunken stepfather as a child that he is as full of hate as he is now." Two of the men I said this to responded by saying that they, too, had been beaten as children. One man was an inventor and had chosen to be a healer and a helper in his community. The other man had connected with his spiritual nature in the study of science. Neither had ever chosen to be mean, spiteful, or violent as they grew up. They had chosen to be different from those who raised them. Each had recognized that hate and anger were the time bombs which could create future violence. It seems that the choice to hold on to anger is a choice to become insane, eventually, or physically sick.

One student who came to me to see if I could help relieve his headache said to me rather forcefully, "I have a right to my anger!"

"Yes, you do," I answered him, "and you have the right to the pain in your stiff neck that goes with it. Perhaps you can think of a more creative way to use your adrenaline than clenching your jaw. Forgiveness usually works rather well." He hadn't yet realized how closely connected his emotions were to his muscle tension.

When childhood memories are relatively happy, a person may have easy access to all of them, including the moment of birth as well as the emotions surrounding conception. When certain of these memories are traumatic, all of them may be blocked, including the happy ones. To find them all, strong determination by the individual and guidance from a knowledgeable practitioner may be needed. A child might have been happy until the age of eight, when something frightening happened. Until the emotional blocks are lifted, even the happy memories before that time may be unavailable to the pre-conscious. However, we do find that the past is malleable, especially through hypnosis. A damaging childhood perception can be reframed so that a positive response can be re-created. Old memories can be changed by altering our reactions to them. Old angers can be relieved by the act of forgiveness. Old fears can be lifted by confronting them instead of hiding from them. Old griefs can be softened by the realization that consciousness belongs to eternity. This lifetime is our school for life on Earth. When we learn to own our memories and at the same time to release our physiological and emotional reactions to them, we can be more comfortable with ourselves and others in our future. When this process has been completed, the future we project is also changed. This is good therapy.

Even without the therapist, a good family discussion during a less emotional time may reveal to us that the event which formed our most fearful memory was actually exciting to a sibling, and transcendental to a cousin. The preparation for what we expect to perceive has a lot to do with what is perceived. When concept precedes percept, the actual event probably will be warped to fit. I have seen that each person's memory of a dramatic situation is different when we all compare notes at a later time. Each person put into the scene his/her expectations, hopes, fears, or mythologies about it. As time goes by, each of those projections gets amplified to protect a particular personality within the personal maze. The actual event was totally different for each of us. A dramatic example of the projections and reflections that make up memory is seen in the Japanese movie *Rashomon*. It is a classic tale, marvelously told, about how each participant of a tragedy held a very different memory about what had happened. Even the ghost of the murdered man was asked to tell his story, and that was also very different from those who lived through the event.

That is one reason why attempts at telepathy can become so useful. They stretch out that misty edge between the external object and the internal projections which make up our "reality concepts." We can watch the shifts take place from the external through the internal maze, instead of just being caught up in our own thoughts on the one side, as though they were the only reality available.

**2. Thinking About Thinking and the Different Types of Perception** — The problems that arise in telepathy when early memories dominate has always intrigued me. Once I had a real problem with it when Russell Targ asked me to draw pictures for Uri Geller, who acted as the receiver. Geller was in an electromagnetically shielded room at Stanford Research Institute (SRI), monitored by Hal

Puthoff. Targ and I were several rooms away. Targ opened a dictionary to find a noun that could be drawn as a picture. (130) On this occasion, I was asked to draw a camel. I was shocked to realize that there were no images of camels in my mind. The drawing (below) did not come out well.

Earlier, when I was a young mother, my occupation (besides raising children) was painting murals for homes and commercial businesses in and around San Francisco. These were not grand public works-type murals, just simple pictures (such as the SF skyline, Yankee Clippers for DiMaggio's restaurant, leopards for the Leopard Cafe, and zoo animals for a children's dental office). That meant that I spent some time at the zoo pushing my baby in her stroller and sketching lions, tigers, bears, and yes, a camel. Below is an example of one of the camels I drew. It was a sketch from life, drawn over again to fit into the small preliminary drawing, and again directly on the wall of the waiting room in the office. Later I included one of the camel sketches in a mural for a child's bedroom (below).

Despite those experiences of painting camels at age twenty-seven, when I was asked to draw a camel while in a semi-trance state to "send" to Geller, there was no image in my mind of a camel. (I had never seen a camel until I was about twelve years old. We lived far out in the desert, with a one-room school, no library, no zoo, and there had been no camels in that area for 10,000 years.) Eventually an image came to me of a very tiny gold camel on a package of cigarettes that my uncle had left on the kitchen table when I was very young. I had not paid much attention to the details then (only the shiny gold caught my attention), and my vague memory of that image helped only a little with this SRI drawing. Disgusted with my drawing, I turned the paper upside down to try to draw a better one. That one was worse. Suggestions were made to try to help

The mural below was nine feet long and four feet high. I painted this one for a children's room in 1956.

**Uri Geller - REMOTE VIEWER**

Above left are the scribbled camels I tried to draw for the SRI experiments in 1973. I never saw a live camel as a child. During the experiment, I had no idea why there were no images of camels in my mind. It was somewhat embarrassing at the time.

Above is a detail of the painting. I didn't even remember doing this mural until long after the SRI experiment was over. My memory provided only my first image of a small picture of a camel, not this large one that I drew from life at age twenty-seven.

Geller drew a horse with a saddle that curves down over the animal, instead of a camel with a hump which curves up.

me. How embarrassing! We did laugh about my problem, and I remarked that Mark Twain had once said, "A camel is only a horse that was put together by a committee." Geller's response was a horse, with the upward curve of a camel becoming the downward curve of a saddle blanket (illustrated bottom right on the opposite page). At no time during that experiment did I even remember my journeys to the zoo and the sketches of a live camel, nor did the memory of the murals I made ever cross my mind. It was only later, when the experiment was over and I had gone home, that I remembered the painting. I always wondered why. The question remained with me for some time after that. Why didn't I see a camel in that situation?

One answer to the camel question might be found in the research done with continuation high school students by Marge King. (131) She asked them to write about their first memories of various things, such as how they might remember their first telephone number. Here are some examples quoted from her report *On Ways of Thinking:*

*GOAL: To discover personal memory systems.*

A.  Think of a number from one to ten but don't say it, just think it. How did you get it?

1.  It just popped into my head.
2.  I heard it!
3.  I saw it. It glowed kind of yellow.
4.  It was black and white—a block print.
5.  It was an orange seven on the back of a green football jersey....

B.  How do you remember the alphabet?

1.  I saw it. It was in one of those little trains that goes around the top of the first grade room with three letters in each train car.
2.  It went up and down and it looked like that alphabet strip that my mom had stuck to the refrigerator when I was little.
3.  I remember by that dumb little song we learned in kindergarten....
4.  Daddy gave me a book with colored letters.

C.  Think of a telephone number. How do you remember it?

1.  I saw it in my own handwriting by the telephone.
2.  I heard the first three numbers, but the last four I knew by the way my finger goes to dial it.

3.  I heard the whole number in a sing-song kind of rhythm....
4.  I heard my friend's voice telling it to me.

King's class project was designed to show the students how each one of them thinks very differently. It also shows us how important are those very first memories. An adult may remember his first steps as a one-year-old by the way his body felt at the time, another may remember them by the way her father was there to catch her when she started to fall, or how proud the parents were that she took those first steps by herself.

The examples from King's project help us to realize just how very different our thinking processes are. The growth of computer education has facilitated learning for those who are less verbal and more visually or kinesthetically gifted. Melissa Jeffress sent this e-mail to King about an Aboriginal student in Australia: (132)

I've been working as a teacher's aide...I do like working with these *[Aboriginal]* students.... Many of the older students speak English as a second language and come from remote communities to board and go to school.... I helped them in remedial reading, using a *[computer]* program.

One day I was asked to help a high school student with her homework. It was very interesting to watch a student, who could only write very simple English sentences, turn on a computer, open the word processor, create a file, name it, title her essay and center it, enter the sentences (painfully slow—that part is the only place I helped), then save it to her own disk. So there's literacy and then there's literacy!

Her story was a short description of *How to Hunt a Dugong.* As I remember you need a canoe, an anchor, paddles, hook and a wap. You can guess what the wap is for! Dugongs are...*[very large]* sea-cows.... They are protected, although Aboriginal people can hunt them in a traditional manner in some areas.

We may not be aware of the number of concepts that we take for granted in our own culture. Many years ago there was a story about Peace Corps volunteers who had gone into the jungles of Africa to help with health matters, especially to help prevent diseases carried by mosquitos. Films about these issues were shown to the natives. Since at that time, these people had never seen lights and shadows move around on a flat screen before, they did not seem

The sketch of the mud hut (center) is a similation of one I made for the children before I saw the drawing (far left) that the young boy had made. When he brought it to me, he saw my sketch and went back and drew the picture on the far right. (His drawing was *much* smaller than mine.) What I believe we see here is the fact that his first drawing came from his knowledge of how the building was constructed; he had not "seen" it as an outsider would see it until he looked at my drawing. We could not see the symbols at the top while we were sitting on the ground, but he drew them because he knew they were there.

to comprehend what the whole film was about. So the workers made a film of the chief of the tribe walking along the road in front of the huts. When he came to a standing container of water, full of mosquito larva, he tipped it over, emptied it and stomped on the larva. The natives were amazed to see the chief's head grow larger. While the camera focused on the chief, who seemed to walk in place, the people were equally amazed to see their huts sliding sideways behind him. We have adapted to our symbols to such an extent that we don't notice that they are symbolic representations. It would never occur to us in this information age to look at a movie with that set of eyes. Yet logic tells us that any movie can be interpreted in that way.

I had an opportunity to observe another different way of seeing when I went to the village of the Abinticua (pages 100 to 104). As I sat on the ground to draw pictures for the native children there, one young boy began to draw pictures for me. For him the mud huts were something that everyone in the village helped to build. He knew that they were very tall and round, and that the thatched roof was added afterward (above left). As soon as he saw my sketch (center), he drew a very careful (and very small) drawing of the mud hut by looking at it from the outside (above right). He added the cap and symbols at the top, which he knew to be there, but which I had not seen. The transformation in his way of looking at the building was immediate, and to me, quite amazing.

Learning to see and learning to draw from life are essential ingredients for the advancement of the evolution of intelligence. When we ask the average child to draw some-

thing from memory today, we are likely to get a drawing of a Mickey-type mouse, a purple Barney, or some other popular cartoon character. Our visual information gathering systems can be expanded during childhood (and later as well) if children are encouraged to do so. Intelligence is expanded through memory, and memory is encoded more accurately when exposed to nature. Color books with distorted line drawings of people and things are not good for this development. Flat screen images (whether 2-D or the implied 3-D of television and computer monitors) distort visual memory away from moving our own bodies in 3-D space. Children should be encouraged to draw from life, yet so many "art" classes for the primary set are of the cookie-cutter variety (e.g., the teacher cuts out a snowflake or a pumpkin or other shape, and the children decorate it). The relationship between visual observation of the 3-D world and the representation of it is sadly neglected. Visual images on TV and computers become symbols to represent the "real" world. Symbols can be manipulated into other meanings. When there is no relationship between observation and actual things, intelligence about them can be compromised.

For a few years I was an art teacher. I had a variety of classes with different age groups and social groups, so I had an opportunity to watch what was happening to the development of the visual intelligence systems of children from primary grades to high school. Most could learn to "see" with the proper opportunity to draw from life and to exercise the visual intelligence systems. I only found three students in all that time who could not (or would not) learn to visualize. However, one of them was very good in handling mathematical abstractions. The need to develop an ability to visualize in 3-D space is essential for anyone who chooses to be a builder, architect, or scientist. Why do I mention scientist here? Because it is necessary for one who would be called "scientist" to be able to observe nature accurately. When the education of the intelligence of the visual system has been neglected, the ability to observe nature can become warped. Then it is possible that we may only see the reflections of the internal concepts that we project onto it.

At one time I also worked with young people (from adolescent though teenage) who had been diagnosed as schizophrenic. They were living in a special home developed for their care. The managers and therapists of this home were open to many different approaches to help these young people, including biofeedback, which is why I was invited to work there. During that time, I had an opportunity to examine the drawings some of the children made in response to the flickering lights from the old variable-speed 8-mm movie projector. I adjusted the frames per second (FPS) to flicker in brainwave range, and asked the young people to draw whatever they saw. Some of their responses to the different frequencies looked very much like the ones I had already collected from the college students and adults (see page 112 and 113). However, a few were just scribbles. I wondered whether those young people were just bored and didn't want to be bothered with all the dots, or if they might have some undiagnosed neurological confusion in their visual system, in their motor activity, or in their hand-eye coordination.

This drawing of an angel and a devil was made by a young boy after he watched a light flickering at approximately 8 FPS. This frequency corresponds to the lower alpha brainwave range at 8 cycles per second (8 Hz). The boy had been diagnosed as being schizophrenic and lived in a home that was organized to care for young people with such problems.

The response illustrated below indicated to me that the emotional problems of this young man were rooted in the hyperspace. He, like others, saw the moving dots during his exposure to the light at approximately 8 FPS. Unlike any of the others, his vision also included figures of an angel and a devil. The devil has wings, a tail, and a pitchfork. The angel is confined in a smaller space. He tried to write "devil" across the chest, but his writing is not that clear. The devil is smiling, the angel is not. When he gave me his drawing he explained to me that they both spoke to him, but that the devil liked to mock him.

It would seem that if his therapy included discussions of the dualities of the archetypes, it might help him resolve his obvious conflicts in that realm. Memories, even for the young, include the whole range of multidimensional consciousness, though it may be rare for them to be able to express this. Some young children have even reported memories of past lives. They may forget them as they get older, but return to those memories after the age of twenty-five. At that time, some of the most dramatic memories might begin to impose themselves onto the life style of the individual unconsciously. Imagine what it would be like to grow up with an accepted concept of having lived before in a different body. Some of this memory might come into awareness more easily through drawing than through storytelling. The developing memory needs pictures as well as language to express its independent information.

**3. Developing Visual and Motor Activity to Expand the Memory of Vision** — Rhoda Kellogg was able to collect and study a million drawings made by young children around the world while she was working with the United Nations. She found a sequence to motor development, hand-eye coordination, and types of imagery which evolve naturally, regardless of cultural differences. She found that children seem to enjoy aesthetic sensitivity from the first free scribbles right up to the emergence of images from the external world. (133) Scribbling is a biofeedback device for the observation of the perceptual brain organization as it develops. The child is establishing the space/ frame that s/he is inhabiting. (134) That frame begins with the nose, extends to the hands holding a crayon, and ultimately stops at the crucial point of interaction between the crayon and the drawing paper. The eyes are then focused on the paper and the marks being made with the motion. The motor activity is an essential part of the perception, as the child enjoys the body sensations while the whole arm moves, and the body position changes. The child that is allowed to scribble is participating in his/her own brain development, his/her own evolution of intelligence. The word here is "allowed," because parents or "sitters" must make scribbling possible with the space and the materials. The child rarely needs to be encouraged to scribble. It is a natural activity unless they are already addicted to television. This sequence of development seen through the child's scribbles goes more or less like this:

1. At first there are a few attempts to hold a pencil and make a few marks. The child explores the pencil and the paper and often stabs at the paper, and then is surprised at the mark. Then the child will make many marks and want to share the delight. (This is between fourteen and eighteen months old, but any age the child becomes interested in the activity is the time to start.)

2. Soon the child discovers that the hand and arm move easily in circles, and s/he will draw circles many times, both for the fun of seeing them and for the fun of the body movement. It is important to have lots of paper and always put the new one up on the wall (refrigerator or something). This may go on for weeks. You may tire of seeing scribbles hung on the wall, but be patient—these efforts are part of the development of intelligence.

3. While moving arms around and around, the child discovers the pattern of the circle. Eventually the circle becomes a face with two straight lines coming out of the head for arms and two more for legs.

4. Then two circles emerge, one for the head and one for the body. Arm lines now might include some fingers, and perhaps some scribbles will be added to suggest hair on the head.

5. It is only then, after the motor activity has been worked out and the internal imaging has been completed, that the child can begin to look outside of himself and start drawing from life.

6. Do not provide children with coloring books! The distorted line drawings of people, animals, and things create a perceptual distortion between the 3-D and 2-D spaces which can cause children to lose self-confidence in their own drawings. At that point they may lose interest in developing their own internal perception or in attempting to draw from life, and shift into the symbolic world of coloring books instead. The interaction between seeing and representing what is seen on a flat surface may become

arrested. Even at age forty or more, people will still draw the same cat or rabbit in exactly the same way they learned to draw it from the coloring book or from the first-grade reader. It is not a picture from nature, it is only a memorized symbol. Symbols have their place in our education, but other intelligences can be developed as well.

7. Those first efforts to draw from life are crucial to the development of perception. They are not to be thought of as exhibition art. Those first drawings are personal, internal exercises for the development of the visual intelligence system. Pure sensitivity to shape and color should be allowed to dominate. This is not the time to exert pressure on the child's ego to compete for some prize. Just encourage the process, and make the supplies available.

8. For the child who just enjoys color for its own sake, the coloring books that contain mandala patterns or other geometric shapes can be used to help center the vision without destroying the child's direct visual response to nature.

9. Modeling clay is an excellent way for a child to respond directly to the 3-D world; to the way solid objects in space look and feel; and to the sensuous feeling of clay in the hands.

10. Any healthy activity designed to stimulate seeing, thinking about seeing, and the expressions of visual thinking should be encouraged.

By the time a child learns to read with the word-picture symbols, without being encouraged to draw or make models from life first, the sense of personal relationship between the 3-D and 2-D representation may not develop properly. It can be re-trained, but this is rarely done in the average elementary or middle school classroom. For that reason the opportunity to expand the visual intelligence system may have been greatly diminished, along with the ability to express unconscious or pre-conscious visual information.

In my art classes, I insisted that the students draw from life. When their efforts were timid, I asked them to make a study of a strong, but simple, face by Michelangelo, Degas, or one from the pink period of Picasso. After studying the way the eyes were drawn, and the nose and mouth, the student would be able to see more details in the face of their model than they had before. When children move from scribble directly to coloring books, or to cartoon characters, those images may become symbols for visual responses for a long time to come. Ask an older student who did not study art to draw an animal, and s/he may provide you with a crude Bugs-type bunny or a Garfield-type cat. The actual response to nature may have become seriously inhibited in the visual system.

Several other problems can cause difficulty with vision as the child matures. Television and lack of exercise are prime targets of criticism. Before we had television in rural areas, my children rode bicycles, visited their friends, worked on private creative projects and played with the animals. For a while, the grandchildren sat draped over chairs, slack-eyed, glued to the TV, and they seemed to ignore the world around them. (Fortunately, they were encouraged to get over it.) The screen is flat, so the eyes don't get the muscle exercise they would when the children are physically active in a 3-D environment. The computer monitor is also flat, and some monitors flicker. Is there a wonder why so many children become near-sighted by the age of twelve? Part may be caused by too many hours staring at the television. Another large part of it is caused by the emotional pressure to study reading and writing on a flat surface under the flicker of fluorescent lights, which are in most school classrooms. (135, 136)

There are many other problems with television and memory, besides the potential for implanting trance induced suggestions. One of them is the afterimage, which the eyes remember even if you don't pay any attention to it. When you have watched for an hour or more, turn down the lights, or go outside, and notice that wherever you look there is a greenish, luminous, television screen-size glow over everything. When you close your eyes, it is still there. Notice what color it is for you. Ask those around you to describe how it looks to them. Just for your own information, keep track of the time it takes for that haze in your vision to fade.

I applaud education for doing the massive job it undertakes to develop literacy, scientific knowledge, and the abstract concepts of mathematics. However, it is only by looking at the 3-D world and attempting to respond to it that visual perception will be developed as a true form of intelligence in itself independent of the verbal and symbolic intelligences. Intelligence involves not only the mind, but the whole body and our access to the information from the hyperspace as well. Our first memories and the first time that we learned something new are always there in the form that we learned them. That moment is precious.

Those memories will be around for a very long time. They shouldn't be dominated by flat images.

**4. Effects of Repetitious Ads from Radio and TV on Long-Term Memory** — We have already discussed the hypnotic effects of TV advertisement. Now here is a personal example of how long the effect of repetition can last on memory. My first years were spent on a farm in the middle of the Great Basin near a town called Wabuska, Nevada. Before the copper mines closed, it was a Wild West town with several bars, gambling tables, gun fights, and seven red light districts. But that was all gone when we moved to the ranch there during the Depression. Only one bar remained by the railroad tracks, and the one small grocery store had a small corner set aside for a post office. Our school hired one teacher for all eight grades and fourteen students. We had the benefit of individualized instruction.

My older sisters all started school before I did, and since our farm was at least two miles away from any other farm, there was no one to play with. Even when I went to school, there was only one other girl my age. We didn't have any libraries and there were only a few books at home. So I played with cats, the dog, the baby lambs and tiny pigs that sometimes needed to be fed on a bottle when there were too many in the litter for the mother to feed. Later, I got to ride the horse to bring the cows home at milking time.

Television even for city folks was twenty-five years away. Our radio was battery-operated and used by our parents for news and weather. My sisters and I did get to hear *Little Orphan Annie* after school. Nevertheless, this old fashioned radio did have a long-lasting effect on my memory. I memorized its sing-song repetitious ads easily, especially one for a soap that was used in washing machines. In those days lots of suds were considered necessary to get the clothes clean. Now, of course, with automatic washers, suds are very bad because they clog the working parts. So the old slogan is obsolete. But "Super suds, super suds, lots more suds with super suds-u-uds" still runs around my head from time to time. Sometimes I can see the humor in it, but generally I am disgusted by the intrusion. However, it does demonstrate how invasive such things can be sixty years later. They are not useful for your mind, your memory, or your intelligence.

Now TV uses sound and flashing lights and actors to sell their products. People who are susceptible to hypnotic suggestion will most likely be stuck with unwanted memories for the rest of their lives. They can process their emo-

| OOLA: | "OOP'S GONE FROM MOO!" |
|---|---|
| PROFESSOR: | "BUT HE HASN'T SHOWED UP HERE!" |
| DOC: | "WHAT'S HAPPENED TO HIM?" |

OOP: "NOW WHERE'N TH' JUMPIN' BLUE BLAZES AM I?"

"I SUPPOSE SUMPIN'S GONE WRONG WITH DOC'S OL' TIME-GADGET AN' I'M STRANDED AGAIN — "

tional and physiological reactions to them, but the actual memories will still be around. I don't expect anything to change in television programming—after all, it is very profitable. However, I can recommend that we attempt to become more conscious about the effects of trance and hypnotic suggestion on our health as well as on our long-term memories. There was a time when students were taught by rote memorization. Understanding and thought were not included in the process, so it was abandoned by educators. However, it was eagerly adopted by radio and television advertisers and sound bite news programs.

**5. Old Memories that Are Attached to Specific Space-time Frames** — We have seen that as a person gets older, those early long-term memories are the ones that last, long after the short-term memory system begins to fail. We have seen that the earliest memories are kept in the form that they were first perceived. Today's memory may be elusive for the elderly, but stories of their early days are still told with the same words and emotions as though they had been recorded on tape. Memories that have accumulated over a long lifetime are evoked by certain associations. A song or a sentence spoken by another person may trigger a whole memory train from another time and place. We may even lose track of the present conversation, because the intruding memory of the past is so strong. The other person may have to remind us what we were talking about to get us back on track in present time.

I may be thinking about what I am writing while I go to the pantry to get something for supper. My verbal mind is totally involved with its own dialog. Unless I see what I want when I open the pantry door, so that the visual memory kicks in, I may forget what it was. If I don't see it, I may have to go back out and this time verbalize what it was I was going to get, to reinforce the memory when the image is not available. While attending a social gathering of enlightened, active, literate senior citizens, I was told that such a lapse in memory is now called "a senior moment." We all laughed about the latest terminology for our embarrassing lapses, but I can recall having "senior moments" when I was very young as well. More than once, when I was trying to introduce two dear friends of mine, I was so full of images that I could not speak the name of either well-known friend.

Close to the end of her life, my mother would allow her consciousness to drift, or even to leave the body from time to time. She didn't really understand what was happening to her at those times. Her religious training had not prepared her for out-of-the-body experiences, or for space-time travel. When she was in an unfamiliar environment, she might come back from such a journey, or from a moment of unconsciousness, and feel totally disoriented. At those times, I could remind her where she was. Her whole set of memories associated with that period would be retrieved. It is not so much that our memory becomes lost, but that our spacetime coordinates have become shifted.

One Christmas we visited my daughter in Hawaii. Mother, who was then eighty years old, had not seen Mara or her children for several years. When mother woke up from a nap in an unfamiliar house, her adolescent great-granddaughters asked her if she wanted some exotic tropical fruit from Mara's garden. Mother said yes, but while they were gone, she quietly said to me, "I think I must be related to those beautiful little girls, but I can't remember who they are." I reminded her that we were in Hawaii, and these were Mara's children. "Oh, yes, of course," she answered. After that she "clicked in" to her present spacetime frame and spoke gently to each of the girls by name when they returned. She always appreciated being able to rely on my "ground control" at such times.

Unfortunately, many people assume that their parents are losing their memory in such situations. If they behave toward the older person as though it were true, the parent also becomes fearful about it, until the actual memory loss becomes exaggerated. This fear may not be necessary. Except for serious cases of brain degeneration, as can occur when a person has Alzheimer's disease or severe dementia, there are many situations in which all the older person needs is a gentle reminder about which spacetime frame s/he is in. Then the whole memory train that belongs to that particular spacetime coordinate becomes readily available.

The illustration on the opposite page suggests some of the confusion that people can feel when they wake up in the wrong spacetime frame. (137) However, Alley Oop *expects* to be traveling in time. He always seemed to make the best of any time warp he found himself in, and we always enjoyed his adventures there. It would be a help to people who suffer a minor stroke, or who just blank out for a moment (i.e., stepped into the hyperspace) to realize when they come back into awareness that their spacetime coordinates can get mixed up. A person, with fifty to eighty or more years of life's memories to choose from, can easily become confused. In these situations, there may not be a loss of memory, as many fear. *Each spacetime frame has its own complete set of memories.* When the older person is in an unfamiliar environment, this confusion can happen more often.

A person might also experience this problem after an operation, when an anaesthetic wears off. One woman told me she was worried that her husband might have suffered brain damage during his illness, because after his second trip to the hospital, he was talking about going home to the place they had lived before, during the first event. He didn't seem to remember that they had moved since then. Her doctor hadn't reassured her that he would be all right. I told her that since the anaesthetic had confused his spacetime coordinates, the hospital room had stimulated his old memory. All she had to do was to remind him and thereby save his confusion as well as her own. This worked well.

**6. Learning to Express the Memories of the Various Senses Directly** — There are other aspects of memory that also need to be addressed here. Memory includes a vast network of sensory systems (each with its own set of memories), electromagnetic frequencies of neuron firings, and the multidimensions of the hyperspace. The ability to *express* whatever memory comes into awareness is often judged to be the memory itself, so the expression of memory is just as important as the memory.

If you want to remember something—e.g., "Where did I put my keys?"—one way to do it is to try to visualize where you saw them last; another way is to feel in your hand where you used them last. If you become emotional about having lost them, your chances of finding them are somewhat diminished. The exercise of taking a deep breath and allowing the brainwaves to become synchronized allows the nonverbal sensory systems to communicate with the verbal expression of awareness through the pure wave forms of the EEG. If you continually ask yourself, "Where did I put my keys? Where did I lose them?" you will defeat the ability of memory to integrate itself. Verbalization also creates an asymmetrical pattern in the EEG. (Language may be global, but the areas of verbal expression are dominant in the left hemisphere.) Becoming emotional about the loss creates flashes of high-amplitude slow waves in the EEG which are also asymmetrical (usually in the theta range). In both cases, the memory is blocked from arising into awareness or into the expressions of awareness. So if you need to make the memory work, sit down, close your eyes, take a deep breath (or five of them), and focus your mind in the center of your brain. An extended period of establishing a brainwave pattern of phase-coherent alpha may allow the information to rise to the surface.

Here are some examples: A friend picked me up to go to a meeting about memory. When I arrived, I realized that I did not have my set of keys which included keys for my car, house, and office. I felt a wave of mild panic energy flow over me. One of the exercises the teacher at the meeting presented was visualizing two blank television screens. On one, you visualize the thing you want to find. On the other you look to see where it is. I saw my keys lying under a pile of orange and brown oak leaves in the driveway. Then I realized that as I got into my friend's car, my keys had fallen out of my pocket onto the ground. The wind blew the leaves over them after we left. When I got home, I went out with a flashlight, turned over a few leaves, and found my keys right away. They were exactly where I had visualized them to be. I couldn't have said where they were unless the image had been given first.

A student called me long distance to ask if I could help him find his lost keys. He told me that he had looked everywhere in the house and could not find them. He said they had to be there because he had driven home the night before, parked the car in the garage, and he remembered bringing the keys into the house. So I said I would look for them and call him back. I put my brainwaves into phase-coherent alpha, moved from there into a light trance state and waited. The vision of his keys came to me right away. I called him back to say that they were in the chair by the front door. He complained that he had already looked there. I said that they had dropped below the cushion onto the black cloth which covered the springs of the chair. But I saw that the black cloth was ripped in one place, and that the keys had fallen through it and landed over one of the springs. That is why they hadn't dropped to the floor. He would have to turn the chair upside down to find them. He did so and found his keys draped over the springs, exactly where I had "seen" them fifty miles away. He was very pleased and very thankful. Nonattachment is best. Becoming emotional doesn't help. Learn to use more of the intelligence that is available from your visual system.

EEG synch is a way of accessing memory. A woman who had attended a meeting at the WRI started to walk down the stairs when it was over. She stopped to talk to a friend and was trying to remember something to tell a friend, who was standing at the top of the stairs. Where she was standing, her head was just lower than mine, and I asked her if she would like me to help her remember. She looked surprised but agreed. I reached over, put one hand at the center of the back of her head and two fingers on the "third eye" location on her forehead. I said, "Take a deep breath and image a light going between both hands." She followed my instructions and soon her eyes popped open. She told her friend whatever it was she had been trying to remember, and then remarked with some amazement, "She just put her hand on my head, and now I can remember!" I chuckled at the success of my experiment. The theory worked in this case. It doesn't always work, because the person is unwilling, or unable, to become nonattached to busy thoughts long enough to just let them go in favor of a wordless vision of light in the center of the head.

The intelligence and memory of the individual sensory systems can be used to a much greater advantage than is generally acknowledged in our society today. Parapsychology is not pseudoscience and education of only the three "Rs" misses a major potential of developing all of our intelligent systems, including psi activity. While some people can only do one thing at a time, others have been able to learn to do many things at once. Perhaps there is one advantage of television and computer games and that is the rapid hand-eye coordination and rapid shifts in focus of attention that the games require. While this may contribute to Attention Deficient Hyperactive Disorder (ADHD) in some children who eat a lot of junk food and have toxic amounts of aluminum in their systems, for others it may the appropriate training for the needs of young fighter pilots of the future—those who must be able to think as fast as their high tech planes can fly through space.

Multi-tasking comes easily to some high energy people (though others of us are quite content to focus on just doing one thing at a time). For example, watch a mother with four children. She can fix several things for dinner simultaneously and have them all finish cooking at the right time. While doing this she can carry on a conversation with each one of the children individually, and answer the phone if it rings, carrying it around between her shoulder and her ear while she stirs the soup. Energy is the key.

Once friends of mine were invited to play music on a national television program. Since I had volunteered to be the designated driver for the evening, I was allowed to be backstage during the performance. As I wandered around, I saw rooms full of the technological wonders that it took to broadcast this program live to all parts of the country, and I marvelled at what I saw there. The most interesting thing to me was to see people who were able to perform many tasks at the same time. One man was watching *twelve* TV monitors at the same time, while he wore a microphone and an earphone. He was able to talk to the different video camera crews, and to direct them to zoom their video cameras in or out. He was in charge of switching from one camera to another, and would tell the leader of each crew when that should happen. The results of his ability to pay attention to all these activities simultaneously would be the seamless, smooth-running show that the people at home saw on their TV sets. I doubt that very many people are able to do multi-tasking in the fast-paced way that this director was able to do. But since one person can do it, others can learn to do it when the job requires it to be done. (However, at my age, I no longer desire life in such a fast lane, even if I could do that much multi-tasking.)

Gottlieb spent many years operating what he called an "Eye Gym." I watched him work with children and adults. He had each one jump on a trampoline while reading letters written on a white board on the wall. They would have to do a knee drop when they came to certain vowels, and clap their hands when they came to certain consonants. The trampoline jump required that the person do all this within the rhythm of each jump. Gottlieb used this technique to integrate certain mental and physical functions along with color therapy and other physical exercises. A young boy who could only read three lines on the eye chart at the start of his work with Gottlieb was able to read three more lines within one month of therapy. I watched it happen as the boy's life changed, socially and academically. His whole personality softened, as he became friendly, cooperative, and less rebellious. His mother told us that he had formed new friendships at school, whereas before he was sure that no one had liked him. The other boys made fun of him because he couldn't catch a ball. Now at least he could see the ball when it came toward him, and he was beginning to be able to play well on a team.

Gottlieb has said, "Vision is more a function of the mind than of the eyeballs.... It is possible to teach an individual to see twice as fast and to remember twice as much. When that happens a profound change will occur in the quality and consciousness of that person's life."

Once you know that your intelligence can evolve to a more advanced level, you can allow it to happen. These exercises can facilitate the process:

1. Recognize that much of your perceptions of the outer world are mixed up with the reflections from your own internal projections.

2. Study the multidimensions of your personality, and clear up the projections that are not useful. For example when someone near you is distressed, can you be concerned and helpful but nonattached? Note the following possible reactions and consider how they might be caused by a reflection from your own internal projection, or from taking a clear look at the other person's situation:

A) *"What did I do wrong, now?"*
B) *"How dare you speak to me in that tone of voice!"*
C) *"That is your problem, I don't want to get involved."*
D) *Walk away so you can avoid the situation.*
E) *"You seem to be very upset, how can I help?"*

3. Through biofeedback training in the various modalities (GSR, EMG, skin temperature, EEG)

you can learn voluntary control of your nervous system as needed. Explore the ways that your electrical activity responds to your different thoughts and emotions. Change the electrical signal and see if it changes your thoughts.

4. Emotions can color your perceptions. However, you can learn how to make creative use of the extra high energy stirred up by your emotions.

5. Practice expanding the sensitivity of all of your senses to receive more information from each of them.

6. Explore different ways to express the intelligence as it is received by the various senses.

7. Practice meditation for itself and for the peacefulness it provides.

8. Practice meditation as a gateway to the multiple dimensions of the hyperspace.

9. Accept the concept that access to non-local spacetime is your rightful mental activity. Practice using psi and double check all responses to sort actual incoming hyperspace information from your own internal projections that originated in memory.

10. Share your knowledge with those who ask for it without forcing it on them.

11. Really listen to your family and friends. Find out who they are, how they think, and what they think about. Compare with them the different ways that each of us perceives the world and with what different dominant cognitive processes.

12. Practice kindness and explore joy.

13. From time to time go out to a mountain top and listen to the birds, or the rocks, or the wind in the trees, and let your mind drift where it will. Intelligence can be absorbed on many levels in such an environment.

14. Find gratitude in your heart for all of creation and express it openly.

15. Explore the deeper meaning of Love and its expressions of compassion.

16. Learn the ways of accessing a higher intelligence when you need guidance. This is available to everyone. Formal religions like to interpret how this might be done and to describe the "only true" ways to find it. However, each person comes into this world with their access to higher intelligence built into the system as standard equipment. Finding your own path requires an attitude of humility, respect, and gratitude knowing that a higher intelligence (beyond each individual's multiple personalities) is available upon request through intention and the practice of internal silence.

Perhaps intelligence is not evolving so much as it is becoming integrated. Our ancient ancestors learned to communicate with each other and with the spirits of plants and animals before the extensive development of language. Literacy for the majority of the population is very recent. It was only two hundred years ago when only the men of the upper classes and even fewer women were educated to read and write. The soldiers of the American Revolution signed up for the war by making a mark where their names should be. As literacy increased through public education, overall intelligence has taken a large step forward, along with a step backward, as well. Nonverbal communication gradually became thought of as nonexistent in the established institutions of learning. Now we know that mind-to-mind communication across time and space has always been a latent ability within us. After many thousands of years, we can acknowledge this ability again and expand all types of intelligence as we choose.

As individuals learn to increase the intelligence of their visual systems, for example, what might we expect from the visual arts? Art is philosophy made visual. For one thing, the artist philosophers of the materialistic age will no longer hold the public interest. The old commercialized galleries, which inflate prices and create mythologies to glorify the bizarre for the tax advantages of their supporters, may begin to wonder what happened. But their flat-painted Soup Cans, large Floor Burgers, along with their currently precious "drip and blob" paintings will become merely historical curiosities of an old materialist culture that is gradually evolving to include a few more dimensions in its perception of reality. Artists must express what is happening to them as images of the multidimensional nature of the world surge through them.

The artists whose work announce the directions that philosophy is taking in the 21st century are those who show us the multidimensional aspects of nature. The nature films from National Geographic, Nova, NASA and others that show us outer space, time-lapses, electron microscopic images, are thrilling. Those artists who create movies that are set in multidimensional realms also come to mind, since we all know them: *Yellow Submarine, Dr. Who, 2001, Star Trek, Star Wars, Powder, Ghost, Phenomena,* and many others. Among the best film animation is the art of Yoichiro Kawaguchi. He has done pioneering research in applying Artificial Intelligence to a free-form generation of computer animation.

But what will be the paintings that will dominate the galleries and our homes in the future? They will come from such artists as: James Dowlen and Tom Byrne who can manifest their images directly from the hyperspace; Jesse Allen who shows us the energy between plants and animals; Alex Grey who shows us with great aesthetic detail the multiple energies in and around our bodies; Susan Seddon Boulet who demonstrates our integral relationship with animal spirits; and Ingo Swann. Swann was one of the best remote viewers for the CIA and his paintings show us a multidimensional world that enlarges our concept of the psyche. While old-guard museum directors still worship the material age and can't or won't exhibit the new art, it means there are many other artists whose paintings most of us will not have seen yet. I know this because the time is right for the best artists among us to manifest such multidimensional visions that will light the way our evolution must take as we seek to build a sustainable way of life on sacred planet Earth.

Artists have always illustrated the way we look at ourselves and the world around us. They can help our civilization become conscious of how our memories develop and illustrate the different paths that the evolution of our intelligence might take, consciously or unconsciously. It is time to take another look at traditional educational processes, along with the commercialization of television trance states for profit. It is time to make conscious choices as individuals about the ways we would like our intelligence to evolve. It is time that individuals and the best of our dedicated scientists begin to explore the vast potential and extensive abilities of the multidimensional mind we share with all life in the infinite domain of the Great Spirit.

# CHAPTER SEVEN — LOGIC AND THE REALMS OF NON-LOCAL SPACETIME

Precognition defies the ordinary logic of linear time. Yet, once in a while, some of us do have experiences of precognition. It may have been trivial, such as dreaming about seeing an unusual animal in a certain place, and the next day you see exactly what you saw in your dream. On the other hand, people have reported that their precognitive visions of disasters motivated them to warn others in time to save their lives. For many who have given up on the idea that *fate* controls our lives or that there is such a thing as a predetermined destiny, precognition just doesn't make any sense. If they strongly believe that we have free will, and that many events in our lives are caused by random circumstances, it is impossible to believe that we could have a vision of an event that has not yet occurred. Yet we do have them, and I shall describe one such event.

I had been at Stanford Research Institute (SRI) in Menlo Park while Russell Targ and Hal Puthoff were conducting experiments with Uri Geller. That night I was to teach a class at 7 PM for Santa Rosa Junior College (SRJC) at a high school classroom in Cotati. It was a two-hour drive, more than that if the traffic was heavy. Yet, events were interesting and I didn't leave Menlo Park until 5 PM. As I rushed out to the car, I had a very strong image of an old gray sedan with a crumpled rear fender. It was driving across the road directly in front of me. I was irritated with the image and brushed it away with my hand, saying aloud though there was no one to hear me, "Just because I am late, I do *not* have to have an accident!"

I jumped in my car and started off. The best route from Menlo Park to Cotati is Highway 280. Just south of San Francisco, it joins 19th Avenue which goes all the way through the city to the Golden Gate Bridge on the north. The traffic at that time of night is heavy, with many stoplights, any one of which could have changed my travel time. After the bridge, US 101 becomes a freeway, passing several towns. Just south of Petaluma the road is still a divided highway, but traffic can enter it from side roads. When I reached that stretch, it was already dark.

I must confess I was moving faster than the speed limit allowed. Just then, the same gray car of my earlier vision, including the dented rear fender, drove slowly onto the highway from the left, without looking, and pulled directly in front of me in the slow lane, the right one of two northbound lanes. It was the exact broadside image I had seen before. There was a car parallel to my left fender, so I could not pass on the left. Fortunately, I had already decided that I would not hit this car, because there was no time to question that possibility now. However, the only place for me to pass it was on the right shoulder, something I have never done or even thought of doing before. As soon as I did that, I saw a culvert blocking the shoulder, and I swerved immediately back onto the highway, just in front of the gray sedan. The swerve was so fast that my car tilted and wobbled before it stabilized. I had avoided an almost-certain collision directly in front of me, as well as a very possible one on the left, or a head-first smash into a ditch.

When I arrived at class, shaken to the core, students teased me about being five minutes late. A very lively discussion about precognition ensued. Many had experienced it and were eager to share their stories and questions about what might be the cause. I felt that my higher consciousness had warned me about the problem ahead of time, so those precious split seconds that it might have taken for me to decide whether or not I could avoid a collision did not delay my actions. I just reacted to the situation without any emotions until later. However, a two-hour drive through city traffic at rush hour could have changed my arrival at that exact spot in the road just enough to put me in front of the gray sedan, or behind it far enough to stop or to slow down. But the clarity of the vision and the exact timing of the actual event, with all of its potential for change, stirs up many unanswered and puzzling questions about logic, linear time, and the actual nature of time and consciousness that allows us to see such a vision before it happens.

The class decided that they would write their next paper on their personal feelings about "Fate vs. Free Will." The next week, some students volunteered to read their papers on the subject, and a rousing discussion was generated. A few were definitely on the side of **fate,** stating that if "God said..." something would happen, then it must. A few were strongly on the side of **free will**, insisting that they had control over their lives. Most of the rest of the class expressed belief in a mixture of fate and free will. They knew they were free to decide about some things, but other events in their lives seemed to be preordained. Naturally, the class did not come to any conclusions, but the discussion did stir up our thinking. Most of us rarely question our assumptions about linear time. But when we are confronted by powerful experiences of precognition, then we must reconsider those assumptions. In that instant, the logic of linear time falls apart, and we are left staring into the unknown. And in spite of the advances in physics and quantum mechanics, we may be facing the unknowable.

## LINEAR TIME AND TIMELESSNESS

We have already seen how each of the sensory systems can cooperate to enhance information, or how they can operate independently. When some images are difficult to express in words, and some concepts, such as the idea of timelessness, defy imagery, symbols are created. For example, the symbols used to celebrate New Year's Eve have two images. The new year is shown as a baby and the old year is shown as an old man, or Father Time, with a long beard and a sickle in his hand. Both images are needed for the concept of the extension of time.

The illustration above, right is from Team #8. The sender expressed, "...Life long lived...." This is a verbal expression of the present as an extension of the past through time. Her receiver drew a watch with no hands, which carries the idea of timelessness very well. Because he did not draw a portrait of a person, this response was not matched by the judges. Few receivers ever know why certain images, and not others, arise in the mind during these trials. Twelve out of this receiver's thirty responses were intensely symbolic, so only six of the thirty were matched.

One receiver may frequently get matching responses just one trial late. Since the response is given during the same set of five, and there has not yet been any feedback given about actual targets used, the receiver seems to have a problem with linear time. This happened with the receiver of Team #2, who wrote that she "kept going back..." to the previous trial because she perceived a hand with a gun in it. Had she drawn that, the judges might have matched it. Unfortunately, her drawing for the previous trial included a castle and a reference to "Snow White and the 7 Dwarfs." Her comments about a "...train—something powerful, straight and black like a gun or a train" were added to the back of the card. That was not enough. She

did not develop the idea of a hand with a gun in it until the next trial. That was too late for it to be matched. The actual target was a man holding a long walking stick (with a metal cap on it) over his shoulder the way someone might hold a rifle. This is what I call the "ringing effect" of one strong target over the next one.

*Team #8 TARGET Trial #1 December 20, 1974*

*Old magazine reproduction of a portrait by Thomas Eakins.*

**BMS = 0**
**SMS = cn**

Another example of the ringing effect was seen when the receiver of Team #12 (a spiritual healer) accurately responded to an image of a hungry child on Target #2. However, for Target #3 (an ad for a new car) he responded with a mother serving food to her children. This was not matched by the judges. However for the healer, it might have been a way to resolve the pain from the ringing effect of the previous image.

The ringing effect was more common for Team #5. We have already seen the receiver's late response to the mountain, when she couldn't smoke in the subject room (page 41). Here the same receiver has provided a response of lightning for a target of lightning one trial late. Her direct response of an axon to Target #6 has similar shapes to the lightning, but because of the direct reference to lightning in her next response, both trials were matched by the judges in reverse (below). Lightning only became a target this one time in the first 290 trials, and twice during the later study. In the later study, one of the lightning *targets*

**Team #5 - TARGET - Trial #6**
**December 16, 1974**
*Painting by Santore. See Appendix A..*

**BMS = 0 — SMS = d, s, m**

**Team #5 - SENDER - Trial #6**

"Thunder clouds,
Dark Blue / Dark Brown"

**Team #5 - RECEIVER - Trial #6**

"Spider web or roots of tree
or neuron, axons, etc."

**Team #8
SENDER
Trial #1**

"Wisdom—
deep feelings
of inner
knowledge.
Pain in eyes.
**Life long
lived.** Hair
reminds me
of Mercury."

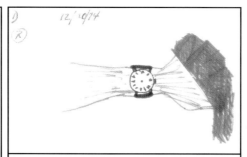

***Team #8 - RECEIVER - Trial #1***

"Wrist watch— only part of an arm showing.
No time on watch."

When attempting to receive messages telepathically, it is essential to clear the mind as much as possible. Even then we find that the images and thoughts that come bubbling up first were our own pre-conscious thoughts just under the surface of our awareness. If we don't recognize them as our own, they take on the guise of the message being sent. If we don't stop with the first image, but look again and again for the message, we may actually find what is being sent. We may be late in receiving it, because the sorting-out process takes time. However, when we learn more about our own inner pre-conscious material, we can improve our ability to distinguish between it and the information that is actually being sent to us.

was a photograph of lightning. It could be matched because the receiver referred to darkness and night. A response to the other, a painting of lightning, was "the joker" with similar colors. It was not matched. Lightning was given as a *response* by three different receivers. The other two were matched only in shape to unrelated targets.

Some judges criticized our practice of doing five trials in one sitting before any feedback was given. However, students were asked during the preliminary sessions whether they wanted to do one trial at a time, five in a row, or all ten at once. Most felt that they were just getting warmed up in a session of five, and that to stop after each one would be a distraction. One team wanted to do ten at once, but we all finally agreed to do five at a time. Some responses were given late in the series, and some were early. Both the examples of the ringing effect, as well as those of precognition meant that at least two responses out of five would be mismatched. The final scores would reflect those as errors, since judging considered only those matched in sequence. Perhaps the statistical correlation between the team's *IP synch* and blind matching scores (page 111) might only indicate their ability to be in present time.

This problem of late response is not unique to our study. It has been reported by many others over the years when several trials are attempted at one sitting before feedback is given. Within my own personal experience this has occurred several times. During the winter of 1969-70, I was staying in New York, far away from my home in California. While there, I practiced my psi ability by checking on the relatives each night during my evening meditation. However, there were four days when I was very busy organizing a group telepathy experiment. When that was finally over and I could rest, I had a dream that my mother had suffered a heart attack. I called her the next morning. She had experienced a mild heart attack three days before and was now resting comfortably. I had missed the information because I had been active instead of receptive. I believe the information was in the hyperspace in the actual time, but it did not enter my awareness until I was clear enough to receive it. In this case, clarity came during sleep.

**Team #5
TARGET
Trial #7
December 16,
1974**

*Photo of a
molded plastic
chair from an
architectural
magazine.*

**BMS = 0
SMS = s, cl**

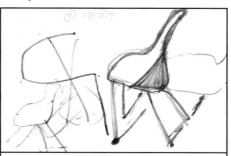

***Team #5 - SENDER - Trial #7***

"Shadow,
Black, Chair"

***Team #5 - RECEIVER - Trial #7***

"dark sky - lightning flash illuminating tree
in full leaf - maybe mountain there, too."

## PRECOGNITION CHALLENGES
## THE LOGIC OF THE LINEAR MIND

It is the responses that are given *before* the target is randomly chosen from the pool of one hundred cards that provide us with the precognitive phenomena. If the target and its response are among the common types of targets (such as flowers), we classified the early match as just a curious synchronistic event. But when the target is unique among the four hundred trials and the early matching response is also unique, then we classified the response as though it were actually precognitive. This did not occur often in our study. However, we did find eight such events which are worth examining in greater detail.

There may have been a ninth occurrence among the trials of Team #9. They may have had a precognition and a reversal, or just a mixed-up numbering on the cards. For example, their Target #6 is a picture of a person with his face painted white and blue, wearing a red turban. The sender describes him as a *"magician."* The receiver's Response #7 is a drawing of a white circle with red lines and a blue triangle. He writes, *"The Magic Triangle. Sorcerer's circle. Hermes Trimegistus."* Target #7 is a painting of an old castle. The receiver's Response #6 has no drawing at all, only the words *"Bryn Mawr College."* After seeing the targets, the receiver felt that he may have given his responses on the wrong numbered cards. This set is interesting regardless of whether the two responses are matched or mixed, though they were not counted in the final scores because of the confusion about the numbering. Even without these two possible "hits," Team #9 was among our three top scoring teams in both the blind match scores for telepathy (BMS) and in their interpersonal alpha phase-coherent ratio (APCR).

One of the most dramatic of the eight examples of precognition occurred during the second session for Team #14 (both trials are illustrated on these two pages). Target #2 (not shown) is a picture of Paul Revere riding a horse. The receiver's response during Trial #2 is the planet Saturn (right). The image is labeled the same way the sender labels her drawing for the actual target of Saturn which came up for Trial #5. This is the *only target* of Saturn in the entire set of four hundred targets. The receiver drew the head of the Big Bad Wolf for Trial #5. Astrologers may find a subtle relationship, since Saturn is considered to be a heavy influence in people's lives, but all five judges quite naturally matched the Saturn target with the Saturn response, and they all matched the wolf with Paul Revere and his horse.

The planet Saturn was given as a *response* only one other time in the four hundred trials, and that was during the first study five years earlier. That target associated with Team #8's response of Saturn was an advertisement for a TV program. It was a picture of a man being hanged with a rope around his neck. In the receiver's response, the planet with a ring around it was small on the card, approximately the same size and shape as the rope and the man's head in the target photo. The receiver of Team #8 wrote, "...Picture of some area in space—Saturn-like planet with a ring around it—stars all around giving off different colors—sparkle." This response was not matched with its target, either. The shape is obviously similar, but the mood and concept are very different from the sender's comments about the hanged man.

What is the difference between precognition and prediction? When a sequence of events has already begun, the outcome might be predicted. For example: when NASA sends a mission to Mars, the space vehicle is programmed to land at a much later time. If nothing changes, the probe lands as predicted. In another type of prediction, a woman dreams that a light fixture lands on her baby's crib, crushing her baby. She runs into the nursery and takes the baby into her own bed. When the light fixture eventually does crash on the empty crib, her dream might be classified as a psychic prediction, even though the woman did not know (nor did any other person know) that the wires holding the fixture were probably already loose and ready to fall. It is enough that her concerns for her child opened her awareness to receive information from the hyperspace in time to prevent a tragedy.

Another type of psychic prediction occurred when I participated in the parapsychology studies at SRI in 1973. Uri Geller and his cousin Shippi were both inside the electromagnetically shielded room on this occasion. Russell Targ had asked me to draw a picture representing the word "homeland" to transmit to him. At the time I lived in the small town of Fair Oaks. My first thought of my own homeland included oak trees, so I drew one. Since Geller's homeland is Israel, Targ drew a menorah on the page. After a time, Geller said

**Team #14 - RECEIVER**
**Trial #2**
*September 13, 1980*

"The Planet Saturn"

he would pass. He said that he and Shippi started talking about politics, and he wasn't confident in his response. He had drawn pictures of several military tanks traveling across a desert. Flying above them were flags of different Islamic nations. A few weeks later, on October 13, 1973, Islamic nations did attack Israel. Geller's drawing was not precognitive, since the attack was, no doubt, already being planned and known by the attacking military. His drawing was a psychic prediction, although he didn't know that at the time. Later Geller did do some remote viewing for his homeland.

A friend told me the following story which seems to be an example of precognition. She and her companion planned to drive up the highway from San Jose to Berkeley to visit me. A few days before that time, she dreamt about a green Chevy with license plate JUS 6...approaching them on the opposite lane. Just as that car came near them, it crossed over the center line and crashed into them, killing them both. She woke up and wrote down as much of the license plate number as she remembered. She was so shaken that she told her friend about it. Later, when they did drive to Berkeley, she saw the green Chevy and yelled for her friend to pull over. They were far enough over on the shoulder of the road that when the Chevy did cross over the center line briefly, just as it did in her dream, it missed them and continued down the highway. They noticed that the license number was the same. When they arrived at my house, they were both quite shaken by the dream and the actual event, which was surely precognitive. Nothing about it was predictable. When she had the dream, she had not decided just when to take the trip.

Why are some of us warned of impending disaster and others are not? I think the warning must depend upon our personal karma, or the flow of the dharma in the

experience of this life, along with our willingness to pay attention to the still small voice within.

I once met a woman who consistently did not pay attention to, or even expect to hear a friendly small voice within. She believed in her own "bad luck." Three of us were in her car and watched in disbelief as she slowly let her car collide with a parked car. Since she was turning around in a quiet residential area, the event could have been avoided easily. Instead of putting her foot on the brake and continuing to turn the steering wheel, she threw her hands in the air and shouted, "Oh, no! We are going to crash!" She just let it happen. The force of her fear projected into her perceptions and created havoc around her. Though no one was hurt or even shaken up, the fender bender was costly. A pattern of believing in bad luck had been set in her psyche and would be projected endlessly onto the world around her. A guide might be able to help her change her patterns of negative thinking, which could change her future, but she would have to ask for such help. Without help one might easily predict future problems for her, and they would not have to evoke their psychic energy to do so.

When I was given a vision about an old gray sedan pulling in front of me seventy miles up the road, that could not have been predicted. Even the driver of the old sedan might not have known when he would begin his journey. That vision would have to be called precognitive. Physicists have provided the words "non-local spacetime" to explain such shifts in the perception of time. Since I believe that consciousness is eternal, I think that the vision that came to me outside of linear time might have been allowed in the concept of karma. My own consciousness has its unfinished karma, and it (or my spirit guide) gave me an image of impending disaster. I made a choice to avoid it. I might have chosen to freeze in fear instead—in which case I would have crashed and (alive or dead) I may then have called the accident fate or bad luck.

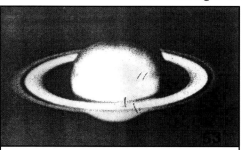

**Team #14 - TARGET - Trial #5**
**September 13, 1980**

Photocopy of NASA image of Saturn

Box scores for both Trials #2 and #5

BMS = 0 — SMS = 0

**Team #14 - SENDER - Trial #5**

"The Planet Saturn"

head of big bad wolf from Walt Disney movie 3 little pigs

**Team #14**
**RECEIVER**
**Trial #5**

"head of Big Bad Wolf from Walt Disney movie— 3 little pigs"

*Team #7 - TARGET - Trial #8*
*November 26, 1974*

*Color photo of a hen. See Appendix A.*

**BMS = 0 —— SMS = cl**

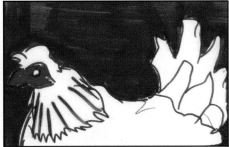

*Team #7 - SENDER - Trial #8*

"The male rooster
feathers—colors
Proud Bird"

*Team #7 - RECEIVER - Trial #8*

"Something round & yellow in foreground left
Brownish line intersecting it
**Statue of Liberty**."

*Team #7*
*TARGET*
*Trial #9*
*November 26, 1974*

"LIBERTY
IN GOD WE
TRUST"

*Photograph of a Liberty Coin.*

**BMS = 0**
**SMS = s, m, cn**

*Team #7 - SENDER - Trial #9*

"**LIBERTY** — 1945
Mercury the messenger—1st Planet
The winged one—Communication

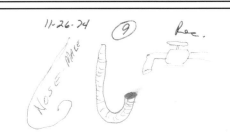

*Team #7 - RECEIVER - Trial #9*

"1.  **J** or plumbing
2.  Male nose, large
3.  Faucet"

The receiver of Team #7 completed two precognitive responses; the example illustrated above is from the team's first session, and the other example, illustrated on the opposite page, is from the second session a month later. In the illustration above, the precognition of the Statue of Liberty comes just one trial before the target of the Liberty coin. The precognition of the eagle illustrated on the opposite page was given four trials before the target of the large bird, which the sender names "eagle."

In the one above, the sender seems to think that the hen is a rooster. The receiver draws the Statue of Liberty with something that looks like a net. (With the imagination of a cloud watcher, it looks like a net we used for catching chickens, back on the ranch.) Nevertheless, during the next trial the receiver struggles with the metal nose of the image on the actual Liberty coin target. He can't seem to decide whether the image is a nose or a faucet, and it does not occur to him that the nose is made of metal. This is another example of what can happen when only part of a target is received. The brief image, brought from the hyperspace,

cannot be tracked by the physical eye for additional detail. It is natural to try to combine logic with memory, but this is rarely useful. Only clearing the mind to find more information, or another image, can help. Often the beginner is so happy to "see" that first image that s/he will quit looking after that.

The only other drawing of the Statue of Liberty given as a *response* in our study was by the receiver of Team #12. He drew it in response to a target picture of a football player with his arm in the air. The position of the figure on the card was so similar that three of the judges matched the football player with the Statue of Liberty quite easily.

The coin above was the only *target* of Liberty used in the study. There was one other coin pulled from the target pool, but the image on it was George Washington. That one was matched with "red ... white ... and blue" and the archetypal duality concept of God and the devil (page 61). Team #7 got the only two targets with coins used in any of our studies.

The sender's response to the drawing by Raphael in Target #4 is very personal (illustrated below). She identifies with the person in the portrait and talks about her own memory and resentments of things past. Her drawings of ribbons in the hair and on the dress have the same type of thin, curved lines that the receiver's drawing of the "eagle" seems to have. His response was given one score for shape similarity to the real-time target.

However, when the sender sees the large bird in the picture of Target #8, she refers to it as an "eagle," even though it isn't one. There are only two *targets* of large, dark birds in the entire set. The other one shows only the head, and the response to it was similar only in shape and color. The *response* of an eagle, named as such, was only given this one time in the four hundred trials.

By the time the picture of the bird is *sent* as the target, the receiver, who already drew an eagle as a response, is ready for the session to be over, because he is worried about his studies. This session is only a few days before the end of the semester, and he still has a term paper to write. He draws books and a globe in a study room for this response, just as he drew a stack of books during the first session which was just before midterm exams. His partner is not a student. She seems to have very different concerns about their relationship, which show up in what she writes in the messages she attempts to transmit to him.

Just which card might be chosen as the next target out of the one hundred cards in the pool could not have been predicted by anyone. Neither the *monitor,* the *sender,* nor the *receiver* in another room could know what target might be chosen. The examples illustrated here do seem to show precognition (events in non-local spacetime). Of the eighteen teams in all, only six of them provided the eight precognitive responses. They seemed to occur for the receivers in our study when they felt pressured in some way, either by time, outside obligations, or by problems in their relationship with the sender.

**Team #7 - TARGET**
**Trial #4**
**December 17, 1974**

*Magazine reproduction*
*of a drawing by Raphael.*

**BMS = 1 — SMS = s**

**Team #7 - SENDER**
**Trial #4**

"Remember when I looked like this
years and years ago—
long dresses and strict fathers—
✝ churches and mean people"

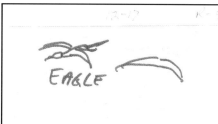

**Team #7**
**RECEIVER**
**Trial #4**

"Eagle or other
large, dark bird.
Turbulent weather,
overcast, ominous."

**Team #7 - TARGET - Trial #8**
**December 17, 1974**

*Color photo of a large bird. See Appendix A.*

**BMS = 2 —— SMS = cl**

**Team # 7 - SENDER - Trial # 8**

"The **eagle** flies high into the sky—
The **eagle** is the east.
Eagle Eye"

**Team #7 - RECEIVER - Trial #8**

"Books
globe
Study room."

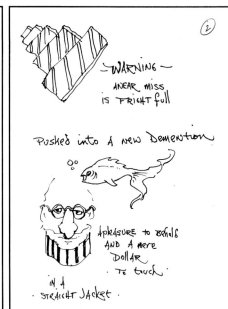

***TV Team JTJ — SENDER***
***Trial #2 — March 25, 1977***

"Nude in waterfall—
attempts to feel cool water—
contrast with hot lights
in the studio."

***TV Team JTJ — RECEIVER***
***Tom Byrne — Trial #2***

" — WIDE DECK
— WINDSHIELD"

***TV Team JTJ — RECEIVER***
***James Dowlen — Trial #2***

"WARNING —
A **near miss** is frightful
Pushed into a new dimension.
A pleasure to behold and a mere
Dollar to touch. In a Straight Jacket."

The following example of precognition was provided during the recording session at the video studio. There the protocol was a bit different because there was one sender and two receivers. This was planned so we could record two people drawing the same shape simultaneously on one video tape, if that occurred. (See page 32.) The director Bob Budereaux was in the mixing room where he could chose where the two video cameras should be focused. He could tell the camera operators through earphones where to move their video cameras during the experiment. The old 1970s black and white, reel to reel video technology left a lot to be desired, but we were able to see events happening in real-time, and I hope such an experiment could be done again with modern color equipment.

The target for this second trial of the session is a photo of a nude woman, standing in water up to her waist with water falling all around her. Since we don't know where the photo was taken and don't have a credit line for either the photographer or the woman, this drawing by the sender will have to suffice to show the pose (illustrated above).

Byrne's response to this target is a boat moving through water. The head of the skipper is seen behind the windshield. While Byrne's response is considered to be a miss, the lady in the waterfall was the only *target* in this session that involved splashing water. It is Byrne's only *response* in this set that included splashing water. Some possible similarities seem quite remote, because the targets and their responses have such different primary subject matter. That is why we asked different judges to match similarities, so that color, shape, mood, etc. could be seen independently from the subject matter of the targets. The brain constantly attempts to match percept with pre-conceived concept. However, the brief flashes that are received during telepathy are often conceptualized prematurely by those unfamiliar with the natural mental processes of psi. Telepathy can become more accurate through frequent practice, through constantly checking your own responses for errors and types of distortions, through discovering your most accurate sense for reception and through being as totally honest with yourself as you can be about your inner projections that tend to be dominant .

Dowlen's response to the nude lady in the waterfall is more complex. He had not yet met the lady he would call his soul mate. He is unaware that he is creating a word pun when he writes, "A near miss is frightful," combined with

**TV Team JTJ
TARGET
Trial #3**

*March 25, 1977*

One fish, two fish, red fish blue fish.

"One fish, two fish, red fish, blue fish."

Drawings and story by Dr. Seuss
Copyright © Theodore S. Geisel 1959 (138)

*We used a color copy of the original picture from the book as a target. Since permission to reprint the original is unavailable at this time, this is only a rough sketch of the colorful drawing to show the target with the response. (With apologies to T. S. Geisel.)*

**RECEIVER - James Dowlen - Trial #2**

**"Pushed into a new dimension"**
(Precognitive detail)

**TV Team JTJ — RECEIVER
Tom Byrne — Trial #3**

**TV Team JTJ
SENDER
Trial #3**

"Dr. Seuss

One fish,
Two fish,
Red fish,
Blue fish.

Children's story

memory of
reading it to
the children."

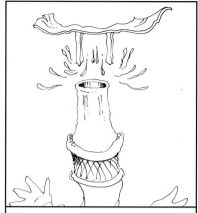

**TV Team JTJ — RECEIVER
James Dowlen — Trial #3**
*(no comment by receiver)*

*(Since splashing water is included in this response, it may actually represent a ringing effect from the previous target.)*

*(Tom Byrne made very few comments on his drawings during this session, and none on this one. Here he has drawn buildings instead of fish, but they are reminiscent of the style used in the drawings in other books by Dr. Seuss.)*

his comments, "A pleasure to behold and a mere dollar to touch...." Perhaps it is his inhibition to "see" the target directly that causes him to provide us with a precognition. Perhaps it is the pressure he feels while under the hot lights of the video studio with a camera focused on him that causes it. In any case, the fish that he draws for Trial #2 is extremely similar to the Dr. Seuss fish in Trial #3. (138) When he also writes that he feels "pushed into a new dimension," that statement provides us with a clue to the experience of receiving an image precognitively. The retrieval of information from non-local spacetime seems to involve moving one's thoughts into the multidimensional realms of the hyperspace.

Dowlen's next response, when the target of the fish comes up, is a hose with splashing water (above right). Perhaps this is an example of a ringing effect of the previous strong target. Since he already "saw" the fish, he is not expecting to see it again. Perhaps the splashing water is a resonant response to his friend's drawing. The actual influences that occur during a strong psychic soup event may not be possible to trace accurately.

Byrne's response to the Dr. Seuss fish target has no

relationship to fish. However, his drawings of buildings are very reminiscent of the way Dr. Seuss draws buildings in some of his books. Just what part of memory is functioning and just what part of our multiple selves is dominant at the time we attempt telepathy is not predictable, as yet. The process is so complex that only the individual may be able to trace the lines of memories that lead to a response, but only after s/he sees the target picture. Even then, this comment is often given: "I have no idea where that came from." The precognition examples we have mentioned here were all given spontaneously. We did not set out to test precognition until some time after we had seen some of these examples.

There were also some spontaneous precognitive examples given during our remote viewing experiments. The most prominent among them were done by Dowlen, especially if he felt pressured about time or had "tuned-in" late. Dowlen wasn't sure just when he would be home on April 19, so we had agreed the day before that the outbound team would go to the site, wherever it turned out to be, and stay there until sunset. This meant that the team would be at the site for an hour or more, which is much longer than they usually spent at target sites. But Dowlen did want to partic-

ipate in this session, and his contribution to RV was always so extraordinary that we were eager to have him take part any time he could.

On that day the randomly chosen target site was the water storage tower in Cotati. It was difficult to focus on a featureless uninteresting site for an hour, so it wasn't long before my mind wandered to other major concerns. When we arrived at the site, I parked the car at the side of the narrow road near the fence. Previously I had borrowed a camera from a friend so I could take better pictures of our target sites. After photographing the tower (above), I locked the camera in the trunk, because I didn't want to carry it all the way up that hill. For this session, my remote viewing partner on the outbound team was F.B. He, being a young man, charged up the hill with great enthusiasm. I, being a plump, middle-aged lady, slowly chugged along at my own pace, reciting to myself an old favorite poem for such an occasion, which was "We're off, we're off, like an elephant herd. An elephant herd of turtles...." (When my children were small, I had written several stories and poems for them. This was the chorus of one of them. Often since then, while getting a slow start to go somewhere, the children or I would repeat those lines. This time, the rhyme was automatically in my head.) As you can see in the illustration at right, Dowlen had caught my slowly moving mood along with the turtle when he finally returned to his studio to "find" us at the remote site. We were already up on the hill before he arrived home, but he was able to include it and my concern for the borrowed camera among several pages of drawings that he made from this session.

Most of his drawings related to my own personal concerns, since my mind had wandered, but the rest of his drawings for this session are precognitive. This collection is the largest set of drawings that Dowlen made for any session. Since I did *not* expect to be involved in a precognition, I wondered about these drawings for several days until the events he described actually occurred.

*James Dowlen REMOTE VIEWER April 19, 1976*

"Sunset remote viewing, 6:10"

*(There was no tripod for the borrowed camera. Dowlen provided his usual embellishment. The turtle on my head, however, is a direct response to the poem I recite to myself as I walk uphill slowly, as usual.)*

Dowlen's second page of drawings is illustrated on the page opposite, above left. It includes the question "A story unfolds?" This is the beginning of a strange series of events, and over the next few days of remote viewing sessions, he added more images about the potential event.

The next two RV sessions were on April 29. The first one was at the ice cream parlor, and Dowlen responded to that with, "The glimmer of a round shining thing reveals its hiding place." (Illustrated on the opposite page, above right.) This, of course, could not be matched with the target site of the ice cream parlor, which was an indoor site. The image of a car and something lying in the grass had no relationship at all to that site. The session that followed was the duck pond at CSUS. (See pages 76 and 77.)

I was able to photograph the ice cream parlor and the duck pond series, but when I needed to use the camera again, I discovered that something had broken. I took it to Santa Rosa to have it fixed, and later went back to pick it up. While in town, I had planned to buy inexpensive used

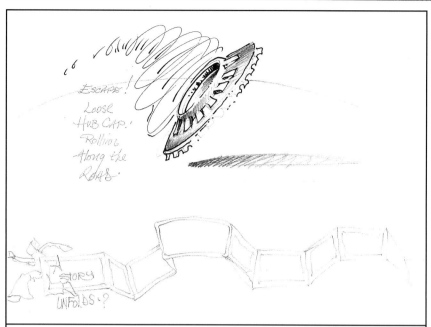

*James Dowlen — REMOTE VIEWER — April 19, 1976*
**Water Tower Target Site**

"Escape! Loose hub cap rolling along the road. A story unfolds?"
*(Dowlen told us he heard a "*zinggg*" sound when this image came to him.)*

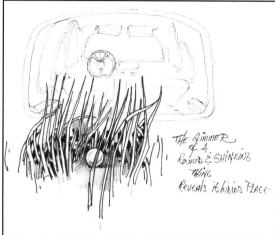

*James Dowlen — REMOTE VIEWER*
*April 29, 1976*
*Ice Cream Parlor Target Site*

"The glimmer of a round & shining thing
reveals its hiding place."

tires for my car, but when the camera repairs took all my available cash, I had to get new tires where I could charge them (more expensive, naturally). The service man on duty on Saturday, May 8, seemed to me to be a bit spaced and somewhat clumsy. As I was driving home, south along US 101, I came to the place where I could see the water tower on my right. The drawings Dowlen had pulled from my personal life during the water tower session on April 19 continued to amaze me. Just at that moment, while I was driving parallel to the water tower, I heard the *zinggg* sound (that Dowlen reported), and knew what I would see when I looked back. The service man had not put the right rear hubcap on securely after he changed the tires. If any of the other hubcaps had come off, they would not have appeared to me in the perspective that Dowlen had drawn his hubcap nineteen days before (above). So I parked along the edge of the freeway and walked across to find my hubcap in the weeds that divided the north and south lanes. It was shining in the grass, just as Dowlen had drawn it during our session at the ice cream parlor on April 29, nine days before. So I took a picture of it there with the newly repaired camera, and picked it up to walk back to my car.

There was no other traffic until a highway patrol car came by. The patrolman seemed irritated. I didn't know that it was against the law to stop for a lost hubcap. He was going by the rule book and planned to move his car across

the lanes so it would be safe for me to walk back over the divided highway to my car. I pointed out that he didn't need to do that. It was safe, because there was no other traffic on the road. So he didn't move his patrol car, but he didn't like me pointing it out to him and wrote a ticket (parts of that are illustrated below). At first I was angry because I could not afford a traffic ticket. But as he was writing it, I realized that this would be a confirmation that Dowlen had drawn a series of images that were actually precognitive. It made me laugh, and the officer thanked me for being so

---

**CALIFORNIA HIGHWAY PATROL**

**NOTICE TO APPEAR    W797191**

DATE 5-8 19 76   TIME 4:30 P.M.   DAY OF WEEK SAT
NAME (FIRST MIDDLE, LAST) JEAN BEERS MAYO
VIOLATIONS (S) 2146/.5 V.C. Disobeying official traffic sign. Pedestrian on freeway retrieving hubcap

---

DATE— 5 - 8 - 76 /TIME—4:30 PM /DAY OF WEEK— SAT

NAME — JEAN BEERS MAYO *[Now Millay]*

VIOLATIONS — "2/46/.5 V.C, Disobeying official traffic sign. Pedestrian on freeway retrieving hubcap."

good-natured about the whole thing. He did not realize that he had become an outside, independent, "objective observer" for a spontaneous precognition experiment.

The story continued to unfold. Two days later, on May 10, our RV session was held at the train tracks before we all had dinner together at my apartment. I showed the hubcap to F.B. and told him about the traffic ticket. I then took a photograph of him holding the hubcap while we were near the train tracks (illustrated below). Dowlen drew a man throwing a frisbee (shaped like a hubcap?) beside the train tracks, and this is illustrated on page 82, in the remote viewing chapter. It is shown again below for the convenience of the reader's comparison of images.

The next chapter in the unfolding story occurred when I decided to go to court to try to get the ticket dismissed. I took Dowlen's set of drawings and tried to explain to the judge why I absolutely had to retrieve that hubcap, because it was important evidence for our remote viewing experiments. He dismissed my case but admonished me that in the future parapsychologists should be more practical. I didn't laugh at the idea of a "practical parapsychologist" until I reached home. In 1976 a person who chose to study parapsychology was not at any time considered to be practical (it was becoming more politically incorrect as time went by). Even my family, who were basically supportive of me, were dismayed by my dedication to such an occupation. Since my teaching assignment at SRJC was only part-time, I was, of course, constantly broke, and often in need of family assistance. Still, we did learn a few things about

psi activity during those many years of study.

Though these examples of precognition from our studies were spontaneous and unexpected, Rauscher, (139) Harary, Targ, and others had all designed experiments to test specifically for precognition. In one, a well-known Russian psychic, Djuna Davitashvili, was able "see" where Harary would be in San Francisco fifteen minutes before his actual location was chosen by random processes. (140) In another, there was an attempt to predict the direction of the prices of silver futures. (141) These began with a series of successful predictions beyond statistical probability, and then something changed; the wrong predictions continued beyond statistical probability. In a later study in 1995 by Targ, Katra, Brown, and Wiegand (142), the protocol to predict the direction of silver futures was improved. Targ writes, "Of the nine trials carried out, two were passed for various reasons, and seven were recorded as traded in the market, although no purchases were actually made. Six of the seven trade forecasts were correct."

*F.B. holds the hubcap so I can photograph it for the record. This was done while we were at the train tracks target site on May 10.*

***REMOTE VIEWING TARGET SITE***

*May 10, 1976*

**The Old Train and Tracks**

*(The flagpole next to the train track is in a similar place in the picture as the light pole is in the RV response by James Dowlen far right.)*

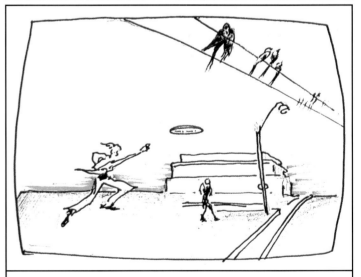

**James Dowlen — *REMOTE VIEWER*
*May 10, 1976* —
*The Old Train Tracks Target Site***

## SUCCESSFUL EXPERIMENTS
## IN PRECOGNITIVE DREAMING

One of the best examples of a formal study of precognition in dreams was reported by Stanley Krippner, Phd. He is a Professor of Psychology and holder of the Chair in Consciousness Studies at Saybrook Graduate School and Research Center. He has written over 500 articles and numerous books about dreams, telepathy, and precognition. The following is an excerpt from his report about one study conducted at the Dream Laboratory at Maimonides Medical Center in Brooklyn, New York, by Krippner, Ullman, and Honorton: (143)

The emerging neuroscience of dreams provides factual support to the innately creative nature of the dream process, and the necessity for the dreaming brain to make sense of the images evoked during the night. To me, it is apparent that, in addition to all the other functions they may serve, dreams are a royal road to the human condition.... Dreams, by their very nature, are imaginative and creative, helping dreamers see what they are and what they can become, making wise decisions that will leave their world a better place than it was when they arrived on the scene. The role of dream life in articulating these visions and anchoring them in waking life is finally assuming recognition both by scientists and laypeople....

The experiments that Montague Ullman and I conducted at Maimonides Medical Center attempted to study telepathic, clairvoyant, and precognitive dreams in a laboratory setting. For example, Malcolm Bessent, a British sensitive, was well known for his purported ability to dream about future events. In 1969 we attempted to explore whether or not he could dream about a waking life experience which we would arrange for him after his night of dreaming was over. When Bessent was awakened after his final period of rapid eye movements (REMs), an experimenter who had not been present during the night selected a random number which directed him to a list of dream images.... An experience was created around the randomly selected image, again by people who had not been present during Bessent's night in the laboratory.

One morning the image "parka hood" was randomly chosen by a toss of dice, and the experimenters had an hour to prepare a post-sleep experience based on the image. When Bessent left the soundproof sleep room, he was taken to an office draped with sheets (to resemble snow). As he inspected a photograph of an Eskimo wearing a parka hood, an ice cube was dropped down his back. Several hours earlier, Bessent had dreamed about ice, a room in which everything was white, and a man with white hair. In fact, his dreams on each of the eight nights of the study were congruent with the following morning's experience, and outside judges were able to match the correct dream with the correct post-sleep experience with an accuracy that was statistically significant.

Bessent returned the following summer for a similar experiment, but one in which the controls were even tighter. For example, a dozen experiences were "packaged" by an experimenter who left for Europe shortly after he selected the props and wrote the instructions. Again, a team of EEG specialists put Bessent to bed and collected the dreams. In the morning, another experimenter selected a number randomly, and located the sealed container to which it corresponded. Outside judges (without knowing the correct match) were able to detect traces of the post-sleep experiences in Bessent's pre-experience dreams, and their judgments again yielded statistically significant results, indicating coincidence was highly unlikely. (144) One night Bessent had several dreams about birds, one of which he reported as:

> *Just water...A few ducks and things. It's fairly misty, but there are quite a lot of mandrake geese and various birds of some kind swimming around in rushes or reeds....*
> *I just have a feeling that the next target material will be about birds.*

The following day, Bessent was taken into a darkened room, sat before a screen, and watched several dozen slides of birds—birds in the water, birds in the air, birds on the land. And an accompanying tape played bird calls!

Some skeptics criticize the study of anomalous dreams, stating that these accounts support "magical thinking" and "irrationality." However, our group at Maimonides, as well as most parapsychologists with whom I am acquainted, fully support scientific methodology. I consider these dreams natural not "super-natural," normal not "paranormal." So little rigorous work has been conducted with anomalous dreams that the mechanisms of their operation are currently unknown. At least a dozen possible explanations have been proposed, ranging from models based on quantum physics to those evoking geomagnetic fields. (145)

Montague Ullman, for example, believes that dreaming sleep is a natural arena in which creativity is at play. Dreams tend to arrange information in unique and emotionally related ways. They depart from rational thought, grouping images together in bizarre associations, and making liberal use of metaphor in constructing the dream story. As a consequence, new relationships emerge that sometimes provide a breakthrough for a waiting and observant mind. Dreams serve a vigilance function—like a sentry alerting the dreamer to whatever may intrude into his or her dream consciousness. (146)

Ullman's "vigilance theory" of dreaming posits that during REM sleep, the dreamer scans not only the internal environment but also those aspects of the external environment that he or she can perceive by anomalous means. During sleep, hunters and gatherers were vulnerable to attack. Contemporary human beings respond to symbolic threats, rather than to physical dangers. Yet vigilance still operates, and REM sleep, perhaps because of its linkage to a primordial danger-sensing mechanism, provides a favorable state for anomalous communication. (147)

Ullman's theory is not incompatible with J. A. Hobson's proposal that, during REM sleep, the brain is activated internally by random neural firing from lower brain centers that stimulate higher brain centers. For Hobson, the dream results from a knitting together of these neurologically evoked memories and images. (148) I would propose that the random nature of this neurological firing provides an opportunity for parapsychological effects to operate, either influencing the portions of the cortex that are stimulated or the images that are evoked.

In Ullman's vigilance theory, however, the brain activity that produces the dream narrative reflects recent emotional residues and explores these residues from a historical perspective, connecting them to the past and projecting them into the future. Ullman implies that there is a collection of dream stories waiting to be told while Hobson suggests that dream narratives are created "on the spot." But parapsychological anomalies could enter both types of dream production, either finding their niche in a carefully constructed, metaphorical tale which contains an emotional linkage to the anomalous element, or filling a gap in a story that is creatively but

haphazardly put together to make sense of a barrage of randomly evoked images.

While research results slowly accumulate, and while theoretical propositions are checked out, the data base on anomalous human experiences slowly grows.... Someday the study of anomalous dreams will be granted respect and recognition as well.

These precognitive dreams reported by Krippner provide us with fine examples of of Malcolm Bessent's ability to apply visions from non-local spacetime in a scientific laboratory under controlled conditions. From that research and from our own spontaneous examples, we decided to explore the possibility of doing a formal study of precognition, not through dreams, but through hypnosis.

## PRECOGNITION EXPERIMENTS USING HYPNOSIS

When Mark Elliot heard I was doing research in psi phenomena, he wondered if psychic information could help him. Elliot enjoyed betting on sporting events. He checked with the published odds from Las Vegas and received computer print-outs of every player's batting average, pitching records and RBIs. He wanted to know if we could predict the winners any better, and he was willing to fund a small study in 1982. This was our opportunity to do a formal study of the phenomena. While spontaneous precognition may be a special case, during a formal study, the results might be skewed if there were emotional or monetary attachments to the outcome.

My own feelings about precognition (whether obtained spontaneously or through formal research) are these: personal karma frequently has more influence over the extended accuracy of precognition than the statistics of probability. Since we did not have a laboratory with a well-equipped dream lab, and our own brainwave analyzers were not designed to do dream research, we decided to use hypnosis as a way of altering the consciousness of our participants so that they could travel in time. In addition, we decided to use many viewers, hypnotizing them one at a time, and then compare their responses. (Three years later, Puthoff was successful in over thirty trials, when he used several viewers and chose the results from the most similar responses that were made by the majority.) (149)

Since we had no idea, really, just what the results might be, we would not guarantee correct results for Mr. Elliot, even though we were excited to try a formal precognitive experiment. He seemed to agree with that arrangement at the time, because of his own curiosity about the possibilities. He knew we would be working with amateurs. (No one with a track record like that of Malcolm Bessent happened to be available to participate.) I was interested, because I thought that, theoretically, *anyone* might be able to bring information from non-local space-time under the right circumstances, and so I chose participants who had no knowledge or any particular interest in ball games.

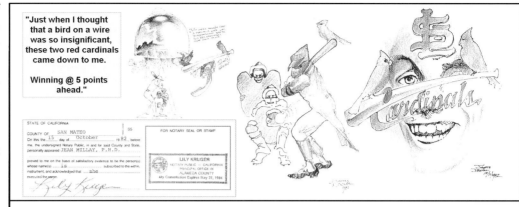

**PRECOGNITIVE DRAWINGS BY JAMES DOWLEN — OCTOBER 11, 1982**

Notarized on October 15, 1982, in San Mateo County by Lily Kruger, Notary Public.

*(Subsequently, the Cardinals won the pennant and then went on to win the 1982 World Series.)*

This is the way we decided to conduct the sessions. I invited twenty people to participate—men, women, and adolescents. Each claimed to have no interest in ball games whatsoever. None had investments in the stock market or any idea of the price of gold. We used guided relaxation and age regression with each of them separately to establish an internal concept of time travel. A few had emotional problems to resolve in the past, which were first resolved as well as possible in one session. Then, as each person was guided from the past back into present time, the journey continued into the future while each was still in a light trance state and comfortable with time travel. We asked each one to explore different times and to look at the TV, or a newspaper headline, for the price of gold, and the score board of five different ball games on specific days.

Our average success at predicting winners over losers was 10% above chance. Our records showed only a random relationship to the actual final scores of the games. One really beautiful exception are the drawings by James Dowlen shown above. Before this series of drawings, Dowlen did not even know the names of the teams who would be playing. After he was informed about this, he drew his vision of who would be the winning team of the World Series for 1982, without hypnosis. He drew the Cardinals on October 11, days before they had even won the pennant that year. The set of drawings was notarized on October 15 (above). My own feeling about predicting ball games is this: if the winner could be known, there would be no reason to play the game. They are played to determine (through skill or error) just who can win. That is the reason for the game. Gamblers insert enthusiasm as well as an element of greed into the energy surrounding the games,

as they have done for centuries. (The Romans placed bets on the gladiators in the ancient Coliseum.) Nevertheless, we were interested in the experiment for its own sake. There is so much we don't know (and perhaps cannot know) about precognition that trying to do it in this way was great fun.

After the baseball season was over, Elliot wanted us to attempt to predict the scores of football games as well. After only two sessions, one participant saw only cobwebs over a darkened scoreboard. This was a strong indication that the threatened NFL strike would not be prevented as hoped. There would be no game on that day. On the basis of that one very strong vision, I informed Elliot and cancelled the rest of the hypnosis sessions that we had previously scheduled.

However, there was one football game still to be played, and Elliot wanted to bet on it. He didn't want me to use guided visualization on the twenty people as I had done before. He only wanted one response from the best psychic. I told him that was not our protocol, and it was not the way to expect an accurate precognition. He was insistent, so I put him in touch with Dowlen directly and refused to participate, or to accept any money or any responsibility for the result, right or wrong. Elliot put pressure on Dowlen, telling him that this was the most important one. (This was exactly the wrong approach, since it piled an emotional element onto the viewer.) Dowlen's drawing was wonderful as always. He sent it to Elliot himself, and the bet was made. Unfortunately, the drawing was of the losing team this time, and the wager was lost. Elliot became very angry and that was the end of his interest in our precognition experiments.

Had he paid attention to our precognition about the amazing rise in the price of gold, he might have been able to recoup his losses. For example, several participants saw that the price of gold would rise dramatically to more than $500 an ounce by February 1983, and that did occur. Remember, my participants did not follow the gold market and had no interest in it (only a couple of them had any money to invest). The price of gold soon dropped again to around $400 and remained there for some time, eventually falling below $300. These reports in the rise of gold prices seemed outrageous to us at the time, but all reports were dutifully recorded.

There were many other results of our experiment. We had tape recordings of each participant reporting their impressions of newspaper headlines, the elections, as well as the price of gold, for months and years in advance. These predictions, made in the summer of 1982 reached five and ten years into the future, into 1987 and 1992. The outcome of these reports obviously could not have been done when we completed our first report for Elliot on August 28, 1982. He was mainly interested in the ball games, and apparently ignored the rest of the report.

The project was then dropped. I needed to take a full-time job and so I devoted myself to the new work in computer graphics. For that reason I did not track the events that had been precognized to occur in five or ten years. At this time, however, in order to make a full report of those predicted events, it would take a great deal of time at the library, finding old news stories for those dates and making a comparison and a statistical analysis. From up here in the hills with no access to a good library within forty miles or to the World Wide Web, that research will not be done. However, no matter what those statistics might eventually have revealed about the percentage of "hits" vs. "misses" in that study, there are some reports that stand out in my mind. And these defy explanation, even if there was only one correct one among a hundred that might have been incorrect, simply wish fulfillment, or even silly (as a few seemed to be at the time). Just as one person's strong image of the cobwebs over the scoreboard was enough to tell us to discontinue the series of hypnosis sessions for the rest of the football season, some of the images for the distant future were strong enough for me to remember them. The old reports were also filed away where I could find them. For example, one participant took a look at the elections ten years ahead to 1992 from her hypnosis session in 1982. She "saw" the newly elected president with light or silvered hair (obviously not Bob Dole). Of course in 1982, no one knew who the candidates would be in 1992.

In early August, one person reported "seeing" a newspaper headline that reported a hurricane in San Francisco on November 17, 1982. On the night of the November 16, I was watching the last TV newscast of the day. The weather man showed a hurricane off the California coast on the satellite map. He said that it would miss the city. It was too late at night to call him and tell him that he was wrong. Anyway, would he take me seriously if I said that a psychic predicted last August that a hurricane would hit San Francisco on November 17? Would he just laugh? (Who listens to psychics?) San Francisco is not a hurricane-prone city, and such things rarely happen there. How such strange weather would have been precognized at all, let alone three months in advance, was also strange, but the precognition was correct. The hurricane did hit San Francisco with some force the next night. Even the weather report for the 18th that the *San Francisco Examiner* printed on the 17th (150) was the following: "BAY AREA FORECAST: Cloudy tonight with light rain or showers likely...." One of the headlines on the following day, however, was "RAIN CAUSES FLOODING...." The news report by Don Lattin began this way: "Thousands of Bay Area residents woke up without power this morning, nine commuters were injured in a 13-car accident in Contra Costa County and several highways were closed today as a fierce storm dumped more than five inches of rain...."

Of course that is not the first or the last time that a weatherman or a psychic missed a prediction. But how is it possible for a hypnotized person to read such a heavy weather report three months in advance? It could not have been the headline of the paper that the hypnotized subject "read" during her session, because the headline did not use the word "hurricane." She had said that she saw the headline on a newspaper in her vision. So "feedback" from the future headline may not have been the cause, unless it was from a smaller, local newspaper that I did not find. In any case, more unusual weather was ahead for that year. As it was revealed later, the 1982-83 winter season had already started for that very wet El Niño year.

Other reports of the future from that summer of 1982 may have been the result of good guessing, such as a decrease in availability of medical care due to costs; and an earthquake in San Francisco in 1983 (earthquakes are always expected in SF, but a big one didn't come until later in 1989). And looking ahead to 1992, there are: more class struggles, as class distinction widens; more conflicts in the Middle East; more computers in the schools and a nationwide computer network. The use of fiber optics was reported to be more common in 1992, and there would be more space travel. One young man (age 11) reported, "...before the year 2001, there will be a space station and people will travel back and forth from there. I don't see any landings of extra-terrestrials." Since this boy was especially interested in reading about and looking for ETs, I thought his hypnosis report, which cut through the popular media hysteria about "aliens among us," was noteworthy.

## PRECOGNITION AS A RESULT OF A NEAR-DEATH EXPERIENCE

My active interest in predictions was not re-kindled until after I had retired from my job designing images on the computer. In 1997, I was introduced to a man who often predicted the outcome of sports events, especially football, baseball, and basketball. He had been totally disabled from a gunshot wound, but his aura was radiant, and his story an inspiration. (His photo is at right.) He was born of an African American father and a Cherokee mother, the fourth one of six boys and two girls. He was raised in Mississippi and that became his nickname. As a young man he worked as a cook at a club in Las Vegas. One night he was lucky at gambling and decided to use his winnings to drive back to Mississippi to visit his family. On the way, he stopped at a midwestern town, found a card room in the back of a bar, and won some more money. While walking back to his motel at night, the two men who had lost money to him earlier drove up to him, pulled a gun, and shot him in the neck. He remembers asking God to let him live and he would be a good person. The two men stripped him, took his money and identity, and abandoned him by the side of the road. Later, a young boy on a bicycle discovered him and reported it. Mississippi was taken to a hospital and remained there in a coma for three weeks. "I died and saw heaven," he recalls. No one knew who he was, but eventually he regained awareness and found himself in the hospital, a quadriplegic. He spent years learning to walk again, which he does, but very slowly and with a cane. He can use one hand, but the other is curled up. It will hold things as a hook would do, but it is immobile. He is happy to be alive, and has forgiven his attackers. (151)

Mississippi believes that from that time, he was given a gift of psychic ability. He feels that if he charged money to use that gift, he would lose it. So he has become a psychic reader for free to his friends who request some information about their lives. His own favorite hobby is studying the odds of ball games. He told me about a happy dream. In this dream he saw young twin boys walking down the street. He walked up to them and said, "I know who will win the Super Bowl, do you?" Both boys looked

straight at him in his dream and both said, at the same time, "The Denver Broncos!" (Denver had been a thirteen-point underdog with the gamblers in Nevada.) After that very vivid dream, he told all of his friends to bet on Denver, and the ones who did won varying amounts of money, depending on the point spread they chose. On July 22, 1998,

*Spiritual psychic Mississippi in 1997*

(Photo by Millay)

Mississippi told me that the Denver Broncos would go to the Super Bowl again that year. He hadn't yet had a vision about whether they would win again or not, he just felt sure that they would be playing in the Super Bowl. By November, 1998, he told me that he had a vision that the Denver Broncos would again win in the Super Bowl, which they did. By March he said they would be in the playoffs the following year as well.

At the time I met him, he lived in Reno and he told me that he spent much of his time on the top deck of the Cal-Neva gambling casino. His many friends frequently asked him for advice about betting on the teams. He told me that if he picked up a ticket (that was bought to bet on a team) and if that ticket felt warm to him, he knew that one would win. Other times if he does not get a feeling while he is holding a ticket, the person may or may not win on that one if s/he bets on it anyway. So I decided to interview him about his actual rate of successes in predicting wins vs. losses, but he had not kept any records, partly because it was so difficult for him to write with his crippled hand.

However, he did show me his system for playing the nickel keno machine, and told me that he had helped his friend win three jackpots in one week. So I bought a $5 roll of nickels and he dropped the first half of them in the slot to show me his system, but his system didn't work for me. Months later, I found him at the same place and since he was feeling lucky, he had played and won two jackpots on the nickel keno machine that same day. He said he once put his hand on a slot machine and told a friend that it was about to pay off. She played it for a while and hit the jackpot. These are the stories about Mississippi that he and his friends like to tell and I enjoy listening to them. But Mississippi doesn't predict that I will win a lot of money. I don't think that it is in my karma, and anyway I rarely gamble or even go near the casinos except to visit him, or unless an out-of-town guest wants to see "Glitter Gulch," which is what we call The Biggest Little City in the World.

Mississippi has many friends who come to share his contagious smile. Some come to ask him to read their palms, or a photograph. He seems to be very accurate in reading futures for people by looking at their palms or at photos, probably more so than in predicting the outcome of ball games, though he never takes any money to do either of those predictions. Mississippi is a truly dedicated spiritual psychic reader. He is one of the most colorful characters in a city that has a notorious history of colorful characters. I gave him a photo to "read" and his description of the man in the picture was extremely accurate. He looked at the photo, closed his eyes, put his hand over the image and then put the image on his forehead. After that he began to report several things, including the detail, "this man likes trees." Unknown to him that man had planted and nurtured four hundred trees—one hundred every year for four years. I gave him other photos and his accuracy was remarkable.

## THE DEBATE OVER THE CAUSE OF PRECOGNITION REMAINS UNSETTLED

Physicist Elizabeth Rauscher, PhD, has attempted to define the possibility of precognition in terms of physics (152). Her report is complex. The question of whether "fate" or pre-determination exists so that we can look ahead and see what is already scheduled to happen has lost credibility with physicists. I am most interested in several other major issues. One question asks if the actual mental reception of an event before its time depends upon some inexplicable connection to individual karma. (My friend's story about the green Chevy might apply here.) Another question asks if we actually travel in time—that since chance is in full operation, we simply step into the future to see what the results of a series of chance events turned out to be. (The prediction of a hurricane months in advance of one that hit SF might apply here.) So we can enjoy the questions about the process without getting too serious or upset when our precognition or prediction is not correct.

Consider the person who has a dream about an airplane crashing and later cancels his flight. When the plane does crash, the incident is reported and even dramatized on TV.

However, how many people refuse to ride in a plane because of fear of crashing, when that rarely happens? What about the other people who do go on the plane and die in the crash? Did they also have a dream and ignore it? Or were they totally unaware of the impending doom? These are important questions that delineate a fine line between paranoia and premonition—or between free will, chance and personal karma. How do you know when to pay attention to a precognition? When do you know it is a future event and not just an unfounded fear? Even the famous Oracle of Delphi, which was honored for its precognitions for hundreds of years, did not answer that question. The Oracle did readings only nine times per year. The women who did them prepared themselves carefully for the intense trance state that the job required. But even then, they were able to give only partial predictions. The rest was up to the belief system of the supplicant to decipher. During the early years of the Christian era, Delphi was declared to be a place of evil and, since precognitions were believed to be the work of the devil, it was totally demolished.

Today, we see that the old predictions of disaster made by Nostradamus hundreds of years ago are being promoted again for profit. We can buy video tapes and books outlining just when the calamities will fall according to today's calculations. It is amazing to me how many people can get caught up in worrying over such predictions about the end of the world, or worse, feeling so fatalistic about it that they are willing to help make it happen. Since our brightest physicists and theologians have no definitive answers about the real problems of precognition, why bother with Armageddon or Nostradamus? And while the sun spot cycle may cause havoc for a time, it has yet to spell the end of the world. Consciousness is eternal, and if human life is destroyed by hate and prejudice, other life forms will develop in the environment that is left. Evolution does not guarantee that life forms get "better" necessarily, but that they change and adapt to the environment they find. We can make a difference in that process by the choices we make now. We can try to preserve the quality of the environment before it is destroyed by our drive to live "better."

Precognition is tricky, like the coyote of Native American mythology. Accuracy is not guaranteed, though sometimes a vision is precise to the smallest detail. Other times we are tricked by our own projections of fear or desire. The cultivation of mental clarity allows the evolution of our awareness about our multidimensional consciousness to progress beyond our projections of fear and paranoia into the higher levels of love and compassion. Whatever the future holds, this prediction is true: love helps, hatred hurts.

# CHAPTER EIGHT — THEORIES RELATING TO PSI PHENOMENA

As we approach the end of the 20th century, a mass of confusion exists about psi phenomena. As you stand in line at any grocery store, you are bombarded with large headlines on the tabloids advertising wild stories about unbelievable events, e.g., aliens are about to invade Earth, and there is a new way to lose twenty pounds in five days. There are also articles about psi events tucked in among other improbable stories (over-exaggerated to seem impossible, and therefore miraculous). For example, information from a dream may have saved someone's life.

TV dramas about angels seem to be more popular than ever. Some church groups have achieved success through their practice of spiritual healing. Some people find solutions to problems through meditation, but most people just don't give the subject of telepathy or other psi phenomena much thought unless some unusual event happens to them personally. And then, they're not sure just what to think. That's partly because psi phenomena are still regarded as pseudoscience by major institutions. Many good research reports have been published, especially in the last twenty-five years, and parapsychologists share this information with each other. Yet little real information about psi goes beyond those who study the phenomena seriously.

However, a variety of theories contribute to our understanding of psi from other disciplines besides parapsychology. Below is a list of some of them. This is by no means a complete list of belief systems which include theories about psi, but it represents some of the major concepts. In the following pages, each of the ten on this list is discussed separately.

## 1. SHAMANISM

Psi phenomena have been natural manifestations of shamanic rituals of various cultures around the world for uncounted centuries. Shamans access information directly from the hyperspace to perform healing rituals for individuals and/or the whole tribe. Shamanism seems to include a combination of ideas about God. There is an external one who speaks to the shaman during rituals and trance states, and there is a belief that all beings, plants, and the Earth are an intrinsic part of divine manifestation.

## 2. *THE TIBETAN BOOK OF THE DEAD*

*The Tibetan Book of the Dead* has been taught for at least 2,500 years. It is read to people who are dying to guide them through the realms *(bardos)* of the hyperspace toward liberation.

## 3. *THE YOGA SUTRAS OF PATANJALI*

*The Yoga Sutras* were collected by Patanjali in the sixth century AD. Written in Sanskrit, they contain the wisdom of earlier centuries. Telepathy is one of the powers *(siddhis)* available to the one who practices meditation.

## 4. PSYCHOLOGY FOR THE 21st CENTURY

Humanistic and transpersonal psychologies include the concept of spirituality, which many of the 19th and 20th century theories and practices of psychology seemed to ignore. When we stop the internal dialog to clear the mind in meditation, we can begin to transcend the personal (transpersonal). The focused human psyche can reach into non-local spacetime to provide the mind with information the eyes do not see, the ears do not hear, and with body sensations from a loved one who may be far away.

## 5. PSI PHENOMENA IN DREAMS

Carefully controlled scientific studies have proved that psi phenomena are included in dreams.

## 6. THE PHASE-CONJUGATE BRAIN

*"We may be beings of conjugated light dwelling in the watery caverns of the brain's ventricles."* (Gottlieb, 153)

## 7. RESONANCE

Various types of resonating frequencies may accompany psi events. The rhythms of music can bring thousands of people simultaneously into the same resonance. The Earth-ionospheric waveguide frequency is constant at 7.8 Hz, which is in the alpha-theta range of human brainwaves. Sidereal time may exert an influence on the results of telepathy, as might geomagnetic fluctuations caused by sun spots.

## 8. THE EARTH AS A CONSCIOUS ENTITY

We may all be connected to people, animals, plants, and the Earth through fields of consciousness.

## 9. QUANTUM MECHANICS

Ordinary reality is imbedded in a higher-dimensional reality, which some believe includes consciousness.

## 10. INFINITE UNIVERSE COSMOLOGY

The Big Bang theory claims that the universe began only a few billion years ago. The space telescope has found globular clusters that are older. Perhaps the words *Infinity* and *Eternity* actually mean that the universe has always been here. Let us consider that there was no beginning.

## SHAMANISM

The practice of shamanism is very ancient. The word "shaman" is of Tungus origin. (154) The Sanskrit word "sramana" originally meant "ascetic" and refers to a novice rather than to a priest or medicine man. The word "shamanism" is used as a generic term for shamanic practice in other parts of the world. However, other cultures have different names for their shamans (e.g., "mamu" for the Abinticua in Colombia). The shaman can be either a medicine man or a medicine woman. In some cultures, the shaman is the one who will go into an altered state of consciousness in order to enter the spirit world to find the cause of illness in the patient. In other cultures, the shaman will provide a chemical aid to the patient to alter his/her consciousness. This will allow the patient's deep fears and angers to come to the surface. The illness may have become physical so that medicines and herbs are also needed, but if the subconscious source of illness is not rooted out, the illness will return in another form.

The shamans use the guidance of spirits, and some will allow themselves to be possessed by a spirit. The spirit may be an ancestor, a powerful entity or god, or a protective animal spirit. Many psi events have been reported to take place during shamanic journeys, such as direct mind-to-mind transference of specific visions, spirit communication, psychokinetic events, out-of-the-body experiences, and dramatic, instantaneous, spiritual healing. In some cultures the entire village will participate in ingesting a sacred plant so they can all enter the hyperspace together to help bind the community in love, cooperation, and friendship.

Western Christianity officially regarded all the ceremonies of native peoples as evil witchcraft, and banned all such practices. As a result, much of the knowledge of the healing uses of herbs and of altered states of consciousness was lost. The enforcement of Christianity over the tribes destroyed their traditions, languages, and most of their people. Today, enlightened anthropologists are attempting to record what is left of these cultures. Some members of the tribes are themselves becoming educated in Western colleges, so that they can use the authority a college degree provides to help educate and save their own societies.

Rolling Thunder, a medicine man from Nevada, told me, "Some Native Americans have chosen to reincarnate into the dominant white race to help save the Earth from commercial destruction. I have met many good people who have done so consciously." (155)

## THE TIBETAN BOOK OF THE DEAD

This book has been taught continuously for at least 2,500 years. It is read to the dying person and continued after death for 49 days, because the sense of hearing is still thought to be a path to the superconscious. The Tibetan belief system is that the dead can be guided past the illusions which arise as the released consciousness moves through the bardos (hyperspace) of archetypal gods and demons. The person is told to avoid being attracted or repelled by them, and to recognize them as products of his own creation. If he accepts the guidance, his soul can then be free of the cycle of births and deaths. (156)

During this process, the person might feel he can communicate telepathically with his relatives. Since they are generally grieving rather than becoming receptive telepathically, the dying one is cautioned not to waste his remaining energy on this, but to continue his journey through the bardos until he reaches enlightenment. In this situation, telepathy is seen as a hindrance to enlightenment.

However, while the adept is still alive, telepathic communication often takes place between a student and his teacher. Tibetans believe that when a high lama dies, he is reincarnated to become the student of his former pupil. The location of the child (lama) may come in a dream. Once the child is found who remembers his past and can identify objects he once used, he is trained to be the lama again.

## THE YOGA SUTRAS OF PATANJALI

These were written in Sanskrit about 500 AD, a thousand years after the most recent Vedas. Though Patanjali followed the *Upanishads* in spirit, these sutras are more like a "how to" manual for meditation, rather than a metaphorical presentation. Yoga means *"yoke."* The concept of yoga is to tie one's consciousness with the divine through a precise practice of breathing and meditation. One of the practices involves learning to perform *"sanyama,"* which is a state of "resonance" or "merging" between an adept's mind and other minds, places, or things. *The Yoga Sutras* state that an adept must stabilize the *citta-vritti* (mind waves) in order to attain the state of *sanyama* (also translated as "becoming totally involved with someone or something in a flow of light"). According to Patanjali, "By observation through sanyama of the content of the mind arises knowledge of the content of another's mind," as well as knowledge of "the subtle, the hidden, and the distant." (157)

## PSYCHOLOGY FOR THE 21ST CENTURY

Major researchers and teachers from the fields of humanistic and transpersonal psychology have demonstrated how our beliefs help create future reality. (158) Therefore it is not useful to cling to the old, overused, and tired tale of Armageddon. In a truly free society, each of us can examine our own thoughts and beliefs. As we evolve our ideas about the true nature of consciousness, we can change our reaction to the past, recreate our mythologies, and create a new vision for a brighter future.

In 1993, Willis Harman, PhD, wrote about a necessary shift in the concept of science. (159) We can think about this shift as an evolution not only of the species, but of our concepts of reality, which are adapting to the rapidly changing world. The 21st century impels us to evolve. Humanity seems to have its own agenda, and some of us will adapt to it and some will try to force the agenda into the same old direction, based on our past mythologies. Who knows? An evolution in the concepts of reality may even affect the evolution of the species as well.

Harman eloquently defined a positive path for us to choose, if we have the will to do so. He wrote that we need:

...to recognize that the problem is not with the paranormal, but with our concept of science— more specifically with the metaphysical foundations adopted in the course of modern science's evolution....

If science were to be recast by building on the oneness assumption rather than on separability, it would appear not only to accommodate the paranormal, but also to respond to other complaints. For one thing, although the reductionistic science would still be available for the purposes to which it is suited, it would no longer have the authority to insist that we are here, solely through random causes, in a meaningless universe or that our consciousness is merely the chemical and physical processes of the brain.

---

**"The time is ripe to insist on a reexamination of the metaphysical foundations of modern science."**

Willis Harman

---

Transpersonal psychology grew out of the needs of many people to come to terms with their own transcendental experiences which were not included in the "official scientific definitions" of human experience. Behaviorism, for example, excluded even the idea that we have a consciousness. Stanislav Grof, MD, became the founding president of the International Transpersonal Psychology Association (ITP). He is a psychiatrist with a solid training and background in Freudian and Jungian psychology. His work soon expanded beyond the limitations of those early theories. In 1992, he spoke at the ITP conference in Prague, Czechoslovakia, and outlined those disciplines which are included in the study of transpersonal psychology as follows: (160)

Transpersonal psychology...accepts that an important dimension of the human psyche and of the universal scheme of things is *spirituality*. It also honors the entire spectrum of human experience, including various levels and realms of the psyche that manifest in non-ordinary states of consciousness; in systematic meditation and other forms of spiritual practice; in spontaneous, mystical experiences; in psycho-spiritual crisis...called spiritual emergencies; in psychedelic sessions; during various powerful forms of experiential psychotherapy; or in near-death experiences....We are talking here about such phenomena as sequences of psychological death and rebirth, experiences of divine light, of cosmic consciousness, of mystical union with other people, nature, and with the entire universe, encounters with archetypal beings, visits to mythical realms, karmic experiences and others.

Transpersonal psychology has been in existence for almost a quarter of a century and has been enjoying steadily increasing influence and popularity. In the last fifteen years the transpersonal orientation has expanded into other scientific disciplines, including quantum relativistic physics, biology, medicine, anthropology, art, ecology and politics....

Grof has increased our understanding of the expanding potential of mind and the spiritual realms of human consciousness as science, not limited to religion. Through his workshops, books, and the founding of the ITP, his influence has pushed the frontiers of psychology beyond its stormy beginnings as a science. Grof's contributions are among the essential foundations for the future of 21st century psychology. The Spiritual Emergence Network (SEN) founded by Christina Grof is also providing therapeutic concepts and information about our multidimensionality.

> **As we evolve our ideas
> about the true nature of consciousness,
> we can change our reaction to the past,
> recreate our mythologies, and begin to
> create a new vision for a brighter future.**

Charles Tart, PhD, is also a founder of the ITP. At that same conference in Prague he discussed the way our models about the mind, and our basic beliefs about the world, also shape our ideas about reality: (161)

...There is reality and then there's the place where the rest of us live practically all the time. We won't deal too much with reality today, because while finding reality is probably our goal in a sense, most of the time we live in a world of concepts, of ideas, of beliefs, of conditionings, of things that channel our energies, that channel our life.

So while finding reality is an important goal (it's one I think I'm involved with much of my life), you can't just assume you can go ahead and do that; you have to take account of the fact that most of the time our belief systems channel our energy. And some metaphysical systems recognize this. Some metaphysical systems say, you can't directly control a lot of things, but you can control your thoughts, you can start affecting your beliefs, and that in turn will control your energy and maybe someday you can actually transcend beliefs.

So we have a lot of beliefs. We have models of reality that we live in. The sad thing about that is by and large we don't know we have any models of reality; we think that we're just attuned to what actually is. We look out there and we see trees and flowers and stairs and planters and wastebaskets and we have the naive view that somehow the reason we see those is because they are out there, and that's about it. We are simply tuned into the world the way it is. That's partly true—we are at least partly tuned in to the way the way the world is or we're dead. Now if there is a truck bearing down on you and your beliefs and models about the world do *not* tell you to get the hell out of the way, you don't live to come to transpersonal conferences. So there is a limit to how much *our belief systems can tune us out of reality,* but...we can get tuned out quite a bit.... Models have a function of guiding the way we think about ourselves...but we know they are not really true.

Tart continued to describe the different models of the mind as they have changed through the century. Humans have tended to mold themselves into each model as it came along, fitting their behavior and their belief systems about themselves to each new model. As new technologies are developed, there is a tendency to compare its mechanical workings with the body. Freud thought of the steam engine as the Id, which builds pressures of desire, causing dreams of wish fulfillment. When the Id builds up too much stress a person has to let off steam, or blow up (as in a psychotic break). When the telephone was invented, the mind was compared with a telephone operator making the switchboard connections in the brain. The computer gave rise to cognitive science. Now "virtual reality" is revising some models again. Daniel C. Dennett, PhD, thinks that computers can be made to be conscious. (162) But in each of these models the soul is left out. Spirituality is often still separated from scientific models. Fortunately, the fields of humanistic and transpersonal psychologies include this essential part of us in their studies. We are more than a collection of behaviors, more than a collection of neurons. We can experience being one with the human family, and one with the universe.

There are two sides to it, of course. We can feel that we are totally alone (sad and lonely), or we can feel that there is only oneness and we and all beings are an integral part of it. Eventually, we must come down from the mountain cave of our enlightenment to interact with other people and things. But the way we project our concepts of reality onto that stage of people and things will determine our perceptions, and dictate to some extent our karma. Being able to study beliefs other than our own is the great gift our founding fathers made possible with the laws that separated church from state. Rising from our somnambulism to take advantage of that freedom to think and to question beliefs requires each of us to make a conscious choice. While we honor the traditions that bind families and communities together, some traditions (followed blindly) can become the source of pollution and disease and must be changed.

> **How I think is what I see.
> Focus defines *Reality*.          (Plato)**
>
> **Beyond the things I choose to see
> Are other realms of *Reality*.   (William James)**
>
> **Since each one chooses differently
> Who should explain *Reality?*   (Thomas Paine)**

## PSI PHENOMENA IN DREAMS

The psi research of dreams, that was carried out at the Maimonides Dream Lab by Krippner and others since 1969, has been among the most important parapsychology work in this century. It opened the field for new ideas and expanded our thinking about dreams and consciousness. Krippner determined the exact time of dreaming from real-time EEG measurements of the dreamer. The dreamer's report often contained elements of the messages being *sent* by someone at a distance.

From my own experience there is an example which seems to combine the Ullman vigilance theory (pages 181-182) with the idea that the dream story is created on the spot, combining a present event with one's own subconscious fears. My children and I were living in Venice, California, in the late Sixties, within a few blocks of the beach. I taught school in east LA and students told me about their riot clubs, where they learned to make pipe bombs. There was not as much violence in our neighborhood as in east LA, but I was concerned about the safety of my children. One night I dreamt that I could hear two different sirens. Screaming fire trucks and police cars were rushing toward our neighborhood. In my dream the riots were just down my street and I couldn't find my children so we could jump in the car and go. I felt a great desperation to leave, now!

Soon, however, I woke up, only to find that a stray cat had come in through our cat door and was trapped in the kitchen by our own cat, defending his territory. They were yowling at each other (like the two different sirens of my dreams). The stray female cat wanted to leave but was blocked by our larger animal standing in front of the cat door. As soon as I walked into the kitchen, our cat was distracted, and the stray bolted out the door. In my dream, I seemed to have identified with the female cat who felt trapped in a dangerous place. The "vigilance" source of the dream sirens was revealed. My deep pre-conscious feeling of being trapped was also revealed. My children did not like their over-crowded classes. My son said, "Mom, there is nothing in a big city that I ever want." The dream brought all of this into focus, so I developed a plan to change jobs so we could move at the end of the semester.

Even though dreams are frequently just a jumble of re-arranged past events, they have often provided me with guidance and information for problem solving. When I needed some inspiration for various projects I was working on, I often discussed them with my father. His advice was, "Well then, get busy and dream."

## THE PHASE-CONJUGATE BRAIN

Often brain theories have been based on conceptions of nature and on the latest technology known to the brain theorists at the time. Thus at one point in history when brain philosophers were excited by new technologies for controlling the flow of water, brain theories were based on hydraulic models. Similarly there have been mechanical, magnetic, electrical, telephonic, photographic and holographic conceptions of the brain.

The concept that "the mind is a form of light energy that has been radiating for billions of years" was a message given to me by two spirits at a séance in Brazil in 1976. I wondered about it at the time, but now the idea that some aspect of consciousness is light may be more fact than metaphor.

Ray Gottlieb, OD, PhD, is the Dean of the College of Syntonic Optometry. He has been successful in using light in healing for years (pages 113-114). He writes that modern technology offers a new possibility, also suggested by ancient philosophers, that "we may be beings of conjugated light dwelling in the watery caverns of the brain's ventricles." Recently he reported on his theory about the phase-conjugate brain in the *Journal of Optometric Phototherapy*. The following is an excerpt from that paper:

...No one can explain how brains gather scattered sensations into whole, meaningful perceptions. Shape, size, color, distance, motion, name, associated memory and effective meaning are widely separated, yet awareness seems instantaneous. Perceptual unity has long perplexed neuroscientists.

Phase-conjugate mirrors (163, 164) suggest a possible mechanism for this unity. Four-wave phase conjugate "mirrors," suggested by the early pioneers of holography in the 1960s, and specifically proposed by Robert W. Hellwarth in 1977, are constructed from three lasers; two meet head-on, creating a holographic-like structure of hot and cool spots caused by the interaction of the two light sources. If a third laser, the object beam, is aimed into this configuration it reflects off the hot spots much as rain drops reflect sunlight to make a rainbow.

Ordinary mirrors reflect light according to the angle the light strikes the mirror, but P-C mirrors "self-target"—the reflection retraces the path back to its source at any angle of incidence. Self-targeting happens automatically without lenses or precise focusing. Even through a cloudy medium like fog or frosted glass, the reflection remains undistorted because the light retraces its path perfectly.

The reflection merges spatial and temporal information from all three input beams so data from several sources can be combined and fed back to a specific location. Mirrors of different light frequencies cannot interact so many can function at the same site. Mirrors form and vanish instantly as the lasers go on and off. No threshold power of the object beam is required for conjugation to occur.

In optics laboratories, P-C mirrors are used to compare, categorize, and recognize incoming and stored data instantly. They can resolve partial or "fuzzy" images into known categories and associated data images.

Here we see how this light apparatus might mirror actual brain function. Imagine millions of coherent packets of light traveling through white and gray matter, meeting in strategic places, creating millions of P-C mirrors that synthesize and reflect information automatically and accurately to meaningful sites.

And where might we find an ideal medium for such light works? The ventricles come to mind. They're four in all, linked into a winged structure. The two lateral ventricles are centered in the cerebral hemispheres, the third between the two halves of the thalamus and hypothalamus, and the fourth between the cerebellum and the brain stem.

Modern scientists have assumed the ventricles are shock absorbers or waste depositories for the brain, but for most of modern history, until the 18th century, the ventricles had been identified as the centers for reason, imagination, and memory.

Two centuries of neuroscience have failed to find the locus of consciousness in gray matter. Finding the fabled "engram," the bit of memory that can be deleted, hasn't happened. Perhaps they're looking in the wrong place. Might consciousness be somehow mediated through the cerebrospinal fluid in the ventricles?

This isn't as far-fetched as it might sound. There is increasing evidence that DNA and other protein structures radiate coherent light (165, 166, 167) and that photic energy can travel through brain matter outside of nerve pathways without dispersing or losing coherence.

The brain actually develops from its ventricles.

Neurons sprout in the neural tube and then migrate to precise locations to form the embryonic brain. In this process the neural tube distorts its shape and grows to become the ventricles. It makes sense that data would be routed to and from its root structure. And this might explain how hydrocephalics, who have huge ventricles and a very thin cortex, can sometimes function normally.

Phase-conjugate mirrors with instantaneous communication back to the tiniest source, undistorted by the inhomogeneous brain medium, able to combine temporal and spatial information from several sources, make partial images whole, correct for phase errors, adjust timing, filter noise, amplify weak signals without degradation, instantly recognize, categorize, and associate images and memories—these are perfect for describing brain function. Many of our scientific and spiritual cravings would be satisfied if the three-dimensional dynamic hologram made of light energy at the mirror's core—not quite "spirit," not quite matter—turns out to be the central processing mechanism for consciousness.

Gottlieb's suggestion that the brain communicates with itself as a phase-conjugate mirror is provocative. The idea that coherent light energy is involved with the processes of translating information from the hyperspace into sensory memory, then into awareness and to the ability of expression, is also thought-provoking. We have demonstrated in our years of study with biofeedback that coherence in brainwaves can lead to profound insight, a sudden remembering of things forgotten, and can become a doorway into trance or out-of-the-body states. Because electromagnetism can be blocked in certain ways, we know that it is not the carrier wave for psi. However, biofeedback training in phase-coherent brainwaves facilitates the focus of attention needed for the information transfer, even though the actual transfer may occur in a very different way.

> **"There is increasing evidence that DNA and other protein structures radiate coherent light and that photic energy can travel through brain matter outside of nerve pathways without dispersing or losing coherence."**
>
> Ray Gottlieb
> Dean of the College of Syntonic Optometry

## RESONANCE

We have already discussed resonance in Chapter Four, but it is so important we have chosen to include it again here among the other theories about psi phenomena. The blending of concepts between physics and psychology allows many ideas to be considered seriously at this time. Some of these ideas were formerly relegated to religion, and therefore "off limits" to scientific study. All the known physical force fields are an essential part of the study of psychology (the strong and the weak nuclear forces, gravity, and especially the electromagnetic properties of life).

Perhaps communication of any kind does not exist without some form of resonance. Neuroscientist Karl Pribram, PhD, of Stanford, suggested a number of years ago that our primary reality may be in the frequency realm. He proposed a model of the brain as a hologram interpreting a holographic universe. (168)

Physicist David Bohm, PhD, suggested that our brains mathematically construct the "solid" reality we measure in our three-dimensional manifestation (the *unfolded* aspect of things) by interpreting frequencies from the hyperspace, beyond spacetime (the realm of the *enfolded* order), which is an inseparable interconnectedness. (169)

Among these frequencies are those which encourage entrainment with brainwaves. We are all familiar with the way different kinds of music create different moods. We choose our CDs to achieve a special musical environment—for meditation, for dancing, for background music for social events, or for focusing on the drama of the music for its own sake. Television causes its own kind of entrainment, until some people are hypnotized by whatever program is being broadcast.

But we can also resonate with the natural environment, wind, trees, birds, animals, and the Earth. Marsha Adams, PhD, reported on a correlation between remote viewing experiments and the geomagnetic activity of the sun. (170) The results of her study were similar to those reported by Persinger, previously mentioned. She wrote that better results could be obtained if "...a remote viewing experiment *[in California]* might be scheduled about thirty-six hours after a quiet *[sun spot]* period...while in New Jersey, the best time may be about four days after a quiet period. Other types of psi experiments may be done on the day of a quiet period." Sun spots affect radio waves, the weather, and the extremely low frequency range (ELF) of the electromagnetic spectrum. Brainwaves are in the ELF range.

## THE EARTH AS A CONSCIOUS ENTITY

The idea that we are not separate from the Earth nor from its animal and plant populations has been around as long as humans have lived on this Earth. Native American leaders enjoyed telling stories about our other relatives. The spiritual leader Black Elk (171) often spoke about our interconnectedness with the concept that the Earth is our mother, the sun is our father, the moon is our grandmother, and all beings who crawl, swim, fly or walk on or under this Earth are all conscious entities to whom we are related.

Brainwaves that occur in the lower alpha range (8 Hz) and in the upper theta range (7 Hz) do coincide with the Earth-ionospheric wave guide as measured at 7.8 Hz. It is possible to be in nature, to stop thinking, and to experience a resonance with the Earth. This is an experiment anyone can try for oneself. It is best to go out beyond the city with its smog, noise, and electromagnetic pollutions and sit quietly on the ground to feel its energies. One method is to stop thinking until you can *feel like* the rock or the tree.

In the summer of 1980, I attended a festival led by the Native American medicine man Sun Bear. This was called a "Medicine Wheel Ceremony." We gathered in an open place which was part of a conference center located about fifty miles north of Los Angeles. At first we just listened to Sun Bear speak. I was inspired to see his loving light and to hear him tell about our relationship to the Earth and all things. I remember especially one of the things that he said: "I don't care what your religion is, if it doesn't include planting corn, it won't support your future generations." (172) Of course, the Native American tribes have been on this land for more than 10,000 years. Those who have tried to destroy them, who follow the newer religions, have been on this land for only a few hundred years.

After Sun Bear had introduced us to the meaning and symbolism of the Medicine Wheel Ceremony, we gathered in a circle. We were each to place a rock on different parts of the wheel while expressing our reverence for the Earth. This was a very moving ceremony, and it served to open our hearts to a new understanding of Earth consciousness. The ceremony continued as drums played and we danced around the circle, sometimes holding hands, sometimes turning around. It was during that part of the ceremony in the late afternoon that my problems developed. The late summer pollen and dried grasses whirled up in the dust as we danced around upon them. I began sneezing uncontrollably, and knew I would have to go home and not be able to participate in the evening ceremonies.

During the break before supper, I decided to ask Harley Swiftdeer, a respected healer, if he could help me. He graciously agreed to see me, even though he was resting at the time. I didn't have to tell him about my hayfever; it was quite evident. He pressed some acupuncture points along my nose and brushed them with an eagle feather. I was still sneezing continuously when he told me, "There is some way that you are thinking that is hostile to the plants in their exuberant sexuality." (173)

It had never occurred to me that my hostility to the plants was the source of the problem. I blamed the plants for causing my allergies. So I went home, still sneezing. The next day I did not return for the rest of the ceremony. I stayed home and drew pictures of different flowers to show my respect for them. By midday, my sneezing had stopped. Of course, I had rested, taken a lot of vitamin C with water, and had eliminated the stress of driving the 100-mile round trip on the LA freeway. Still, I was amazed by the way Swiftdeer had re-framed my problem and made me aware of my relationship to the plants. I had always felt connected to our animals, but not to the plants.

Rupert Sheldrake, PhD, studied animals that seemed to develop similar habits in different places simultaneously. He proposed a model called *morphogenic fields* that might explain how life forms are connected to each other. (174)

In 1987, Dennis Bardens traced the accounts of psi phenomena attributed to animals, from ancient times to the present, in his book *Psychic Animals.* (175) He reported the remarkable ability of dogs and cats to travel many miles to find their human companions; the loyalty of many different types of animals to save their human friends from danger; and the apparent ability of many animals to communicate telepathically. He wrote, "...The mounting evidence in favor of the belief that animals may, like humans,

possess extra-sensory perception should sober us a little; we are not separate, nor immune to what they think and feel."

The Native American spiritual leader David Monongye was quoted as saying, "The original instructions of the Creator are universal and valid for all time. The essence of these instructions is compassion for all life and love for all creation. We must realize that we do not live in a world of dead matter, but in a universe of living spirit. Let us open our eyes to the sacredness of Mother Earth, or our eyes will be opened for us."

James Lovelock, PhD, chose the Greek name for the Earth goddess, Gaia, for his theories about the Earth as a superorganism. (176) The system of the material Earth and the living organisms on it evolves so that self-regulation is an emergent property. "...In such a system active feedback processes operate automatically and solar energy sustains comfortable conditions for life. The conditions are only constant in the short term and evolve in synchrony with the changing needs of the biota as it evolves." Since life and its environment are closely coupled, the idea that the whole Earth may be a living entity is worth exploring.

Brian Swimme, PhD, discussed "The Universe as Sacred Story...." with Benjamin Webb. (177) "...the human future depended upon the activity...[of our ancestors, the worms] back then. The same thing is true for us. We're making these immense decisions about our community and the future of all these vast creatures. We can't imagine them, but somehow we must take them into account. So this sense of inter-communion would be one of the major discoveries of the new story."

When I was a child we climbed on the haystack to watch the sunsets, the highlight of the day. The glorious oranges and red colors of cumulus clouds faded into pink and into dark blue and then into night. On nights when the moon was dark, the sky would roll out forever and fill with sparkling stars. I was a very small person on an enormous Earth which supported all the life upon it, but it was small compared to the sun. And Earth and sun were also very small compared to the Milky Way. My family taught me that all within The Great Mystery is truly sacred.

## QUANTUM MECHANICS

In 1973, Jacob Bronowski wrote in *The Ascent of Man:* "One aim of the physical sciences has been to give an exact picture of the material world. One achievement of physics in the twentieth century has been to prove that the aim is unattainable." (178)

Physicist and Sanskrit scholar Dean Brown agrees with that statement, because he believes that the universe possesses three domains of reality: physical, mental, spiritual. He writes: (179)

It is a kind of blind religious faith on the part of dogmatic scientists if they expect to find explanations of the higher planes from considerations of the material. Physicists since Neanderthal times have hunted in vain for material connections of inner experiences, jumping to conclusions that have led to blind superstitions that were propagated by the people of that time as well as by the academics of today. Technology, a by-product of physics, has turned out to be useful, but it has not contributed to our fundamental understanding of the universe, nor of life, nor of art, nor of healing, nor of animal migration, nor even of intuition.

Physics cannot even understand Life, common everyday burgeoning life, the fundamental fact of the universe, let alone mind and consciousness. But the situation is not symmetric—consciousness can indeed understand physics!

Perception. No physical event occurs in the moment when we perceive something. We do not gain or lose weight when we experience a cognition. No amount of mentation can lead to spiritual experience. Each domain has its own laws and processes. The best that we can hope for are parallels, analogs, that cannot bear the burdens of proof.

I consider quantum mechanics to be the pinnacle of thought in physics, the acme that will lead to the unfoldment of new revelations. Bohm, the consummate quantum mechanist, points out that the wave equation has a mysterious term in the potential function that is independent of time and space, that is, *non-local.* Most contemporary scientists agree on this point and "non-local" is very much a by-word today in the journals.

Of course, non-local means infinite and eternal. This is the domain of visionary art and psychic perception and expression. It is also the domain of synchronicity and the place where the "hundredth monkey" effect, entangled particles, and mass hysteria can be understood. William Blake dealt with this process when he said, *"Eternity is in love with the productions of time."*

No doubt, every mental event correlates with the physical, and physical events with the mental. The wisdom traditions say "not-two." We take pills to change our moods. We meditate for healing.

Physics is the science of processes that can be understood in the context of mass, energy, space, and time. By contrast the science of mind, psychology, cannot be quantified nor understood in physical terms because the processes are immaterial and transcend the frozen domain of mass.

One cannot find the sublime impact of a Schubert Lied *[song]* by cutting up the piano! Mind is to brain as the Lied is to the piano. The Lied uses the piano as a vehicle. Mind uses the brain as a vehicle.

Physics can never enter the domain of the mental and the spiritual because physics, by definition, must be material, quantifiable, reproducible, rational and assume a shared reality. Spirit and mind cannot be forced into that tiny shoebox. At best, we can use parallels to physics to suggest some useful analogies for modelling spirit and mind. And those analogies have been particularly sterile.

The one jumping-off point that will be fruitful is in bridging the concept of energy between the three domains. The broad concept of light, for example, is now being extended far beyond the limitations of physics. A further understanding of light and energy will lead to the new "physics" of the next millennium. Psychic research, and the psychology of perception and expression, are the main ways to get there.

There are important and well-confirmed correlations between physics and psi ($\Psi$). In 1989, Michael Persinger and Stanley Krippner studied the relationship between sun spot activity over a ten year period of dream telepathy studies. The "telepathic dreams were most accurate *[when]* associated with significantly quieter planetary geomagnetic activity." (180) In 1997, James Spottiswoode studied free-response telepathic experiments conducted over a twenty year period. (181) Those completed within a specific period of Local Sidereal Time (LST) were statistically more successful than those done when the Earth was not in that same position in relationship to the outer celestial bodies. Such celestial influence on our thinking may be more profound than anyone could know.

## INFINITE UNIVERSE COSMOLOGY

The prominent cosmological theory in modern scientific communities today is that the universe began with a big bang from an extremely tiny condensed vacuum point around fifteen billion years ago. Our Earth was formed somewhat later than that and, around four billion years ago, life on Earth began accidentally and has been evolving ever since, until it reached today's life forms.

What does this idea have to do with the theories of psi phenomena? The words are the key. There is in our vocabulary a word for *infinity* and another one for *eternity*. Infinity means **without beginning or end**, unlimited space. Eternity means **existing through all time, forever**. It implies that forever extends into the past as well as into the future. In our practice of meditation, the concepts of the *infinite* and the *eternal* are intensely meaningful.

However, the Bible states that "God created...." Everything began at a specific time in the past, and devotees argue about when (i.e., 8,000 years or so ago, counting all the begats since Adam and Eve, or fifteen billion years ago during an incredible Big Bang event).

The Hubble Space Telescope (HST) has given us a picture of dust and gases being spit out of a black hole. It had been said that nothing can escape a black hole, but there it is (captured on film), 40,000 light years across and extending far into space—nearly the distance of the radius of our own galaxy. (Perhaps one big bang was just our galaxy.)

The Hubble Space Telescope has also photographed an area near the handle of the Big Dipper. That is one of the few places in the sky dark enough for HST to focus into deep space. HST can't see anything on the other side of our own Milky Way, because there is too much light from other stars in most of the sky. However, behind the Big Dipper's handle, 1,500 galaxies were counted in that one picture. That is at least 1,500 more than Edwin Hubble himself expected to find when he first discovered a galaxy other than our own at the Mt. Wilson Observatory in 1924. Using the mathematics of the Doppler effect, Hubble made an **assumption** that the galaxies were traveling away from us, and that led to another **assumption** that the whole universe must have started with a big bang. (The Doppler effect is a mathematical formula used to explain why a sound traveling toward you seems higher than a sound traveling away from you. The length of the wave is longer when it is traveling away.) Hubble and other astronomers came to the conclusion that stars must be traveling away, because their

"Non-local means infinite and eternal.
This is the domain of visionary art
and psychic perception and expression.
It is also the domain of synchronicity...."

Dean Brown

atomic signatures were shifted toward the longer wavelengths—that is toward the red end of the spectrum. The farther away it is, the faster it is moving away, as determined by where its observable light (in its own specific bands) has shifted toward the red. Astronomers established a formula for determining how far away and how fast the stars were traveling because of their specific *red shift*. That formula is based on the Doppler effect and includes the "Hubble Constant." (When a number of stars were judged to be older than the calculated age of the universe, cosmologists said it was because the Hubble constant was not a big enough number. The big bang could still be explained by the formula.)

Now consider a young man in a souped-up car with a *very* loud sound system. He and his girlfriend are parked a few blocks away, but you can hear his music. He is not traveling anywhere, but the distance is enough to cancel the higher notes (shorter wavelengths). However, the deep boom, boom of the low notes can easily disturb your sleep. In a similar way, let's assume for a minute that the distant star doesn't have to be moving for its light to have shifted toward the red end of the spectrum.

"Wait," my physicist friend told me. "Sound is different from light, because it is filtered. The shift of specific bands of light along the spectrum provides a very compelling argument for the idea that the distance of stars is related to their motion as well. The Doppler effect provides the simplest explanation for the red shift that is observed. Therefore, by Occam's Razor, that is what is used."

"But," I said to him, "how can Occam's Razor apply when the logic of such thinking leads to the conclusion that the whole universe was created in a big bang and will all be squashed again into a big crunch? The concept that this whole vast, yet to be revealed, universe could have come from a tiny point, and may (or may not) condense again into a tiny point, is **NOT** the simplest explanation for the observable. Occam's Razor should not apply to the methods used to measure distance and speed, if the results are as complex as a big bang would have to be. It might be useful to consider a different explanation for the red shift."

My arguments didn't convince anyone. I am not an astronomer, or a mathematician, but as an old school teacher who enjoys stirring up thoughts about old assumptions, I submit the following suggestions for your consideration: Suppose the words "**infinity** and **eternity**" actually refer to the universe which has always been there; suppose the idea that the *entire* universe was created all at once at a specific time in the past is just an old mythology that mathematicians have found a way to support; suppose the big bang was just a local event which is repeated again and again at different times in different places in the endless spacetime of the universe. While individual galaxies may contract into black holes until the pressure pushes them out again, with their particles condensed and recombined (as in the picture taken by HST), it is not too difficult to imagine that the endless universe is full of stars and galaxies exploding, collapsing, and reforming at different times throughout eternity. It is too difficult for me to imagine that the whole universe itself, as it is now, could have burst forth from a vacuum point all at once during a specific time in the past.

The Big Bang theory disturbs me and many other people I know, no matter how well educated. An honored teacher told me that I was confusing the spiritual with the material. He explained to me that people, animals, and planets (including the whole universe) of the material world are all born and will all die. It is only the spiritual universe that is eternal and infinite. That idea is one of the arguments used to support the suppression of education about our multidimensional minds. "Spiritual" ideas have to be left to the church, not to public education. These are issues that need a lot more open-minded discussion.

Alexander Shulgin, PhD, and his wife Ann Shulgin have written about this in their book *TIHKAL* (182):

...As this fun essay progresses, I hope to offer an alternative to the concept of origin. There might have been no origin. **Our universe has always been here, it is infinitely old,** and so God just might have been with us much longer than anyone ever suspected. All the weird observations that are part of our science will fit another explanation just as well, or even better, but the veil of prejudice must be put aside for a moment for us to see it....

Let me paint a brief word picture of the Big Bang religion first, using the vocabulary of the faithful. We have interpreted the evidence from our instruments to support a theory that the universe is expanding, and expanding at a remarkably rapid rate....This is our way of being at peace with the observation that the further away a light source is, the more the spectrum of that light is shifted to the red....The resemblance between this dynamic picture and an explosion has provided us an irresistible model for the origin of our universe. This is portrayed as a super explosion, and what we see now is the debris, the shards and fragments, still flying away in every direction....With this model in front of us, let us pretend that we can watch the passing of time in the reverse direction. Let's run the movie projector backwards. Each frame takes you to an earlier point in time, so that the flying fragments appear to be coming together again, with the volume of the universe getting progressively smaller and the matter (or whatever it is) that is in it getting progressively hotter. As the film continues to roll backwards, everything appears to condense to a smaller and smaller volume, and then even this shrinks further to what looks like a point, and that point is so hot the matter can't even exist at all. Stop the projector right there. Look at that birth frame. If you closely inspect the image before you, you should see an extremely small something, at a temperature of a fantastically large number of degrees centigrade. The movie is said to have started from this point in the normal time direction and that is what the physicists call the Big Bang. From that miniscule source came all the stuff that constitutes this universe: the energy, the eventual mass, the stars and the galaxies, the forces of gravity and of life....

But here is the faith aspect of this particular cosmological religion. Look at the one frame again...and ask to look at the frame that immediately precedes it....The question has no meaning, some will say...which avoids the original question....What lit the fuse? Who said, "let the games begin?" Listen carefully and you just might hear someone speak the name so frequently invoked by the biblical creationists: God.

---

"Tao is a vast immeasurable void....
Without beginning, without end,
infinite, indefinable...."

F. J. MacHovec (183)
1962 English translation of *The Book of Tao*

So **the Big Bang is presented within our present day science as a miracle,** nothing more and nothing less....Scientists...fit all observations into a theory that will support, or at least be at peace with, this Big Bang miracle....Examples abound of the capitulation of the scientific community to this canonical cop-out. Two recent articles appeared in the local *San Francisco Chronicle* that are superb illustrations of this mindset.

On March 4, 1995, there was reported the discovery of the sixth and last quark, the top quark. I do not wish to detract in any way from the beauty of fundamental particles, the various forces, the laws of physics, and all the related entities that are the ultimate building blocks and operative rules of the matter that constitute the universe. I'm all for chemistry, and physics, and thermodynamics and quantum mechanics. They are real; they are essential; they are inescapable. What I am against is the blind attachment of everything to the Big Bang nonsense. Let me make a parallel between the biased reporting that is so much in vogue now (let's call it Big Bang Bias, or BBB), and how it might have been phrased in non-biased language (called IOU for Infinitely Old Universe), in the matter of this quark report.

**BBB**   "Scientists have managed to isolate a bit of matter providing a major clue to the origin and evo-

"I THINK YOU SHOULD BE MORE EXPLICIT HERE IN STEP TWO."

"I think you should be more explicit here in step two."

Copyright © 1994 by Sidney Harris (184)

lution of the universe."
**IOU**   "Scientists have managed to isolate a bit of matter providing a major clue to the structure of the universe."
**BBB**   "Quarks vanished as independent entities at the very beginning of time when the original Big Bang that created the universe began to cool."
**IOU**   "Quarks have never before existed as independent entities, as the extreme conditions of heat and energy needed to release them are not known in nature."
**BBB**   "...have found the missing link in our theoretical model that tries to understand how the universe **evolved from its birth.**"
**IOU**   "...have found the missing link in our theoretical model that tries to understand what the universe is and of what it is made."

...How much simpler life would be if we just dropped the concept of the Big Bang, and the insistence upon there being a point of origin. Rather than continue a search for a beginning, **simply assume that everything has always been here.** And rather than fret over when it all might crunch, **simply assume that everything will always remain here.** Our space and cosmos has been around forever, and will stay with us forever.

...Suddenly a number of things that seemed to be uncomfortably hurried in the BBB world become quite relaxed in the IOU world. The most obvious of these issues is the question of the origin of life.

The time period allotted for the creation of life, in our current philosophy, is absurdly small. This carries the arguments that presume the origins to be on earth. We have an extraordinarily complex DNA system that encodes the ultimate details of the living organism. It is complex today and there are indicators that three billion years ago, when the earth was just cooling down enough to support life, it was just as complex. When did it have time to evolve from something simple to something less simple to something as complex as it is today (just as it was back then)? If you accept evolution, then you must assume that we leapt from a zero level (no life) to a ten level (life as we know it today) with the nine levels having been reached while the earth was still new and relatively uninhabitable....

For those of us who meditate, who feel the Earth and stars with the heart instead of the intellect, we KNOW that the universe is ETERNAL. It is intensely experiential. Perhaps you had been meditating for years, perhaps you had a near-death experience, perhaps you were just doing the dishes one day, not thinking about anything in particular, and suddenly you were filled for a moment with a profound connection to the light of ETERNITY. The experience stopped you absolutely still and stunned you with its power. You may have had to spend days or weeks attempting to express the ideas of that moment. Some have spent a lifetime interpreting the wealth of information that was given with such a gift. Books have been written and inventions have been created on the basis of a personal experience with that moment of knowing that ETERNITY is absolutely real. These realms of timelessness and endlessness may be experienced by anyone who devoutly seeks such knowledge. The term *Grace* has been used by some for such a moment when the gift is given.

For many years I was privileged to live at the Washington Research Institute. It was the center of exciting meetings and lively discussions about world events, psi phenomena and the possible nature of reality. Physicists, psychologists, doctors and philosophers met frequently at the WRI to exchange ideas. Among their discussions were questions about the age and geometry of the universe, the Big Bang, string theories, hyperspace and origins of life. Some were very patient with me, knowing I had no background in math or physics. They exuded so much enthusiasm for their theories that I was caught up in the flow of energy and I really wanted to understand. For twenty years, I listened. In the city as I sat each day at a computer, I could almost believe that the universe was once only a vacuum point, out of which burst forth particles of dust and gases, hydrogen, helium, and eventually stars and galaxies.

However, we are now retired and are no longer living in a city. Instead we are living at the edge of the Great Basin, a mile high, away from any smog-filled area and artificial lights, both of which obscure the sky. When our own lights go out, there is not another light bulb shining anywhere that we can see. Behind us, to the west, is a sweet smelling Jeffrey Pine forest. In front of us, to the east, are wild flowers in the summer and the glistening white of snow in the winter. Beyond that are miles of the sacred sagebrush and bitter brush. In the daytime, we can see the hills fifty miles away on the other side of the valley below us. They glow blue and purple in the clear air.

At night we watch the sky, as I did as as child lying on the haystack. No matter what I have learned, I find it impossible in my heart to think that all those stars that I can

**Out in the desert, a mile high, above most of the smog and pollution, the awesome night sky rolls out forever. It is filled with more stars than anyone can ever see through city lights. Beyond the stars we can see, there are the thousands of galaxies that we can't see. We can't know what is on the other side of our own Milky Way. For twenty years honored teachers have patiently tried to share their knowledge with me about how the universe started from a vacuum point. I must reverently apologize to them. I have tried to follow their teachings, but out here under the endless sky, I am unable even to imagine that everything in this whole unimaginably vast universe could have come from one single, very, very, small something.**

see, and the thousands of others that I can't see, could have come from a vacuum point. And so lovingly and reverently I apologize to all the honored teachers who tried to explain this to me. I would like to believe what so many intelligent people, for whom I have great respect, have stated to be true. But belief may or may not be connected to an intellectual activity. When I look at the vast array of stars out here where the sky is clear my reaction is visceral.

I have often repeated these verses from *The Tao Te Ching* that were written approximately 2,500 years ago: "There was something mysterious, without beginning, without end, that existed before the creation of the heavens and the earth...." For me, the word *"before"* does not mean before in time. It means *before* as in the organizing principle. Because the Tao is also described as "Unmoving; infinite; standing alone; never changing. It is everywhere and it is inexhaustible....**Tao is a vast immeasurable void.... Without beginning, without end, infinite, indefinable.** It is the form of the formless; it is existence in non-existence; it is the greatest mystery...." (183)

It is clear to those of us who explore the multidimensional regions of the hyperspace that we can identify within ourselves the realms of timelessness and eternity, the endlessness of space and infinity. We can explore and expand the intelligences of our sensory systems. We can expand our ability to *express* what our sensory systems perceive. We can explore the realms of non-local space-time. Through resonance we can feel the world around us.

I can believe that the heavier elements in our bodies (iron, calcium, magnesium et al.) were created in the nuclear furnaces during the explosions of stars long before the Earth itself was formed. I can believe that we (our cellular beings) evolved along with the changes in our environment. I also can believe that we are more than all of that.

The cells in our bodies may be made up of star stuff, but our inspirations come from hyperspace stuff and are interpreted through our own memory stuff, as we enlarge our awareness of Self to include it all: the subconscious, pre-conscious, multiple awarenesses, and the multidimensionality of the superconscious.

# CHAPTER NINE — BELIEF SYSTEMS AND THE POLITICS OF SUPPRESSION

Mind-to-mind communication and remote viewing are the main topics here, not the different and mutually hostile concepts of God. Yet every community struggles with the political and educational battles over the existence or non-existence of an external God, and the instantaneous creation vs. the evidence of evolution. Because these issues dominate so much political energy they have created a climate of political suppression of funding for research in psi phenomena. It is for that reason that I have chosen to examine some of the background of this suppression. This discussion is intended to expose these political issues beyond their dogmas. There is no intention to offend anyone.

One of the hotly debated political issues in education today is whether or not life began by accident or was created in seven days in exact accordance with the chapter of Genesis in the Judeo-Christian Bible. There is much resistance to the idea of accidental life. This is an extremist idea which has not been proved by science, though it has become "official doctrine" in science classes. Creationism is another extremist position in defiance of atheism. Both sides battle it out in the courts and in the election booths, and raise great sums from ordinary people to wage this war. Some beliefs are so long-standing that their adherents no longer question the source, but just blindly repeat what they were taught. For some of these people, psi can be included in their belief system (with specific qualifications, such as evoking the name of Jesus Christ first), but for others it must be rejected totally, as though it were impossible.

Many arguments (and sometimes violence) can be traced to whether or not people choose to believe that an *external* God exists. The idea of a white-haired old man floating about the sky, zapping clay into life to create the first two people, immaculately conceiving an *only* son, whose name now stands for the entire, much older, universe, is quite unacceptable to those who study science. A prevalent idea, preached in scientific communities, is also unacceptable to many of us, even though we have no relation to the creationists. That idea is: God does not exist; life began merely by accident; our own consciousness began only at birth; our memories cannot begin until the hippocampus is formed; and our consciousness ends when we die. Many of us know from experience that there is something more to life, and we resist both extremes. Science has been a guiding light for intelligent people for hundreds of years. However, when the dedicated atheists in the scientific community continue to deny the fundamental wholeness of humanity in favor of a mechanistic explanation of our separate parts, thoughtful people naturally question the "reality" as well as the wisdom of such thinking.

The first issue to examine openly is whether we believe that God is external to His Creation or intrinsic to everything in universe. These two concepts lie at the heart of *all* theories:

**1.** God is **external** to His Creation. He created everything in six days and rested on Sunday. (Or was it Saturday?) He created Adam and Eve in a garden that He designed especially for them, became angry when they disobeyed Him, and sent them away. We pray to Him to be with us, and to provide help and favors. If we promise to be good and obey His rules, we are allowed to go to Heaven when we die.

**2.** God is **intrinsic** to all creation. The fundamental laws of nature that our best science has revealed over time are among the **Laws of *Its* Own Nature** (e.g., the fundamental equations concerning electromagnetism, waves, particles, the strong and the weak nuclear forces, gravity, $E = MC^2$, $Z = Z^2 + C$, et al.). Those laws not yet discovered remain within the Great Mystery.

A legend tells of a wise old teacher named Lao Tzu who lived in China around 2,500 years ago. When he left the palace and his post as advisor to the emperor, he planned to retire to the mountains, but the guards were ordered not to let him go until he wrote down all he knew. *The Book of Tao (Tao Te Ching)* is said to be the result. (183) Frank J. MacHovec's poetic translation in 1962 has been my favorite. It is quoted in Chapter Eight and again here:

...There is something mysterious, without beginning, without end, that existed before the heavens and earth. Unmoving; infinite; standing alone; never changing. It is everywhere and it is inexhaustible. It is the mother of all.

I do not know its name. If I must name it, I call it Tao and I hail it as supreme.

Supreme means never-ending; never-ending means far-reaching; and far-reaching means returning. Thus Tao is supreme, the heavens are supreme, earth is supreme, and man is supreme. There are four supremes in the universe; man is one of them.

Man is subject to the laws of the earth, the earth is subject to the laws of the universe, the universe is subject to the laws of Tao, and **Tao is subject to the laws of its own nature....**

From *The Tao Te Ching*, we can explore the concepts of God (Tao) as being intrinsic to us and to all things, rather than being external to us and to all things. There are many religions other than the Judeo-Christian ones that follow this belief. In our own land we have, in our ignorance, tried to convert the Native Americans from their own profound understanding of life. Yet they who had never heard of Lao Tzu believed that all people were related to the Great Spirit, and that all beings, including Earth, sky, animals, and ourselves, are related to each other. Today, a growing number of us are beginning to show a new respect for those ideas.

It is the denial of or the belief in the **external** God that is most likely to suppress the concept of psi phenomena. The political battles on both sides prevent proper research and education about human consciousness:

1. CREATIONISM
ESP is the work of the devil. Those who accept what the church preaches will be *SAVED*. All others will go to Hell. When psi phenomena (healing, RV) manifest as the result of prayer in Jesus' name, it is *a miracle of Divine will*. Satan is the power behind all psi phenomena that *did not* come directly from Jesus as an answer to prayer. (Deuteronomy 18: 9-13)

2. ATHEISM
There is no God. Life began by accident. ESP cannot exist, therefore it does not. Life begins at conception, but the mind is a blank slate, and memories can only be formed after the brain develops sufficiently as the infant matures. Death is the end of consciousness. Only the material world that can be measured is "real."

3. UNFOUNDED BELIEFS
When psi events have saved lives, and science refuses to acknowledge that psi exists in the natural world, such events have been called "miracles." Unfounded ancient prophecies about the end of the world have been feared by each generation for centuries, and still cause fear today.

Psi research has been blocked, repressed, or ridiculed throughout most of this century. Atheists believe that all psi phenomena must be the result of fantasy, since the type of consciousness that such experiences require is nonexistent in their understanding of the material world. It has been called "religion" in order to ban the study of human consciousness from public school. The popular media promotes stories of "fantastic miracles" because people will pay money to read about them or to watch them on TV.

## CREATIONISM

Three religions that have their roots in the old testament of the Holy Bible—Muslim, Jewish and Christian. Each has different sects and different interpretations of *The Word*. The fundamentalists among each of them are the ones who attempt to affect our science and politics the most, in spite of our laws for the separation of church and state. In Iran and Iraq, for instance, the internal problems there are based in part on a lack of separation of church and state. The political powers attempt to control, define, and impose a fundamentalist interpretation of Islamic religion by force and violence against their own people, and to inspire acts of terrorism against the West. Whereas the Sufis of the Islamic religion are the ones who carry the deep spiritual traditions, it is the fundamentalists who rule the country. In Israel, where a democratic attempt to separate church and state is practiced, a part of the Jewish population (which clings to its own brand of fundamentalism) is quite resistant to political attempts to make peace with their traditional enemies among the Islamic peoples. When they make war on each other, as they have for countless centuries in that part of the world, our government is also affected. Dogmatic fundamentalism anywhere creates fear, hatred, and limited thinking, and can become the breeding ground for war and violence. These are hardly the peaceful intentions which lie at the heart of most religions.

However, when a belief system is shared in a group, that combined resonance builds power. In the US Christian fundamentalists use this group voting power politically. They work to win school board elections so that creationism can be taught in public school. Evolution is thought to be an evil idea designed to disrupt the teachings of the Bible. For them the King James version of the Bible is the only book that is the direct revelation of God. *Genesis* (as translated over the centuries through Hebrew, Greek, Latin, and finally into English 1,600 years later) is taken word for word on faith. The world was created in seven days, about 8,000 or so years ago. The fossil records in the rocks (which are billions of years old) were created in the same seven days to maintain the eternal mystery of God. Adam was the first and only person. Eve was created from the rib of Adam in the form we see humans today (white, of course). When the son of Adam and Eve took a wife no one questions where she might have come from. Humans did not evolve from monkeys, they were created in the image of God (implying that He looks like us). Eternal hell fires of the devil await all non-believers and eternal heaven await the faithful. For them, only the future is eternal, but the past had a definite beginning.

As translations of the ancient Bible were made through several languages, each version was copied over and over by hand through the centuries until the printing press was developed around 1450 AD. About 160 years after that, the King James English translation became a major undertaking by scholars at the time. It is poetic as well as it is a fundamental contribution to the history of literature. If one were to make an English translation directly from the Hebrew today, one might find the story of Ruth, for example, as well as some of the other Old Testament stories, to be richer in content. Some things were inevitably lost or changed over time, as the translations of Dead Sea Scroll suggest. (185) Nevertheless, an English translation was essential for the people then, and the version that James I authorized is a truly remarkable accomplishment.

Before he was crowned King James I of England and the head of the Church of England, he had been the King James VI of Scotland, a land which was predominately Catholic. His great uncle, Henry VIII had broken with the Catholic Church for his own reasons, and though Henry's first daughter Queen Mary tried to bring the country back to Catholicism, she failed. His second daughter Elizabeth I was in power for over forty years, long enough so that going back to Catholicism was out of the question. She left no heirs. Her Catholic cousin Mary Queen of Scots would have ascended the throne, but she was accused of plotting to overthrow Elizabeth I and was beheaded. So Mary's son became King James I in 1603 AD.

However, during his reign in Scotland James believed in the reality of demons and wrote about them. He had many people tortured to confess they were witches and to name others who might be witches. He then had them all burned alive at the stake. (Unfortunately, he did not have the Tibetan knowledge that demons are an integral part of consciousness. Tibetan demons become manifest through karma and can be dissolved through understanding, right action and meditation.) When James was crowned King of England, he encouraged Shakespeare to write a play about wicked witches to gain public support against anyone else he decided to call a "witch." Shakespeare did a great job with the "unnatural hags" in *Macbeth*. He dramatized how predictions of the future were the work of the devil. This is wonderful theatre! At the same time, Shakespeare also revealed the natural workings of precognition—that only

> ### "ESP IS THE WORK OF THE DEVIL."
>
> Quoted from a pamphlet by Jehovah's Witnesses.

part of a prediction is received. The rest is created by one's pre-conscious desires. Macbeth killed King Duncan and others, but it is the witches who are blamed for his wickedness. We might say that James I used the power of the media to influence public opinion for his own purposes and to defend his own questionable actions. (We are complacent to think that using the power of the media to distort truth deliberately doesn't happen in our democracy. Yet, multibillion dollar commercial enterprises do use this power.)

Because James I had been taught to believe in demons and the need to be saved from them, he continued those teachings, passing the concepts along with that first translation of the Bible into English. Fundamentalist Christians continue to preach the need to be *saved*. Within the bonds of their community, members provide comfort and support for those who are also willing to believe it. The combined resonance of those who are *saved* can be so powerful that some who are sick are healed in Jesus Christ's name. Some have said that their true work in this world is the "healing of hearts." They do charitable work with the poor and homeless, the sick and the lost children. Some leave the comforts of home to go where people are oppressed to help them and to save them. Dedicated missionaries are even willing to live in extreme discomfort to do this work. Some feel guided by holy spirit to do this, while others do it from fear of the devil. It is the fear that can limit critical thinking and logic. When the famous healer Olga Worrall was successful in her spiritual healing without evoking the name of Jesus, fundamentalists condemned her as being in league with the devil. She responded with this question: if the devil is making people well, who then was responsible for making them sick? (186) After her husband Ambrose died, he continued to help her in her spiritual healing work.

A confusion in logic for some believers exists when Jesus and the devil are seen as nearly equal in power. A believer might be unable to feel the oneness of consciousness, because the devil is in it, too. With the experience of oneness comes the understanding that all dualities are derived from the one, and the balance of duality is essential to the action of the universe. During the early exaggerated New Age fuss over positive and negative, Bob Beck said, "Well, if I can get the good (positive) side of my battery to cooperate with the bad (negative) side, I may be able to start my car." (187) That is not to say we encourage evil behavior among us, but the understanding of the nature of our own lights and shadows allows us to deal with the world and its complications. The 21st century demands that we evolve beyond the old limitations of dogma and blind rituals that grew out of a different age.

## ATHEISM

Those who are caught up in atheism believe that there is no God, no intelligent Creator of Life. Life on Earth began *only* by accident. Perhaps a few amino acids drifted into the same place in the vast ancient seas and created a protein. Eventually, perhaps because of lightning storms, a cell developed that was able to divide and reproduce itself. Gradually, through evolution and survival of the fittest over billions of years, humans walked on two feet and learned to build fire. For years Western science thought that the human mind begins at birth as a *tabula rasa,* a blank slate on which experiences are recorded, though not remembered until the brain develops sufficiently for real thought. We exist only between birth and death. The end of life and mind coincide with the death of the body. Only those things that are measured in our three-dimensional world are considered to be real. Telescopes, microscopes, computers, satellites can expand the capacity of humans to see and know about the world, but extra-sensory perception cannot exist, and therefore it does not. Anyone who thinks that it does is deluded.

It is true that medical scientists have not found a specific *extra sense* in the body that is dedicated to psi activity (e.g., precognition, psychokinesis, telepathy, conversations with those who have died or communication with angels of the heavenly realm). And so I have agreed with the atheists on this one point. *Extra-sensory perception* does not exist. However, the abilities of the sensory systems we know are much more extensive than previously realized. *Telepathy and other psi phenomena do exist,* and have been recorded by many civilizations over the centuries. The senses we use to attempt to communicate telepathically are not *extra* but are our ordinary senses. To be able to report our psychic impressions, we talk about subtle feelings, implied sounds, and draw images from visions. In spite of the prevalent idea in academic and scientific circles that psi phenomena is only fantasy, the literature from scientific studies in this area in the last thirty years is quite extensive. (188)

The late Carl Sagan, PhD, and the group of skeptics he endorsed believed that ESP does not exist, and that anyone who found any positive results in tests of it were frauds or at least "sloppy" scientists. Sagan declared many times,

---

**Resistance to psi research
is not based on science, but on politics.**

---

> ## "PARAPSYCHOLOGY IS PSEUDOSCIENCE."
>
> Carl Sagan
> *The Demon-Haunted World*

and again in his book *Demon-Haunted World* (189) that parapsychology was a pseudoscience. In the 1970s there was a flurry of interest in psi phenomena following the publication of parapsychology research done in the Soviet Union during the Cold War. (190) But by the 1980s, the atheistic skeptical backlash began to dominate the politics of science. All classes of parapsychology in publicly supported community colleges across the US were cancelled with no public debate allowed. This could be compared to the burning of the books in other repressive civilizations in the past. In spite of Dr. Sagan's other scientific achievements and his dynamic contribution to the TV series *Cosmos* he was partially responsible for this repression, because of his own prejudices and his great influence in government and scientific circles.

Today the public might be shocked about another event in the 1980s which went almost unnoticed. Two people with higher degrees (one in physics, the other in biophysics) published the results of their astounding independent study. It was a very careful, double-blind study of psi phenomena with positive results. Their scientific methodology was impeccable. (191) The biophysicist was a teacher in a state college at the time, and she was summarily fired. The only reason given for her dismissal was that she had published work in the field of psi. If the administrators had been straightforward enough to accuse her of *heresy* to the accepted tenets of atheism, there might have been a public response. However, it was enough to use the word "parapsychology," which was clearly the academic code word for heresy at the time. Even now, a respected professor at a state university could be fired for publishing positive results of research in the field of parapsychology.

No one doubts that there are self-styled prophets for profit all around us. There is a need to warn the unwary about the deliberate fakes and deluded flakes. But the real need is for a re-evaluation of this "science" that rejects all psi events out of hand. An atheistic organization was formed whose members called themselves CSICOP (Committee for the Scientific Investigation into Claims of the Paranormal). They were well-funded and their spokesman was the popular TV magician, Randi, who was well acquainted with the art of deception. He ridiculed all parapsychologists throughout this period, regardless of their substantial data. Finally, Eldon Bird and Uri Geller were successful in bringing a lawsuit for slander against Randi. (192) During this backlash period, even the prestigious scientific organization the American Association for the Advancement of Science hired that same TV magician to speak at their conference in San Francisco. His mission was to debunk the carefully controlled parapsychology studies from SRI that had been published in *Nature* magazine in 1974. After Randi's recorded talk and during the question period, which was not recorded, Randi mentioned my name to this audience as Uri Geller's secret accomplice who slipped him the messages under the door. This self-styled magician could only see the reflections of his own type of deceptions of magic wherever he looked. Though he had never met me and had done no research on his own, he chose to use my name to discredit the entire work at SRI. Since Targ had asked me to draw the pictures for the experiment, which Geller then drew telepathically while locked in a room shielded electromagnetically (often three buildings away), I had to threaten to sue Randi for slander as well. The audience of "good old boy" scientists at this event did not care that Randi was willing to trash others in his rush to debunk good science. It was enough that they were willing to ignore the data from careful scientific research and to believe the magician because he supported their own prejudices. The politics of science has fallen far because of its adherence to atheistic dogma. Can good science survive this type of thinking? Ideally, the new generation will find a way beyond the religion of materialism.

The same dogma dominates the politics of government agencies that will fund one kind of research but not another kind if it is currently politically incorrect. It is clear that resistance to psi research in government funding is not based on science, but on politics. The Defense Department and the CIA did psi research in secret, though not for public information. Only when the Cold War was over and the program cancelled was it acknowledged that the work had been done at all. Then hard line, brainwashed, conservative skeptics complained that tax money was wasted on nonsense. It may take years to undo such prejudicial thinking.

Stephen Toulmin, PhD, is a philosopher and physicist. On a TV series called *Glorious Accident: Understanding our Place in the Cosmic Puzzle* (193), he spoke about the shift of consciousness needed for the next century:

The adventure of the modern world that began with people like Rene Descartes and Newton has failed. We have run aground. We don't know where we are. We are backing into a new millennium eyes lowered....

The myth of rationality and materialism...that had been established ages ago by people like Descartes...the myth that was to be the basis for the modern world...*[because of it]* the modern world may have ground to a halt....

The dream of Descartes and his ilk remains real for many people. It is their dedication to rationality, which once promised intellectual certainty and harmony, that still makes them trust science and industry. It is the world view that looks upon nature, animals, the universe, and everything around us as unconscious matter. Only *we* possess this unique thing, a conscious mind. With that mind we will eventually understand the world around us. That myth of Descartes and his followers has captured and fascinated for decades, just like the other myths of Descartes's days, that our consciousness is located in our head that is formed inside our skull rather than by the world outside. What he convinced people of was the idea that if only we pursued some kind of rational method we could be able to find general recipes for getting ourselves out of these difficulties (or that was the...general impression people carried away)....There was this art of being rational which was going to provide us with general procedures for solving, not only intellectual problems, but also as time went on...technical problems and practical problems as well.

And I think that idea that there is some kind of general intellectual recipe for dealing with problems—what when I was a young man was called *THE SCIENTIFIC METHOD*—was very seductive, especially for people who see the world falling apart around them....

The devoted followers of Descartes have gradually created a new kind of state religion. After the repressive type of domination practiced in Europe by Catholic and Protestant reformers in turn, the concept of rationality was quite appealing. Since thousands of people had been burned alive for not following the dogmas of whatever religious belief had political power at the time, the framers of the Constitution separated public school from religious teaching in order to prevent such battles over the control of human thought. They were not atheists. They did believe in God. Many of them were deists and/or members of the Masonic Order. They believed that the separation of church and state would help ensure personal freedom at the time. However, because atheism could not be considered a religion, its ideas were gradually allowed to dominate our science and education over time. A few of the major tenets of atheism eventually became dogmatic as well, inhibiting any scientific study in the areas of its disbelief. For that reason the "cult" of atheism should be removed from education, along with several of its ideas that have *not been proved* by scientific study. For example, one of the basic premises of atheism is that life on Earth began by accident. This hypothesis has not been proved scientifically.

There is no doubt that science, once released from church dogma and doctrine, has brought us into a far different world than we were in before the Constitution was written. When people were free enough from religious dogma to study the material world with scientific rigor, they began to gain more knowledge than ever before. Consider the major changes in the last two hundred years, or even in the last century. For those who were born in 1900, there were no cars, airplanes, telephones, TV, computers, satellites, or trips to the moon. Many homes had no electricity and no indoor plumbing. If we could pump enough water from the well on the ranch, and the pipes in back of the wood stove had heated the water hot enough while supper was cooking, we could have a bath on Saturday night, but we still had to go outside to the outhouse.

Removing religion from school served the purpose of science (and our comfort) well. But atheism has come full circle. For now it blocks the very premise of research into the most essential of sciences (the potential of human consciousness) by its own accumulated closed-mindedness and dogmas. The idea that this life is all there is and death is the end has helped to give rise to what is now being called "moral decay." Atheistic education has given us technology without compassion, homelessness without community support, a population that is basically unconsciousness about its relationship to the Earth, and mind that is not encouraged to acknowledge its innate ability to explore its true multidimensional nature.

I am definitely *not* suggesting that we return to prayer in our public schools or to teach creationism instead of evolution. There is a way to do this that does not include either the religion of creationism or atheism. The science

---

**The science of the human potential
must be taught with an open mind.
There is a way to do this that is non-religious.
Schools can use biofeedback equipment as
a scientific tool for self-discovery.**

---

**The basic premise of atheism,
that life on Earth began by accident,
has not been proved scientifically.**

---

of human potential should be taught with an open mind. Schools can use biofeedback equipment as scientific tools for self-discovery. When children learn to raise or lower their skin temperature (as needed), gain voluntary control over their brainwaves and the electrical output of their muscles and emotional responses, they soon learn, through good scientific methods, that their minds are truly multidimensional (e.g., "Does the biofeedback tone change when I shift my thoughts from math lessons to music? What happens to the biofeedback tone when I re-feel emotions?"). They can learn to increase their ability to focus attention. When that is learned early in school, the results can lead to their learning to become more intelligent. (194) Evolution of consciousness is happening now. It must not be inhibited by limited ideas about the true nature of mind just because the cult of atheism has political control over what students might be able to learn about their own consciousness in public school. These are *not* religious ideas. They arise from good scientific observation and experiences with biofeedback of the electromagnetic properties of our brains and bodies.

Students at a continuation high school in California had an opportunity to work with biofeedback instruments in Marge King's classroom. These students wrote about their learning experiences. (195) One teenager wrote this rhyme after working with the brainwave analyzer:

*I'm in beta when I add,
I'm in theta when I'm mad.
Therefore, I can't add
When I'm mad.*

One angry young man in her class discovered that one hand was ten degrees colder than the other one. He practiced warming his hand with the help of the skin temperature feedback machine. When he realized that his hand was cold because the muscles in his arm were very tense, he admitted that he was angry with his father who said mean things to him all the time. His arm was tense, because sometimes he felt like hitting back, though he really didn't want to do that. Days later when he came to class, he told King that he learned how to keep his muscles from being so tense and how to keep his hand warm. He told her that, "My dad still bitches at me, but it don't bug me no more."

## UNFOUNDED BELIEFS

*Webster's New World Dictionary* defines a miracle as: *"An event or action that apparently contradicts known scientific laws and is hence thought to be due to supernatural causes, especially to an act of God."*

Experiences have been reported by thousands of people down through the centuries that did seem to them to be *miracles.* Some can be explained by today's science, some are still mysteries. My belief is that the first miracle is Life itself. Beyond that our multidimensional consciousness, which is the essence of the existence of life in the body, is part of the multidimensional universe, and whatever actually happens in that framework must be lawful, whether science understands it or not. Here is a story from my own experience:

Doctors told my mother that she had a cyst on one of her kidneys and that there was no way to remove it. It was not considered life-threatening. At that time I had heard about a spiritual healer, the Reverend Plume. He lived some distance from us, but I persuaded my mother to let me take her to see him. On the way we stopped to see another friend of mine who was having trouble with numbness in her fingers. She had undergone an operation already which had not helped. I invited her to come with us. When the Reverend Plume worked with mother, it seemed that the ends of his fingers disappeared into the back of her body. I was willing to think that I must be wrong, that the cloth or soft tissue hid his fingers. Mother didn't feel anything at the time, and we don't know if her cyst was healed then or not, it was never checked by the doctor. She did live another twenty years after that time. However, my friend had a different experience. This time, I thought I saw the ends of his fingers become transparent and then disappear into her elbow, where there was no place to hide them. I was very close to her elbow this time to watch him. Immediately she felt a tingling sensation in her fingers, and within a day or two, she was healed. Was this a miracle, or a natural law not yet explained?

On another occasion, the spiritual healer Greg Schelkun, whose remote viewing picture is reproduced on page 89, asked me to help him with a young man who had a tumor in his brain. The tumor was blocking the vision of the man's left eye and was pressing on his thalamus. His doctors had told him that it was inoperable, and that he should go home and prepare his last will and testament. In desperation, and with nothing to lose, he sought the help of a known spiritual healer and found Schelkun. The man had

never had an out-of-the-body experience, so Schelkun thought that if I hypnotized him, I could encourage such an experience for him. It might help him to reduce his natural fear of death. During the session, the young man entered into a deep trance state. I asked him my usual question, which was to find the source of his problem. Instantly, he felt he was experiencing a past life as a Greek fisherman out on the sea alone. A storm came up and the mast broke and fell across his forehead. He experienced great pressure there, and then died in that lonely boat so far away from home. We went over and over that experience until he could relieve the feelings of pressure on his head, and leave that old body as a free spirit. I only worked with him once, though he continued to see Schelkun for several months until his tumor disappeared. He did not die as predicted by the doctors. (Then he had new problems. What would he do to earn a living for himself? Living may be more difficult than dying.) Was the process of working with the abilities of the mind enough? Did the mind heal the brain? Was this a miracle, due to divine interference? Attempts to do spiritual healing do not always save the life that doctors have judged to be doomed, but sometimes healing does take place against all predictions.

What happens in healing? The issue here is not whether we actually believe in a past life experience, or even whether we may have brought into this present life the emotions that were dominant when we died in the past. Perhaps consciousness provides us with a drama we invent, subconsciously, to elicit the necessary changes in the electrical and biochemical activity of the brain. Perhaps we just set the drama in the past so that it will not be threatening to us in the present. We can solve problems of strong emotions better in the past than we can solve them today. If I am still angry at the Inquisitor for ordering me to be burned at the stake four hundred years ago, then I may still be so angry today that I unconsciously evoke others to be mean to me now. It may be easier to forgive the evil of four hundred years ago than it is to forgive my employer (or lover or family member) for insults today. But there seems to be a psychic connection between forgiveness of the old pain and the healing effect on the current situation. Is the subsequent release just a fundamental change in attitude and/or a miracle? Whatever the reason, the future is also changed when we change our own response to the dramas of the past. The past, whether it involves a childhood trauma or a past-life problem, is malleable.

Nevertheless, spiritual leaders over the centuries have claimed to have accomplished miracle healings by asking for divine intervention or help from saints or the spirits of those who have died. Today new research shows that modern medicine can use both prayer and technology for healing. (196)

In 1971, doctors thought that Don Westerbeke had an inoperable brain tumor. The spiritual healers in the Philippines were able to relieve his pain and his symptoms. Patricia Westerbeke did a careful study of other cancer patients who went to the Philippines, even though we knew some spiritual healers also used sleight of hand as well. She reported the medical diagnosis of the patients before they went, their own reports of their experiences, and follow-up interviews six months later. Those who changed their life styles *kept* their "miracle" healings; those who rejected it all as fake and a waste of money did not. The Westerbeke study (197) could be considered a precursor to the whole field of psycho-neuro-physiology which followed her study. The use of placebos for centuries show that some "miracle healings" occur within the believing mind itself.

A major unfounded belief today is the one about visiting aliens from another star system. When I first drew the pictures for the remote viewing research at SRI, Puharich was still pushing the idea that aliens from UFOs gave Geller the power to bend metal. (Later, as Geller learned more about his own power, he wrote and lectured about how anyone might develop personal mind power.) Yet in 1973, when I watched a 3/8" steel bar bend as Geller stroked it gently with his fingers, I did wonder how that had actually happened. It was done under controlled conditions and I was sitting by him, close enough to watch very carefully. However, since I firmly believe that all is contained in natural law, I was unwilling to call it a miracle. Later, I even experienced bending a spoon in my own hand, and I still didn't understand why it was possible. However, during the time of the experiments at SRI, Geller seemed to be surrounded by a poltergeist type of activity. When he walked through the halls, I saw magnets, and the pictures they were holding, fall off metal cabinets in the offices near him. Objects fell to the ground in front of him. No one could discover where they came from. That phenomena was not studied at SRI. There was no way to do a controlled study of such unexpected events. It was enough to try to prove accurate remote viewing under controlled conditions with the sensory shielding available.

In 1974, Puharich and Hurtak gave lectures about mass landings of UFOs and an invasion of ETs in three years time. These UFO stories along with the years of reading about little green men from Mars had affected the preconscious imaginings of many. Unfortunately, the members of a well-publicized cult bet their lives on the belief that ETs were coming to take their spirits away in a high-frequency vehicle. Human abductions by the same little grayish-green aliens are described in similar ways through common hypnotic suggestions. The believers and the abductees have formed their own cult. The talk shows are full of their stories. Can it be true? Other star systems are many light years away. It is very difficult to imagine how they can travel here and bring their hardware with them.

Another issue for the believers in miracles is the one of prophecy. *The Book of Revelations* is full of gloom and doom for the future, even though God promises, after the flood of the Old Testament, that the Earth would never again be destroyed that way. The rainbow is a token of His covenant. It is in the later writings that predict God will destroy the world by fire next time. So some feel that our civilization is marching toward the millennium with only doomsday prophecies as guides to an inevitable disastrous future. But the millennium is only an arbitrary number for the 2,000 years since the time of Christ. The Chinese are are counting years over 6,000, so they are not limited by that (except for the Y2K problem with international computers, and perhaps for the heavy sun spot cycle in that year that can affect everyone). Many people have created their own fantasies about the coming *rapture*. Others consider the ways any possible surviving humanity might be able to live after the mass destruction that is predicted.

We can also look to Hindu philosophy for a description of this time—the Kali Yuga. This is the name of an age, predicted centuries ago in India to be a time of confusion and destruction. Only those who are devoted now will remain pure enough to survive the radiation and be able to reproduce the next generation when the Kali Yuga has completed its cycle. To be pure, they must remain vegetarian and celibate, and meditate several times per day.

Dramatic TV broadcasts try to convince listeners that the prophecies of Nostradamus were accurate in the past, and therefore must be so in the future. The prophecies about Armageddon have been around so long that it may be possible for us to replay those myths by constant mental projection. Everyday TV evangelists preach the fears of Armageddon to remind followers that only the "good" are "saved." (And by the way, please send money to keep the evangelists on the air and able to help save sinners from the demons of hell.) In each belief system there are different definitions about what "good" means, but all of them preach that the non-believers of each system will die horribly and they will not be "saved."

> **"You've been living
> In the Kingdom of Balance
> In the century of the sun
> And you can read some Nostradamus
> If you're havin' too much fun"**
>
> Chorus of a Rap Song
> Copyright ©1995, Don Douglas (198)

Our own research of prophecy (precognition) involved many unsolved questions. The ability of people to see into future time was not as successful as their ability to see into distant space (RV). So perhaps the old prophecies are not cast in stone after all, to be played on the human stage while Fate alone determines the action. *The Armageddon is not inevitable.* There are other conscious choices that can be made in our travels toward the future. Let's explore the possibilities with an open mind. Nostradamus could be compared to the witches in *Macbeth.* That which is symbolic and incomplete is interpreted by believers through their own mental projections.

What is reality? What are you willing to believe? What can be proved? What preconceived theories will you automatically attach to the evidence? Sometimes several different theories can be used to "explain" the same pieces of evidence (see page 198). However, if your pet theory must ignore or reject evidence, then it misses an accurate description of "reality." All theories must include all the events of the natural world. If the theory leaves out or cannot account for actual events, confusion and arguments over the true nature of reality continue unabated. Eventually, the political arena becomes involved to support or deny particular events. This creates the mass confusion that a democratic system has to deal with—public opinion. We have seen that public opinion can be roused by the media from the belief system of its advertisers. It is essential to question old beliefs and examine the growth of ideas, before the politics of international commercial interests create indelible belief systems that we no longer question.

One of the major political arguments in this decade has been over whether or not an external God exists. This debate has cost billions of dollars and has engaged the energy of millions of people in every school district in the country. Our Constitution prevails to keep religion out of public schools, especially the nonscientific ideas of the creationists. The evidence that changes have taken place in the life forms on Earth has been written in the ancient rocks. But atheists continue to preach that life is accidental, that we are a collection of cells, and that death is the end of consciousness. Without scientific proof, those concepts must be judged to be the religious doctrines of atheism. It is time that scientists admit that we don't have an answer to everything. There are still many unsolved questions about the Great Mystery of life and the universe. The Great Mystery may reveal a few more of its secrets in the fullness of time and through the dedication of those with open minds. It is the reality of that mystery that can stir the consciousness of the young future scientists. Through biofeedback, children can learn, scientifically, to increase their ability to focus attention, and thus learn to have access to their own higher intelligence, their own cosmic consciousness. This will improve their ability to develop their scientific perceptions.

At the Thomas Jefferson Memorial in Washington, DC, these words are carved in marble around the entablature of the rotunda, "*I have sworn upon the altar of God, eternal hostility against every form of tyranny over the mind of man.*" We are free to form our own beliefs, knowing that "*all men are created equal.*" Yet this statement is a warning that those beliefs that practice the suppression of others (declaring them to be unequal) and those that preach violence against others are forms of tyranny to be avoided.

The explorations into the nature of consciousness demonstrate that our minds are multidimensional. Access to higher intelligence is hardwired into each human system. Our free will involves developing the internal software to find it, and choosing the belief system to interpret it. As we learn to accept that fact within ourselves, our educational systems and our government institutions, our society might begin to be prepared for the next century.

Discussions of *reality* are never-ending. Each century might be defined by a different dominant concept of reality. However, when you become aware of your own relationship between the spacetime body and the hyperspace body, it is easier to feel the essence of the connection of all things.

## SOME LOGIC THAT FLOWS FROM A BELIEF IN PSI PHENOMENA

We can remain blind to the idea that we might be limited by the belief system that we learned to accept as we grew up. Or we can freely choose a belief system that allows us the room to evolve into the wealth of ideas that is expanding into the 21st century. Some of our beliefs are relatively minor and may make little difference in the future. However, there is one major choice that is fundamental to the way *you will be able to think* about your world, and the way *you will create* your way of being in that world. If you didn't think this choice was all that important, think again. Take a look at this non-serious satire of the logic that follows these belief systems and see if you can relate to any of it.

**Find your place on the chart of belief systems, or add your unique choice of belief wherever it fits.**

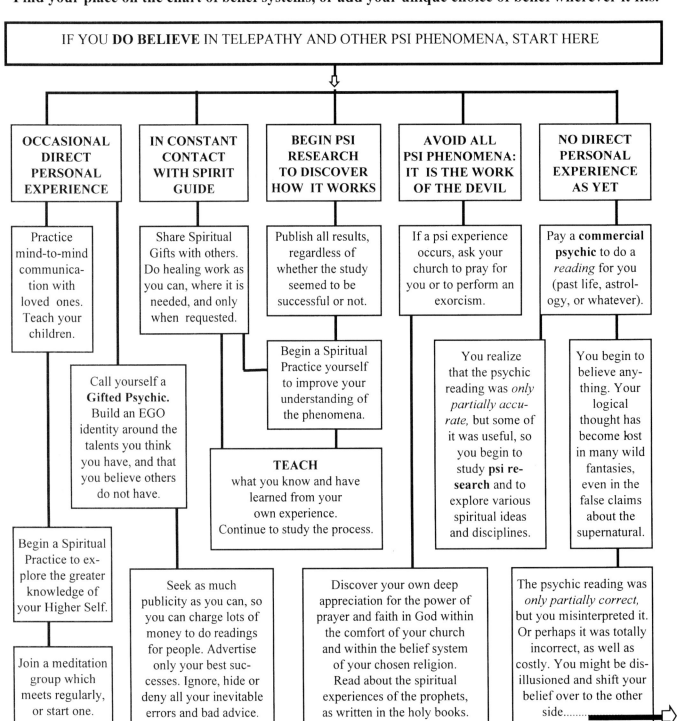

IF YOU **DO BELIEVE** IN TELEPATHY AND OTHER PSI PHENOMENA, START HERE

**OCCASIONAL DIRECT PERSONAL EXPERIENCE**

**IN CONSTANT CONTACT WITH SPIRIT GUIDE**

**BEGIN PSI RESEARCH TO DISCOVER HOW IT WORKS**

**AVOID ALL PSI PHENOMENA: IT IS THE WORK OF THE DEVIL**

**NO DIRECT PERSONAL EXPERIENCE AS YET**

Practice mind-to-mind communication with loved ones. Teach your children.

Share Spiritual Gifts with others. Do healing work as you can, where it is needed, and only when requested.

Publish all results, regardless of whether the study seemed to be successful or not.

If a psi experience occurs, ask your church to pray for you or to perform an exorcism.

Pay a **commercial psychic** to do a *reading* for you (past life, astrology, or whatever).

Call yourself a **Gifted Psychic.** Build an EGO identity around the talents you think you have, and that you believe others do not have.

Begin a Spiritual Practice yourself to improve your understanding of the phenomena.

You realize that the psychic reading was *only partially accurate,* but some of it was useful, so you begin to study **psi research** and to explore various spiritual ideas and disciplines.

You begin to believe any-thing. Your logical thought has become lost in many wild fantasies, even in the false claims about the supernatural.

**TEACH** what you know and have learned from your own experience. Continue to study the process.

Begin a Spiritual Practice to explore the greater knowledge of your Higher Self.

Seek as much publicity as you can, so you can charge lots of money to do readings for people. Advertise only your best successes. Ignore, hide or deny all your inevitable errors and bad advice.

Discover your own deep appreciation for the power of prayer and faith in God within the comfort of your church and within the belief system of your chosen religion. Read about the spiritual experiences of the prophets, as written in the holy books.

The psychic reading was *only partially correct,* but you misinterpreted it. Or perhaps it was totally incorrect, as well as costly. You might be dis-illusioned and shift your belief over to the other side........

Join a meditation group which meets regularly, or start one.

### SOME LOGIC THAT FLOWS FROM A DISBELIEF IN PSI PHENOMENA

These charts attempt to diagram some of the ways different people think about telepathy and other forms of psi phenomena. As one who has had a fairly good education, do you believe it is possible for telepathy and other psi phenomena to exist, or do you think it is impossible, because there is no "scientific" theory at present to account for its existence? Because the emotional conflict about the very existence of psi has obscured scientific research, there is much confusion among many people about what to think.

(These charts are *not* designed to include the beliefs and practices of other religions of the world with practices that are less understood in Western societies, such as shamanism, voodoo, espiritista and ancestor worship.)

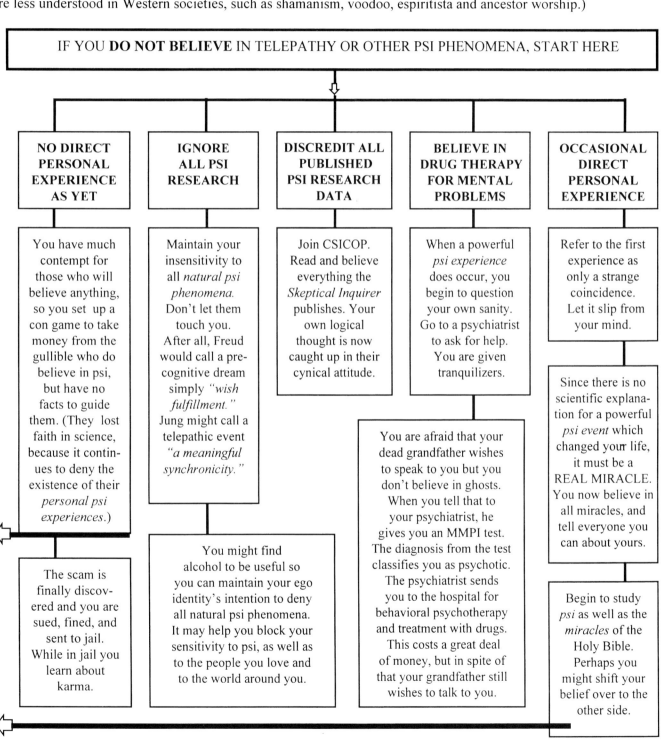

## CHAPTER TEN — SUMMARY AND CONCLUSION

*"We are standing on the edge of the land of beyond..."*
—Gandalf, from *The Hobbit* by J. R. R. Tolkien (199)

The 21st century will find us exploring the light of consciousness in greater depth, like the man who climbs the highest mountain and declares that he does so just because it is there to be explored. From our own research over thirty years we have discovered several things about telepathy and remote viewing:

1. Everyone of us may receive a telepathic message at some time in our lives, especially from a loved one.

2. Everyone of us can receive information about an object or a distant place when we are willing to clear our minds of internal dialog and focus our whole attention to it.

3. Our consciousness operates not only in the four dimensions of space and time but also in the multidimensions of non-local spacetime.

4. It is our senses that bring the information from the hyperspace into our awareness. We can see, hear, smell, taste, feel, and/or identify with whatever it is we want to know about from the distant information.

5. The incoming information is woven into our own memory systems, prejudices, dominant personality at the time of reception, and current emotional state. If we are not careful we can misinterpret everything. The key to accuracy is to be free of emotions and to have a clear mind.

6. Logic is rarely useful in the later interpretation of a partial reception. Trust the senses and try again for a more complete reception. Accept the unexpected—it may very well be the key to the important part of the message.

7. "The events seem unusual because the spacetime projection provides only a partial view of the hyperspace events." (Sirag: page 12, References 19 & 20)

8. The amount of distance (50 feet or 8,000 miles) between sender and receiver does not seem to make any difference to the accuracy of the reception.

9. Distractions in the immediate environment of the receiver can block or confuse the reception.

10. Trance states or hypnotic states can be very helpful for successful transmission and reception of information, but they are not necessary.

11. Strong psychedelics (e.g., psilocybin mushrooms and LSD) can be useful for retrieving information, especially in an emergency. Empathogens (MDMA) can help people establish deeper levels of communication. Marijuana can create a mind state that facilitates telepathy. These are not absolutely necessary, but if used properly, they can be extremely helpful in certain situations for some people.

In comparing our data with those of others, we find that they, too, have come to similar conclusions about the remote viewing process. Targ published his conclusions about his research in a report on precognition. (200) In it he asks: *"What Do We Know about Remote Viewing?"*

One of the hallmarks of the remote viewing process is that shape, form and color are described much more reliably than the target's function, or other analytical information. In addition to visual imagery, viewers sometimes describe other sensory data such as associated feelings, sounds, smells and even electrical or magnetic fields. As a viewer, I (RT) have learned that if I see a color clearly and brightly, or something silver and shiny, then that is the aspect of the target which I am most likely to describe correctly. Several others have reported these unusual and personal responses to target data as well.

Viewers can sense both present and future activities at target sites. There is no evidence to indicate that it is more difficult to look slightly into the future than it is to describe an object in a box in front of you...practice allows people to become increasingly skillful in their ability to separate out the psychic signal from the mental noise of memory and imagination.

We have shown that accuracy and resolution of remote viewing targets are not sensitive to distances of up to 10,000 miles, as demonstrated in our trials with Djuna Davitashvili in the 1984 Moscow-San Francisco remote viewing. *[See page 180.]* Targets and target details as small as 1 mm can be sensed....

Visual or audio distractions, or anything novel in the working environment, may appear as noise or erroneous impressions on the viewer's mental screen during the remote viewing session. Additionally, numbers are usually much more difficult to perceive than pictorial targets. It seems to be harder to guess a number from 1 to 10, than it is to describe a location chosen from an infinitude of planetary locations that one has never seen before. In looking for geographical targets, viewers search their interior mental landscape for a surprise, and this will usually be the correct answer. With a numerical target, there are no surprises since one is already familiar with all the possibilities, and is apt to try to use analysis to rule out the various choices. A prior knowledge of target possibilities, absence of feedback, and use of mental analysis all tend to make remote viewing more difficult.

Factors that enhance remote viewing are seriousness of purpose, feedback, heart-to-heart trust among all participants, and acceptance of *psi*. Experienced viewers learn to improve their performance by becoming aware of their own mental noise from memory and imagination, filtering it out, and by writing down their impressions and drawing their mental pictures. Drawing is especially important because it gives one direct access to his or her unconscious processes.

The use of several viewers can bring additional information of remote viewing targets....

Targ's summary of what seems to work best in remote viewing has been culled from his own twenty or more years of research. His conclusions match our own from work done during that same period of time. In addition, Jeffrey Mishlove has also confirmed this information from his own years of research. (201) If we go back as far as 1930 and read what Mary Craig Sinclair had to say about how she did telepathy with her husband Upton Sinclair (202), we find that her experiences are similar as well:

My experience is that fragments of forms appear first. For example, a curved line, or a straight one, or two lines of a triangle. But sometimes the complete object appears: swiftly, lightly, dimly-drawn, as on a moving picture film. These mental visions appear and disappear with lightning rapidity, never standing still unless quickly fixed by a deliberate effort of consciousness....

Do not fail to record what seems to be a very stray fragment, for it may be a perfect vision of some portion of the real picture....If in doubt as to what the object of your vision is, do not try to guess...guessing is one of the things one has to strive to avoid. To a certain extent one comes to know a difference between a guess and a "hunch."

The details of this technique are not to be taken as trifles. The whole issue of success or failure depends on them. At least, this is so in my case. Perhaps a spontaneous sensitive, or one who has a better method, has no such difficulties. I am just an average conscious-minded person, who set out deliberately to find a way to test this tremendously

important question of telepathy and clairvoyance, without having to depend on a "medium," who might be fooling himself, or me. It was by this method of careful attention to a technique of details that I have found it possible to get telepathic messages and to see pictures on hidden cards, and symbolic pictures of the contents of books.

This technique takes time, and patience, and training in the art of concentration....

From Sinclair's publication of *Mental Radio* in 1930 until now, nearly seventy years later, the techniques of successful telepathic attempts seem to have remained basically the same. Why, we wonder, has the field been so neglected by professional psychologists, educators, and the rest of the mainstream scientific community? It was Albert Einstein who wrote the preface for Sinclair's book. Even he felt that the subject matter was very important. He wrote the following on May 23, 1930. Both his German words and the English translation of it are printed in the book:

I have read the book of Upton Sinclair with great interest and am convinced that the same deserves the most earnest consideration, not only of the laity, but also of the psychologists by profession. The results of the telepathic experiments carefully and plainly set forth in this book stand surely far beyond those which a nature investigator holds to be thinkable. On the other hand, it is out of the question in the case of so conscientious an observer and writer as Upton Sinclair that he is carrying on a conscious deception of the reading world; his good faith and dependability are not to be doubted. So if somehow the facts here set forth rest not upon telepathy, but upon some unconscious hypnotic influence from person to person, this also would be of high psychological interest. In no case should the psychologically interested circles pass over this book heedlessly.
—(signed) A. Einstein

Since 1930, we have seen many fads about reportedly useful therapies come and go in psychological circles while the science of mind has been entangled in the mind reflections of an age that is passing. Mind-to-mind communication, however, is still waiting on the outer edges to be considered seriously. What can be done to include this important field of study? What can be done to get past the barriers set up by hard-line skeptics so that ordinary people across the country are encouraged to accept the reality that their own minds are multidimensional?

The Sidney Harris cartoon at right is a satire on the common rejection of the obvious by science. If that did not occur so often this cartoon would have no meaning and not be funny enough to be printed in *The New Yorker* magazine. When there is no acceptance of honest personal experiences by the scientific community, then it is the sciences that suffer neglect. The steadfast refusal by the leaders of our "official science" to explore all the vital issues of multidimensional consciousness has helped to give rise to the cults of "flaky science." Ordinary people no longer trust the intellectually elite. It is the scientific taboo of all psi phenomena, even though many of us have had experiences with it, that has led, I believe, to the gradual rejection of science by those who would rather swing pendulums, carry charms to ward off negative energy, or ask a deck of cards to tell the future. When there is no real scientific information for actual experiences, old mythologies are dug up to serve the purpose. Many who do seek information about psi will make up elaborate and weird stories to go along with the ancient myths. Atlantis and Mu are still alive in the minds of some people. The old predictions about mass destruction of the world are constantly fed into the media through videos, movies, TV programs, books, and computer games. This stimulates confusion about real psi phenomena. The power of group mind is so strong that it may be possible for the believers to create disasters.

However, it may also be possible to use the power of group mind to create a new and brighter civilization to surpass the old mythologies. It makes sense to give the more positive visions a chance. Even though the next ice age may eventually descend upon us again, humans did survive the last one and left us with marvelous images on cave walls. Imagine for a moment how well developed the senses needed to be for those ice age people to survive. Our senses are probably limited compared to them and very much so compared to other animals. The eagle can see more than we can, the dog can hear and smell more than we can, but we can expand the ability of each of our own senses somewhat through training. Learning the ways to express this intelligence for each sensory system is also important. One key to an *evolution* of intelligence is the ability to sustain a steady focus of attention. The key to the *expression* of intelligence includes the ability to communicate verbally as well as through the appropriate sensory systems. Each sense provides different intelligent information. Another key to an evolution of intelligence is through the integration of mental functions to allow our ancient heritage of sensory awareness and nonverbal communication to merge with our more recent acquisition of symbolic, verbal, and electronic methods of communication.

"Although humans make sounds with their mouths and occasionally look at each other, there is no scientific evidence that they actually communicate among themselves."

Copyright © 1994 by Sidney Harris. (203)

The scientist who is dedicated to the concept that "objective" science is the only way to "know" something may be so brainwashed by abstract symbolism that s/he cannot accept what is there to be seen. That is why I firmly believe that a student needs to learn to draw and learn to expand the intelligence of the visual system in the early years. This is an important part of the education of one who would pursue science as a profession. Otherwise abstract symbols can be manipulated to corrupt scientific information, though it still claims to have been derived by "objective" research. So much of what we perceive is only a reflection of what we project. How objective can one be if one has had no training to actually see the external world or practice in learning how to express those visions?

Perhaps the newer technologies of the World Wide Web can stimulate a people-to-people program to bypass the scientific agencies that refuse to accept psi. As people communicate with each other across the world, without waiting for their governments to make it possible to do so, information transfer accelerates exponentially. People in other countries all over the world are becoming increasingly aware of their own latent mental abilities. This is part of the evolutionary drive into the next phase of life. We are being pushed or driven (some may be kicking and screaming, while others are rushing forward with great enthusiasm) into the next millennium, and we can share our different ways of knowing with each other all across the world.

What is the difference if we call a sudden insight a "hunch" instead of a message channeled from a spirit guide? What if we are conscious enough about brainwave synchronization to trust the pure wave forms of electrical activity to integrate mental functions? What if we learn to do that without calling it meditation or prayer? Does it matter which belief system we use to label our creative inspirations? I don't think it does, unless one gets tangled up in the details of the logic that follow each assumption. They are like different rivers flowing down on opposite sides of a hill from the same source of the mountain lake at the top. The conclusions can develop very differently from the same source, because of the different belief systems attached to them. Try to cultivate clarity about your assumptions. Your logic is based on your primary assumptions about the nature of reality that you choose to accept. If your logic leads to faulty conclusions, go back to the source and question your assumptions.

Those who work with biofeedback can help bypass some of the religious and atheistic taboos about consciousness. Various modalities of biofeedback (GSR, EMG, pulse rate, skin temperature, and audio-video feedback of student interactions in class) are useful at any time. We found that brainwave biofeedback works best as early as fifth grade. (By seventh and eighth grade the girls did *not* want electrode paste in their carefully glued-up hair arrangements. This was no longer a serious problem by the time they were old enough to go to high school or college, if they were beginning to care about learning.) But the fifth graders of my class seemed to be eager to participate in biofeedback, and some learned very quickly how to adjust the electrodes and to test them for the right connection to the scalp. They were delighted to discover their own electromagnetism. They wanted to know how their own energies were related to the energies of the Earth and sun. As they learned to gain voluntary control, as needed, over muscle tension, blood flow, emotional outbursts, and brainwaves, they could begin to identify themselves with more of the dimensions of their reality.

Can students learn to turn anger (with its deep roots in fear) into a transcendental experience, just by concentrating on synchronizing the high-amplitude slow brainwaves of fear into a high state of meditation? The answer for some of them is yes. This type of personal health education has a lifetime benefit, and it serves as a major introduction to the student's multidimensionality. The "self-discovery model" developed by King for her continuation high school classes encouraged creative exploration. (See also page 159.) Students wanted to discover how their private thoughts and emotions directly affected their physiological reactions. Brainwave biofeedback is also an excellent way to learn how different food, drink, and drugs (legal or non-

legal) affect the brain. After students learn some amount of voluntary control over the range of brainwaves of both sides of their heads (and how both sides relate to each other), they can then find out about the effect that food, drink, or drugs have on that control. One continuation high school student came in before class and asked King if he could hook up to the *Light Sculpture* before the other students arrived. He explained, "I just had a couple of Valiums and a six-pack, and I want to see what it does to my brainwaves." After watching his brainwaves scatter the changing patterns of light with no control, he sat quietly for a time and then said, "Oh. Now I see why I have trouble with math when I do that before coming to school."

Currently, EEG biofeedback is being used clinically to alleviate attention deficit hyperactive disorder (ADHD). Part of the treatment for increasing the child's ability to focus attention is feedback in the beta range of EEG. (204) Gottlieb's therapeutic techniques that include the use of the trampoline and light has proved to be useful for this disorder as well. (See pages 113-114) One of the most important issues that contribute to problems with the ability to focus attention seems to be toxic amount of metals in the body (especially aluminum). The detoxification of metals and the rebalancing of the person's metabolism is a primary step in solving ADD and ADHD. (205) The growing evidence of this serious problem might be called the "junk food with TV disorder."

Interhemispheric brainwave biofeedback can provide other benefits as well. Consider the people who want to practice meditation, but their minds wander easily. They have been quietly sitting for some time before they realize that they are planning tomorrow's projects, remembering something from the past, or just talking to themselves, instead of being in the light of the present moment. The tone that indicates that the student has achieved phase coherence stops instantly when the mind wanders from the hum of no thought. To keep the tone on, the student must stop thinking in words and find his/her own unique mental pattern that allows the EEG to remain in phase coherence. We have also found that when the student's simultaneous alpha increased its percentage of phase coherence (for exam-

> **"The answers I seek are all right here**
> **When I'm able to keep my vision clear."**
>
> Shelby W. Parker
> March 22, 1995 (206)

ple, from 50% to 85%), the student frequently responded with an *"Ah Ha!"* reaction, having received a sudden insight. Through the synchronization of the wave forms, the verbal and nonverbal mentations can become integrated. Stereo brainwave biofeedback is an excellent tool to learn how to stop the internal dialog and to be at peace.

In my psychology classes, whenever I conducted a guided imagery session into "past-life fantasies," I reported that if the students followed my hypnotic suggestions about how to focus their energy in their brains, they would experience something unusual. (Participation in this exercise was not a requirement of the course—students could leave at that time, if they chose to do so.) I offered at least three belief systems to the students to account for the phenomenon. One was that their visions were like their dreams. The second was that their visions were pulled from the archetypal unconscious. The third was that anyone could tune into anyone who ever lived and feel, or imagine they felt, what that person felt. The fourth was that the students might be experiencing their own past-life events. No one was expected to believe in a past life, but the fantasy exercise usually revealed some important aspect of their present-life dramas that could be solved by setting it in a context that was less threatening to their present ego identity. Some students experienced sensations and visions that were so powerful that they did believe they had been connected to past lives. Some of these were fearful or painful, and needed to be resolved before class was over. If they were not resolved, the student made an appointment with me, at no charge, to clarify the experience and to integrate the lesson of the drama into his/her present life situation.

Another realm, not accepted by the mainstream of science, involves communication with those who have entered the spirit world. Through our exploration over many years with psychedelics, hypnosis, trance states, and travel among people who speak to spirits as a normal part of their lives, we have learned a few concepts about this realm and feel it is important to share them, even though many psychologists totally reject the idea of spirit communication. We have found that:

1. We can receive information that is important to us from the spirits of those who have died. Sometimes a dear friend or relative chooses to continue to communicate with us and/or to help protect us.

2. The loving communication we receive from the spirits can take any form and be translated through any of our senses.

3. Clarity of mind is essential to keep the received information accurate and not mixed up with favored, but dusty, old mythologies.

4. It is important to find out who it is who wants to talk to you. Some spirits are your ancestors, some are angelic beings of light, some are enlightened beings, and some are just lost.

5. For those who are lost in the unknown dimensions, those who died with no preparation for the extension of consciousness beyond the body, there are prayers and instructions to help them find peace. Different religions have their own ways of doing this. The one below is one I have found to be continuously useful for me. I have modified it from the Leary, Alpert, Metzner version of *The Tibetan Book of the Dead—The Psychedelic Experience.* (207) One can light candles, burn sage to purify the air, enter a light trance and announce to the confused spirit who is present:

*The time has come to seek new levels of reality. Your body has gone and there is no need to continue to identify with it or with its pain. Enjoy the freedom from the body. You are about to be set face to face with the clear light. You are about to experience it in its reality. In this state, all things are like the void and cloudless sky, and the naked spotless intellect is like a transparent vacuum. At this moment know yourself. The radiant light you may be experiencing is the true nature of your reality. You have become pure spirit. You are not limited by your former earthly concerns. Concentrate on the unity of all beings. Maintain the image of the clear light. Use it to obtain understanding and love.*

This type of sincere attempt to speak to the spirit often results in clearing confusion. Most have appreciated the chance to solve emotional concerns for loved ones. Those who were raised to believe that death was the end are surprised when consciousness is still linked to a personality instead of emptiness. Some of those are pleased to learn about the all encompassing light and will be drawn toward it. Some may choose to remain near loved ones to offer helpful advice and comfort as needed.

6. Spirits could be stuck in hateful ideas that were built into of the wars of their time. They could have carried such hate beyond death into the spirit realm. When you can't help relieve a spirit of his anger, if he refuses to respond positively to loving advice, then an exorcism may be needed so you will no longer need to be involved with him. Spirit possession needs to be dealt with when the entity chooses to remain hostile and troublesome.

It is my opinion that many of those who died without prayers during the recent wars of mass destruction may have reincarnated into the war-like ghettos of the large cities of today. While the rise of economic imbalances has contributed to the homelessness, joblessness, poor education, and hopelessness that characterize the ghetto environment, among those who help to maintain that violence may be those who previously died violently. If they seek help for their fearful and violent dreams of war, if they wonder about their past, who can help them? Even those soldiers who survived the war have bad dreams about what they saw and did. Rolling Thunder told me that in Native American tribes, warriors were purified in special rituals before coming back into their communities. The rituals helped them to separate their killing experiences from their life of loving care for their families. It helped them to detach themselves from the guilt of involvement in violence.

The spirits are involved with the living, though they are not often recognized there. When we acknowledge our ancestors, our teachers, and the ultra-dimensional beings who are there to guide us, both realms will feel the benefit.

In our research we have seen that the brainwaves of one person can affect those of another. We have seen that one person with a headache can transmit that to another. And the opposite has been demonstrated—a healer can transmit healing energy to another to stimulate the other's immune system. We have chosen the term "Psychic Soup" to refer to the collection of mental processes shared by a group involved in the same project. It occurs when the harmony is strongly felt and the images are easily shared.

Beyond the idea that we are simply material beings, we are also electromagnetic beings. We can resonate consciously with each other, the animals, the Earth, the sun, the moon, and the heavens. We can play in linear time, and in non-local spacetime. We are more than our four-dimensional manifestation in spacetime; we are a consciousness that is infinite and eternal, and we can explore it all and enjoy it all. Darrell Lemaire has often said, "There are no limits." I used to debate that with him, but as the years and positive experiences accumulate, I find fewer reasons to do so.

Families can also explore *how* each member "thinks" about things. This one visualizes, that one verbalizes, perhaps the youngest of them feels all the emotions, but doesn't yet know how to verbalize them. Try out a family evening on a regular schedule to let each one *be*, not who you demand s/he to be, but who each one really is, and how each one perceives the world in a different way. This is one of the most educational projects a family can do and enjoy together. Parents may be very surprised to learn of the acute perceptive abilities of their offspring. This is one way to develop some flexibility in your collective reality systems. And it is a positive way to show love and acceptance of each other. The family members who can share such experiences have a better chance of learning about their multidimensionality than those who just follow the habit of work or school and watching television. No matter how educational the television programs are, the time that is set aside for inter-family communication is the essential education for parents and children alike.

From our years of study, and from the research of others, we offer a recipe for using our multidimensional minds to create *real magic*. While this recipe doesn't always work the way you want it to—it does often produce amazing results. Look for multidimensions among the results as well. My definition of **real magic** is what happens during mind travel through space and time, such as remote viewing, mind-to-mind communication, spiritual healing, out-of-the-body experiences, and the transmission of love energy between people, animals, plants, Earth and the heavens. Love is the energy of life. Love can be the mechanism for achieving resonance. Love is the organizing principle of the universe. When we focus our intention to tap into that organizing principle from our own source of love and humility, there will be a reflecting response of some kind. You can count on it. We are all intricately woven into the fabric of consciousness. Loving attention to the practice of this magic can enhance the evolution of your own intelligence and that of those who share the dream.

*Real Magic can be created by maintaining a steady
focus of intention through an appropriate belief system.*

*Best Wishes,
Jean Millay*

# REFERENCE NOTES

## INTRODUCTION

1. Krippner, S. (Ed.) *Advances in Parapsychological Research.* (Vols 1-3). New York: Plenum, 1977.

## TECHNICAL AND THEORETICAL CONCEPTS ABOUT OUR MULTIDIMENSIONAL MINDS

2. Gurney, E., Myers, F. W. H. & Podmore, F. *Phantasms of the Living.* London: Trubner & Co., 2 vols., 1886.

3. Sinclair, U. *Mental Radio.* New York: Macmillan, 1930.

4. Rhine, J. B. *Extrasensory Perception.* Boston: Bruce Humphries, 1973 (originally published in 1934).

5. Targ, R. & Puthoff, H. "Information Transmission Under Conditions of Sensory Shielding." In *Nature* 252 (1974): 602-607.

6. Rauscher, E. "Longitudinal Comparison of Local and Long-Distance Remote-Perception Phenomena." In *Silver Threads: 25 Years of Parapsychology Research.* Kane, B., Millay, J. & Brown, D. (Eds.). Westport, CT: Praeger, an imprint of Greenwood Publishing Group, 1993: 64-77.

7. Brown, D. *Cosmic Law: The Evolution of Philosophy.* Los Angeles: The Philosophical Research Society, 1996.

8. Mishlove, J. *Roots of Consciousness: The Classic Encyclopedia of Consciousness Studies Revised and Expanded.* Tulsa, OK: Council Oaks Books, Revised edition, 1993.

9. Hardy, A., Harvie, R. & Koestler, A. *The Challenge of Chance: A Mass Experiment in Telepathy and its Unexpected Outcome.* New York: Vintage Books, 1975.

10. Houser A. & Kloesel, A. (Eds.) *The Essential Pierce Vol. 1 & 2.* Indianapolis, IN: Indiana University Press, 1992-1998.

11. Millay, J. *The Relationship Between Phase Synchronization of Brainwaves and Success in Attempts to Communicate Telepathically: A Pilot Study.* San Francisco: Saybrook Institute, 1978.

12. Heinze, R.-I. *Trance and Healing in Southeast Asia Today.* Berkeley, CA/Bangkok: Independent Scholars of Asia, Inc. and White Lotus, 1988/1997.

13. Kamiya, J. "Operant Control of the EEG Alpha Rhythm and Some of its Reported Effects on Consciousness." In *Altered States of Consciousness.* Tart, C. T. (Ed.) New York: Wiley, 1969.

14. King, M. *Brainwave Biofeedback as a Science Lesson.* Presented at the First Western Area Convention of the National Science Teachers Association. San Diego, CA, Dec. 2, 1972.

15. Vilenskaya, L. & Steffy J. *Firewalking: A New Look at an Old Enigma.* Falls Village, CT: Bramble Company, 1991.

16. Johnston, J. & Millay, J. "A Pilot Study in Brainwave Synchrony." In *Psi Research Review.* Vilenskaya, L. (Ed.) Vol. 2, No. 1. (March 1983): 71-98.

17. Spottiswoode, S. J. P. "Apparent Association Between Effect Size in Anomalous Cognition Experiments and Local Sidereal Time." In *Journal of Scientific Exploration,* Vol. 11, No. 2. (1997).

18. Persinger, M. & Krippner, S. "Dream ESP Experiments and Geomagnetic Activity." In *JASPR* 83 (1989): 101-116.

19. Sirag, S. P. "Hyperspace Reflections." In *Silver Threads: 25 Years of Parapsychology Research.* Kane, B., Millay, J. & Brown, D. (Eds.). Westport, CT: Praeger an imprint of Greenwood Publishing Group, 1993: 156-165.

20. Sirag, S. P. "A Mathematical Strategy for a Theory of Consciousness." In *Towards a Science of Consciousness: The First Tucson Discussions and Debates.* Hameroff, S. T., & Kasniak, A. W. & Scott, A. C. (Eds.) Cambridge, MA: MIT Press, 1996.

## CHAPTER ONE: SENSORY PERCEPTION

21. Targ, R. & Puthoff, H. *Mind Reach.* New York: Delacorte Press, 1977.

22. Freedman, D. Z. & van Nieuwenhuizen, P. "The Hidden Dimensions of Spacetime." In *Scientific American.* (March 1985): 74-81.

23. Sagan, C. *Demon-Haunted World: Science as a Candle in the Dark.* New York: Random House, 1995.

24. Schultz, C. PEANUTS reprinted by permission of United Feature Syndicate, Inc.

25. Allen, J. *Birds in a Brewing Storm: Late Afternoon.* Painting © Jesse Allen. Reproduced by courtesy of The Vorpal Gallery, San Francisco and New York City.

26. Schlitz, M. "The Phenomenology of Replication." In *The Repeatability Problem in Parapsychology.* Shapin B. & Coly, L. (Eds.) New York: Parapsychology Foundation Press, 1985: 73-97.

27. Pritchard, R. "Stabilized Images on the Retina." In *Perception: Mechanisms and Models, Readings from Scientific American.* San Francisco: Freeman, 1972.

28. Thompson, E., Maj. Gen., Asst Chief of Staff of Intelligence, US Army, 1977-1981, Ft. George, Mead, MD. (TV broadcast, 1997 - DIA-CIA RV, code name, *"Real Flame."*)

29. Lubar, J. F. "Neurofeedback for the Management of Attention Deficit Disorders." In *Biofeedback: A Practitioner's Guide, 2nd Ed.,* Schwartz, M. S. (Ed.). New York: Guilford Publications, Inc., 1996: 493-522.

30. Sheldrake, R. *Seven Experiments That Could Change the World.* New York: Berkeley Publishing, 1996.

## CHAPTER TWO: MULTIPLE PATHS THROUGH THE MAZE OF MIND

31. Fadiman, J. "Multiple Personalities: A Way of Understanding Successful Personality Growth." at the 12th Annual International Transpersonal Psychology Conference, Prague, Czechoslovakia, June 1992.

32. Guion, C. "Espiritistas." In *Association for Humanistic Psychology Newsletter.* Guion, C. (Ed.). San Francisco, 1978: 12-13.

33. Brown, D. *The Upanishads.* Los Angeles: Philosophical Research Society, 1996.

34. Targ, R. "A Decade of Remote-Viewing Research." In *Silver Threads: 25 Years of Parapsychology Research.* Kane, B., Millay, J. & Brown, D. (Eds.). Westport, CT: Praeger, an imprint of Greenwood Publishing Group, 1993: 54-63.

35. Dossey, L. *Healing Words: The Power of Prayer and the Practice of Medicine.* New York: HarperSanFrancisco, HarperCollins, 1993.

36. Krippner, S. *Song of the Siren.* New York: Harper and Row, 1975.

37. Kantor, D. & Millay, J. "Past Life, Present Dramas." In *Proceedings of the Tenth International Conference on the Study of Shamanism and Alternative Modes of Healing.* Heinze, R.-I. (Ed.). Berkeley: Independent Scholars of Asia, Inc., 1991: 334-345.

38. Mitchell, S. *Tao Te Ching by Lao Tzu, A new English Version, with Foreword and Notes by Stephen Mitchell.* Translation copyright © 1988 by Stephen Mitchell. New York: HarperCollins Publisher, 1999.

39. King, M. "Biofeedback in the High School Curriculum." In *Association for Humanistic Psychology Newsletter.* Guion, C. (Ed.). San Francisco, June 1975: 20-21.

40. Krippner, S. (Ed.) *Dream Time and Dreamwork.* Los Angeles: Jeremy Tarcher, 1990.

41. Puthoff, H. & Targ, R. "The CIA & ESP: Taking the Wraps off Government Remote Viewing Experiments." In *Noetic Sciences Review.* Sausalito, CA: Inst. of Noetic Sciences, Summer, 1996.

42. Nillsson, L. *Behold Man.* Boston: Little Brown & Co., 1974. Reprinted in *LIFE* magazine, 1965.

43. Mookerjee, A. *Tantra Asana: A Way to Self-realization.* Basil, Switzerland: Ravi Kumar, Publisher, Basilius Presse, 1971.

44. Wilhelm, R. & Baynes, C. F. *The I Ching, or Book of Changes, 3rd Edition.* Princeton, NJ: Princeton University Press, Bollingen Foundation, Inc., 1950.

45. Ullman, M., Krippner, S., with Vaughan, A. *Dream Telepathy.* New York: Macmillian, 1973.

46. Freud, S. *The Interpretation of Dreams.* New York: Basic Books, 1953.

47. Jung, C. G. *Man and His Symbols.* Garden City, NJ: Doubleday; 1964.

48. Campbell, J. with Moyers, B. *The Power of Myth.* Flowers, S. (Ed.). New York: Doubleday; 1988.

49. Warcollier, R. *Mind to Mind.* New York: Farrar Strauss and Strauss & Co., 1948, 1963.

50. Sinclair, U. *Mental Radio.* New York: Macmillan, 1930.

51. Escher, M. C. *The Graphic Work of M. C. Escher.* New York: Ballantine Books, 1960, 1967, 1971, 1975.

52. Thurber, J. *Men, Women & Dogs.* New York: Harcourt Brace, 1943.

53. Evens-Wentz, W. Y. *The Tibetan Book of the Dead.* London: Oxford University Press, 1960.

54. Leary, T., Alpert, R. & Metzner, R. *The Psychedelic Experience, A Manual Based on The Tibetan Book of the Dead.* New Hyde Park, New York: University Books, 1964.

55. Lorenz, L. "Siva, Lord of Destruction." Reprinted with permission. Copyright © *The New Yorker* collection 1982. Lee Lorenz from The Cartoon Bank (cartoonbank.com.) All rights reserved.

56. Puharich, A. & Hurtak, J. Series of lectures on the UFO phenomena. Palo Alto, CA: 1973.

57. Vallee, J. *Revelations, Alien Contact and Human Deception.* New York: Ballantine Books, 1991.

**CHAPTER THREE: REMOTE VIEWING**

58. Kadooka, L. (photographer) "After 116 years, two volcanoes erupt at once." *Tribune-Herald Newspaper.* Honolulu, HI, 1984.

59. Kesey, K. *Sometimes a Great Notion.* New York: The Viking Press, Inc., 1963, 1964. (New York: Bantam Books; 1st printing, 1965, 17th printing, 1972.)

60. Simeona, M. (Hawaiian Kahuna) Personal Communication, Honolulu, HI, April, 1984.

61. Persinger, M. Quoted in *Quest for the Unknown. UFO: THE CONTINUING ENIGMA.* Pleasantville, New York: The Reader's Digest Assn, Inc., A Dorling Kindersley Book, 1991. (Williams, R., Senior Ed.)

62. Pellegrini, L. "O Congresso de Bruxaria de Bogotá." In *Planeta,* São Paulo, Brasil: October, 1975; 104-113.

63. Sannella, L. *The Kundalini Experience: Psychosis or Transcendence?* San Francisco: H. S. Dakin, 1975. Revised and reprinted as *The Kundalini Experience.* Lower Lake, CA: Integral Publishing, 1987.

64. Leary, T. "Probe for Higher Intelligence." In *Spit in the Ocean.* Pleasant Hill, OR: 1975. Kesey, K. (Ed. and Pub.)

65. Rolling Thunder. (Native American Shaman) Personal Communication, Cotati, CA, 1975.

66. Weil, A. "A Bunch of the Bruhos Were Whooping It Up." In *Rolling Stone.* New York: 10/23, 1975; 56-58.

67. Geller, U. *Uri Geller's Mind Power Kit.* New York: Penguin Studio, 1996.

68. Mayo, J. (Millay) "Intercontinental Telepathy." In *Association for Humanistic Psychology Newsletter.* Guion, C. (Ed.) San Francisco: 1975; 14-15.

69. Seucucui. (Abinticua Shaman) Personal Communication, Lake Guatavita, Colombia, SA, August, 1975.

**CHAPTER FOUR: RESONANCE**

70. Neufeldt, V. & Guralnik, D. (Eds.) *Webster's New World Dictionary of American English, Third College Edition.* New York: Simon & Schuster, Inc., 1991.

71. Kamiya, J. "On the Relationships Among Subjective Experience, Behavior, and Physiological Activity in Biofeedback Learning." In *Self Regulation of the Brain and Behavior,* Rockstroh, E. T., Lutzenberger, W. & Birbaumer, N. (Eds.) New York: Springer-Verlag, 1984: 245-254.

72. Green, E. & Green, A. "The Ins and Outs of Mind-Body Energy." In *Science Year 1974, World Book Science Annual.* Chicago: Field Enterprises Educational Company, 1973, p. 146.

73. Fehmi, L. G. "Attention to Attention." In *Applied Neurophysiology and Brain Biofeedback.* Kall, R, Kamiya, J. & Schwartz, G. (Ed.) Trevose, PA: Future Health, Inc., 1999

74. Millay, J. "Education and Music, an Interview with Ali Akbar Khan." In *Association for Humanistic Psychology Newsletter.* San Francisco, CA: May, 1979; 22-23. Guion, C. & Millay, J. (Eds.).

75. Engleman, S., Goodman, V., Herzog, L., Jacobson, A., Mayo (Millay), J. & Ronan, J. *Bio-Feedback Training and Learning of Brain-Wave Synchronization.* California State University at Sonoma. Term Paper, 1974.

76. Johnston, J. "Brainwave Synchronization: Report on a Pilot Study." In *Silver Threads: 25 Years of Parapsychology Research.* Kane, B., Millay, J. & Brown, D. (Eds.). Westport, CT: Praeger, an imprint of Greenwood Publishing Group, 1993: 233-241.

77. Brown, B. *New Mind, New Body.* New York: Bantam, 1974.

78. Escher, M. C. *The Graphic Work of M. C. Escher.* (Translated from the Dutch by Brigham, J.) New York: Ballantine Books,1967.

79. Gottlieb, R. "Healing with Light." In *Association for Humanistic Psychology Perspective.* San Francisco, CA: Nov., Dec., Jan., 1997-1998; 15-16. Hart, (Ed.).

80. Rael, J., with Marlow, E. *Being & Vibration.* Tulsa, OK: Council Oak Books, 1995.

81. Millay, J. "Biofeedback for Self-Discovery." In *Biofeedback in Education To Enhance Intelligence and Help Prevent the Abuse of Drugs.* Millay, J. (Ed.) Doyle, CA: Desktop Publication, 1990, revised 1995. PO Box 457, Doyle, CA 96109.

82. Campbell, D. *The Mozart Effect: Tapping the Power of Music to Heal the Body, Strengthen the Mind & Unlock the Creative Spirit.* New York: Avon Books, 1997.

83. Hart, M. and Liebermann, F. with Sonneborn, D. A. *Planet Drum: A Celebration of Percussion and Rhythm.* New York: HarperSanFrancisco, HarperCollins Publishers, 1991.

84. Millay, J. "Education and Music, an Interview with Ali Akbar Khan." In *Association for Humanistic Psychology Newsletter.* San Francisco, CA: May, 1979; 22-23. Guion, C. & Millay, J. (Eds.).

85. das Gupta, A. Personal Communication at the Monterey Pop Festival, Summer, 1967.

86. Quincy, C. & Alter, J. "Sonic Resonance and Its Interactions with the Dynamics of Cerebral Spinal Fluid in Relation to Focus of Attention and Altered States." In *Proceed ings of the Third International Conference on the Study of Shamanism and Alternate Modes of Healing.* Madison, WI: A-R Editions, Inc., 1987. 164-168. Heinze, R.-I. (Ed.).

87. Klimo, J. *Interdimensional Communication.* Lecture at the Institute for the Study of Consciousness, Berkeley, CA. March 8, 1998.

88. Dakin, H. S. *High-Voltage Photography.* San Francisco, CA: H. S. Dakin Co.: 1974, 1975, 1978.

89. Wirth, D. P. "Significance of Belief and Expectancy within the Spiritual Healing Encounter." In *Social Science Med.* Vol. 41, No. 2, 249-260. 1995.

90. Mikuriya, T. *Marijuana Medical Papers: 1839 -1972.* Oakland, CA: Medi-Comp Press, 1973.

91. Grinspoon, L., Bakalar, J. B. *Marihuana, the Forbidden Medicine.* New Haven, CT and London: Yale University Press, 1997.

92. Douglas, D. Personal Communication, Doyle, CA, 1996.

93. Moyers, B. *Moyers on Addiction: Close to Home.* PBS Television production. March 29, 30 & 31, 1998.

94. Jennings, P. "Pot of Gold." *ABC News Saturday Night.* TV production. 1996, 1998.

95. Weil, A. "Ancient Drugs." *In Search of History.* Produced by Talley, S. R., for The History Channel. Film Roos, Inc. 1995, 1998.

96. Sannella, L. *The Kundalini Experience: Psychosis or Transcendence?* San Francisco: H. S. Dakin, 1975. Revised and reprinted as *The Kundalini Experience.* Lower Lake, CA: Integral Publishing, 1987.

97. Scully, R. T. Personal Communication, 1965.

98. Leary, T. Voice introduction to the 16 mm.movie, *The Psychedelic Experience.* One of two Winners of the Zellerbach Award for "Film as Art" at the San Francisco International Film Festival, CA; 10/1965. (Millay, J. & Willis, A., co-producers.)

99. Wolfe, T. *Electric Kool-Aid Acid Test.* New York: Farrar, Straus & Giroux; 1968.

100. Owsley. Personal Communication by e-mail, fall, 1998.

101. Jahn, R. G., Dunne, B. J. & Nelson, R. D. Engineering Anomalies Reseasrch. *Journal of Scientific Exploration.* 1987; 1:21-50.

102. Radin, D. *The Conscious Universe: The Scientific Truth of Psychic Phenomena.* New York: HarperEdge, 1997. Reprinted in *IONS Noetic Sciences Review.* 46, 20-25, 58-61. 1998.

103. Leary, T. "Seeds of the Sixties." Reprinted in the *Association for Humanistic Psychology Newsletter.* San Francisco, CA: 1976; 62-63. Guion, C. (Ed.).

104. Mullis, K. B. "The Great Gene Machine." In *Omni.* April, 1993. (Liversibge, A., Interviewer)

105. Adamson, S. *Through the Gateway of the Heart: Accounts of Experiences with MDMA and other Empathogenic Substances.* San Francisco, CA: Four Trees Publications, 1985.

106. Shulgin, A. & Shulgin, A. *Pikal: A Chemical Love Story*. Berkeley, CA: Transform Press, 1991.

107. Grof, S. *Realms of the Human Unconscious: Observations from LSD Research*. New York: E. P. Dutton, 1977.

108. Wilson, G. *Relax*. Cartoon copyright © by Gahan Wilson, 1978.

## CHAPTER FIVE: TRANCE

109. Heinze, R.-I. *Shamans of the Twentieth Century*. New York: Irvington Publishers, 1991.

110. Erickson, M. H. *Healing in Hypnosis*. New York: Irvington Publishers, 1977.

111. Grof, S. *Beyond Death: The Gates of Consciousness*. London, England: Thames and Hudson, 1980.

112. Grof, S. *Beyond the Brain*. Albany, New York: State University New York Press, 1985.

113. Hastings, A. *With the Tongues of Men and Angels: A Study of Channeling*. Fort Worth, TX: Holt, Rinehart & Winston, 1991.

114. Mander, J. *Four Arguments for the Elimination of TV*. New York: Morrow Quill Paperback, 1976.

115. Enzenberger, H. M. *The Consciousness Industry*. New York: The Seabury Press, 1975.

116. Garrett, M. and Penny, T. J. *The 15 Biggest Lies in Politics*. New York: St. Martin's Press, 1998.

117. Steele, J. & Barlett, D. "Special Report: Corporate Welfare." In *Time*. Nov. 9, 1998. New York: Time, Inc.

118. Douglas, D. R. "Fat Cat Rule." In *Rhymes for Rap*. Personal portfolio of poetry. San Francisco, 1989.

119. Mahealani Kuamoó-Henry. (Hawaiian Kahuna) Personal Communication, Keaau, HI, 1997.

120. Pearsall, P. *The Pleasure Prescription*. Alameda, CA: Hunter House Press, 1996.

121. Gasparetto, L. Personal Communication. San Francisco, CA, 1980.

122. Winkelman, M. "Trance States: A Theoretical Model and Cross-cultural Analysis." In *Ethos*. 1986.

123. Erickson, M., Rossi, E. & Rossi, S. *Hypnotic Realities: The Induction of Clinical Hypnosis and Forms of Indirect Suggestion*. New York: Irvington, 1976.

## CHAPTER SIX:
## THE DEVELOPMENT OF MEMORY AND INTELLIGENCE

124. Lashley, D. *In Search of the Engram*. Tarrytown, New York: Torstar Books, 1950.

125. Penfield, W. *The Mystery of the Mind*. Princeton, NJ: Princeton University Press, 1975.

126. Grof, S. *Realms of the Human Unconscious: Observations from LSD Research*. New York: E. P. Dutton, 1977.

127. Swann, J. *Sacred Places: How the Living Earth Seeks Our Friendship*. Santa Fe, NM: Bear & Co., 1990.

128. Pearsall, P. *The Heart's Code*. New York: Broadway Books, A Division of Bantam Doubleday Dell Publishing Group, Inc., 1998.

129. Brown, D. *The Upanishads*. Los Angeles: Philosophical Research Society, 1996.

130. Targ, R. & Puthoff, H. "Information Transmission Under Conditions of Sensory Shielding." In *Nature* 252(1974): 602-607.

131. King, M. "View from a Classroom Using Biofeedback and Other Tools." In *Association for Humanistic Psychology Newsletter*, San Francisco, CA: May, 1979; 26-27. Guion, C. (Ed.).

132. Jeffress, M. *Cold in Oz*. Personal Communication by e-mail, fall, 1998.

133. Kellogg, R. *Analyzing Children's Art*. Palo Alto, CA: Mayfield Pulishing Co., 1969.

134. Pasto, T. *The Space Frame Experience in Art*. New York: A. S. Barnes & Co., 1964.

135. Ott, J. N. *Health and Light*. Old Greenwich, CN: Devin-Adair, 1973.

136. Wurtman, R. J. "The Effects of Light on the Human Body." *Scientific American*. July 1975; 69-77.

137. Hamlin, V. T. *Alley Oop*. Copyright © 1963 NEA Services, Inc.

## CHAPTER SEVEN: LOGIC AND THE REALMS OF NON-LOCAL SPACETIME

138. Geisel, T. S. *One Fish, Two Fish, Red Fish, Blue Fish.* New York: Random House, Inc., 1959.

139. Rauscher, E. A. & Mullins, A. J. "The Scientific Investigation of Direct Perception across Space and Time." *Mind Space.* 1977.

140. Targ, R., Targ, E. & Harary, K. "Moscow—San Francisco Remote Viewing Experiment." In *Psi Research*; 1984. Vol. 3, No. 3/4

141. Harary, K. & Targ, R. "A New Approach to Forecasting Commodity Futures." *Psi Research*; December 1985.

142. Targ, R., Katra, J., Brown, D. & Wiegand, W. "Viewing the Future: A Pilot Study with an Error-Detecting Protocol." In *Journal of Scientific Exploration*; 1995. Vol. 9. No. 3; 367-380.

143. Krippner, S., Ullman, M. & Honorton, C. "A Precognitive Dream Study with a Single Subject." In *Journal of the American Society for Psychical Research*, 1971, 65; 192-203.

144. Krippner, S., Honorton, C. & Ullman, M. "A Second Precognitive Dream Study with Malcolm Bessent." In *Journal of the American Society for Psychical Research*, 1971, 66; 269-279.

145. Stokes, D. M. "Theoretical Parapsychology." In *Advances in Parapsychological Research*, 1987, Vol. 5; 77-189. Krippner, S. (Ed.)

146. Ullman, M. "Dreaming, Altered states of Consciousness and the Problem of Vigilance." In *Journal of Nervous and Mental Disease,* 1961, 133; 529-535.

147. Ullman, M. & Krippner, S., with Vaughan, A. *Dream Telepathy: Experiments in Nocturnal ESP, 2nd edition.* Jefferson, NC: McFarland, 1989.

148. McCarley, R. W., and Hobson, J. A. "The Form of Dreams and the Biology of Sleep." In *Handbook of Dreams: Research, Theories and Applications,* New York: Van Nostrand Reinhold, 1979; 76-130. Wolman, B. B. (Ed.).

149. Puthoff, H. E. "ARV Associational Remote Viewing Applications." In *Research in Parapsychology 1984,* Metuchen, NJ: Scarecrow Press, 1985.

150. Lattin, D. Staff writer *San Francisco Examiner*; Thursday, November 19, 1982.

151. Mississippi. Personal Communication, Reno, NV, 1998.

152. Rauscher, E. A. "A Theoretical Model of the Remote-Perception Phenomenon." In *Silver Threads: 25 Years of Parapsychology Research.* Kane, B., Millay, J. & Brown, D. (Eds.). Westport, CT: Praeger, an imprint of Greenwood Publishing Group, 1993, 141- 155.

## CHAPTER EIGHT: THEORIES

153. Gottlieb, R. "Phase-Conjugate Brain." In *Journal of Optometric Photo Therapy.* March, 1997; 8.

154. Lauger, B. "The Origin of the Word Shaman," In *American Anthropologist, 19* (1917): 195ff.

155. Rolling Thunder. Native American medicine man. Personal Communicaton, Carlin, NV, 1983.

156. Guru Rinpoche according to Karma Lingpa. *The Tibetan Book of the Dead: The Great Liberation Through Hearing in the Bardo.* Translated from the Tibetan by Fremantle, F. & Chögyam Trungpa. Boulder & London: Shambala, 1975.

157. Brown, D. The Yoga Sutras of Patanjali in *The Upanishads.* Los Angeles: Philosophical Research Society, 1996.

158. Tart, C. *Waking Up: Overcoming the Obstacles of Human Potential.* Boston: Shambhala, New Science Library, 1986.

159. Harman, W. "Foreword: Shiftin Assumptions." In *Silver Threads: 25 Years of Parapsychology Research.* Kane, B., Millay, J. & Brown, D. (Eds.). Westport, CT: Praeger, an imprint of Greenwood Publishing Group, 1993: xx-xxx.

160. Grof, S. *President's Address* to the 12th Annual International Transpersonal Conference, Prague, Czechoslovakia: June, 1992.

161. Tart, C. *The Spiritual Path for the Scientifically Handicapped.* Presented at the 12th Annual International Transpersonal Conference, Prague, Czechoslovakia: June, 1992.

162. Dennett, D. C. *Glorious Accident:Understanding Our Place in the Cosmic Puzzle.* A 1993 series of interviews conducted by Wim Kayzer for UPRO/ The Netherlands. Broadcast by PBS.

163. Shkunov, Valadimir, V. & Zel'dovish, Boris Ya. "Optical Phase Conjugation." In *Scientific American.* December, 1985; 54-59.

164. Pepper, D. M. "Applications of Optical Phase Conjugation." In *Scientific American.* January, 1986; 74-83.

165. Popp, F. A. "Biophoton Emission: Evidence for Coherence and DNA as Source." In *Cell Bioph.* 1984, V. 6, 33-52.

166. Adey, W. R. & Lawrence, A. F. *Nonlinear Electrodynamics in Biolgical Systems.* New York: Plenum Press, 1984.

167. Reshetnyak, S. A. et al. "Mechanisms of Interaction of Electromagnetic Radiation with a Biosystem." In *Laser Physics.* 1996, V 6, #4, 621-653.

168. Pribram, K. *Languages of the Brain.* Englewood Cliffs, NJ: Prentice-Hall, 1971.

169. Bohm, D. *Wholeness and the Implicate Order.* London: Routledge & Kegan Paul, 1980.

170. Adams, M. "Possible Influence of the Geophysical Environment on Human Health and Behavior." In *Proceedings of the Third International Conference on the Study of Shamanism and Alternate Modes of Healing.* Madison, WI: A-R Editions, Inc., 1987. 164-168. Heinze, R.-I. (Ed.)

171. Neihardt, J. G. *Black Elk Speaks: Being the Life Story of a Holy Man of the Oglala Sioux.* New York: Washington Square Press, 1932. (Pocket Books, 1959.)

172. Sun Bear. Medicine Wheel Ceremony introductory lecture. Ojai, CA, 1981.

173. Swiftdeer, H. Personal Communiction, Ojai, CA, July, 1981.

174. Sheldrake, R. *A New Science of Life.* Los Angeles: Tarcher, 1981.

175. Bardens, D. *Psychic Animals: A Fascinating Investigation of Paranormal Behavior.* New York: Henry Holt & Co., 1987. Barnes & Noble Books, 1996.

176. Lovelock, J. *Gaia: A New Look at Life on Earth.* Oxford, UK: Oxford University Press, 1979.

177. Swimme, B. The Universe as Sacred Story. *Fugitive Faith: Conversations on Spiritual, Environmental, and Community Renewal.* San Francisco, CA: Orbis Books (in press). Webb, B. (Ed.) Reprinted in *IONS Noetic Sciences Review.* 46, 26-30. 1998.

178. Bronowski, J. *The Ascent of Man.* Boston & New York: Back Bay Books, Little, Brown & Company, 1973.

179. Brown, D. Personal Communication. Redwood City, CA, 1998.

180. Persinger, M. & Krippner, S. "Dream ESP Experiments and Geomagnetic Activity." In *JASPR* 83 (1989): 101-116.

181. Spottiswoode, S.J.P. "Apparent Association Between Effect Size in Anomalous Cognition Experiments and Local Sidereal Time." In *Journal of Scientific Exploration,* Vol. 11, No. 2. (1997).

182. Shulgin, A., Shulgin, A. *Tihkal: The Continuation.* Berkeley, CA: Transform Press, 1997.

183. MacHovec, F. J. Translation of *The Book of Tao.* Mount Vernon, NY: The Peter Pauper Press, 1962.

184. Harris, S. *Miracles.* Cartoon. Copyright © 1994 by Sidney Harris.

## CHAPTER NINE: BELIEF SYSTEMS AND THE POLITICS OF SUPRESSION

185. *The Dead Sea Scrolls* were found in a cave that may have been occupied by Essenes about the time that Jesus lived. Many translations and controversies involve them.

186. Worrall, A., Worrall, O. *The Healing-Touch.* NY: Harper & Row, 1970.

187. Beck, R. Personal communication, Los Angeles, CA, 1975.

188. Krippner, S. (Ed.) *Advances in Parapsychological Research.* (Vols 4-8) Jefferson, NC: McFarland & Co., Inc., 1984, 1987, 1990, 1994, 1997.

189. Sagan, C. *Demon-Haunted World: Science as a Candle in the Dark.* New York: Random House, 1995.

190. Ostrander, S. & Schroeder, L. *Psychic Discoveries Behind the Iron Curtain.* Englewood Cliffs, NJ: Prentice-Hall, 1970.

191. Rauscher, E. A. & Rubic, B. "Human Volitional Effects on a Model Bacterial System." In *PSI Research Journal* 1983; 2, no.1.

192. Byrd, E. For more information about Bird's and Geller's slander suits against Randi and others, contact: http://www.tcom.co.uk/hpnet/uga.htm.

193. Toulmin, S. *Glorious Accident: Understanding Our Place in the Cosmic Puzzle.* A 1993 series of interviews conducted by Wim Kayzer for UPRO/The Netherlands. Broadcast by PBS.

194. Millay, J. "The EEG and the Focus of Attention." In *Biofeedback in Education To Enhance Intelligence and Help Prevent the Abuse of Drugs.* Millay, J. (Ed.) Doyle, CA: Desktop Publication, 1990, revised 1995. PO Box 457, Doyle, CA

195. King, M. "Biofeedback in the High School Curriculum." In *Association for Humanistic Psychology Newsletter.* Guion, C. (Ed.). San Francisco, (June 1975): 20-21.

196. Dossey, L. *Healing Words: The Power of Prayer and the Practice of Medicine.* New York: HarperSanFrancisco, HarperCollins, 1993.

197. Westerbeke, P. & Krippner, S. "Subjective Reactions to the Filipino Healers." In *International Journal of Paraphysics*, 14, 9-17. 1980.

198. Douglas, D. "Nostradamus." *Rhymes for Rap.* Personal portfolio of poetry. San Francisco; 1989.

**CHAPTER TEN:
SUMMARY AND CONCLUSION**

199. Tolkien, J. R. R. *The Hobbit.* London: George Allen & Unwin, Ltd., 1937. (New York: 1st Ballantine Books printing, 1965. 6th printing, 1983.)

200. Targ, R., Katra, J., Brown, D. & Wiegand, W. "Viewing the Future: A Pilot Study with an Error-Detecting Protocol." In *Journal of Scientific Exploration*; 1995. Vol. 9. No. 3; 367-380.

201. Mishlove, J. *Psi Development Systems.* New York: Ballantine Books, 1988.

202. Sinclair, U. *Mental Radio.* New York: Macmillan, 1930.

203. Harris, S. *Dolphins.* Cartoon copyright © 1994 by Sidney Harris.

204. Lubar, J. F. "Neurofeedback for the Management of Attention Deficit Disorders." In *Biofeedback: A Practitioner's Guide, 2nd Ed.*, Schwartz, M. S. (Ed.). New York: Guilford Publications, Inc., 1996: 493-522.

205. Brown, J. www.metabolicresearch.com

206. Parker, S. Personal portfolio of poetry. Honolulu, HI, 1995.

207. Leary, T., Alpert, R. & Metzner, R. *The Psychedelic Experience, A Manual Based on the Tibetan Book of the Dead.* New Hyde Park, New York: University Books, 1964.

# APPENDIX A

## SOURCES OF TARGET PICTURES

Since we needed hundreds of pictures for targets, we took them from any source we could find: wrapping paper designs, postcards, greeting cards, personal drawings, and magazines.

Fortunately, I had gathered and/or saved a large collection of magazines by the fall of 1974. Most were *LIFE, National Geographic* magazines, and comic books. The following is a list of magazines we used:

*Archeology*
*Arizona Highways*
*Better Homes and Gardens*
D. C. Comics
*Dr. Strange* (Stan Lee Comics)
*Field and Stream*
*Hustler*
*LIFE*
*Mad*
*Man, Myth and Magic*
Marvel Comics
*National Geographic*
*Newsweek*
*Oui*
*Penthouse*
*Playboy*
*Psychology Today*
*Sunset*
*Time*
*Today's Health*
*U.S. News and World Report*

Newspapers: *The San Francisco Chronicle;*
*The Tribune-Herald* (Hawaii)

US Post Office advertisements
Postcards that came in the mail
Wrapping paper designs
Greeting card reproductions of paintings by:
Jesse Allen
Emil White
M. C. Escher
Photographs on cards by unknown photographers

Many others are reprinted here with permission and these are listed on the Permissions page before the Table of Contents.

Some of these same magazines were used again in the 1980 series, since a substantial target pool had been stored away. Some images were pasted on the cards already, and some were just in a box, waiting for volunteers to trim and paste them. Magazines and papers that had been published between 1975 and 1980 would have been included in the new target pool, as well. The Lennart Nillsson photographs of the fetus were color-copied from *LIFE* so the article would not be destroyed. This was also done with some of the famous paintings and sculpture that *LIFE* had published. The photocopies were not particularly well done in 1974, but they made excellent target pictures anyway. However, we do apologize for the poor reproductions to those artists and photograhers whose images were used as targets that way.

One thing that was done at the time, with no thought to the future, was the use of rubber cement. Over the many years of storage this has managed to bleed through the thin magazine paper to discolor the picture on the front. Some had been color-copied on the primitive (not very good color) copier machines of the time. All had been copied in black and white for the record. These early copies have helped us to restore the main features of the original targets on separate sheets for comparison. Computer reconstruction has made it possible to reprint them in this book. This would not have been possible without that technology.

Fortunately all targets and responses were duly recorded at the time they were completed. After that, their labels had to be covered so the judges could attempt to match them blindly. All this was done before any were judged for similarities. After the first judge completed the comparisons for similarities, the set was sent to each of the other four judges in turn. Of four hundred *targets,* two were lost during this period. Two *responses* were lost somewhat later when they were sent out to be reproduced for the 1981 publication.

Reprinted here with permission are some images from our telepathy and remote viewing experiments were published in *Silver Threads: 25 Years of Parapsycholgy Research*, Kane, B., Millay, J. & Brown, D. (Eds.) Westport, CT: Praeger, an imprint of Greenwood publishing Group, 1993. .

# APPENDIX  B

## FURTHER ACKNOWLEDGMENTS

More than one hundred and forty people graciously assisted with our research over the years, and I am most grateful to them all. Without them, no work could have been done. All were volunteers, since we rarely had the money to pay for such experiments. R. Timothy Scully, PhD, provided the electronic brainwave analyzers and the phase comparator. Stanley Krippner, PhD, sent me the first $500 to build the *Light Sculpture* as a feedback system for the Scully brainwave electronics. George and Grace Beers, my parents, gave me a place to live while I built it and then provided a "grubstake" to move to Cotati, CA, to get started. Saybrook Institute granted me the first Don Parker scholarship. As soon as that move had been made, Russell Targ and David Hurt provided me with a counter for the output of the phase comparator. Tom Etter, PhD, built an electronic feedback AUM tone.

Kate Lang recommended me as a teacher of parapsychology, so I had a part time job while doing research. Eleanor Criswell, EdD, professor of humanistic psychology at CSUS, had set up the environment for students to study parapsychology. Many came from all over the country to study with her. From this group, students volunteered for our 1974-75 studies. Suzanne Engleman, PhD, then an undergraduate student at CSUS, organized the assistant monitors for the project from the statistics class. Their class project also came from the wealth of information we were gathering. With all that background help, the project began in earnest just as the fall semester of 1974 began. Now after many years of pondering the results, I needed to write about it. However, since I am not a writer, verbalizing the nonverbal was a big problem for me. That is when the next series of helpers was needed. Marge King, Don Douglas, Ruth-Inge Heinze, PhD and Kathy Glass provided editorial help at different times. They did struggle with me to try to make sense of the multidimensional realms of the hyperspace and to translate that into a linear format. For the results, I am most appreciative for their advice as well as apologetic to them for my weaknesses. All the people who helped in one way or another are listed alphabetically. A few of the participants in the cannabis studies chose not to be listed. To all, listed or not, I am most grateful to you.

**Volunteers who participated in the telepathy and brainwave synchronization studies conducted between 1974 and 1975:**

| | |
|---|---|
| Kristen Anacker | Tim Lynch |
| Dorothy Bean | Jerry Muehe |
| Nancy Berman | Rickie Muehe |
| Laurie Campbell | Draza Nickolic |
| Curtis Doster | Allan Painter |
| Larry Gerald | Rose P. |
| Mark (Gurumukh) Harris | Sharon Snyder |
| David H. | Stephen Snyder |
| James Hickman | Nancy Tyler |
| Jane Lakin | Wendy Westerbeke |
| Gretchen Lukaszewski | Russell Winkler |

**Monitors, judges (for blind matching and judging of similarities), and those who helped prepare the target pictures for the studies conducted in 1974, 1975, 1980:**

| | |
|---|---|
| Fred Blau | Laura Herzog |
| Bunny Bonewitz | Avreayl Jacobson |
| Phyllis Cole | Shirley Palmer |
| Suzanne Engleman, PhD | James Ronan |
| Vickie Goodman | Andrew Stone |
| Sandra Hayes Rose | Theda Stone |
| Renee Hendrick | Larry Tessler |
| Shaun Hendrick | |

# APPENDIX  B

FURTHER ACKNOWLEDGMENTS

**Volunteers who participated in the telepathy and brainwave synchronization studies in 1980; the remote viewing; and the precognition experiments conducted between 1976 and 1984:**

Tom Byrne
Melissa Jeffress.
James Dowlen
William Dresbach
Maja Evens
Lori Grace
Carol Guion
Mark (Gurumukh) Harris
John Holmdahl
Kristi Jones
Don Kantor
Chris Lenz
Dan Retuto
Gary Sandman
Gregory Schelkun

Priscilla Schelkun
Chris Scott
Robert Skutch
Belle S.
Diane Brown Temple
Marcus True
Cheryl Wells
Will Wells
Linda Zimmerman
(Monica, age 9,
Ingrid and Wesley,
age 10, David and
Robert, age 11,
Mike, age 12,
Phil, age 15)

**Cooperative and/or Supportive Organizations:**

Institute of Noetic Sciences
North Atlantic Books
Parapsychology Research Group
Saybrook Institute
The International Conferences on the Study of
Shamanism and Alternate Modes of Healing
The Thanks Be to Grandmother
Winnifred Foundation
Washington Research Institute
The Holmes Center

**Advisors, teachers, resource people and others who offered moral, spiritual and/or economic support:**

Joel Alter, DO
Bob Beck, DSc
Arthur Bloch
Bunny Bonewitz
William Braud, PhD
Barbara Brown, PhD
Dean Brown, PhD
Charles Brush, PhD
James Bugental, PhD
Susan Campbell, PhD
Mary Lou Carlson
Eleanor Criswell, EdD
Henry Dakin
Alexa Douglas
Don Douglas
Mark Elliot
Uri Geller
Raymond Gottlieb, OD, PhD
Stanislav Grof, MD
Richard Grossinger, PhD
Carol Guion
Ruth-Inge Heinze, PhD
Joseph Hendrick, PhD
Richard Hendrickson, PhD
David Hurt
Harish Johari
James R. Johnston, PhD
Joanne Kamiya
Joe Kamiya, PhD
Ustad Ali Akbar Khan
Marjorie Beers King

Storm King
Barbara Klein
Stanley Krippner, PhD
Kate Lang
Timothy Leary, PhD
Darrell Lemaire
Jose Lucientes
Dorothy Lyddon
Michael Mahon
Mara Mayo
Mitchell Mayo
Tod Mikuriya, MD
Don Parker, PhD
Shelby Parker
Echo Penrose
Reynold J. Penrose
Cheri Quincy, DO
Ustad Alla Rakha
Elizabeth Rauscher, PhD
Lee Sannella, MD
Gregory Schelkun
R. Timothy Scully, PhD
Seocucui
Saul-Paul Sirag
Sola Patricia Smith
Owsley Stanley
Russell Targ
Rolling Thunder
Larissa Vilenskaya, LHD
Patricia Westerbeke
Ronalda Whitman

# APPENDIX C

## LIST OF ILLUSTRATIONS

# APPENDIX C

## LIST OF ILLUSTRATIONS

# APPENDIX C

## LIST OF ILLUSTRATIONS

# APPENDIX  C

## LIST OF ILLUSTRATIONS

# APPENDIX  C

## LIST OF ILLUSTRATIONS

# APPENDIX  C

## LIST OF ILLUSTRATIONS

# APPENDIX  C

## LIST OF ILLUSTRATIONS